NEGIMA!? NEO

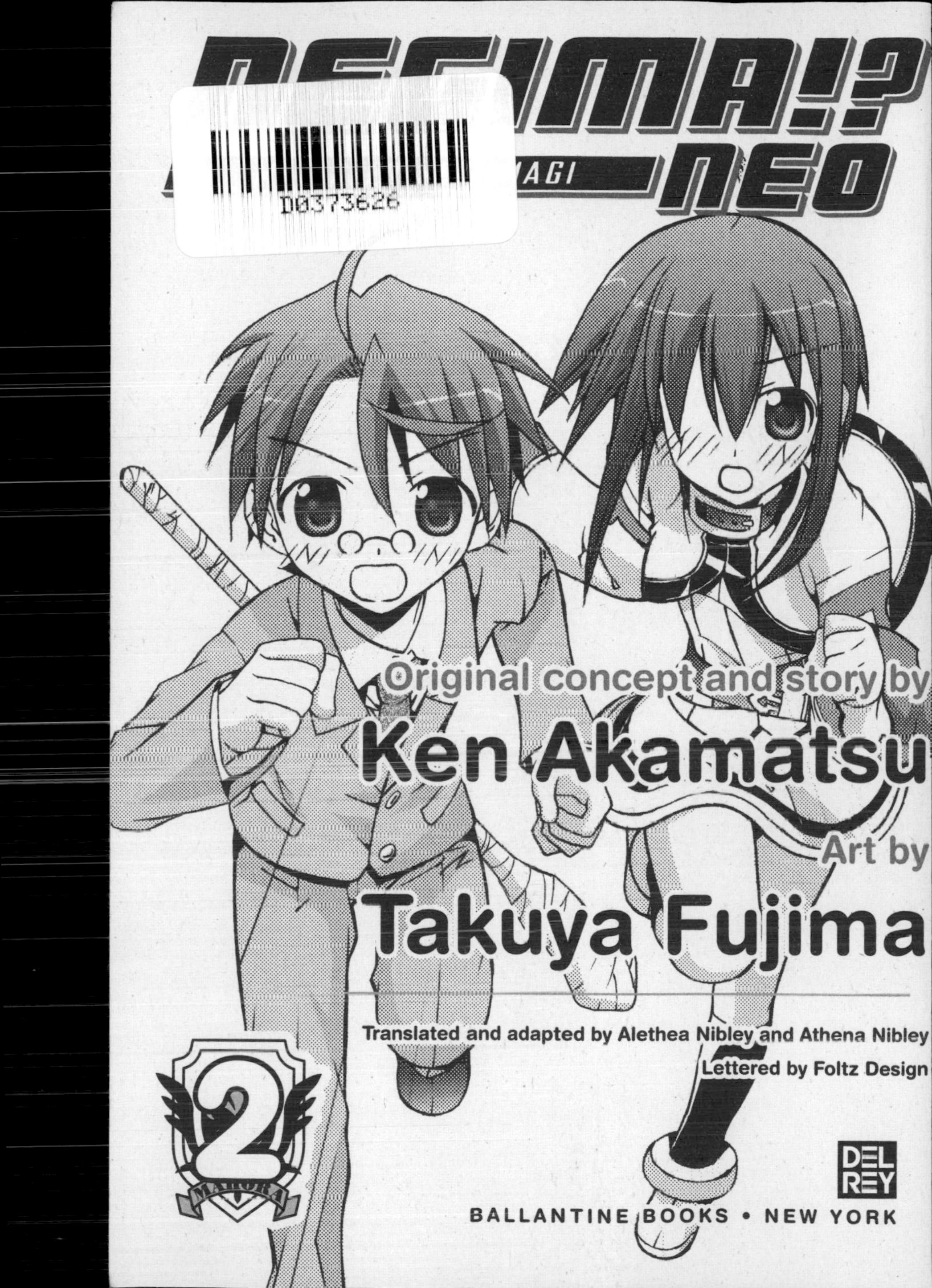
2
MAHORA

Original concept and story by
Ken Akamatsu

Art by
Takuya Fujima

Translated and adapted by Alethea Nibley and Athena Nibley

Lettered by Foltz Design

DEL REY
BALLANTINE BOOKS • NEW YORK

A Del Rey Manga/Kodansha Trade Paperback Original

Negima!? neo volume 2 copyright © 2007 by Takuya Fujima © Ken Akamatsu © KODANSHA/
Kanto Maho Association/TV Tokyo.
English translation copyright © 2009 by Takuya Fujima © Ken Akamatsu
© KODANSHA/Kanto Maho Association/TV Tokyo.

Published in the United States by Del Rey, an imprint of
The Random House Publishing Group, a division of Random House, Inc., New York.

DEL REY is a registered trademark and the Del Rey colophon
is a trademark of Random House, Inc.

Publication rights arranged through Kodansha Ltd.

First published in Japan in 2007 by Kodansha Ltd., Tokyo

Based on the manga *Mahoh Sensei Negima!* by Ken Akamatsu,
originally serialized in the weekly *Shonen Magazine* published by Kodansha, Ltd.

ISBN 978-0-345-51017-4

Printed in the United States of America

www.delreymanga.com

1 2 3 4 5 6 7 8 9

Translators/adapters: Alethea Nibley and Athena Nibley
Lettering: Foltz Design

CONTENTS

A Word from the Artist

Presenting *Negima!? neo*, volume two ★

Releasing a whole graphic novel at this pace while doing work for another monthly magazine...this might be a record for the fastest I've worked without collapsing!

As for the story in this one, we jump right into the sprite, star crystal arc(?) from the anime!

We go into the story little by little, but I hope that when you read it, you enjoy it not just a little, but as much as you can.

Later!
—Takuya Fujima

Honorifics Explained

Throughout the Del Rey Manga books, you will find Japanese honorifics left intact in the translations. For those not familiar with how the Japanese use honorifics and, more important, how they differ from American honorifics, we present this brief overview.

Politeness has always been a critical facet of Japanese culture. Ever since the feudal era, when Japan was a highly stratified society, use of honorifics—which can be defined as polite speech that indicates relationship or status—has played an essential role in the Japanese language. When you address someone in Japanese, an honorific usually takes the form of a suffix attached to one's name (example: "Asuna-san"), is used as a title at the end of one's name, or appears in place of the name itself (example: "Negi-sensei," or simply "Sensei!").

Honorifics can be expressions of respect or endearment. In the context of manga and anime, honorifics give insight into the nature of the relationship between characters. Many English translations leave out these important honorifics and therefore distort the feel of the original Japanese. Because Japanese honorifics contain nuances that English honorifics lack, it is our policy at Del Rey not to translate them. Here, instead, is a guide to some of the honorifics you may encounter in Del Rey Manga.

-san: This is the most common honorific and is equivalent to Mr., Miss, Ms., or Mrs. It is the all-purpose honorific and can be used in any situation where politeness is required.

-sama: This is one level higher than "-san" and is used to confer great respect.

-dono: This comes from the word "tono," which means "lord." It is an even higher level than "-sama" and confers utmost respect.

-kun: This suffix is used at the end of boys' names to express familiarity or endearment. It is also sometimes used by men among friends, or when addressing someone younger or of a lower station.

-chan: This is used to express endearment, mostly toward girls. It is also used for little boys, pets, and even among lovers. It gives a sense of childish cuteness.

Bozu: This is an informal way to refer to a boy, similar to the English terms "kid" and "squirt."

**Sempai/
Senpai:** This title suggests that the addressee is one's senior in a group or organization. It is most often used in a school setting, where underclassmen refer to their upperclassmen as "sempai." It can also be used in the workplace, such as when a newer employee addresses an employee who has seniority in the company.

Kohai: This is the opposite of "sempai" and is used toward underclassmen in school or newcomers in the workplace. It connotes that the addressee is of a lower station.

Sensei: Literally meaning "one who has come before," this title is used for teachers, doctors, or masters of any profession or art.

-[blank]: This is usually forgotten in these lists, but it is perhaps the most significant difference between Japanese and English. The lack of honorific, known as *yobisute,* means that the speaker has permission to address the person in a very intimate way. Usually, only family, spouses, or very close friends have this kind of permission. It can be gratifying when someone who has earned the intimacy starts to call one by one's name without an honorific. But when that intimacy hasn't been earned, it can be very insulting.

NEGIMA!? NEO

MAGISTER NEGI MAGI

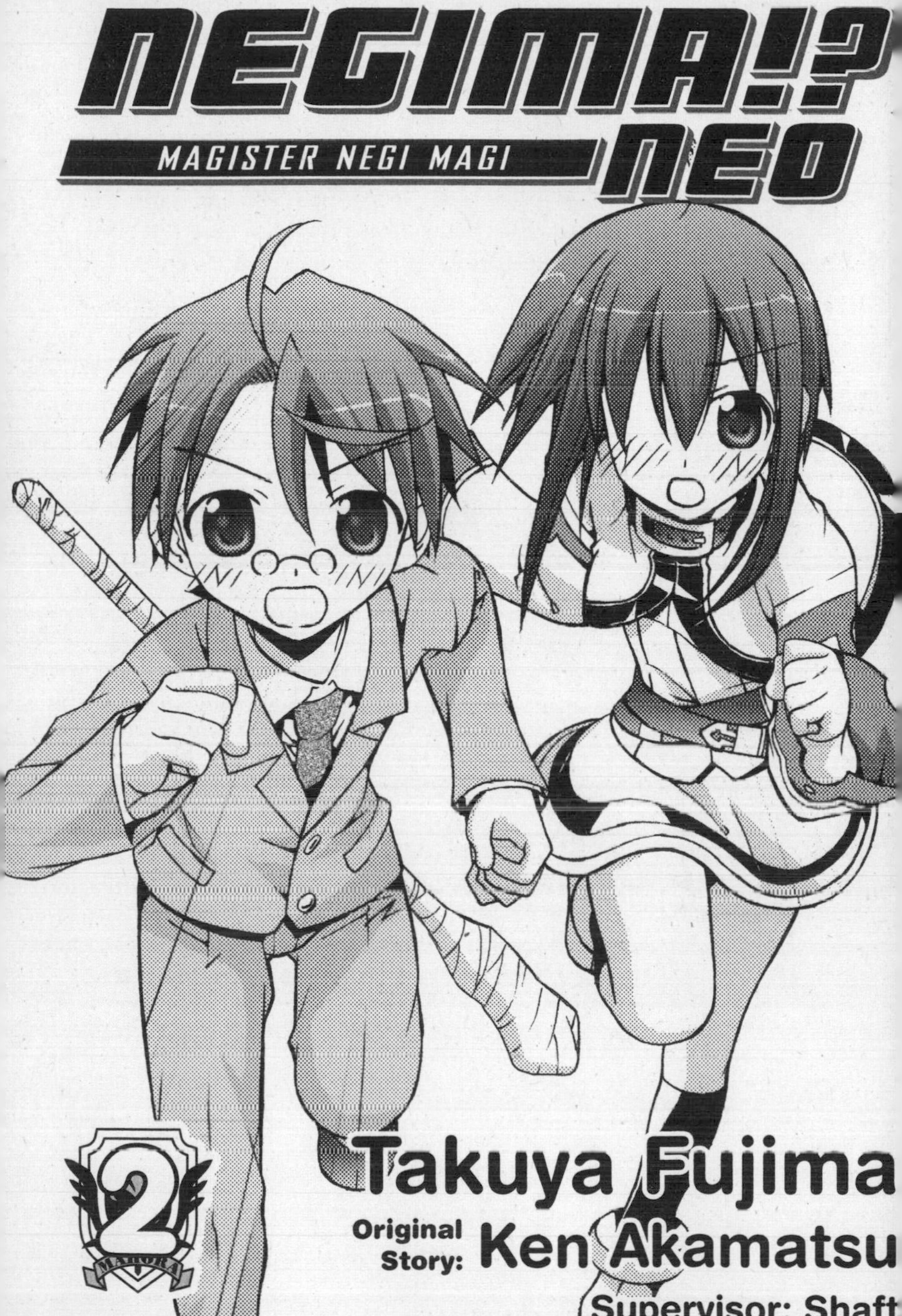
2
MAHORA

Takuya Fujima

Original Story: Ken Akamatsu

Supervisor: Shaft

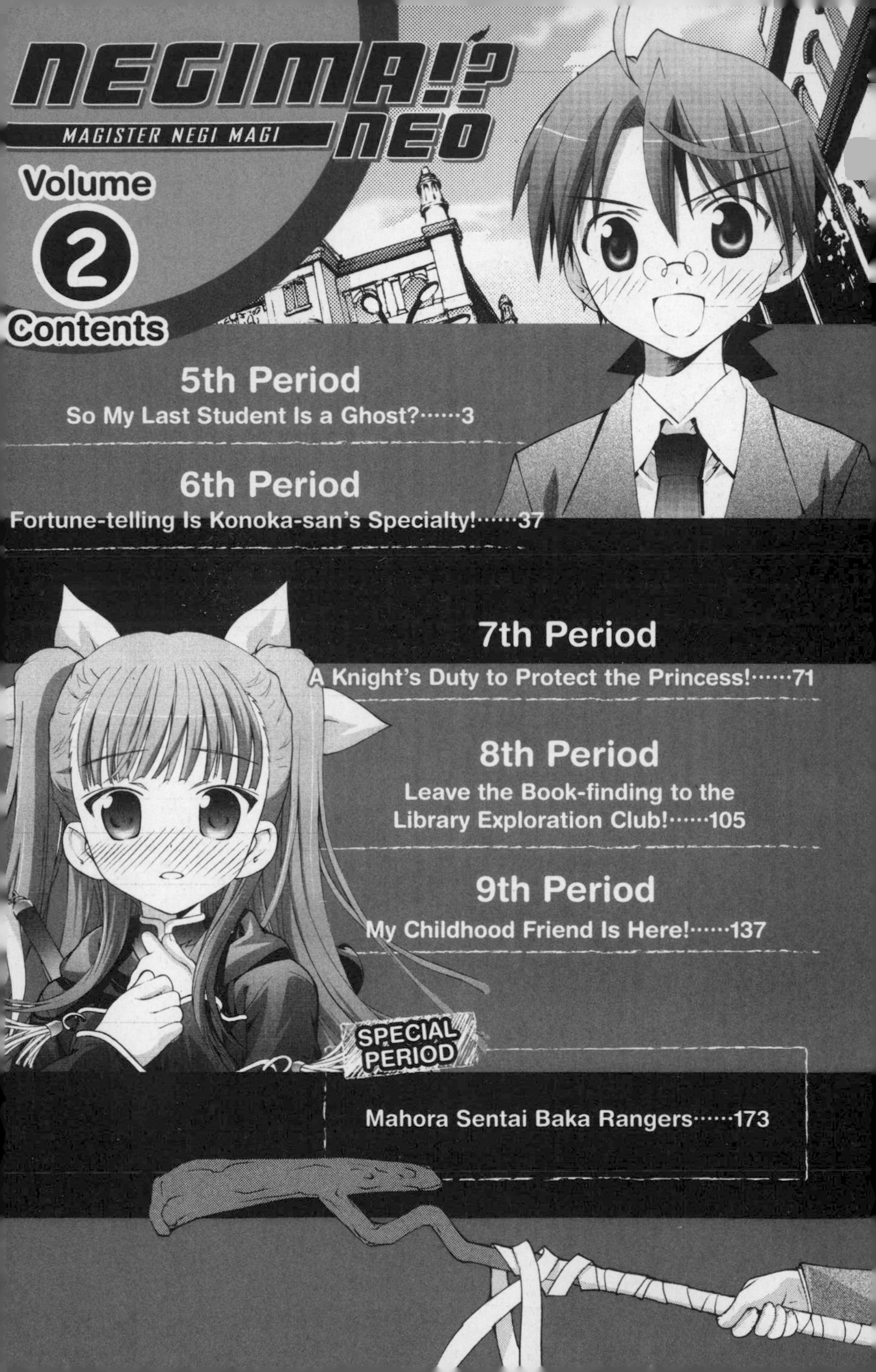

NEGIMA!? NEO

MAGISTER NEGI MAGI

Volume 2

Contents

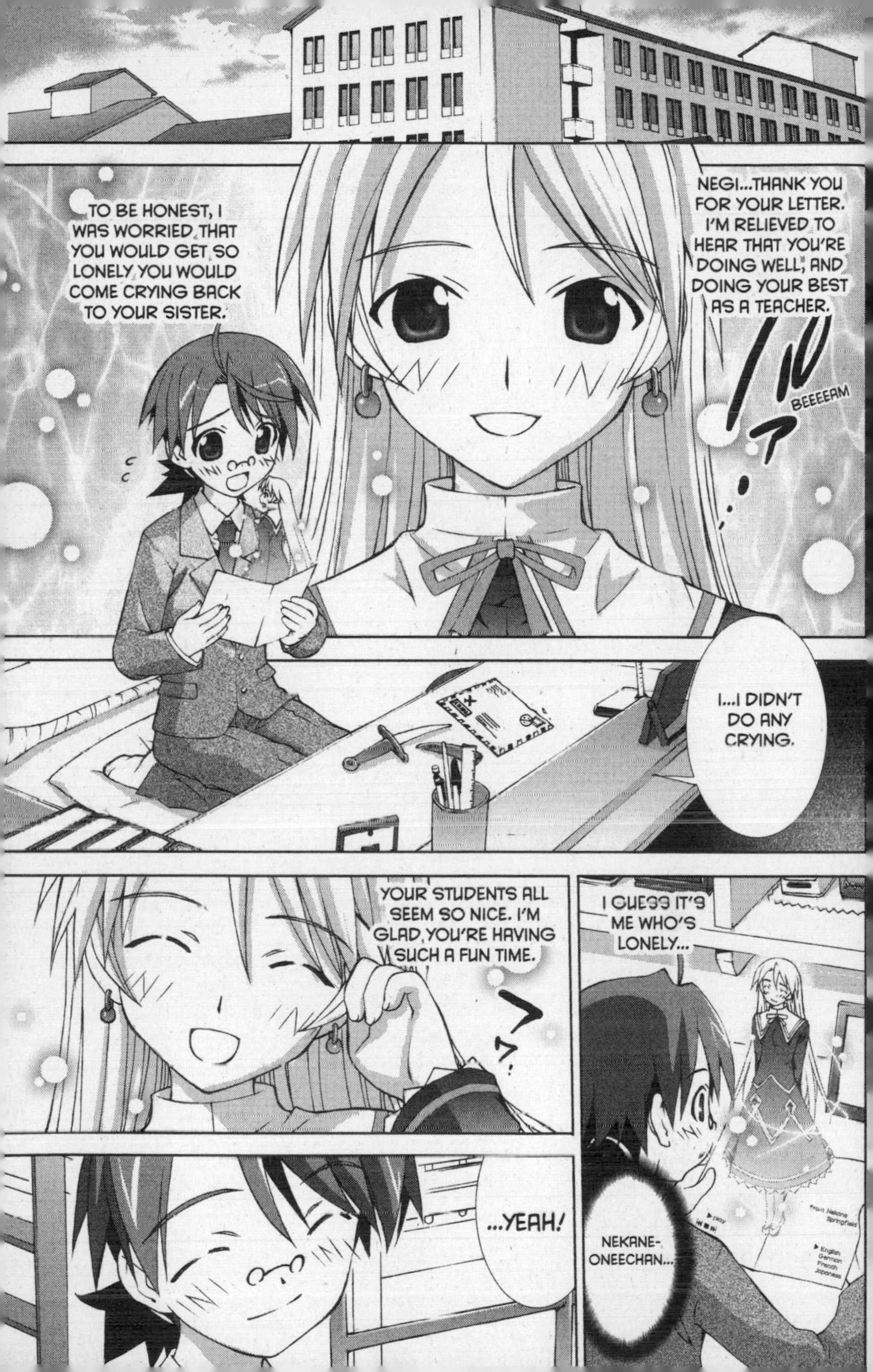
NEGI...THANK YOU FOR YOUR LETTER. I'M RELIEVED TO HEAR THAT YOU'RE DOING WELL, AND DOING YOUR BEST AS A TEACHER.
BEEEEAM
TO BE HONEST, I WAS WORRIED THAT YOU WOULD GET SO LONELY YOU WOULD COME CRYING BACK TO YOUR SISTER.
I...I DIDN'T DO ANY CRYING.
I GUESS IT'S ME WHO'S LONELY...
from Nekane Springfield
play
English
German
French
Japanese
NEKANE-ONEECHAN...
YOUR STUDENTS ALL SEEM SO NICE. I'M GLAD YOU'RE HAVING SUCH A FUN TIME.
...YEAH!

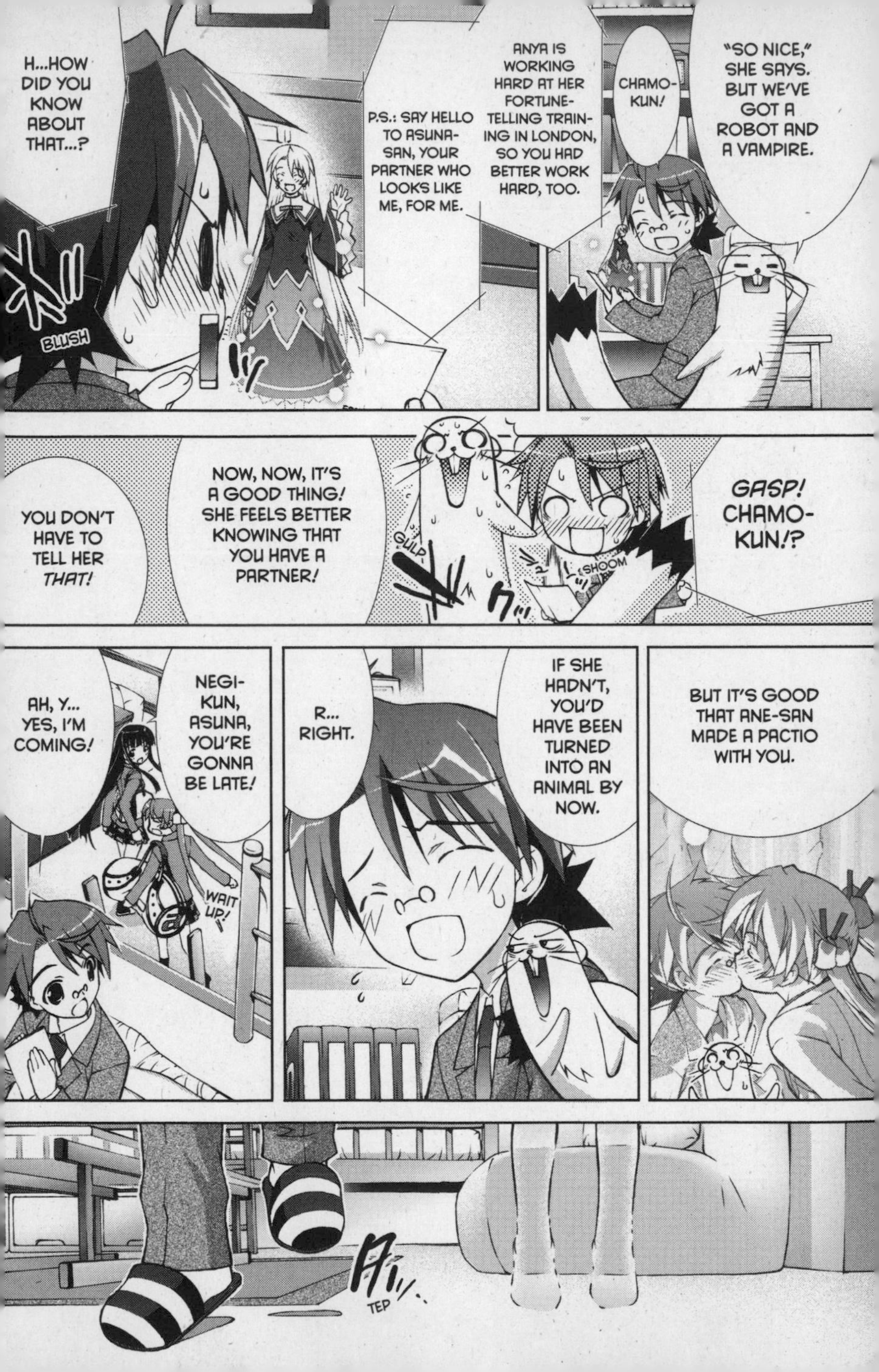
"SO NICE," SHE SAYS. BUT WE'VE GOT A ROBOT AND A VAMPIRE.
CHAMO-KUN!
ANYA IS WORKING HARD AT HER FORTUNE-TELLING TRAINING IN LONDON, SO YOU HAD BETTER WORK HARD, TOO.
P.S.: SAY HELLO TO ASUNA-SAN, YOUR PARTNER WHO LOOKS LIKE ME, FOR ME.
H...HOW DID YOU KNOW ABOUT THAT...?
BLUSH
GASP! CHAMO-KUN!?
SHOOM
GULP
NOW, NOW, IT'S A GOOD THING! SHE FEELS BETTER KNOWING THAT YOU HAVE A PARTNER!
YOU DON'T HAVE TO TELL HER THAT!
BUT IT'S GOOD THAT ANE-SAN MADE A PACTIO WITH YOU.
IF SHE HADN'T, YOU'D HAVE BEEN TURNED INTO AN ANIMAL BY NOW.
R... RIGHT.
NEGI-KUN, ASUNA, YOU'RE GONNA BE LATE!
AH, Y... YES, I'M COMING!
WAIT UP!
TEP

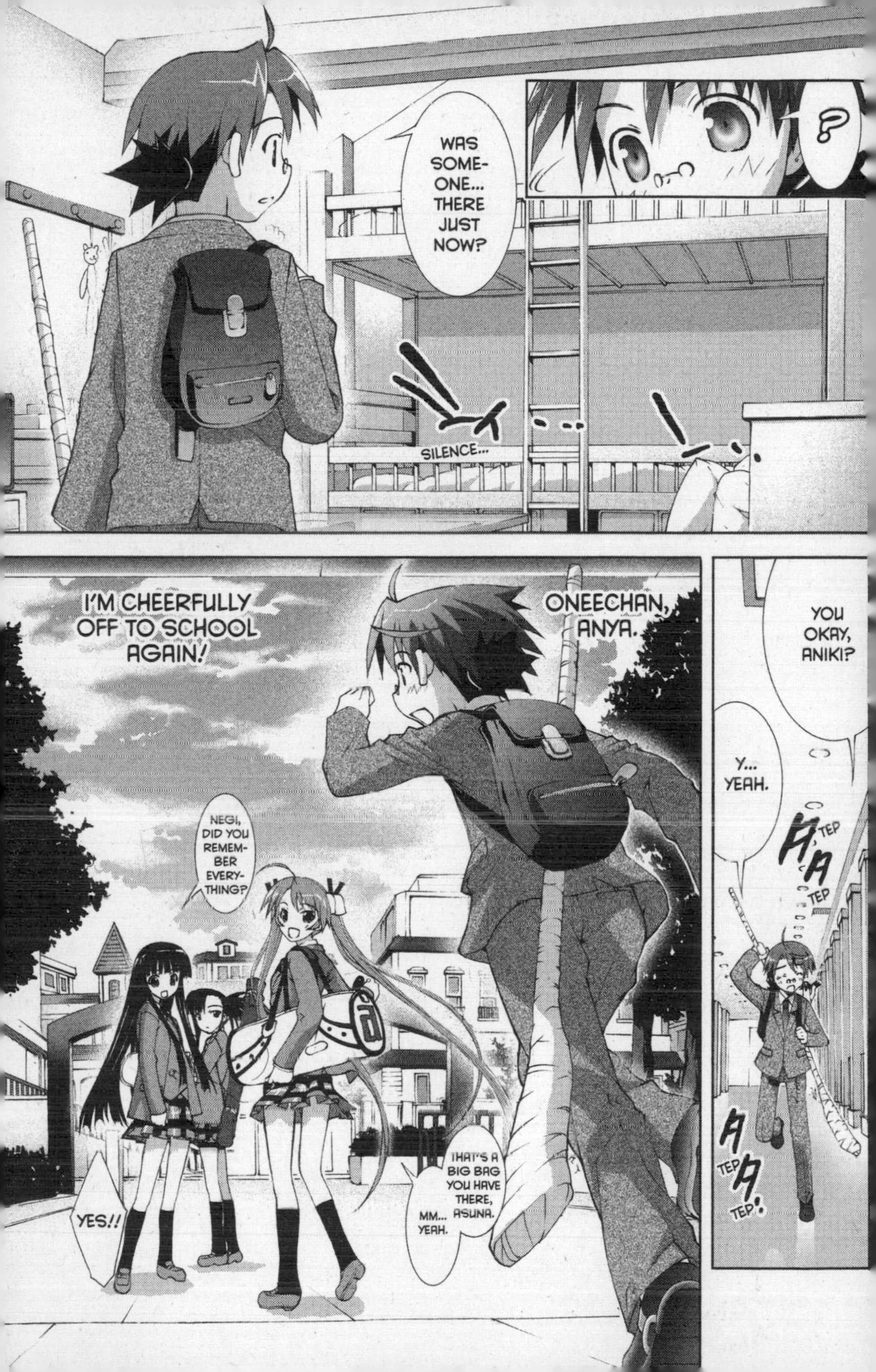
?
WAS SOME-ONE... THERE JUST NOW?
SILENCE...
YOU OKAY, ANIKI?
Y... YEAH.
TEP
TEP
TEP
TEP
ONEECHAN, ANYA.
I'M CHEERFULLY OFF TO SCHOOL AGAIN!
NEGI, DID YOU REMEMBER EVERYTHING?
THAT'S A BIG BAG YOU HAVE THERE, ASUNA.
MM... YEAH.
YES!!

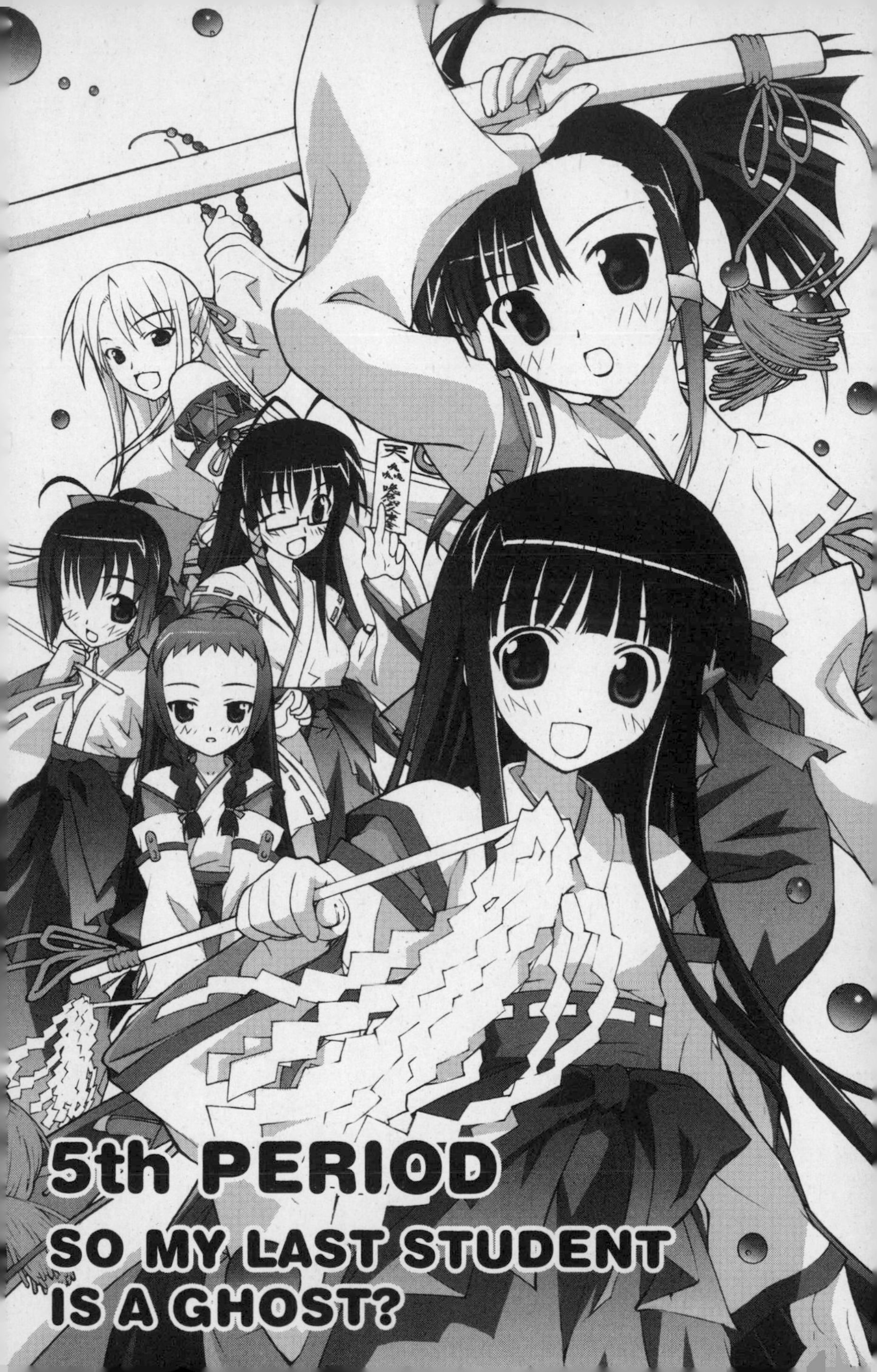

5th PERIOD
SO MY LAST STUDENT IS A GHOST?

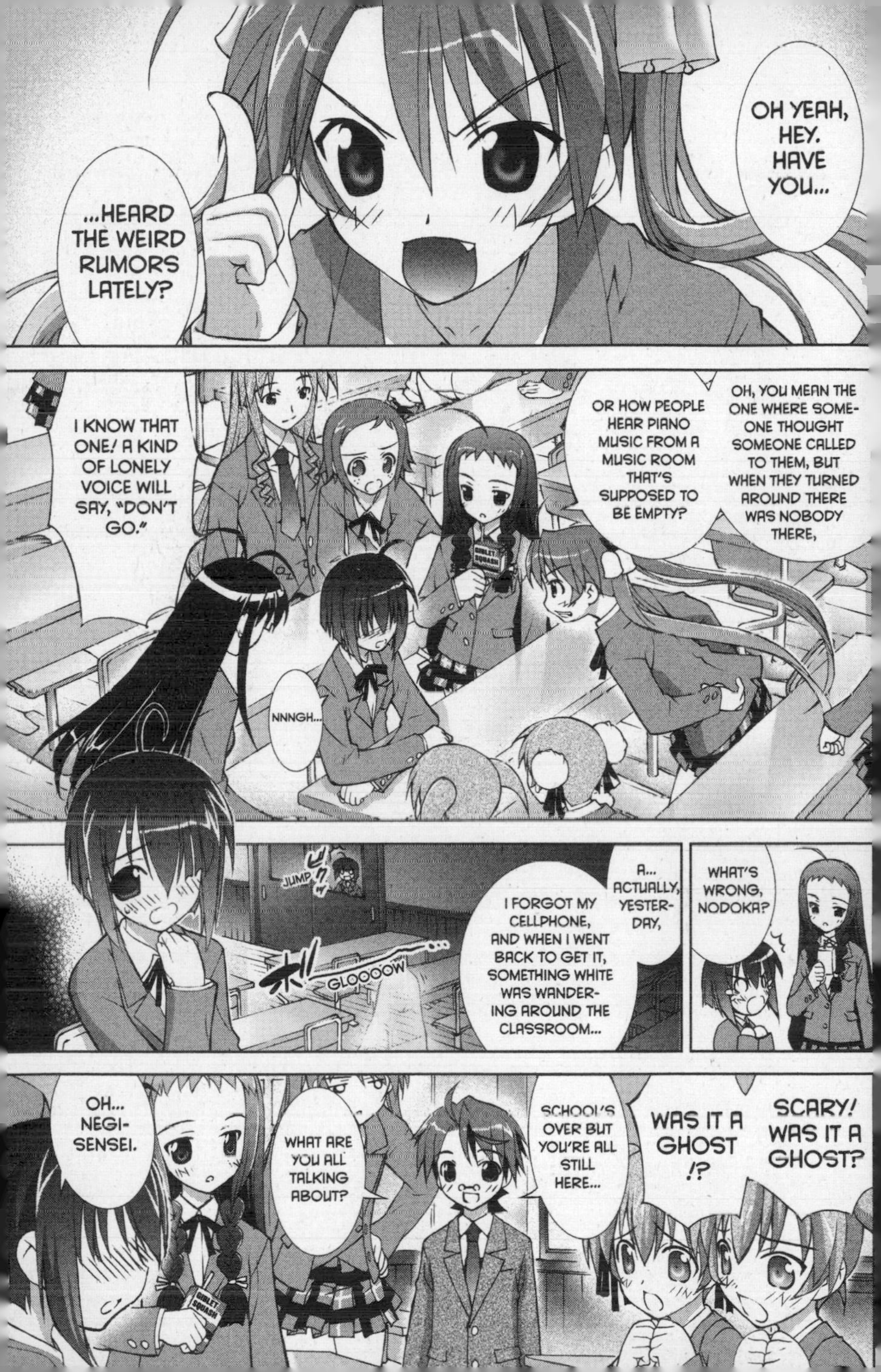
OH YEAH, HEY. HAVE YOU...
...HEARD THE WEIRD RUMORS LATELY?
OH, YOU MEAN THE ONE WHERE SOME-ONE THOUGHT SOMEONE CALLED TO THEM, BUT WHEN THEY TURNED AROUND THERE WAS NOBODY THERE,
OR HOW PEOPLE HEAR PIANO MUSIC FROM A MUSIC ROOM THAT'S SUPPOSED TO BE EMPTY?
I KNOW THAT ONE! A KIND OF LONELY VOICE WILL SAY, "DON'T GO."
GIBLET SQUASH
NNNGH...
WHAT'S WRONG, NODOKA?
A... ACTUALLY, YESTER-DAY,
I FORGOT MY CELLPHONE, AND WHEN I WENT BACK TO GET IT, SOMETHING WHITE WAS WANDER-ING AROUND THE CLASSROOM...
JUMP
GLOOOOW
SCARY! WAS IT A GHOST?
WAS IT A GHOST !?
SCHOOL'S OVER BUT YOU'RE ALL STILL HERE...
WHAT ARE YOU ALL TALKING ABOUT?
OH... NEGI-SENSEI.
GIBLET SQUASH

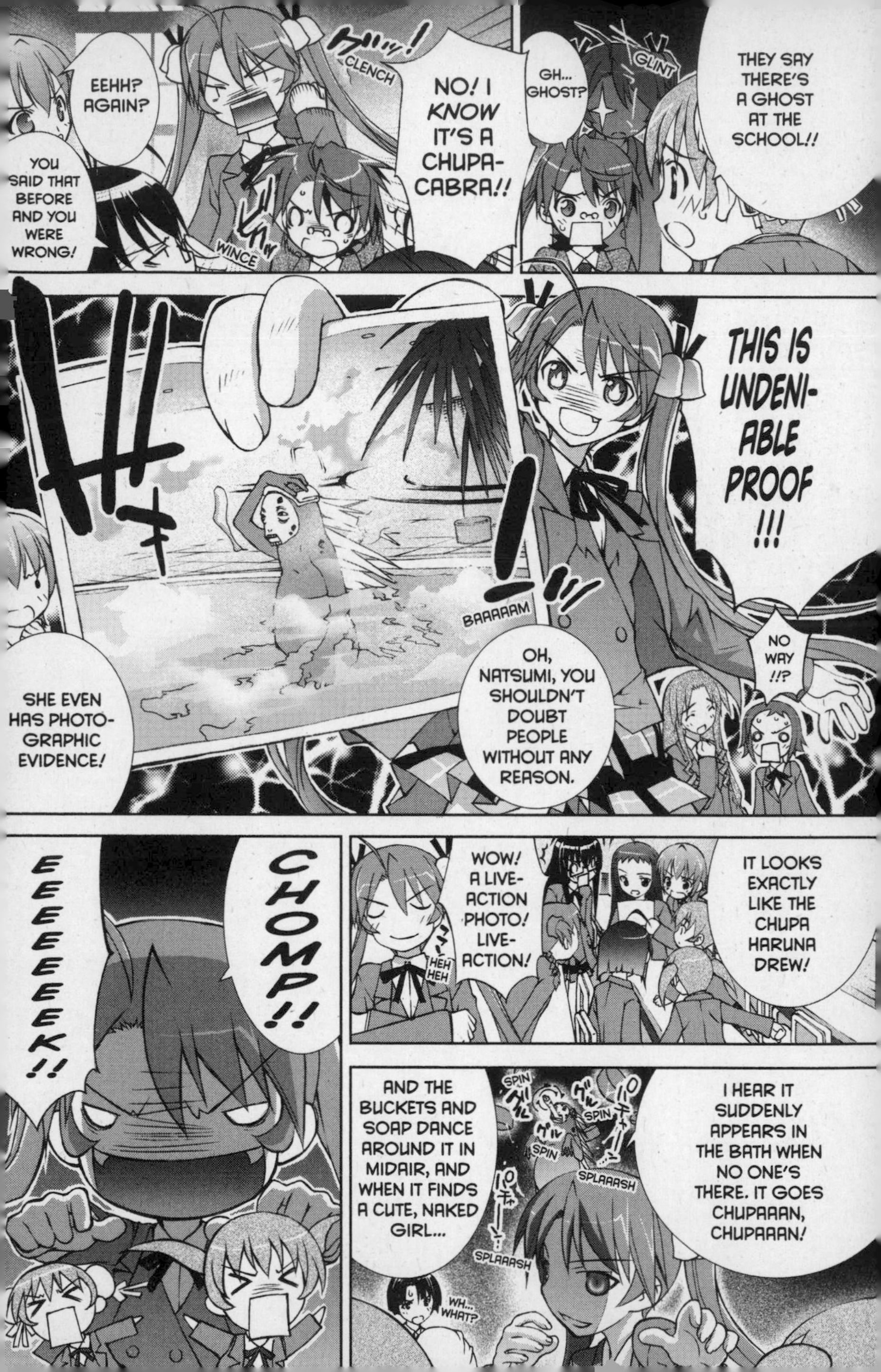
THEY SAY THERE'S A GHOST AT THE SCHOOL!!
GLINT
GH... GHOST?
NO! I KNOW IT'S A CHUPA-CABRA!!
CLENCH
EEHH? AGAIN?
YOU SAID THAT BEFORE AND YOU WERE WRONG!
WINCE
THIS IS UNDENI-ABLE PROOF!!!
BAAAAAM
NO WAY!!?
OH, NATSUMI, YOU SHOULDN'T DOUBT PEOPLE WITHOUT ANY REASON.
SHE EVEN HAS PHOTO-GRAPHIC EVIDENCE!
IT LOOKS EXACTLY LIKE THE CHUPA HARUNA DREW!
WOW! A LIVE-ACTION PHOTO! LIVE-ACTION!
HEH HEH
I HEAR IT SUDDENLY APPEARS IN THE BATH WHEN NO ONE'S THERE. IT GOES CHUPAAAN, CHUPAAAN!
SPIN
SPIN
SPIN
SPLAAASH
AND THE BUCKETS AND SOAP DANCE AROUND IT IN MIDAIR, AND WHEN IT FINDS A CUTE, NAKED GIRL...
SPLAAASH
WH... WHAT?
CHOMP!!
EEEEEEEK!!

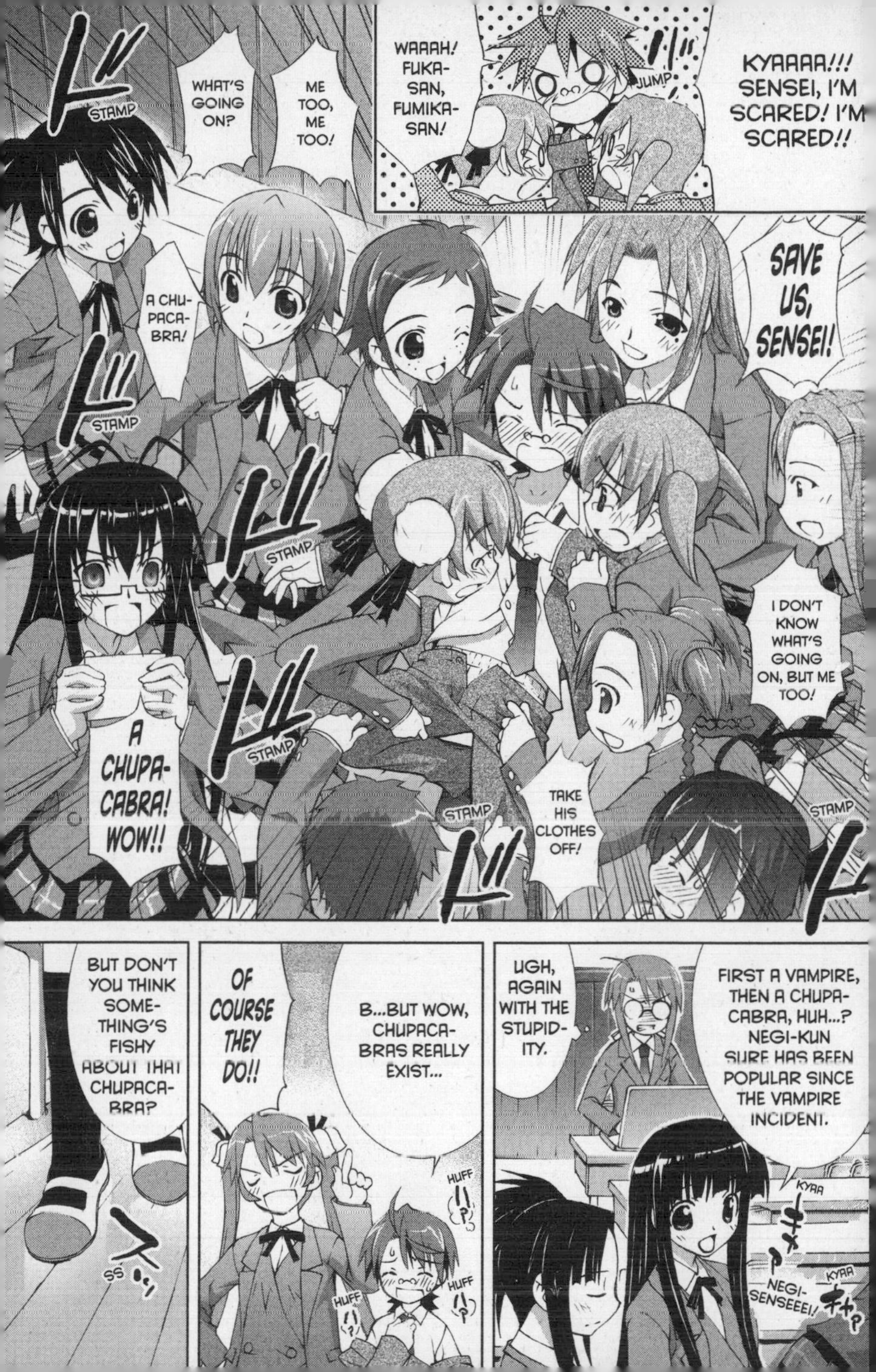

KYAAAA!!! SENSEI, I'M SCARED! I'M SCARED!!
JUMP
WAAAH! FUKA-SAN, FUMIKA-SAN!
SAVE US, SENSEI!
ME TOO, ME TOO!
WHAT'S GOING ON?
STAMP
A CHUPA-CACA-BRA!
STAMP
I DON'T KNOW WHAT'S GOING ON, BUT ME TOO!
STAMP
STAMP
TAKE HIS CLOTHES OFF!
STAMP
A CHUPA-CABRA! WOW!!
STAMP
FIRST A VAMPIRE, THEN A CHUPA-CABRA, HUH...? NEGI-KUN SURE HAS BEEN POPULAR SINCE THE VAMPIRE INCIDENT.
UGH, AGAIN WITH THE STUPID-ITY.
KYAA
NEGI-SENSEEEI!
KYAA
B...BUT WOW, CHUPACA-BRAS REALLY EXIST...
OF COURSE THEY DO!!
HUFF
HUFF
HUFF
BUT DON'T YOU THINK SOME-THING'S FISHY ABOUT THAT CHUPACA-BRA?
SS

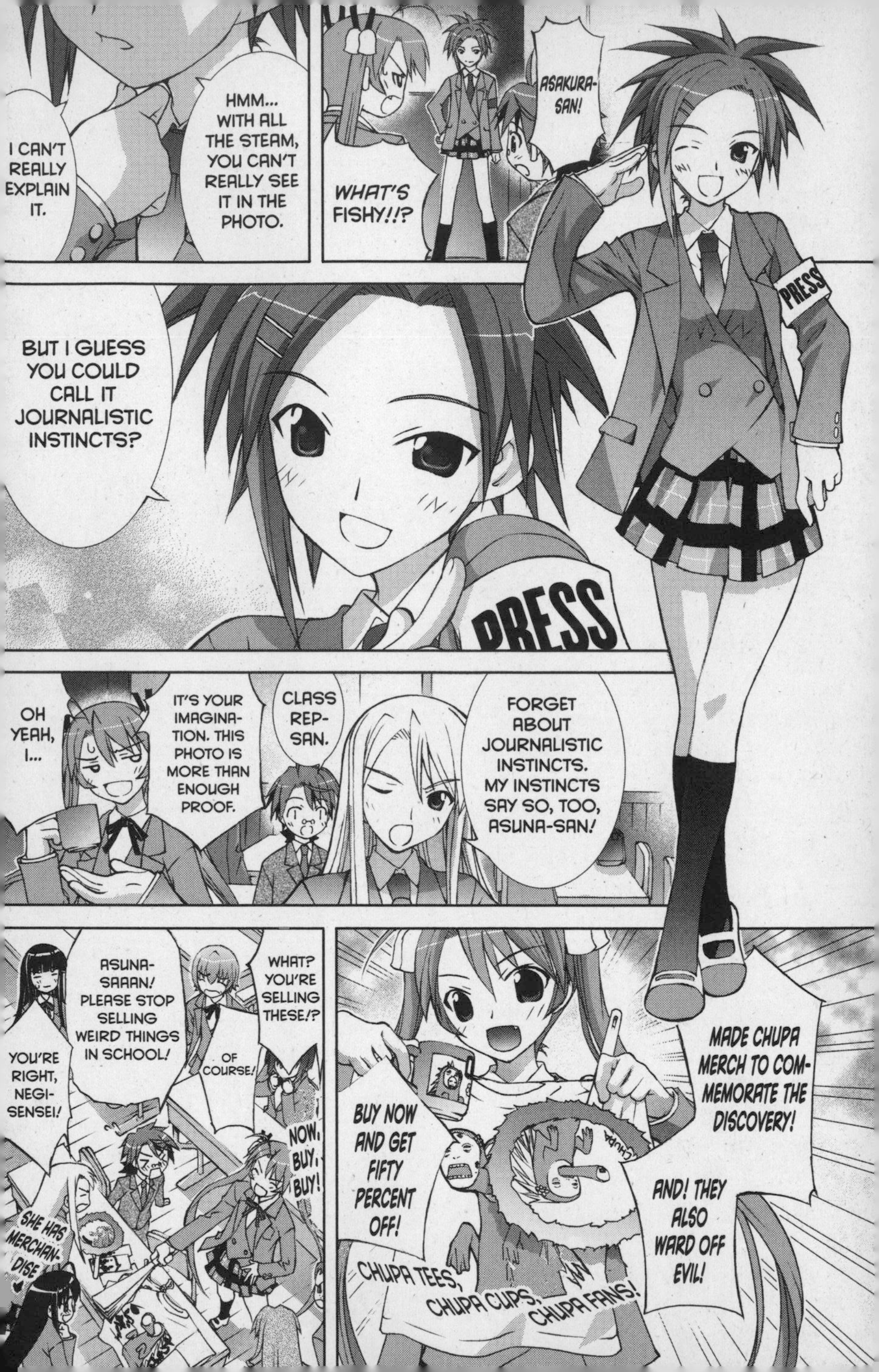
PRESS
ASAKURA-SAN!
WHAT'S FISHY!!?
HMM... WITH ALL THE STEAM, YOU CAN'T REALLY SEE IT IN THE PHOTO.
I CAN'T REALLY EXPLAIN IT.
BUT I GUESS YOU COULD CALL IT JOURNALISTIC INSTINCTS?
PRESS
FORGET ABOUT JOURNALISTIC INSTINCTS. MY INSTINCTS SAY SO, TOO, ASUNA-SAN!
CLASS REP-SAN.
IT'S YOUR IMAGINATION. THIS PHOTO IS MORE THAN ENOUGH PROOF.
OH YEAH, I...
MADE CHUPA MERCH TO COMMEMORATE THE DISCOVERY!
BUY NOW AND GET FIFTY PERCENT OFF!
AND! THEY ALSO WARD OFF EVIL!
CHUPA TEES, CHUPA CUPS, CHUPA FANS!
WHAT? YOU'RE SELLING THESE!?
OF COURSE!
ASUNA-SAAAN! PLEASE STOP SELLING WEIRD THINGS IN SCHOOL!
NOW, BUY, BUY!
YOU'RE RIGHT, NEGI-SENSEI!
SHE HAS MERCHANDISE

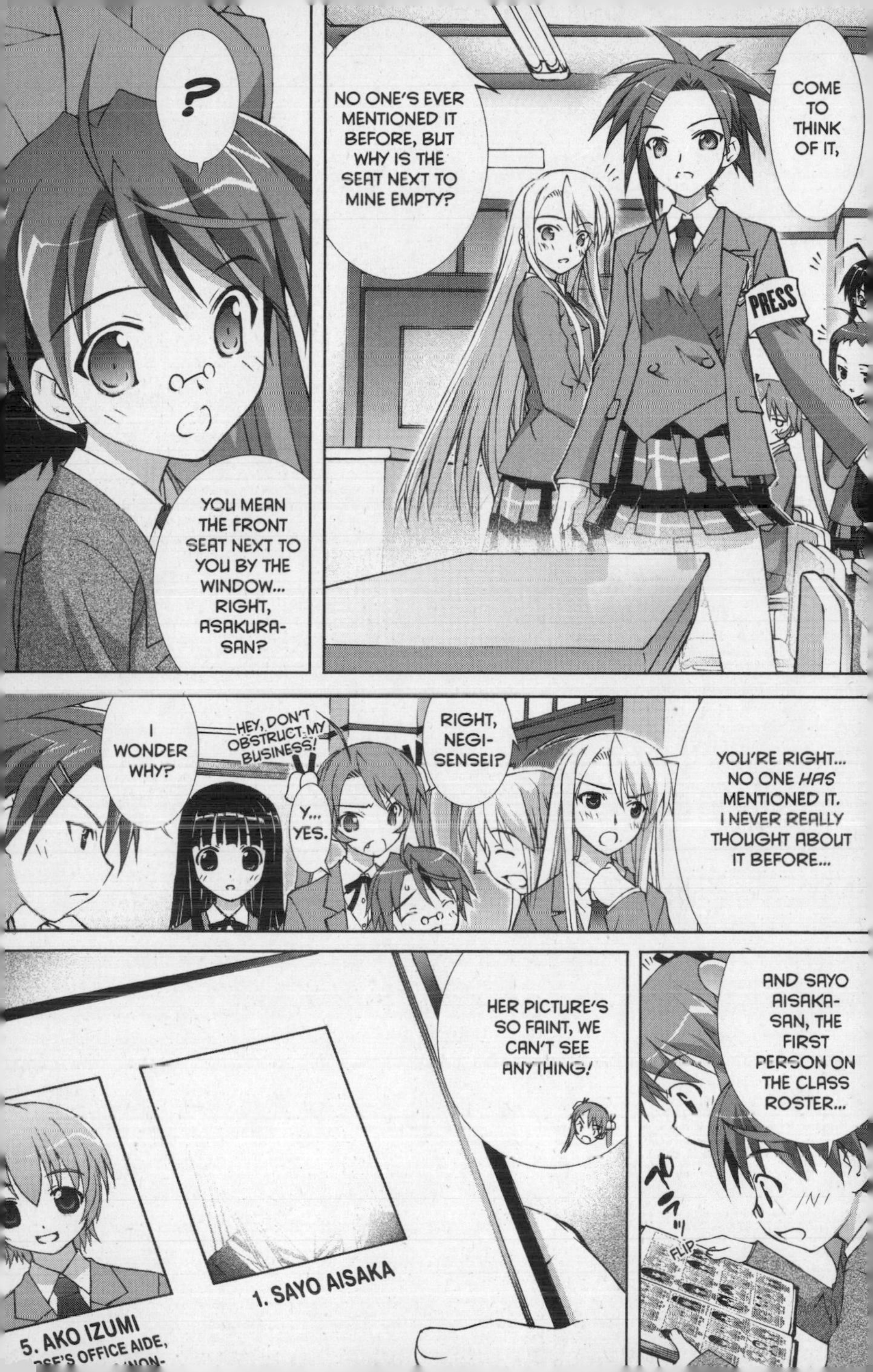

COME TO THINK OF IT,
NO ONE'S EVER MENTIONED IT BEFORE, BUT WHY IS THE SEAT NEXT TO MINE EMPTY?
PRESS
?
YOU MEAN THE FRONT SEAT NEXT TO YOU BY THE WINDOW... RIGHT, ASAKURA-SAN?
YOU'RE RIGHT... NO ONE *HAS* MENTIONED IT. I NEVER REALLY THOUGHT ABOUT IT BEFORE...
RIGHT, NEGI-SENSEI?
Y... YES.
HEY, DON'T OBSTRUCT MY BUSINESS!
I WONDER WHY?
AND SAYO AISAKA-SAN, THE FIRST PERSON ON THE CLASS ROSTER...
FLIP
HER PICTURE'S SO FAINT, WE CAN'T SEE ANYTHING!
1. SAYO AISAKA
5. AKO IZUMI

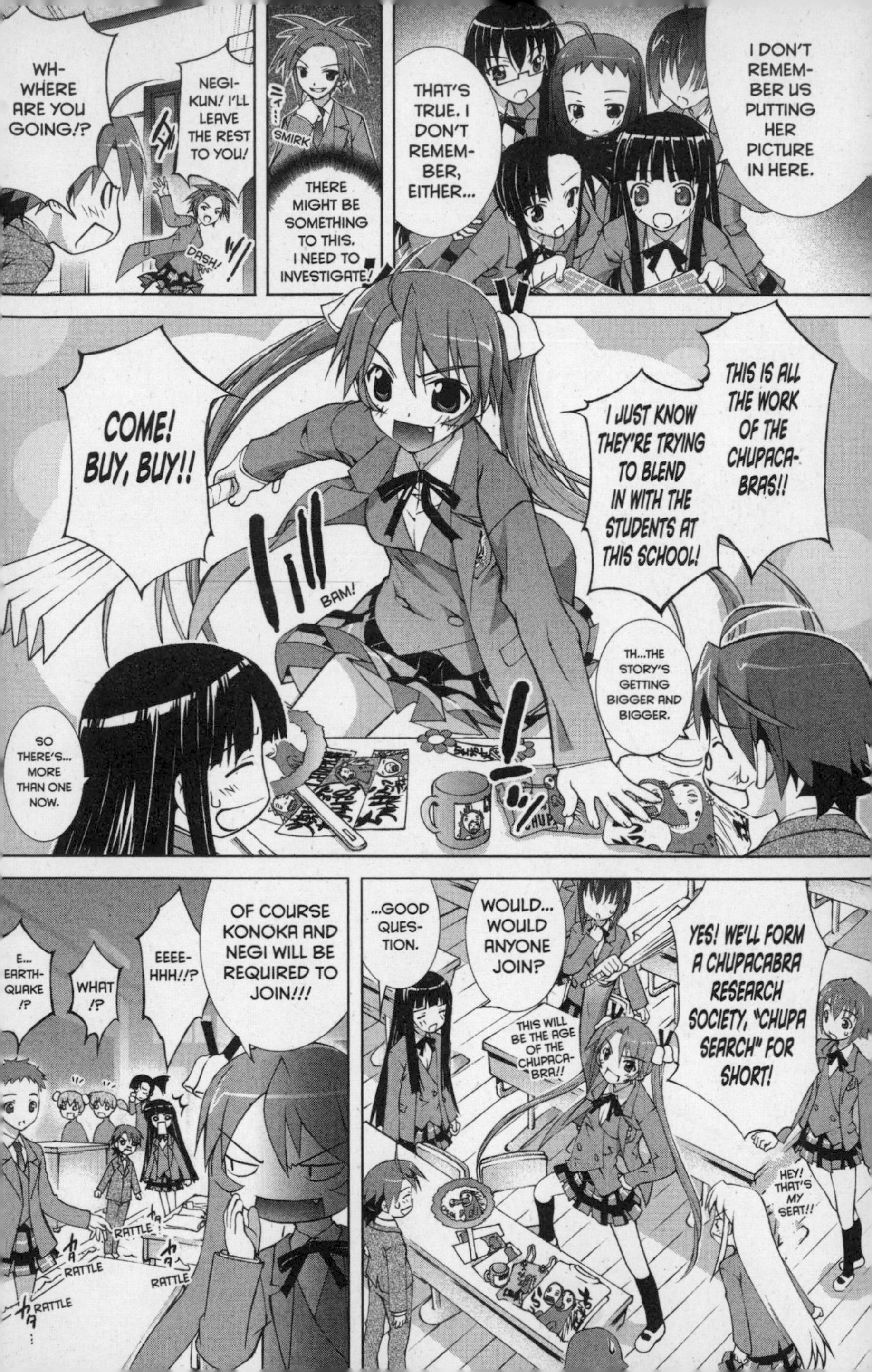

I DON'T REMEMBER US PUTTING HER PICTURE IN HERE.
THAT'S TRUE. I DON'T REMEMBER, EITHER...
SMIRK
THERE MIGHT BE SOMETHING TO THIS. I NEED TO INVESTIGATE!
NEGI-KUN! I'LL LEAVE THE REST TO YOU!
WH-WHERE ARE YOU GOING!?
DASH!
THIS IS ALL THE WORK OF THE CHUPACABRAS!!
I JUST KNOW THEY'RE TRYING TO BLEND IN WITH THE STUDENTS AT THIS SCHOOL!
COME! BUY, BUY!!
BAM!
TH...THE STORY'S GETTING BIGGER AND BIGGER.
SO THERE'S... MORE THAN ONE NOW.
YES! WE'LL FORM A CHUPACABRA RESEARCH SOCIETY, "CHUPA SEARCH" FOR SHORT!
WOULD... WOULD ANYONE JOIN?
...GOOD QUESTION.
THIS WILL BE THE AGE OF THE CHUPACABRA!!
HEY! THAT'S MY SEAT!!
OF COURSE KONOKA AND NEGI WILL BE REQUIRED TO JOIN!!!
EEEE-HHH!!?
WHAT!?
E... EARTHQUAKE!?
RATTLE
RATTLE
RATTLE
RATTLE

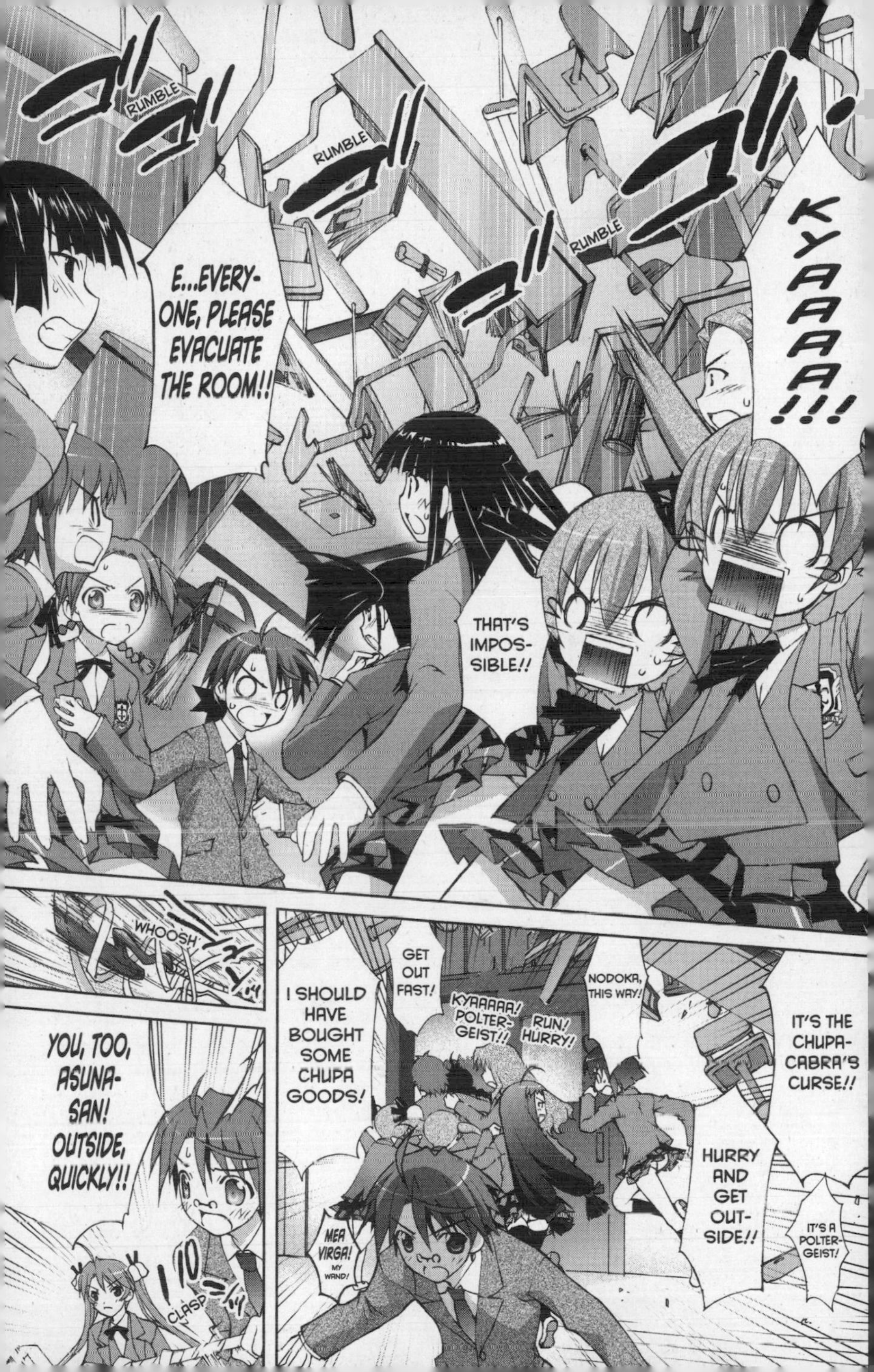
KYAAAAA!!!
RUMBLE
RUMBLE
RUMBLE
E...EVERY-ONE, PLEASE EVACUATE THE ROOM!!
THAT'S IMPOSSIBLE!!
IT'S THE CHUPACABRA'S CURSE!!
NODOKA, THIS WAY!
RUN! HURRY!
KYAAAAA! POLTERGEIST!!
GET OUT FAST!
I SHOULD HAVE BOUGHT SOME CHUPA GOODS!
HURRY AND GET OUTSIDE!!
IT'S A POLTERGEIST!
MEA VIRGA! MY WAND!
WHOOSH
YOU, TOO, ASUNA-SAN! OUTSIDE, QUICKLY!!
CLASP

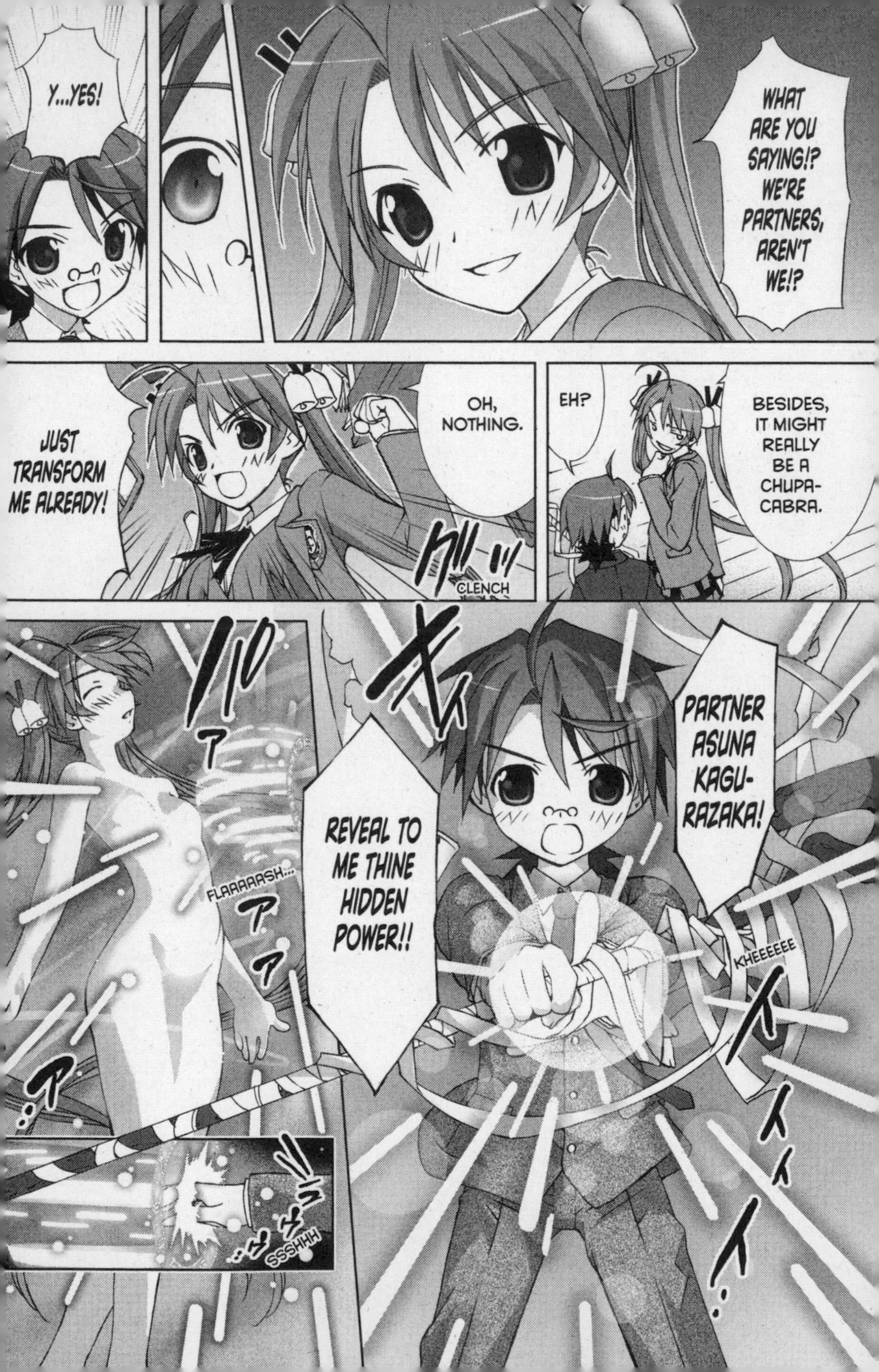
WHAT ARE YOU SAYING!? WE'RE PARTNERS, AREN'T WE!?
Y...YES!
BESIDES, IT MIGHT REALLY BE A CHUPA-CABRA.
EH?
OH, NOTHING.
JUST TRANSFORM ME ALREADY!
CLENCH
PARTNER ASUNA KAGU-RAZAKA!
REVEAL TO ME THINE HIDDEN POWER!!
KHEEEEEE
FLAAAAASH...
SSSHHH

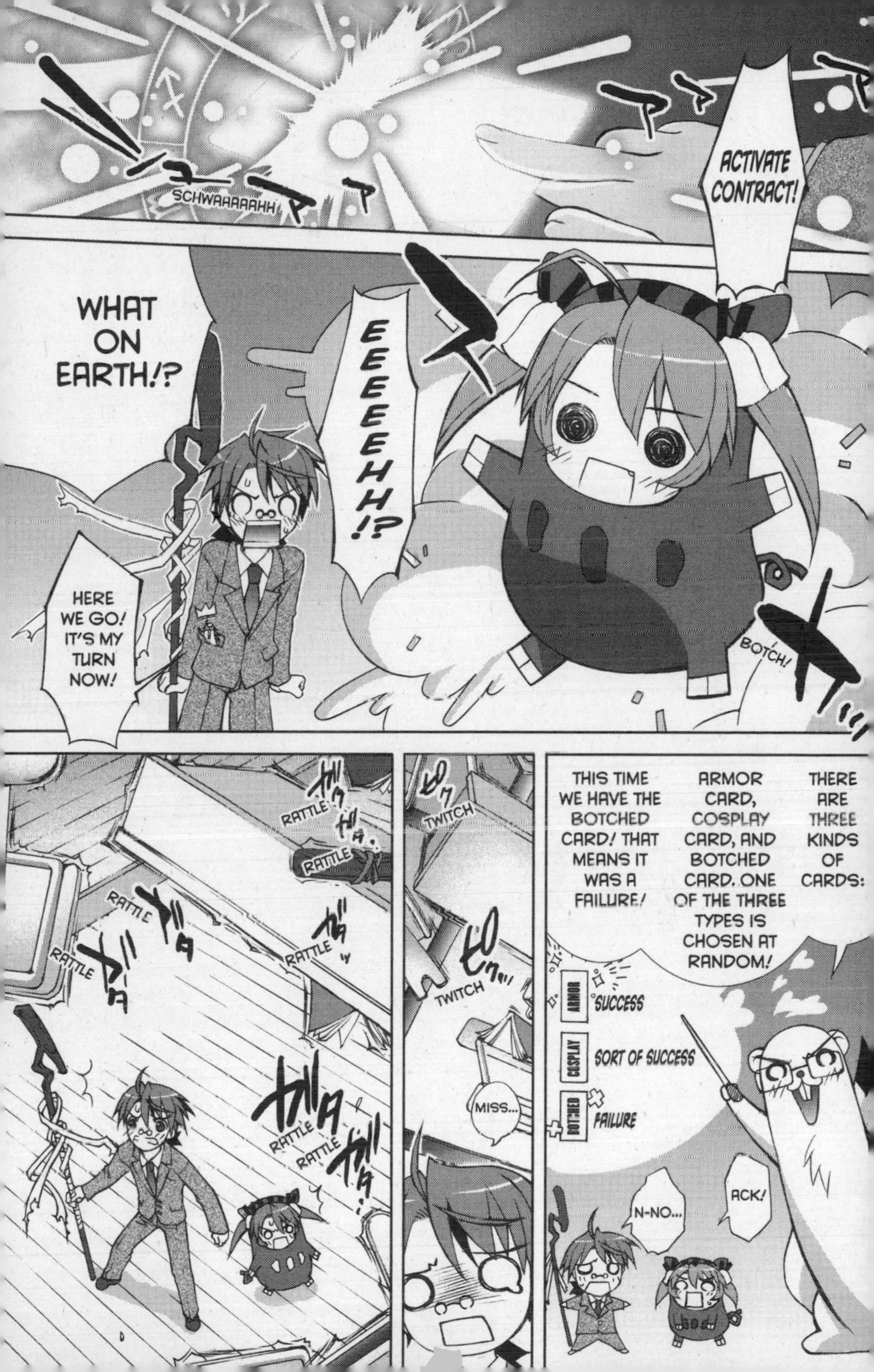
ACTIVATE CONTRACT!
SCHWAAAAAAHH
EEEEEEHH!?
WHAT ON EARTH!?
BOTCH!
HERE WE GO! IT'S MY TURN NOW!
THERE ARE THREE KINDS OF CARDS:
ARMOR CARD, COSPLAY CARD, AND BOTCHED CARD. ONE OF THE THREE TYPES IS CHOSEN AT RANDOM!
THIS TIME WE HAVE THE BOTCHED CARD! THAT MEANS IT WAS A FAILURE!
ARMOR SUCCESS
COSPLAY SORT OF SUCCESS
BOTCHED FAILURE
ACK!
N-NO...
TWITCH
TWITCH
MISS...
RATTLE
RATTLE
RATTLE
RATTLE
RATTLE
RATTLE
RATTLE
RATTLE

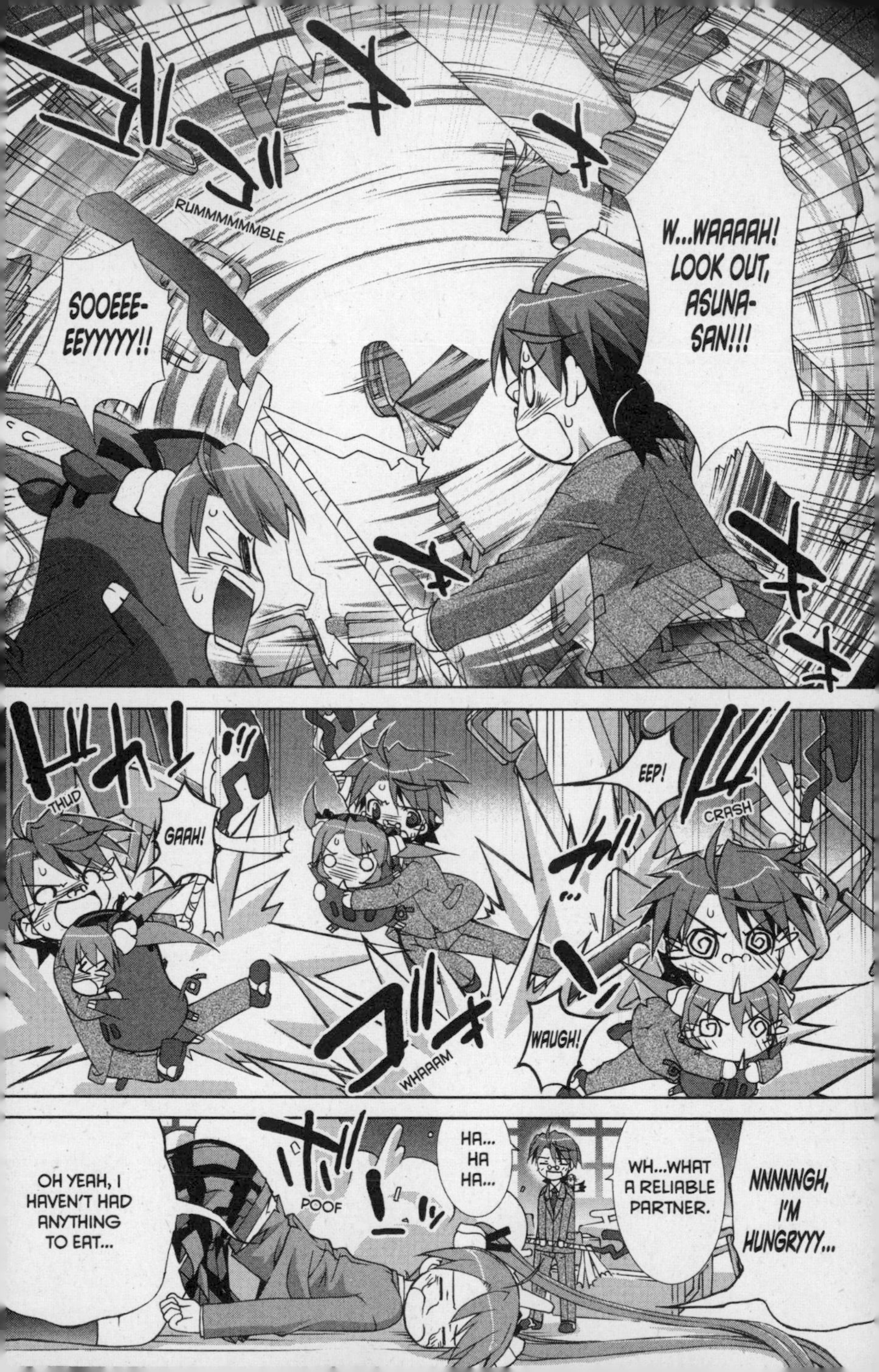
W...WAAAAH! LOOK OUT, ASUNA-SAN!!!
RUMMMMMMMBLE
SOOEEE-EEYYYYY!!
CRASH
EEP!
WAUGH!
WHAAAM
GAAH!
THUD
NNNNNGH, I'M HUNGRYYY...
WH...WHAT A RELIABLE PARTNER.
HA... HA HA...
POOF
OH YEAH, I HAVEN'T HAD ANYTHING TO EAT...

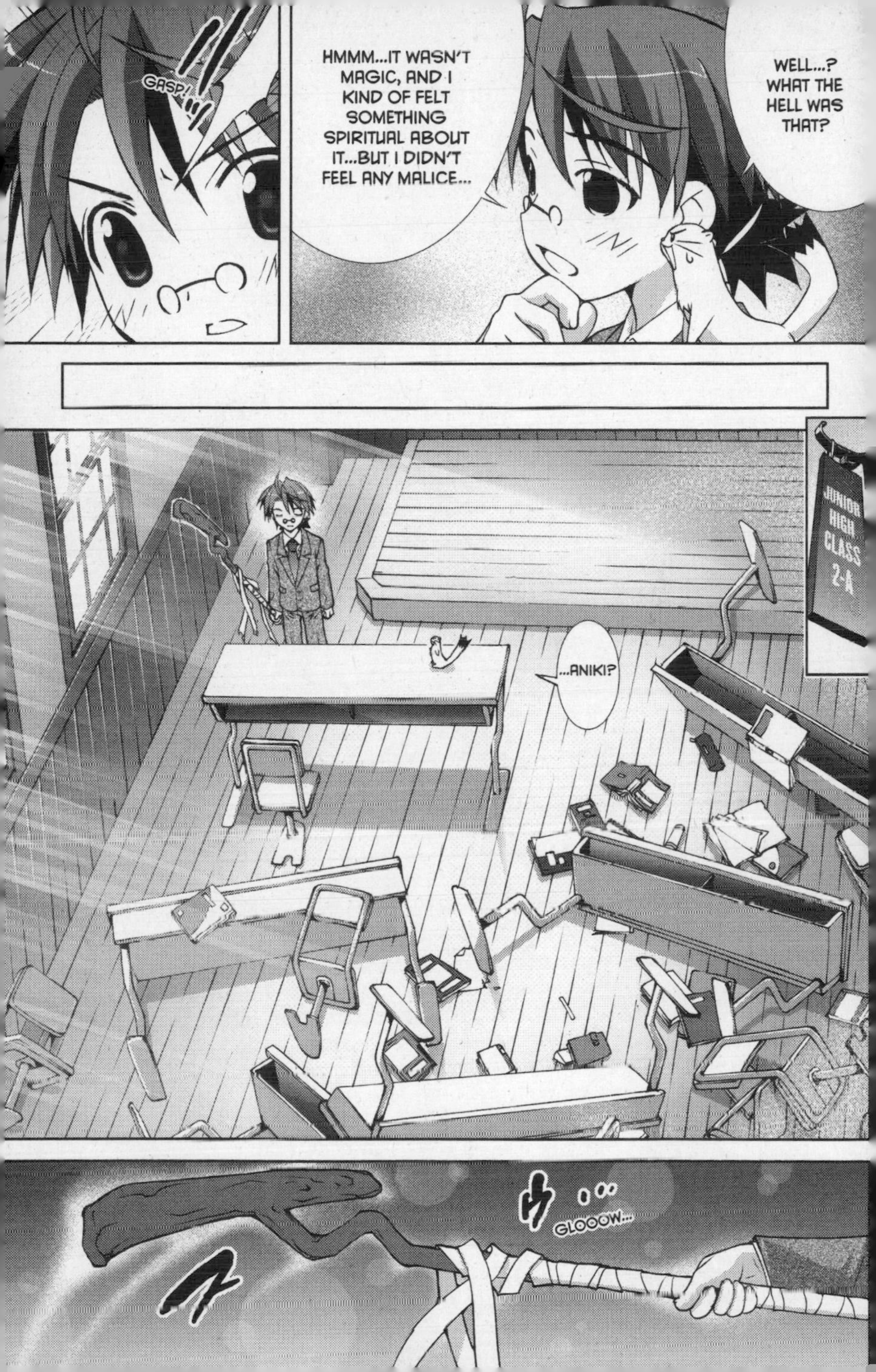
WELL...? WHAT THE HELL WAS THAT?
HMMM...IT WASN'T MAGIC, AND I KIND OF FELT SOMETHING SPIRITUAL ABOUT IT...BUT I DIDN'T FEEL ANY MALICE...
GASP!
JUNIOR HIGH CLASS 2-A
...ANIKI?
GLOOOW...

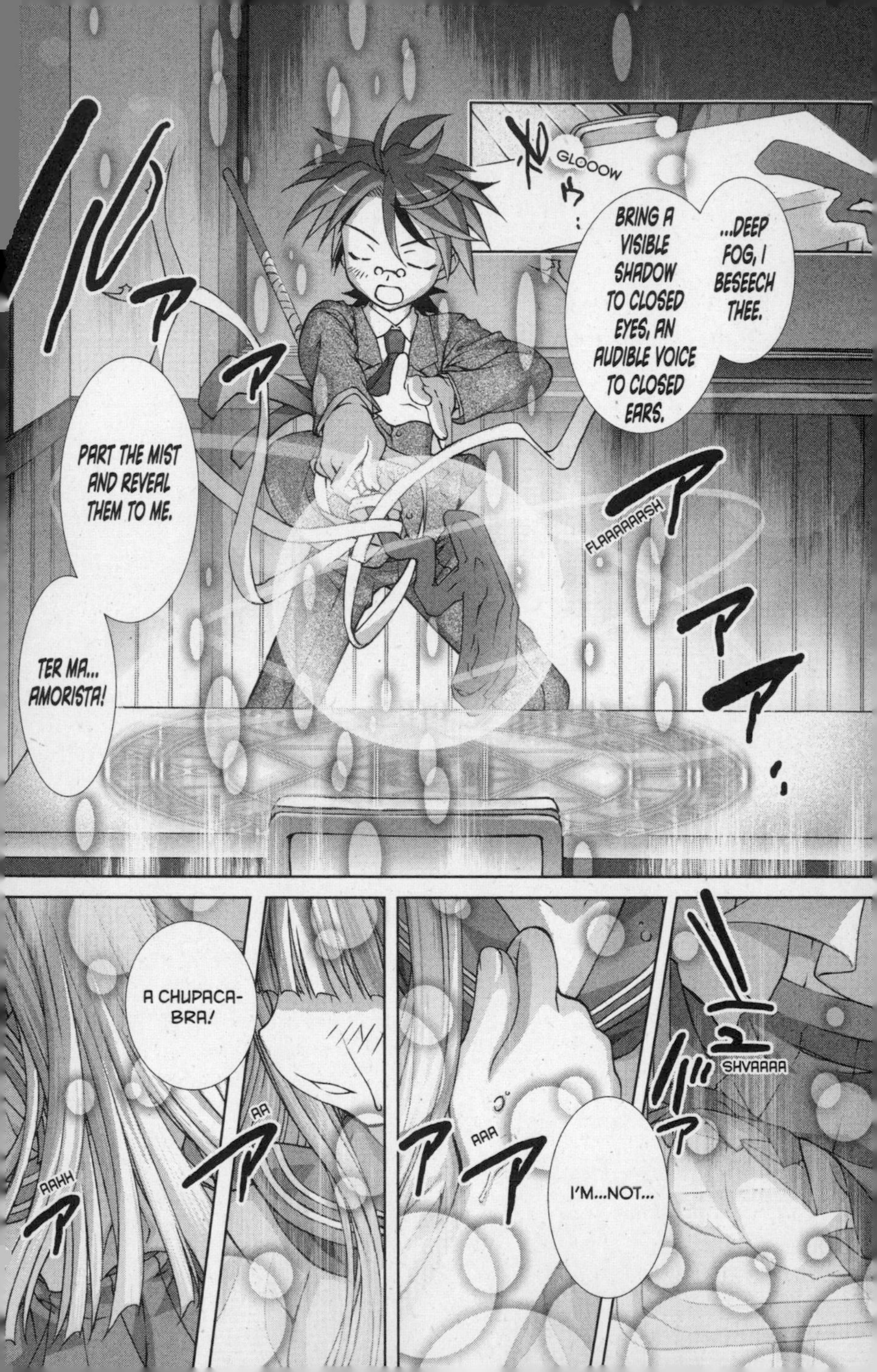
GLOOOW
...DEEP FOG, I BESEECH THEE.
BRING A VISIBLE SHADOW TO CLOSED EYES, AN AUDIBLE VOICE TO CLOSED EARS.
FLAAAAAASH
PART THE MIST AND REVEAL THEM TO ME.
TER MA... AMORISTA!
SHVAAAA
I'M...NOT...
AAA
AA
A CHUPACA-BRA!
AAHH

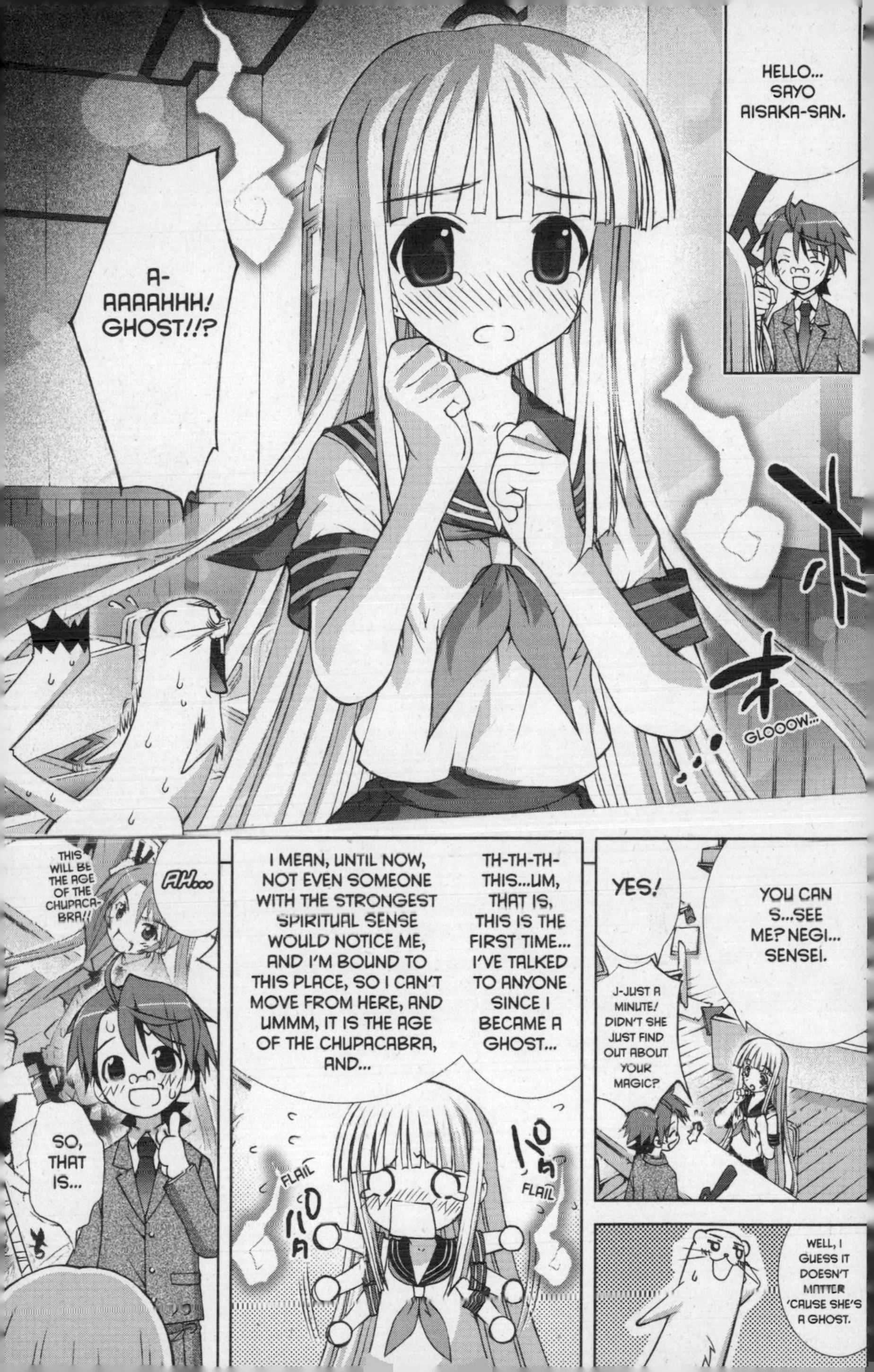
HELLO... SAYO AISAKA-SAN.
A- AAAAHHH! GHOST!!?
GLOOOW...
YOU CAN S...SEE ME? NEGI... SENSEI.
YES!
J-JUST A MINUTE! DIDN'T SHE JUST FIND OUT ABOUT YOUR MAGIC?
WELL, I GUESS IT DOESN'T MATTER 'CAUSE SHE'S A GHOST.
TH-TH-TH-THIS...UM, THAT IS, THIS IS THE FIRST TIME... I'VE TALKED TO ANYONE SINCE I BECAME A GHOST...
I MEAN, UNTIL NOW, NOT EVEN SOMEONE WITH THE STRONGEST SPIRITUAL SENSE WOULD NOTICE ME, AND I'M BOUND TO THIS PLACE, SO I CAN'T MOVE FROM HERE, AND UMMM, IT IS THE AGE OF THE CHUPACABRA, AND...
FLAIL
FLAIL
AH...
THIS WILL BE THE AGE OF THE CHUPACABRA!!
SO, THAT IS...

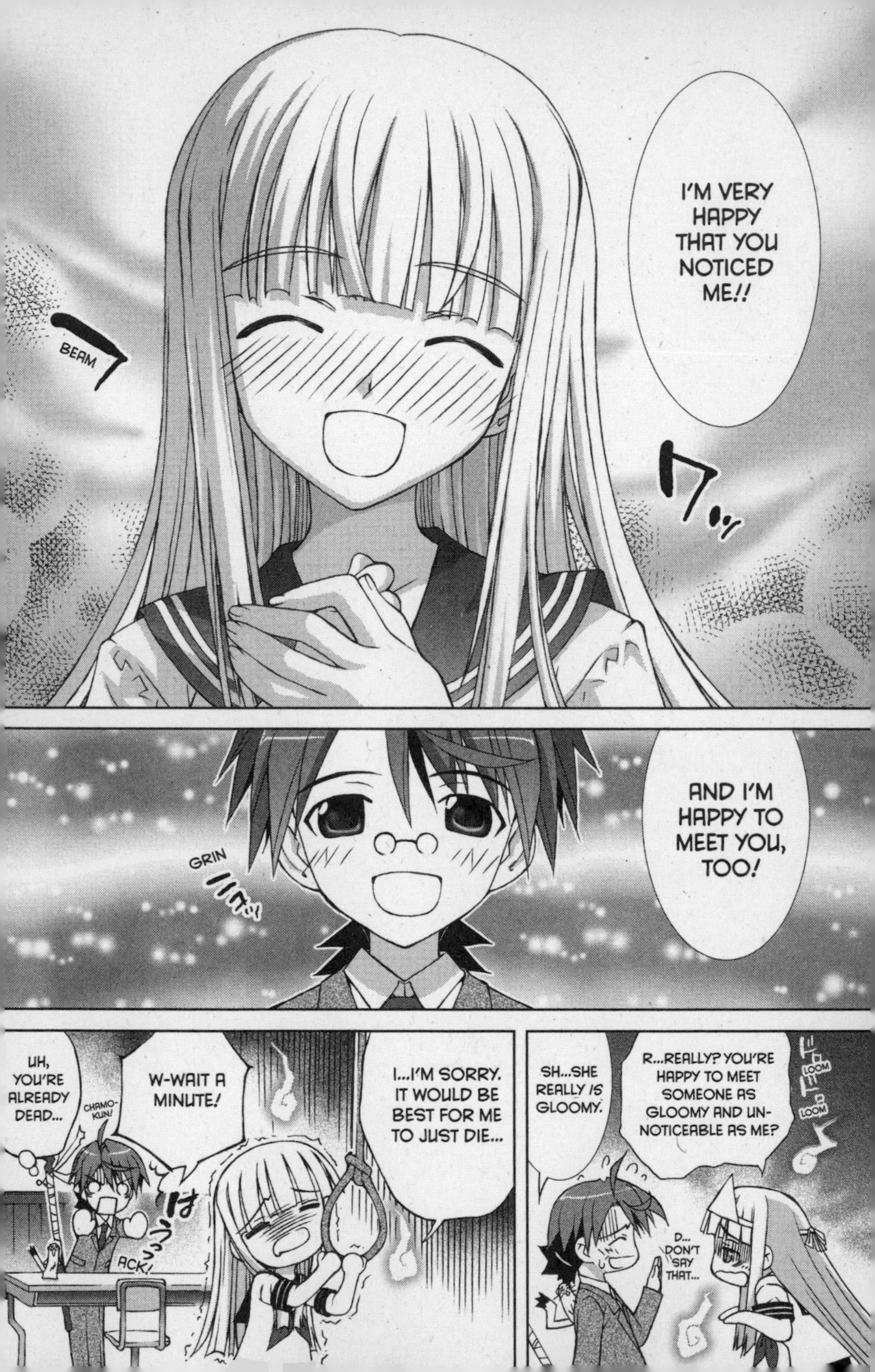
I'M VERY HAPPY THAT YOU NOTICED ME!!
BEAM
AND I'M HAPPY TO MEET YOU, TOO!
GRIN
R...REALLY? YOU'RE HAPPY TO MEET SOMEONE AS GLOOMY AND UN-NOTICEABLE AS ME?
LOOM
LOOM
SH...SHE REALLY *IS* GLOOMY.
D... DON'T SAY THAT...
I...I'M SORRY. IT WOULD BE BEST FOR ME TO JUST DIE...
W-WAIT A MINUTE!
UH, YOU'RE ALREADY DEAD...
CHAMO-KUN!
ACK!

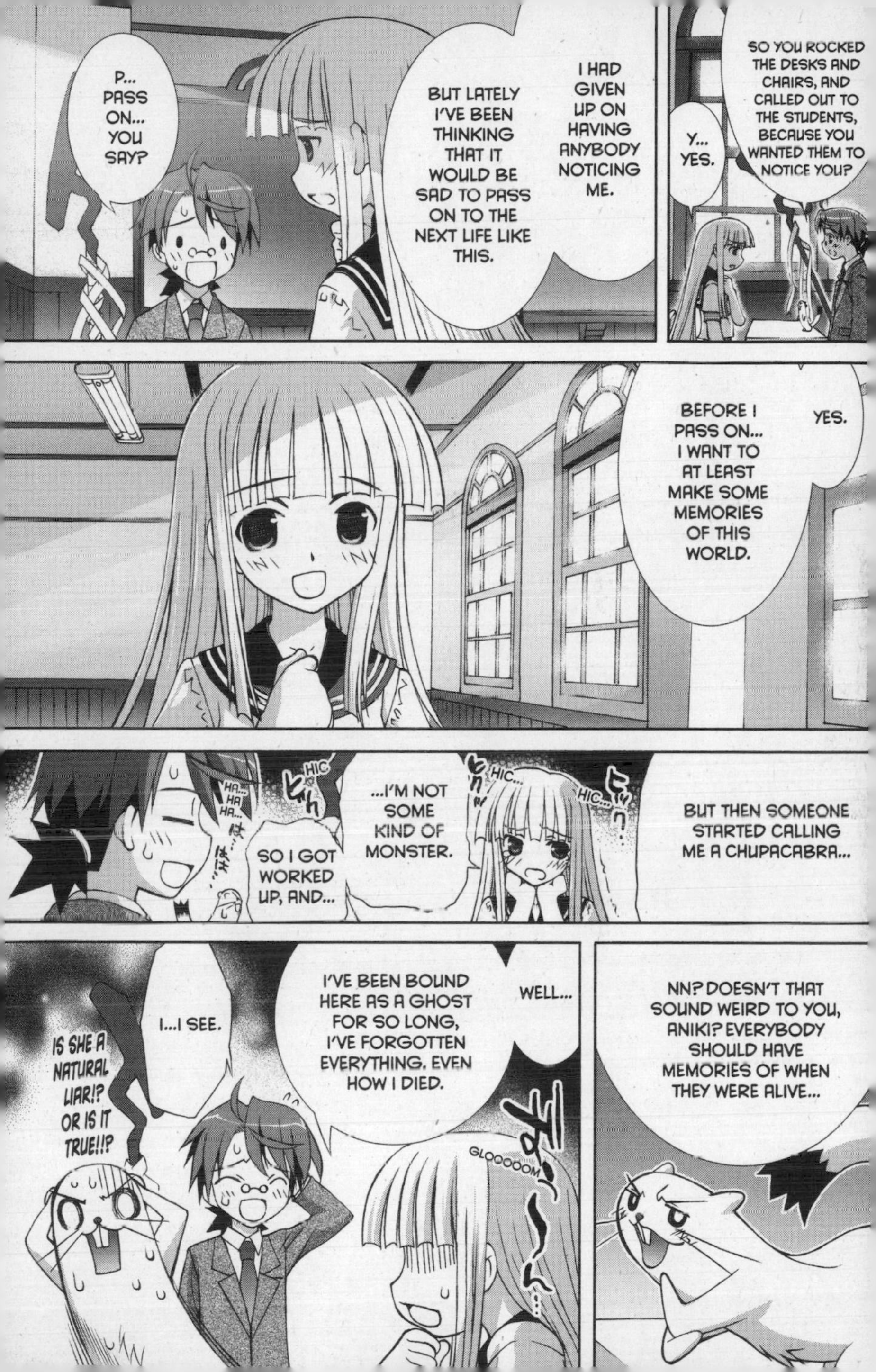
SO YOU ROCKED THE DESKS AND CHAIRS, AND CALLED OUT TO THE STUDENTS, BECAUSE YOU WANTED THEM TO NOTICE YOU?
Y... YES.
I HAD GIVEN UP ON HAVING ANYBODY NOTICING ME.
BUT LATELY I'VE BEEN THINKING THAT IT WOULD BE SAD TO PASS ON TO THE NEXT LIFE LIKE THIS.
P... PASS ON... YOU SAY?
YES.
BEFORE I PASS ON... I WANT TO AT LEAST MAKE SOME MEMORIES OF THIS WORLD.
BUT THEN SOMEONE STARTED CALLING ME A CHUPACABRA...
HIC...
HIC...
...I'M NOT SOME KIND OF MONSTER.
HIC
SO I GOT WORKED UP, AND...
HA... HA HA...
NN? DOESN'T THAT SOUND WEIRD TO YOU, ANIKI? EVERYBODY SHOULD HAVE MEMORIES OF WHEN THEY WERE ALIVE...
WELL...
I'VE BEEN BOUND HERE AS A GHOST FOR SO LONG, I'VE FORGOTTEN EVERYTHING. EVEN HOW I DIED.
GLOOOOOM
I...I SEE.
IS SHE A NATURAL LIAR!? OR IS IT TRUE!!?

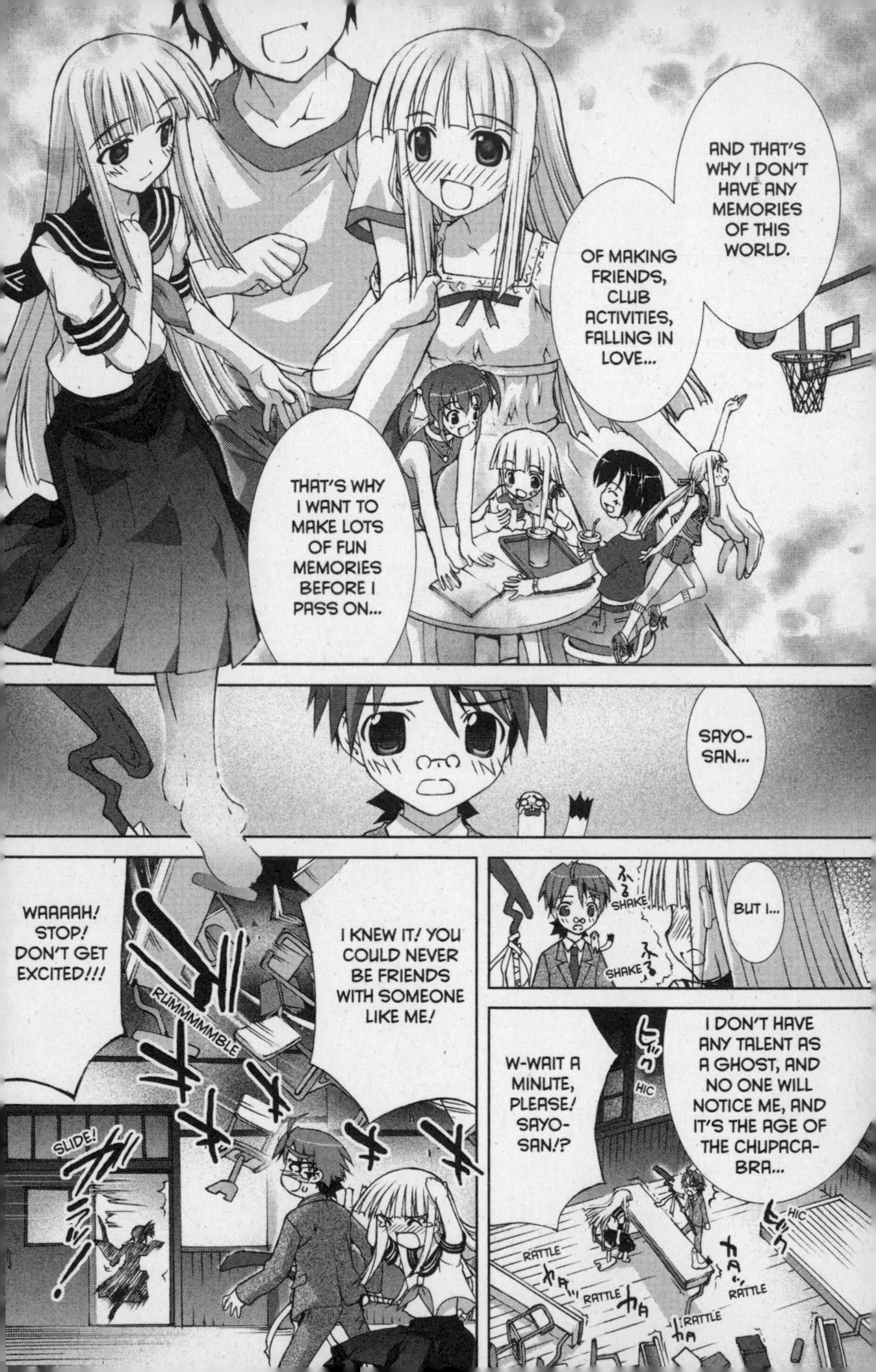
AND THAT'S WHY I DON'T HAVE ANY MEMORIES OF THIS WORLD.
OF MAKING FRIENDS, CLUB ACTIVITIES, FALLING IN LOVE...
THAT'S WHY I WANT TO MAKE LOTS OF FUN MEMORIES BEFORE I PASS ON...
SAYO-SAN...
BUT I...
SHAKE
SHAKE
I DON'T HAVE ANY TALENT AS A GHOST, AND NO ONE WILL NOTICE ME, AND IT'S THE AGE OF THE CHUPACABRA...
HIC
HIC
W-WAIT A MINUTE, PLEASE! SAYO-SAN!?
RATTLE
RATTLE
RATTLE
RATTLE
I KNEW IT! YOU COULD NEVER BE FRIENDS WITH SOMEONE LIKE ME!
WAAAAH! STOP! DON'T GET EXCITED!!!
RUMMMMMBLE
SLIDE!

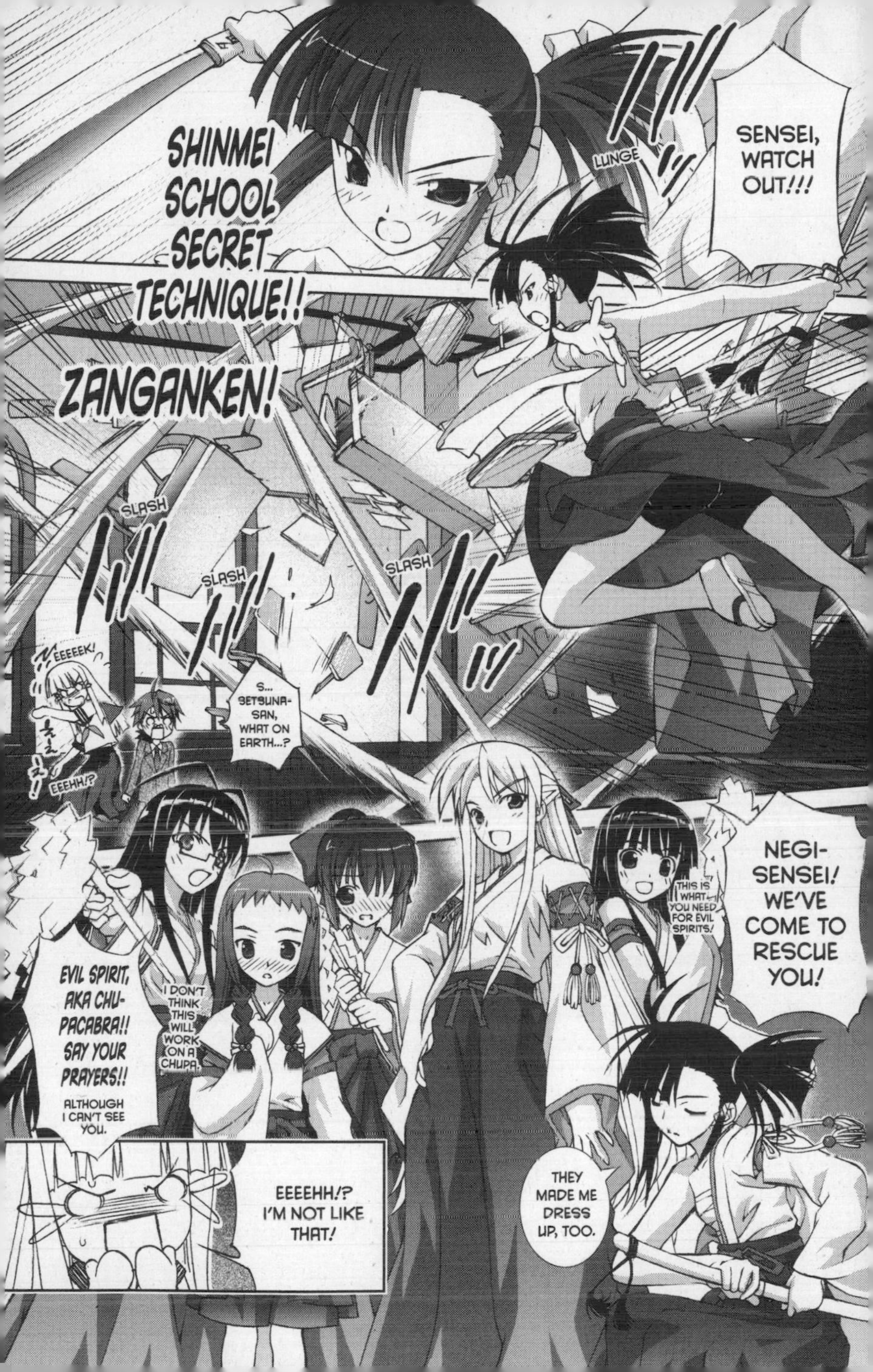
SENSEI, WATCH OUT!!!
LUNGE
SHINMEI SCHOOL SECRET TECHNIQUE!!
ZANGANKEN!
SLASH
SLASH
SLASH
S... SETSUNA-SAN, WHAT ON EARTH...?
EEEEEK!
EEEHH!?
NEGI-SENSEI! WE'VE COME TO RESCUE YOU!
THIS IS WHAT YOU NEED FOR EVIL SPIRITS!
I DON'T THINK THIS WILL WORK ON A CHUPA.
EVIL SPIRIT, AKA CHUPACABRA!! SAY YOUR PRAYERS!!
ALTHOUGH I CAN'T SEE YOU.
THEY MADE ME DRESS UP, TOO.
EEEEHH!? I'M NOT LIKE THAT!

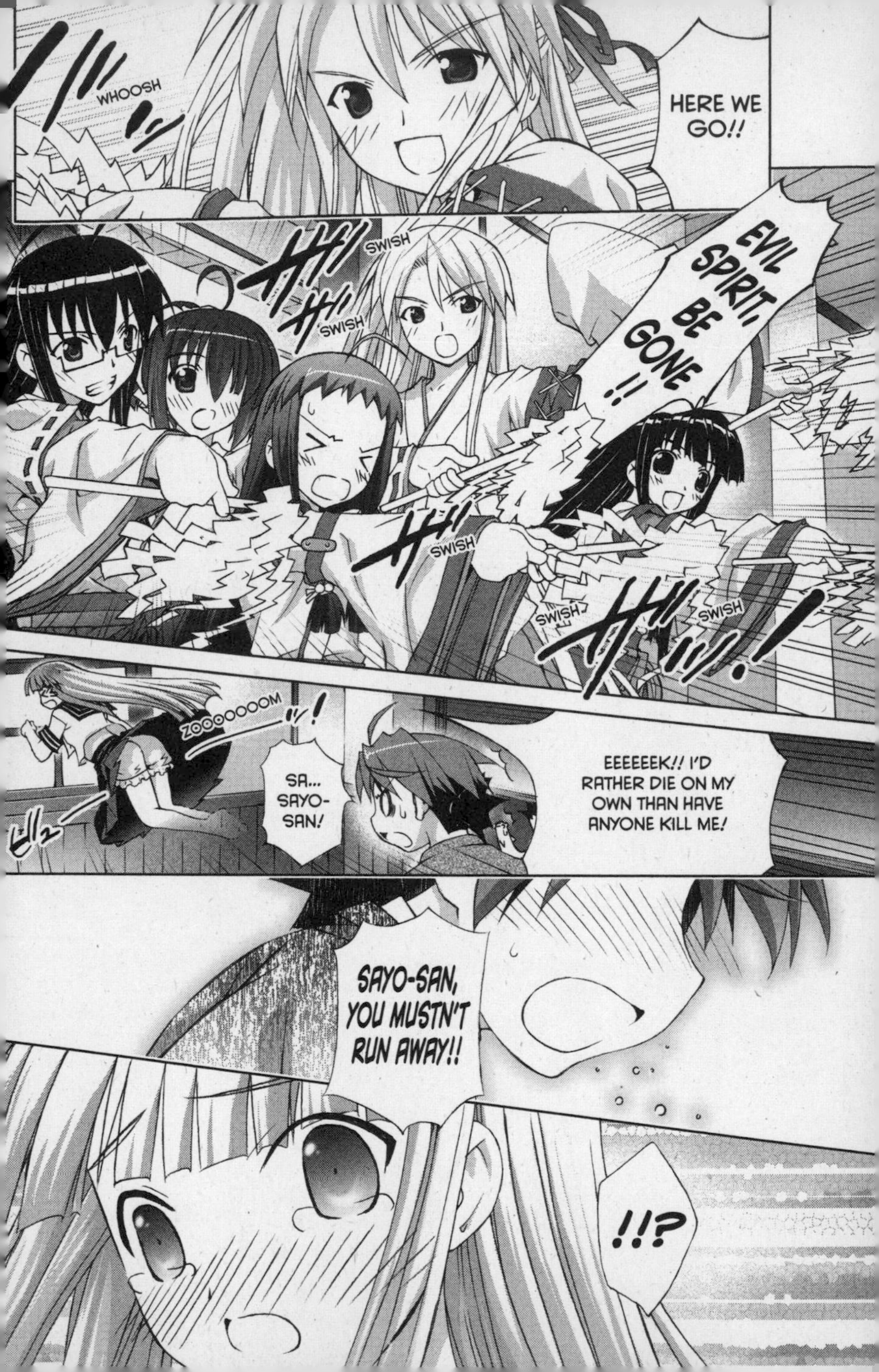
HERE WE GO!!
WHOOSH
EVIL SPIRIT, BE GONE!!
SWISH
SWISH
SWISH
SWISH
SWISH
EEEEEEK!! I'D RATHER DIE ON MY OWN THAN HAVE ANYONE KILL ME!
SA... SAYO-SAN!
ZOOOOOOOM
SAYO-SAN, YOU MUSTN'T RUN AWAY!!
!!?

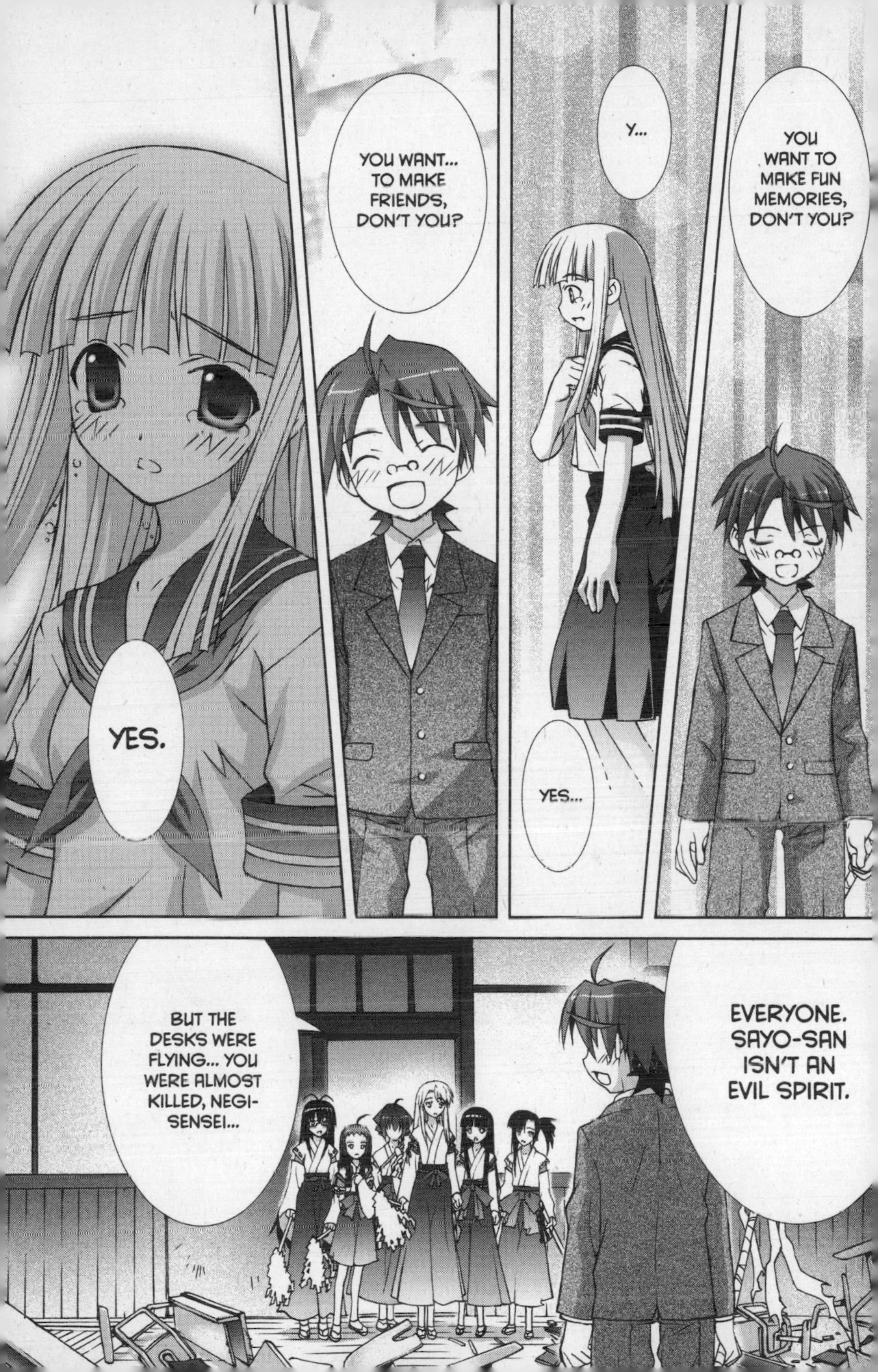
YOU WANT TO MAKE FUN MEMORIES, DON'T YOU?
Y...
YES...
YOU WANT... TO MAKE FRIENDS, DON'T YOU?
YES.
EVERYONE. SAYO-SAN ISN'T AN EVIL SPIRIT.
BUT THE DESKS WERE FLYING... YOU WERE ALMOST KILLED, NEGI-SENSEI...

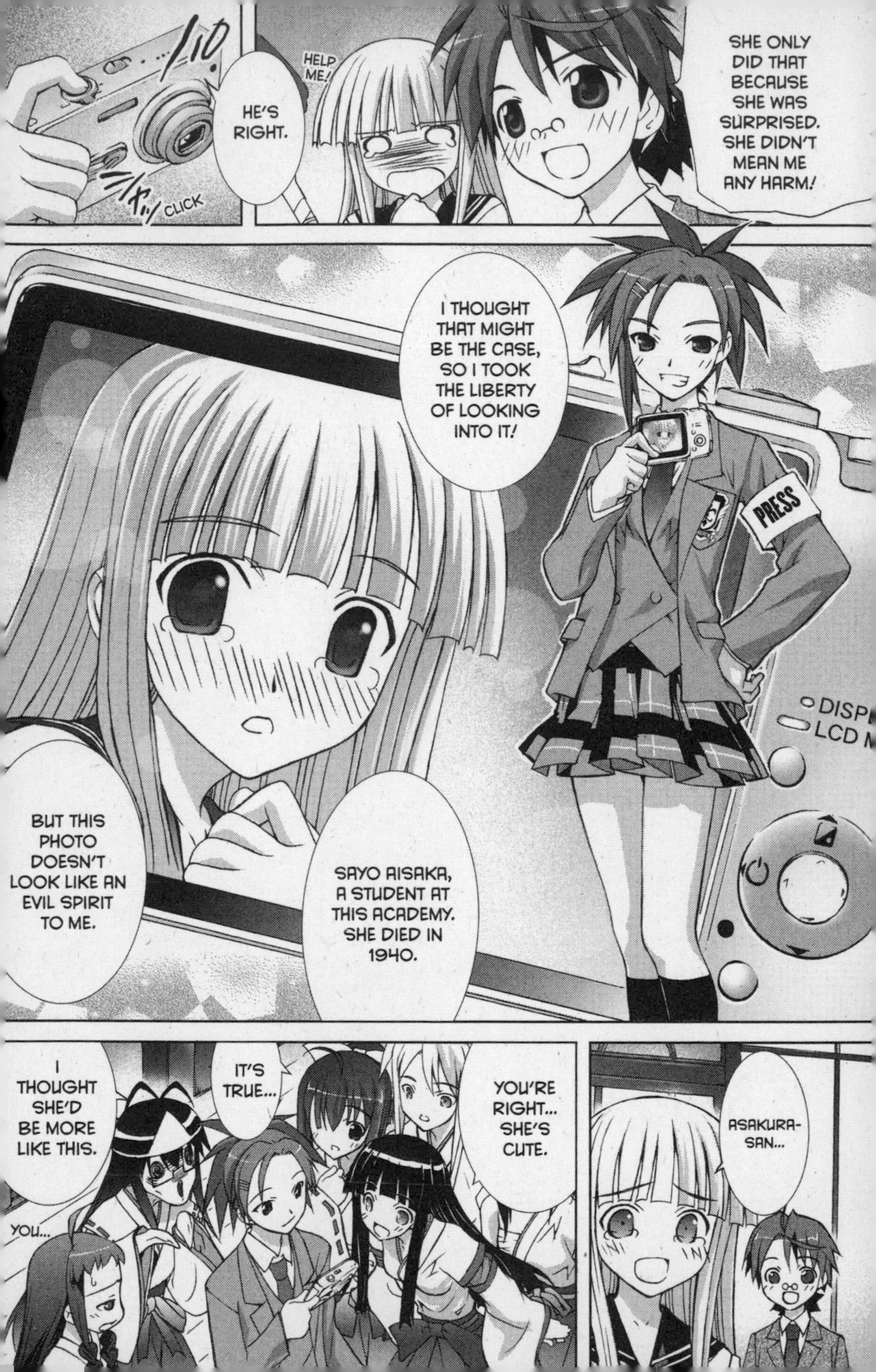
SHE ONLY DID THAT BECAUSE SHE WAS SURPRISED. SHE DIDN'T MEAN ME ANY HARM!
HELP ME!
HE'S RIGHT.
CLICK
I THOUGHT THAT MIGHT BE THE CASE, SO I TOOK THE LIBERTY OF LOOKING INTO IT!
PRESS
SAYO AISAKA, A STUDENT AT THIS ACADEMY. SHE DIED IN 1940.
BUT THIS PHOTO DOESN'T LOOK LIKE AN EVIL SPIRIT TO ME.
ASAKURA-SAN...
YOU'RE RIGHT... SHE'S CUTE.
IT'S TRUE...
I THOUGHT SHE'D BE MORE LIKE THIS.
YOU...

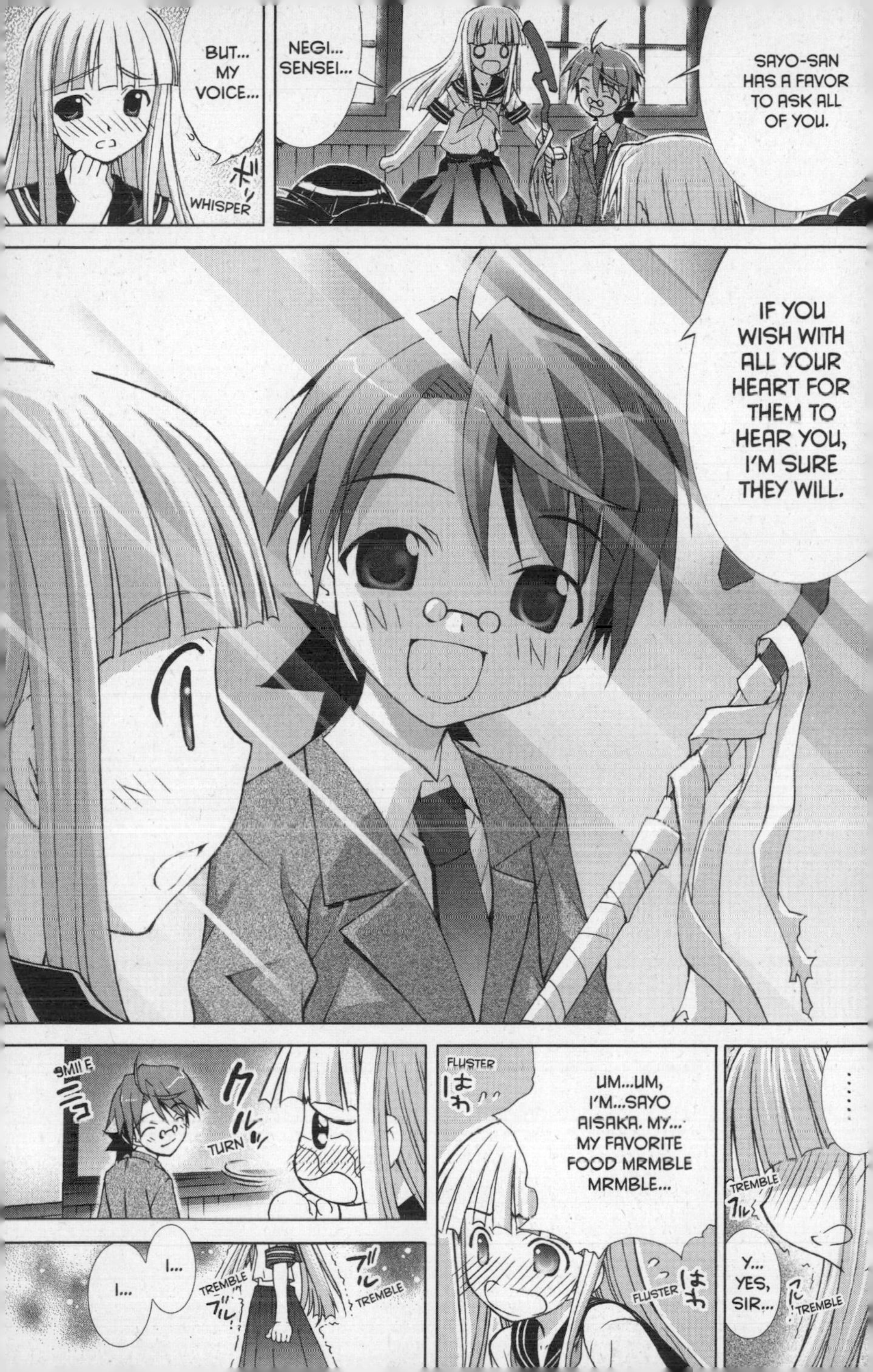
SAYO-SAN HAS A FAVOR TO ASK ALL OF YOU.
NEGI... SENSEI...
BUT... MY VOICE...
WHISPER
IF YOU WISH WITH ALL YOUR HEART FOR THEM TO HEAR YOU, I'M SURE THEY WILL.
......
TREMBLE
Y... YES, SIR...
TREMBLE
FLUSTER
UM...UM, I'M...SAYO AISAKA. MY... MY FAVORITE FOOD MRMBLE MRMBLE...
FLUSTER
SMILE
TURN
I... I...
TREMBLE
TREMBLE

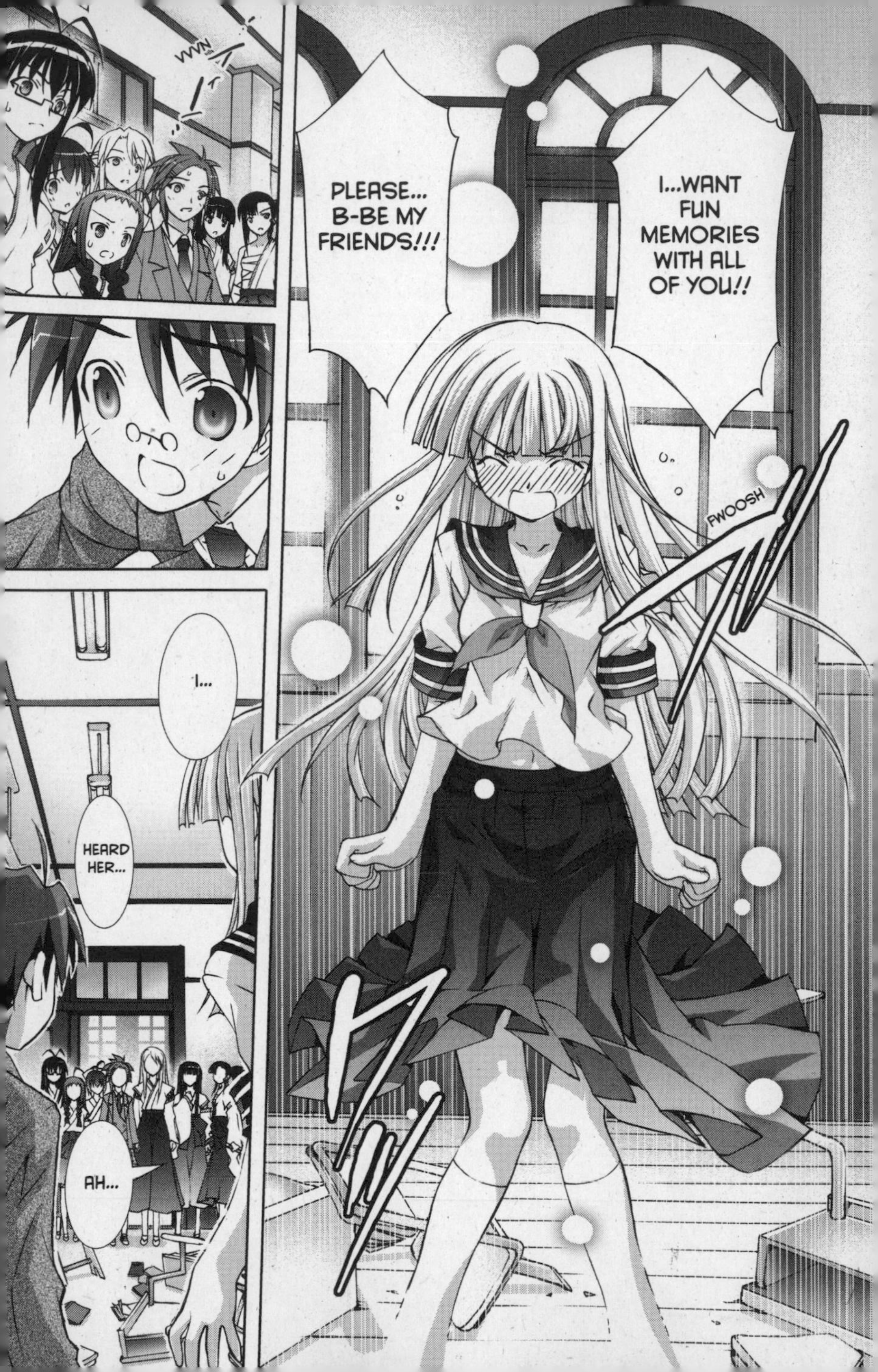
I...WANT FUN MEMORIES WITH ALL OF YOU!!
FWOOSH
PLEASE... B-BE MY FRIENDS!!!
VVVN
I...
HEARD HER...
AH...

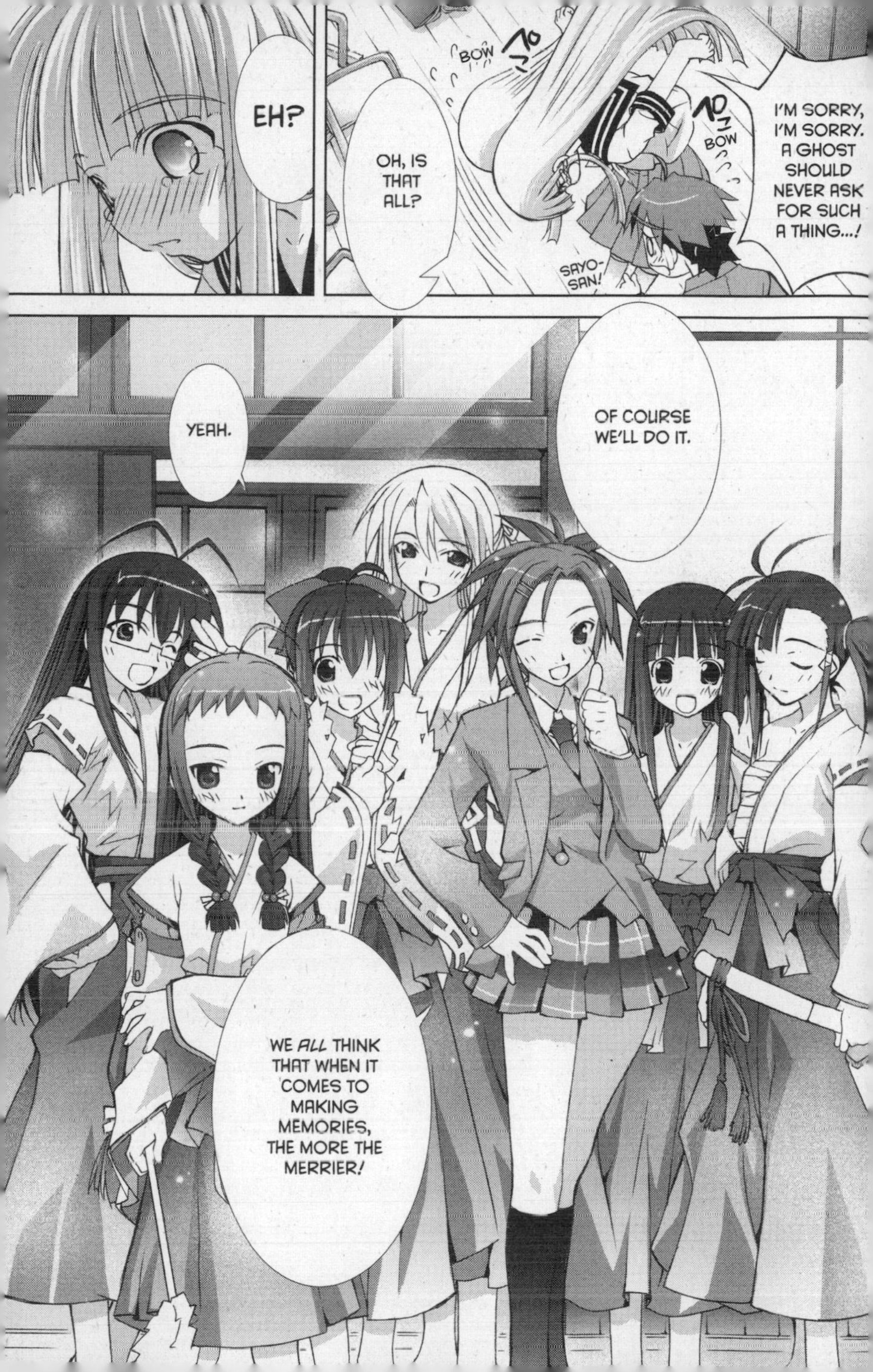
I'M SORRY, I'M SORRY. A GHOST SHOULD NEVER ASK FOR SUCH A THING...!
BOW
BOW
SAYO-SAN!
OH, IS THAT ALL?
EH?
OF COURSE WE'LL DO IT.
YEAH.
WE *ALL* THINK THAT WHEN IT COMES TO MAKING MEMORIES, THE MORE THE MERRIER!

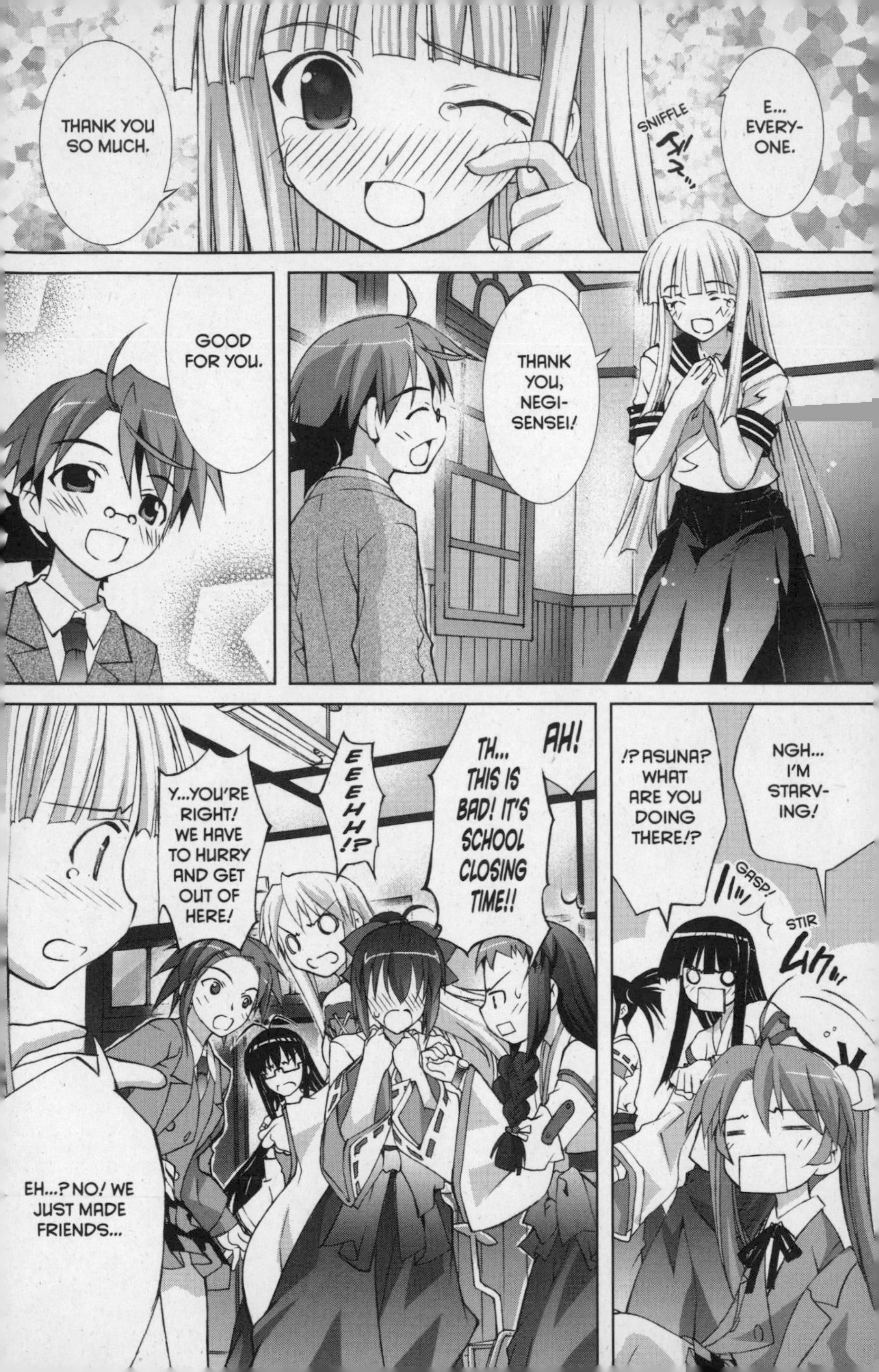
E... EVERY-ONE.
SNIFFLE
THANK YOU SO MUCH.
THANK YOU, NEGI-SENSEI!
GOOD FOR YOU.
NGH... I'M STARV-ING!
STIR
GASP!
!? ASUNA? WHAT ARE YOU DOING THERE!?
AH!
TH... THIS IS BAD! IT'S SCHOOL CLOSING TIME!!
EEEEHH!?
Y...YOU'RE RIGHT! WE HAVE TO HURRY AND GET OUT OF HERE!
EH...? NO! WE JUST MADE FRIENDS...

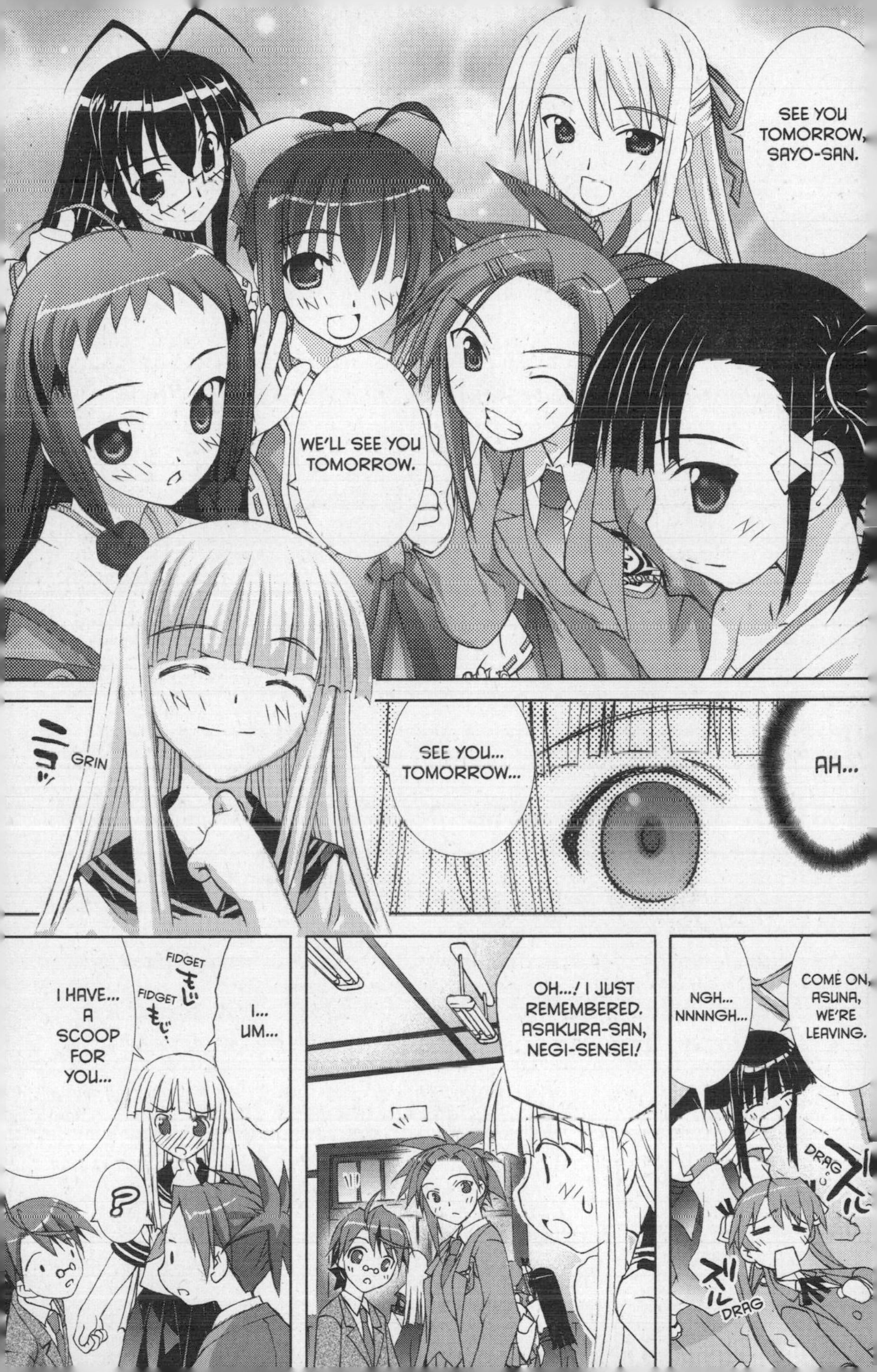
SEE YOU TOMORROW, SAYO-SAN.
WE'LL SEE YOU TOMORROW.
AH...
SEE YOU... TOMORROW...
GRIN
COME ON, ASUNA, WE'RE LEAVING.
NGH... NNNNGH...
DRAG
DRAG
OH...! I JUST REMEMBERED. ASAKURA-SAN, NEGI-SENSEI!
I... UM...
FIDGET
FIDGET
I HAVE... A SCOOP FOR YOU...
?

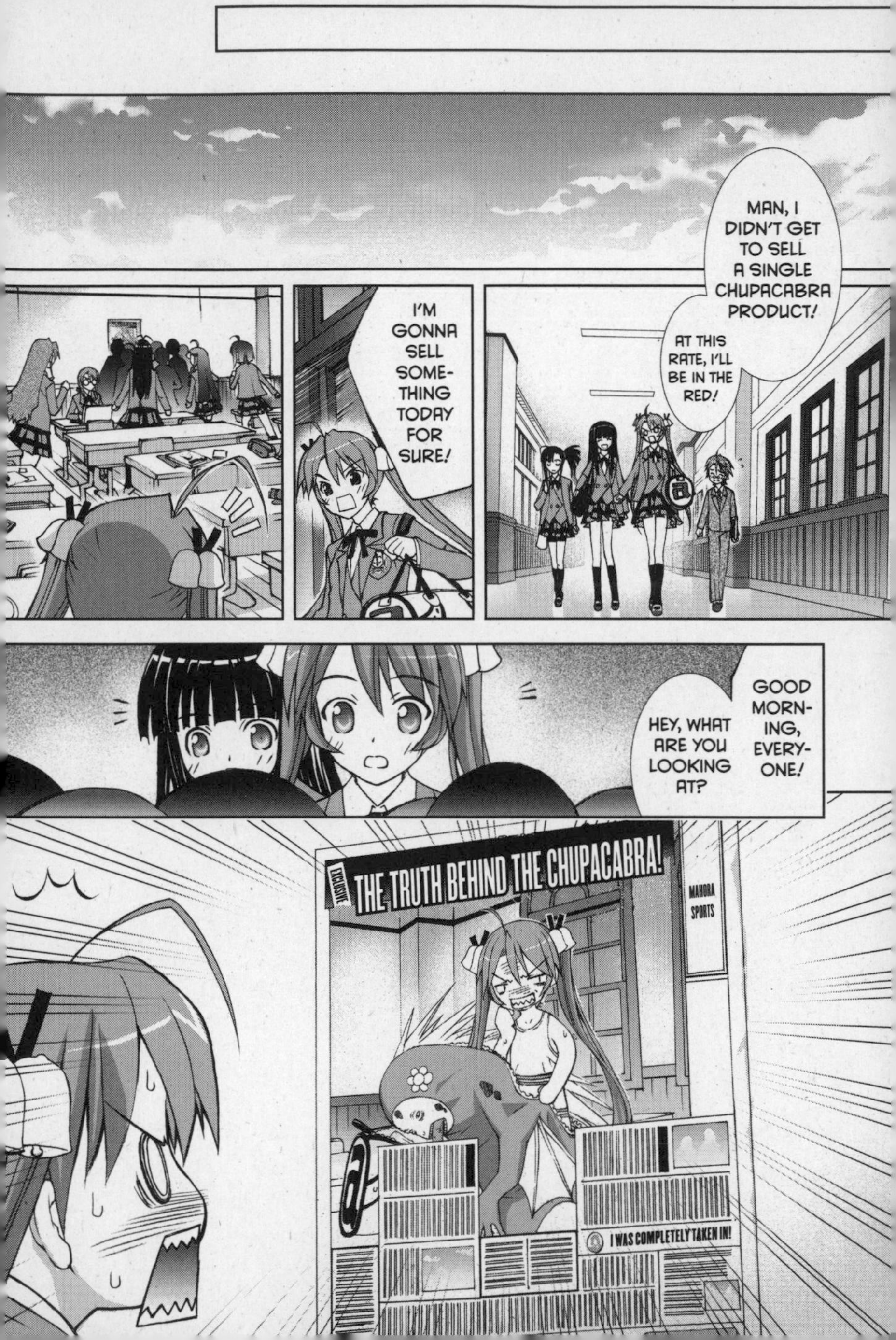
MAN, I DIDN'T GET TO SELL A SINGLE CHUPACABRA PRODUCT!
AT THIS RATE, I'LL BE IN THE RED!
I'M GONNA SELL SOME-THING TODAY FOR SURE!
GOOD MORN-ING, EVERY-ONE!
HEY, WHAT ARE YOU LOOKING AT?
EXCLUSIVE
THE TRUTH BEHIND THE CHUPACABRA!
MAHORA SPORTS
I WAS COMPLETELY TAKEN IN!

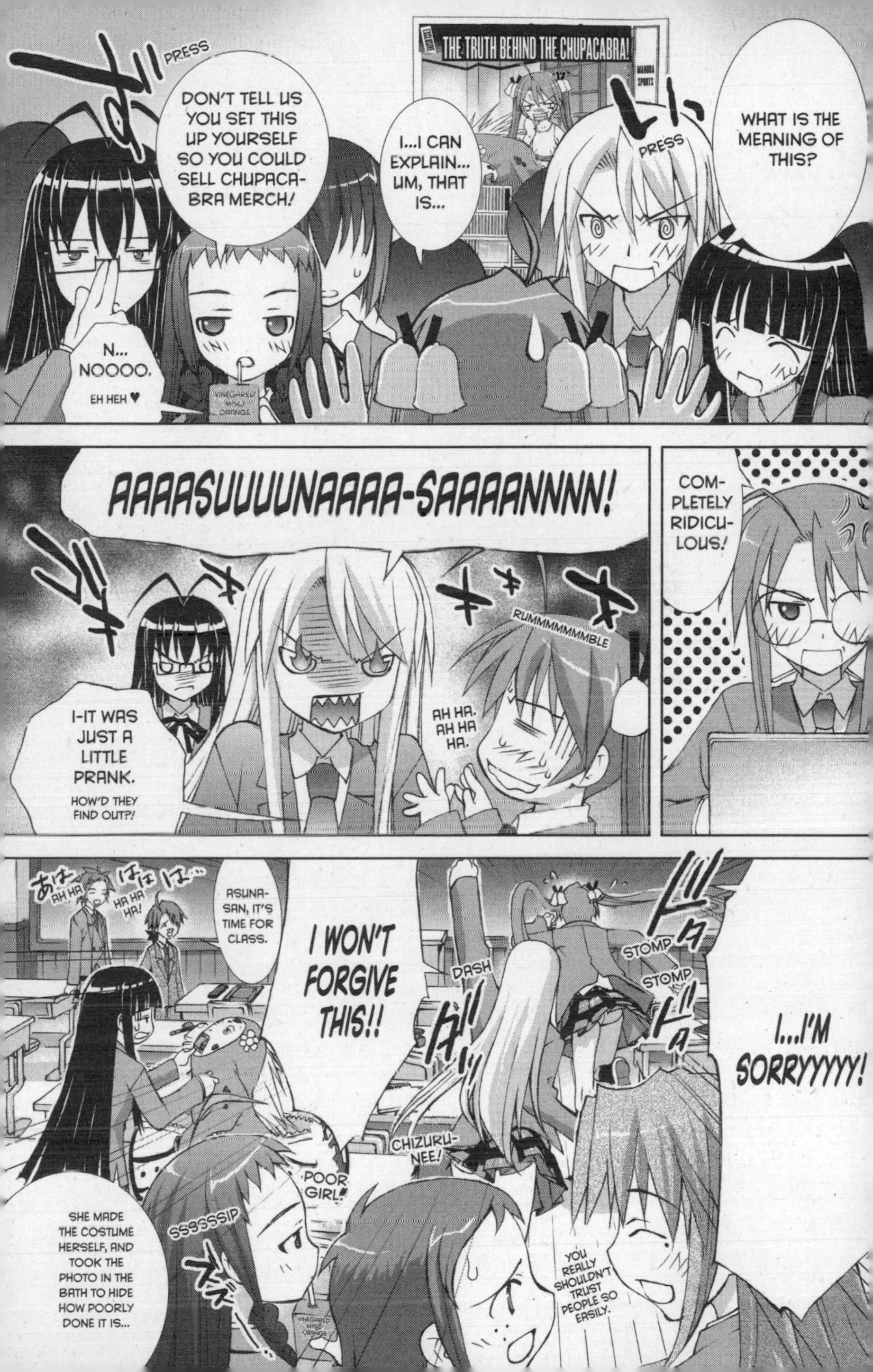
WHAT IS THE MEANING OF THIS?
PRESS
THE TRUTH BEHIND THE CHUPACABRA!
MAHORA SPORTS
I...I CAN EXPLAIN... UM, THAT IS...
DON'T TELL US YOU SET THIS UP YOURSELF SO YOU COULD SELL CHUPACA-BRA MERCH!
PRESS
N... NOOOO.
EH HEH ♥
VINEGARED MISO ORANGE
COM-PLETELY RIDICU-LOUS!
AAAASUUUUNAAAA-SAAAANNNN!
RUMMMMMMMBLE
AH HA. AH HA HA.
I-IT WAS JUST A LITTLE PRANK.
HOW'D THEY FIND OUT?!
STOMP
STOMP
I...I'M SORRYYYYY!
DASH
I WON'T FORGIVE THIS!!
ASUNA-SAN, IT'S TIME FOR CLASS.
AH HA
HA HA HA!
CHIZURU-NEE!
YOU REALLY SHOULDN'T TRUST PEOPLE SO EASILY.
POOR GIRL!
SSSSSSIP
SHE MADE THE COSTUME HERSELF, AND TOOK THE PHOTO IN THE BATH TO HIDE HOW POORLY DONE IT IS...
VINEGARED MISO ORANGE

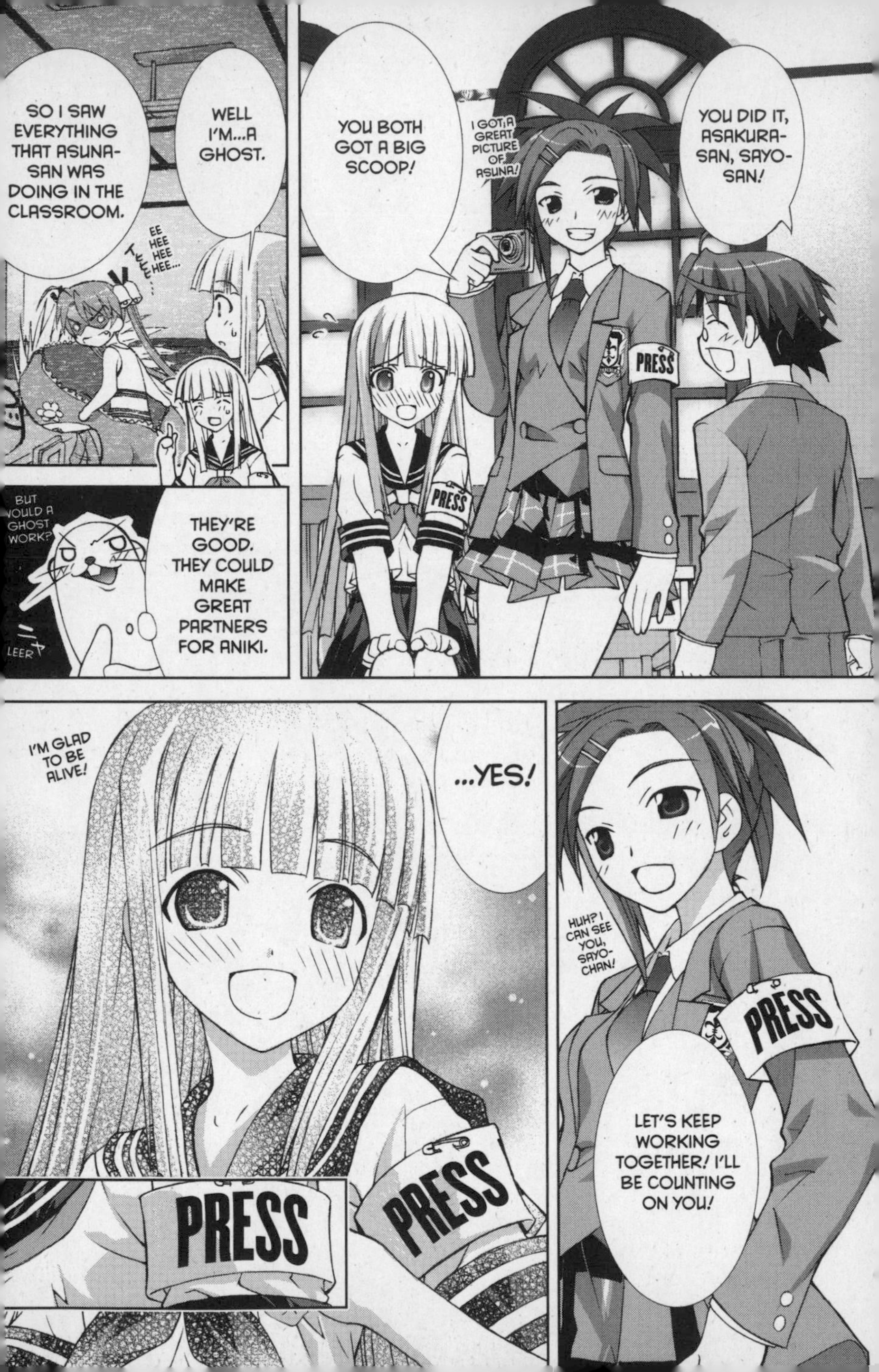
YOU DID IT, ASAKURA-SAN, SAYO-SAN!
I GOT A GREAT PICTURE OF ASUNA!
YOU BOTH GOT A BIG SCOOP!
PRESS
PRESS
WELL I'M...A GHOST.
SO I SAW EVERYTHING THAT ASUNA-SAN WAS DOING IN THE CLASSROOM.
EE HEE HEE HEE...
THEY'RE GOOD. THEY COULD MAKE GREAT PARTNERS FOR ANIKI.
BUT WOULD A GHOST WORK?
LEER
HUH? I CAN SEE YOU, SAYO-CHAN!
PRESS
LET'S KEEP WORKING TOGETHER! I'LL BE COUNTING ON YOU!
...YES!
I'M GLAD TO BE ALIVE!
PRESS
PRESS

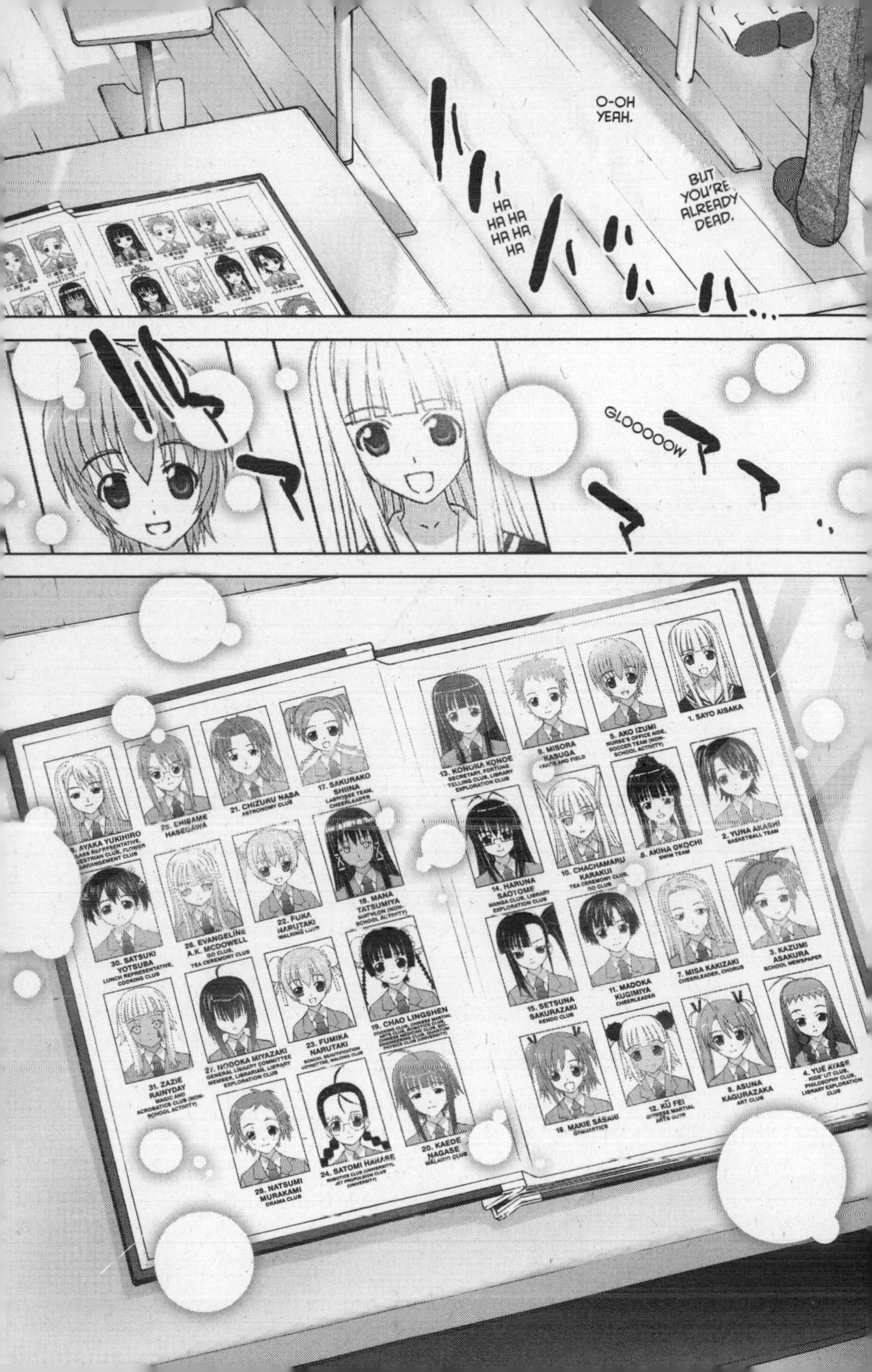
O-OH YEAH.
BUT YOU'RE ALREADY DEAD.
HA HA HA HA HA
GLOOOOOW
1. SAYO AISAKA
5. AKO IZUMI
NURSE'S OFFICE AIDE, SOCCER TEAM (NON-SCHOOL ACTIVITY)
9. MISORA KASUGA
13. KONOKA KONOE
SECRETARY, FORTUNE TELLING CLUB, LIBRARY EXPLORATION CLUB
2. YUNA AKASHI
BASKETBALL TEAM
6. AKIRA OKOCHI
SWIM TEAM
10. CHACHAMARU KARAKUI
TEA CEREMONY CLUB, GO CLUB
14. HARUNA SAOTOME
MANGA CLUB, LIBRARY EXPLORATION CLUB
3. KAZUMI ASAKURA
SCHOOL NEWSPAPER
7. MISA KAKIZAKI
CHEERLEADER, CHORUS
11. MADOKA KUGIMIYA
CHEERLEADER
15. SETSUNA SAKURAZAKI
KENDO CLUB
4. YUE AYASE
KIDS' LIT CLUB, PHILOSOPHY CLUB, LIBRARY EXPLORATION CLUB
8. ASUNA KAGURAZAKA
ART CLUB
12. KŪ FEI
17. SAKURAKO SHIINA
LACROSSE TEAM, CHEERLEADER
21. CHIZURU NABA
ASTRONOMY CLUB
25. CHISAME HASEGAWA
AYAKA YUKIHIRO
18. MANA TATSUMIYA
26. EVANGELINE A.K. MCDOWELL
GO CLUB, TEA CEREMONY CLUB
30. SATSUKI YOTSUBA
LUNCH REPRESENTATIVE, COOKING CLUB
19. CHAO LINGSHEN
23. FUMIKA NARUTAKI
31. ZAZIE RAINYDAY
MAGIC AND ACROBATICS CLUB (NON-SCHOOL ACTIVITY)
20. KAEDE NAGASE
24. SATOMI HAKASE
ROBOTICS CLUB (UNIVERSITY), JET PROPULSION CLUB (UNIVERSITY)
28. NATSUMI MURAKAMI
DRAMA CLUB

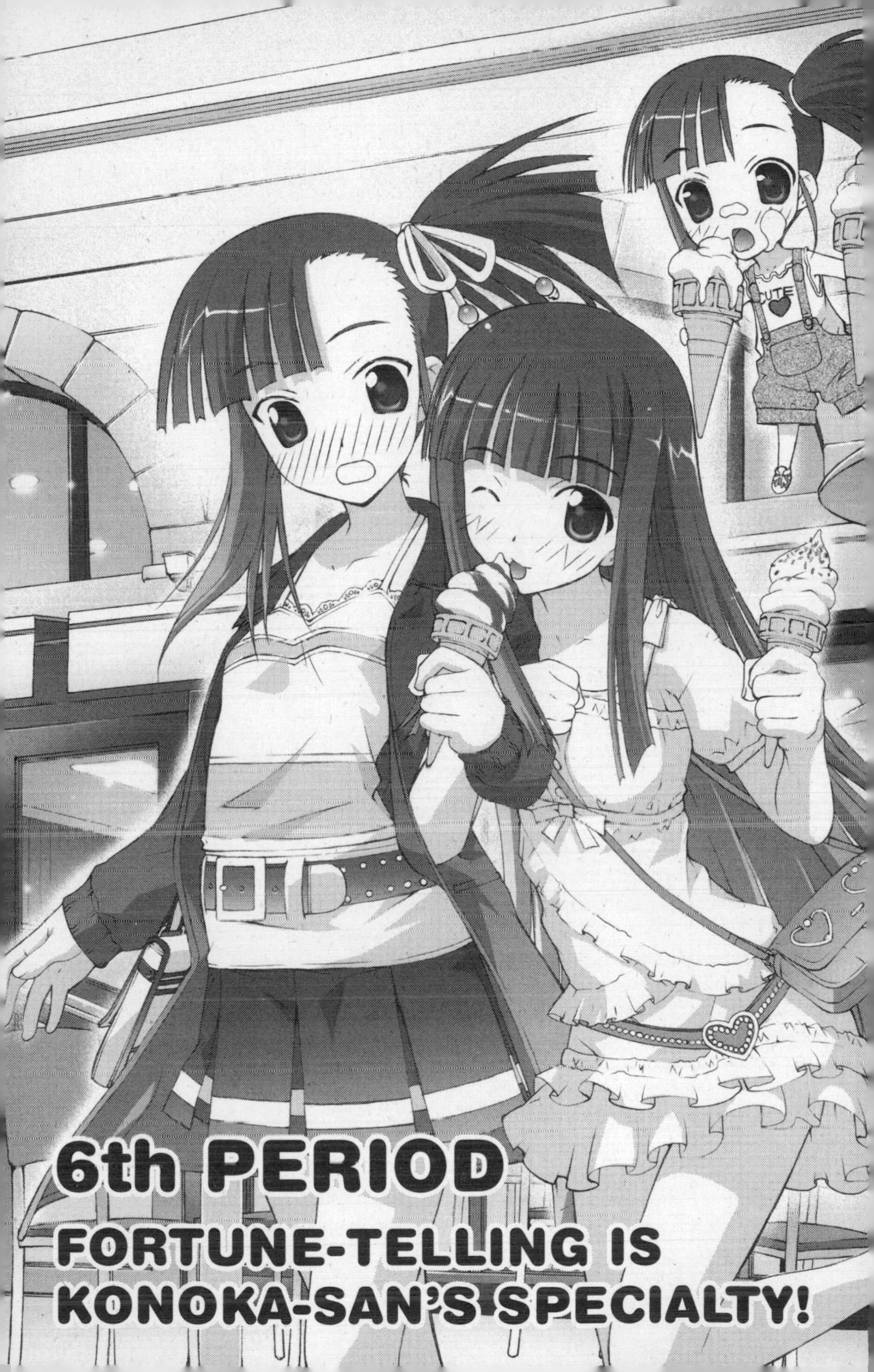
CUTE

6th PERIOD

FORTUNE-TELLING IS KONOKA-SAN'S SPECIALTY!

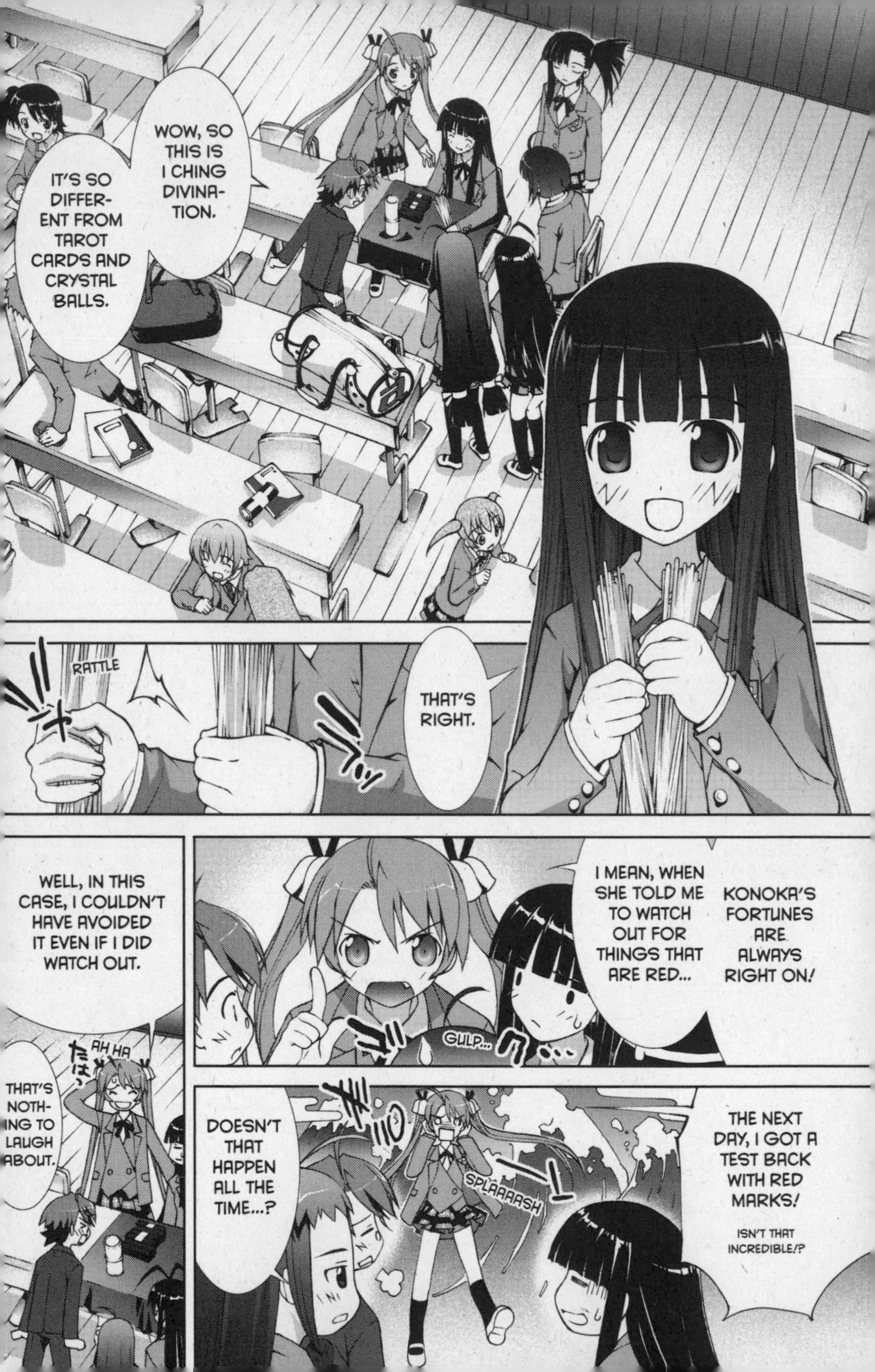
WOW, SO THIS IS I CHING DIVINATION.
IT'S SO DIFFERENT FROM TAROT CARDS AND CRYSTAL BALLS.
THAT'S RIGHT.
RATTLE
KONOKA'S FORTUNES ARE ALWAYS RIGHT ON!
I MEAN, WHEN SHE TOLD ME TO WATCH OUT FOR THINGS THAT ARE RED...
GULP...
WELL, IN THIS CASE, I COULDN'T HAVE AVOIDED IT EVEN IF I DID WATCH OUT.
THE NEXT DAY, I GOT A TEST BACK WITH RED MARKS!
ISN'T THAT INCREDIBLE!?
SPLAAAAASH
DOESN'T THAT HAPPEN ALL THE TIME...?
AH HA
THAT'S NOTHING TO LAUGH ABOUT.

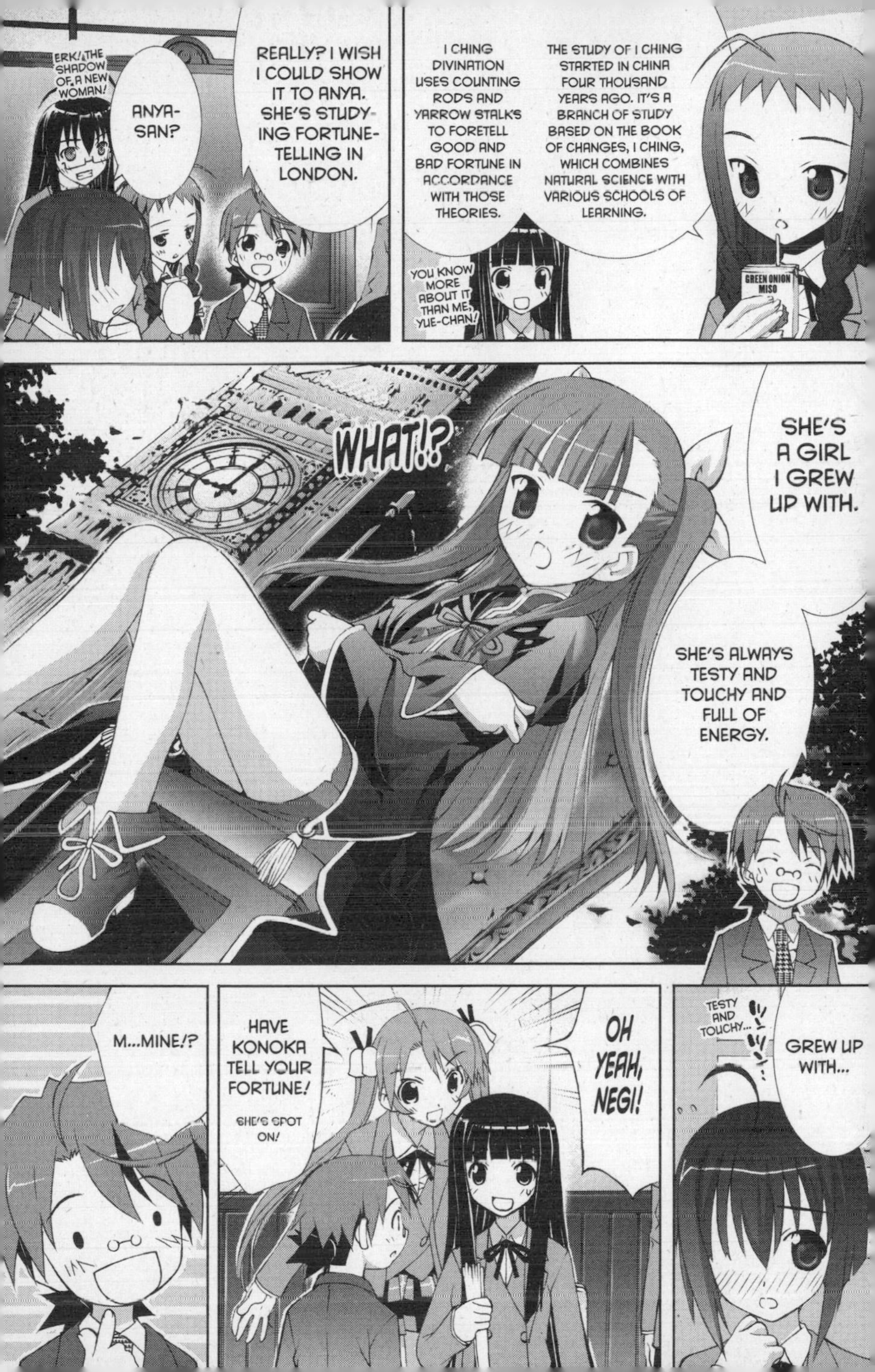
THE STUDY OF I CHING STARTED IN CHINA FOUR THOUSAND YEARS AGO. IT'S A BRANCH OF STUDY BASED ON THE BOOK OF CHANGES, I CHING, WHICH COMBINES NATURAL SCIENCE WITH VARIOUS SCHOOLS OF LEARNING.
I CHING DIVINATION USES COUNTING RODS AND YARROW STALKS TO FORETELL GOOD AND BAD FORTUNE IN ACCORDANCE WITH THOSE THEORIES.
GREEN ONION MISO
YOU KNOW MORE ABOUT IT THAN ME, YUE-CHAN!
REALLY? I WISH I COULD SHOW IT TO ANYA. SHE'S STUDYING FORTUNE-TELLING IN LONDON.
ANYA-SAN?
ERK! THE SHADOW OF A NEW WOMAN!
SHE'S A GIRL I GREW UP WITH.
WHAT!?
SHE'S ALWAYS TESTY AND TOUCHY AND FULL OF ENERGY.
GREW UP WITH...
TESTY AND TOUCHY...
OH YEAH, NEGI!
HAVE KONOKA TELL YOUR FORTUNE!
SHE'S SPOT ON!
M...MINE!?

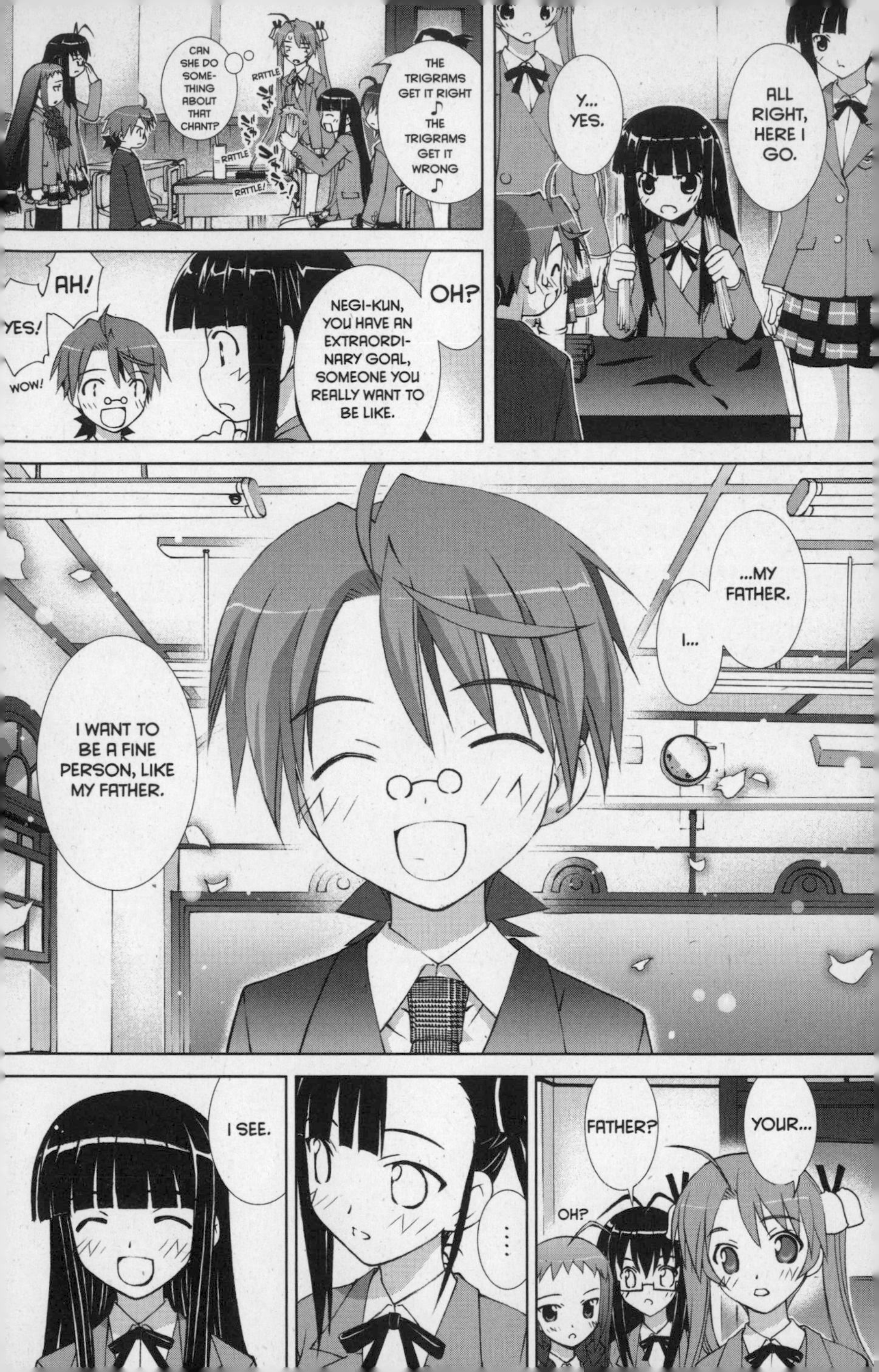
ALL RIGHT, HERE I GO.
Y... YES.
THE TRIGRAMS GET IT RIGHT ♪ THE TRIGRAMS GET IT WRONG ♪
RATTLE
RATTLE
RATTLE!
CAN SHE DO SOME-THING ABOUT THAT CHANT?
OH?
NEGI-KUN, YOU HAVE AN EXTRAORDI-NARY GOAL, SOMEONE YOU REALLY WANT TO BE LIKE.
AH!
YES!
WOW!
I...
...MY FATHER.
I WANT TO BE A FINE PERSON, LIKE MY FATHER.
YOUR...
FATHER?
OH?
....
I SEE.

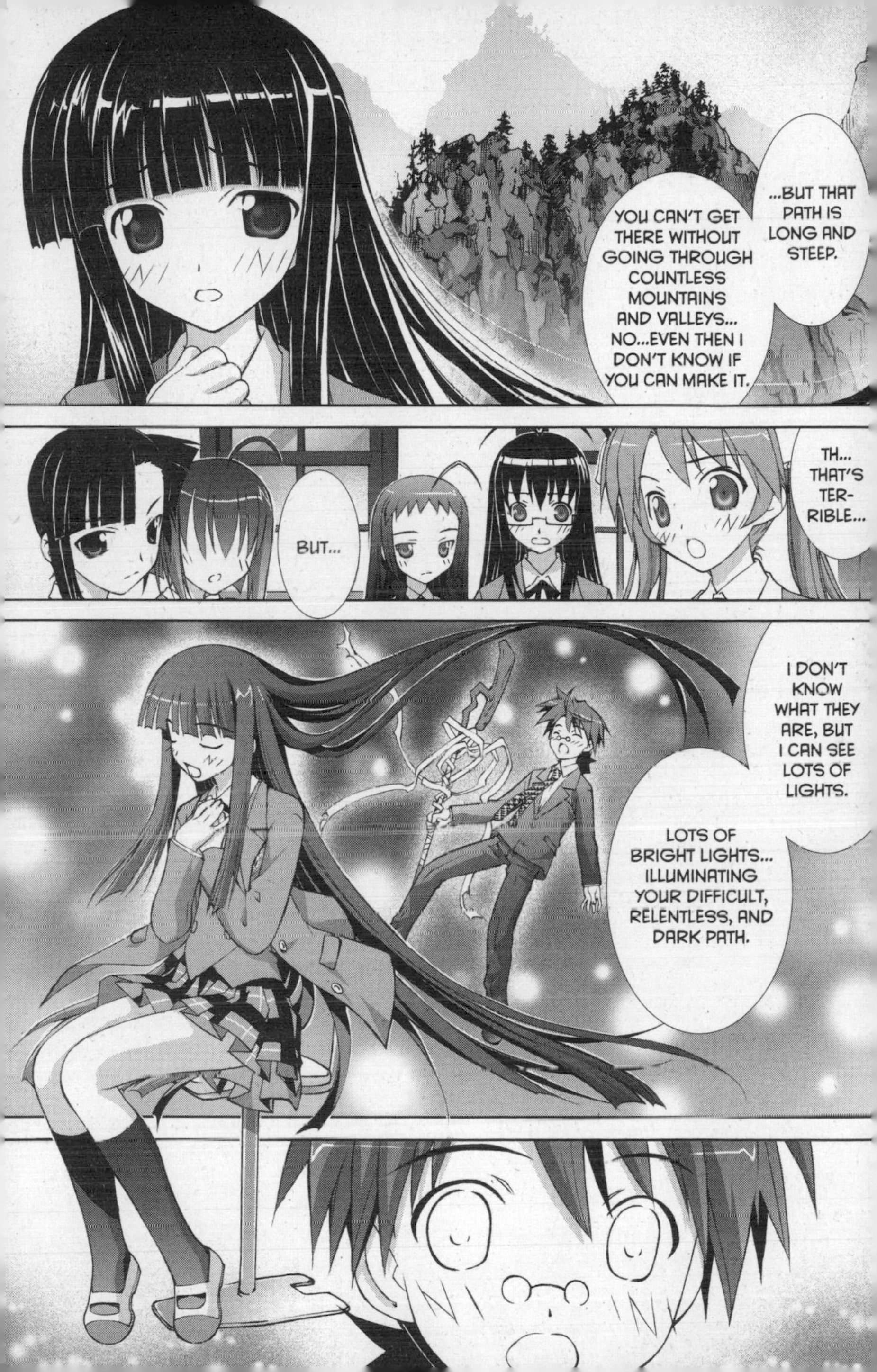
...BUT THAT PATH IS LONG AND STEEP.
YOU CAN'T GET THERE WITHOUT GOING THROUGH COUNTLESS MOUNTAINS AND VALLEYS... NO...EVEN THEN I DON'T KNOW IF YOU CAN MAKE IT.
TH... THAT'S TER-RIBLE...
BUT...
I DON'T KNOW WHAT THEY ARE, BUT I CAN SEE LOTS OF LIGHTS.
LOTS OF BRIGHT LIGHTS... ILLUMINATING YOUR DIFFICULT, RELENTLESS, AND DARK PATH.

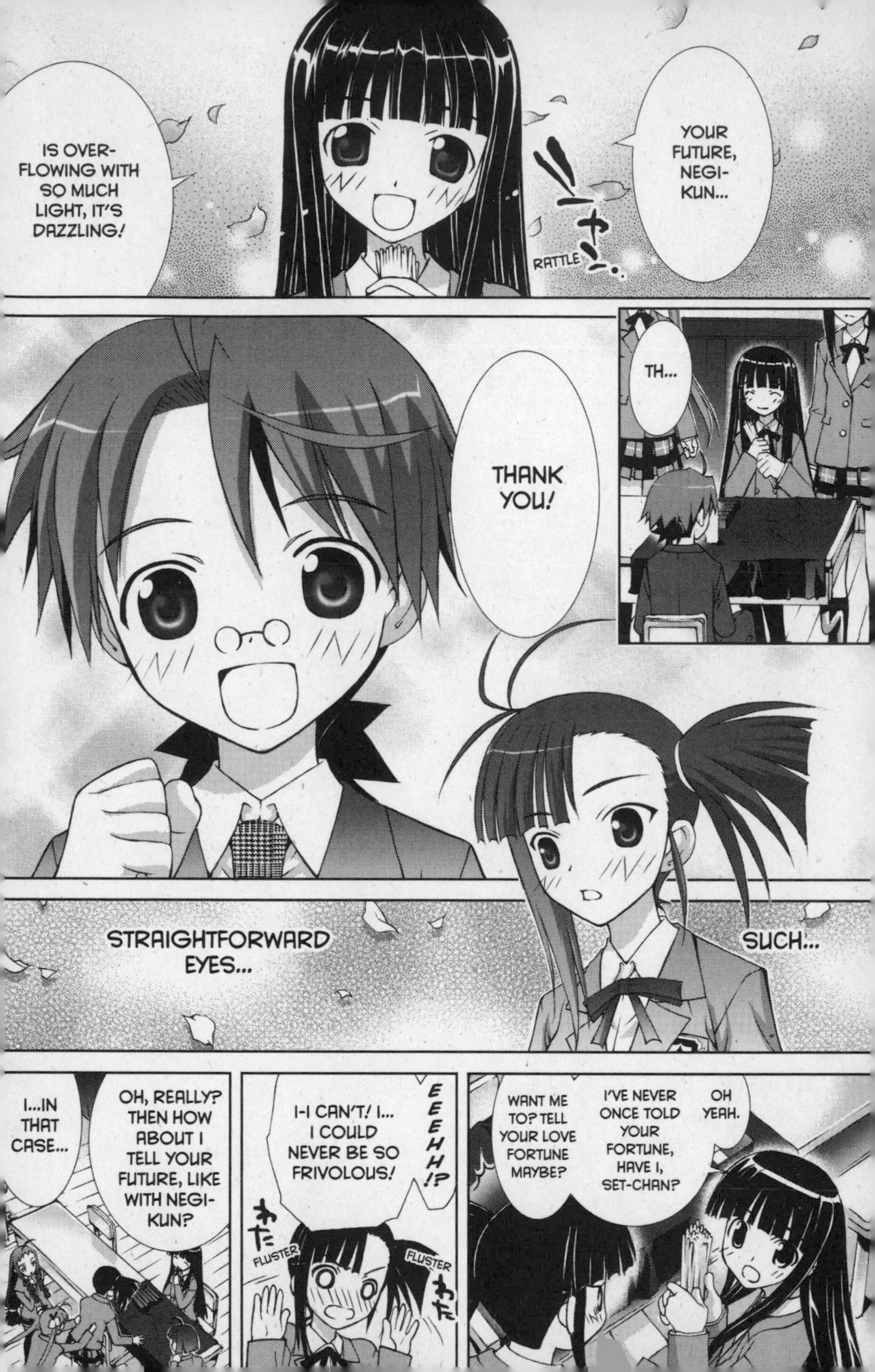
YOUR FUTURE, NEGI-KUN...
RATTLE
IS OVER-FLOWING WITH SO MUCH LIGHT, IT'S DAZZLING!
TH...
THANK YOU!
SUCH...
STRAIGHTFORWARD EYES...
OH YEAH.
I'VE NEVER ONCE TOLD YOUR FORTUNE, HAVE I, SET-CHAN?
WANT ME TO? TELL YOUR LOVE FORTUNE MAYBE?
EEEEHH!?
I-I CAN'T! I... I COULD NEVER BE SO FRIVOLOUS!
わた FLUSTER
わた FLUSTER
OH, REALLY? THEN HOW ABOUT I TELL YOUR FUTURE, LIKE WITH NEGI-KUN?
I...IN THAT CASE...

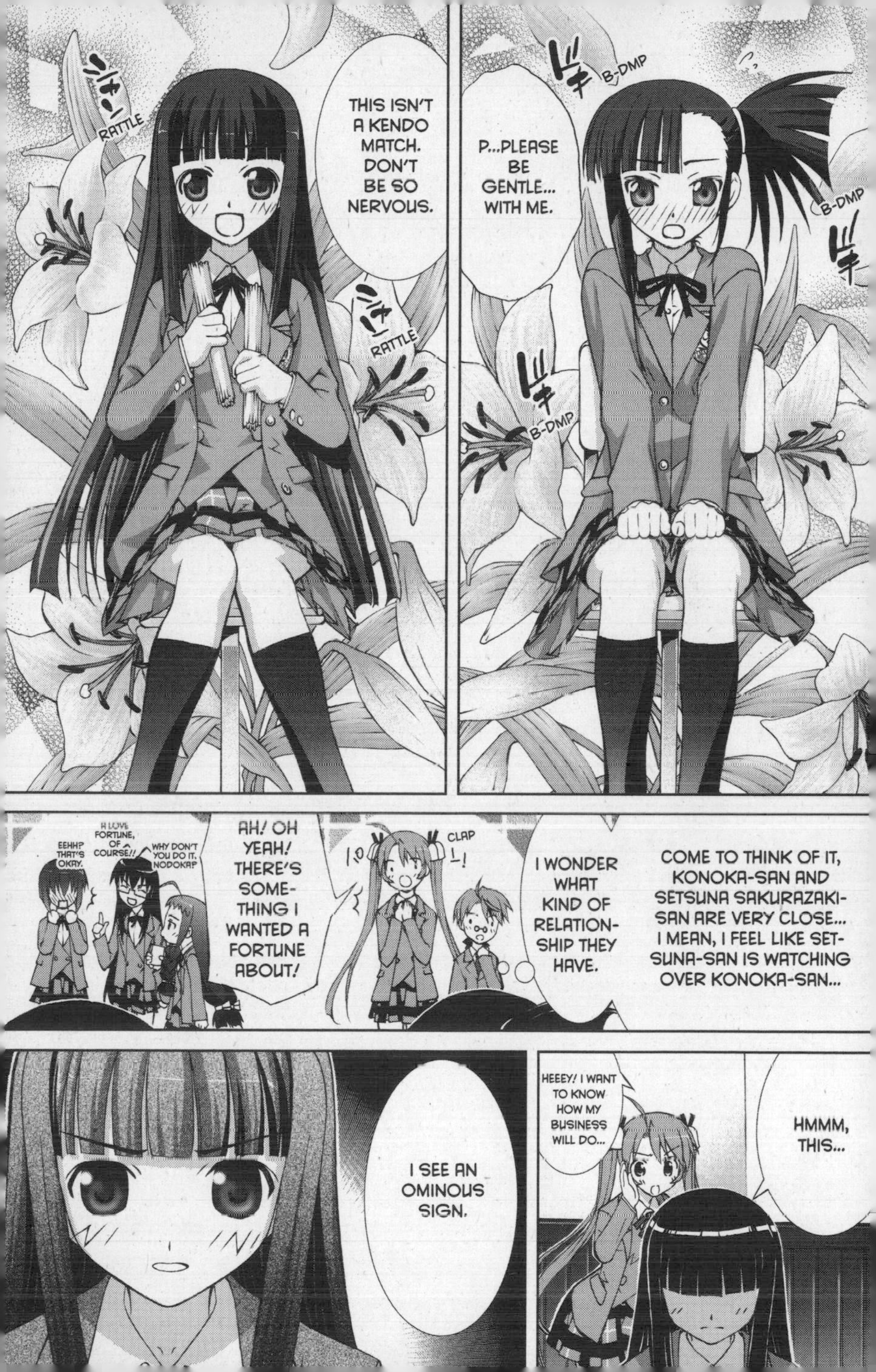
B-DMP
P...PLEASE BE GENTLE... WITH ME.
B-DMP
B-DMP
RATTLE
THIS ISN'T A KENDO MATCH. DON'T BE SO NERVOUS.
RATTLE
COME TO THINK OF IT, KONOKA-SAN AND SETSUNA SAKURAZAKI-SAN ARE VERY CLOSE... I MEAN, I FEEL LIKE SET-SUNA-SAN IS WATCHING OVER KONOKA-SAN...
I WONDER WHAT KIND OF RELATION-SHIP THEY HAVE.
CLAP
AH! OH YEAH! THERE'S SOME-THING I WANTED A FORTUNE ABOUT!
WHY DON'T YOU DO IT, NODOKA?
A LOVE FORTUNE, OF COURSE!!
EEHH? THAT'S OKAY.
HMMM, THIS...
HEEEY! I WANT TO KNOW HOW MY BUSINESS WILL DO...
I SEE AN OMINOUS SIGN.

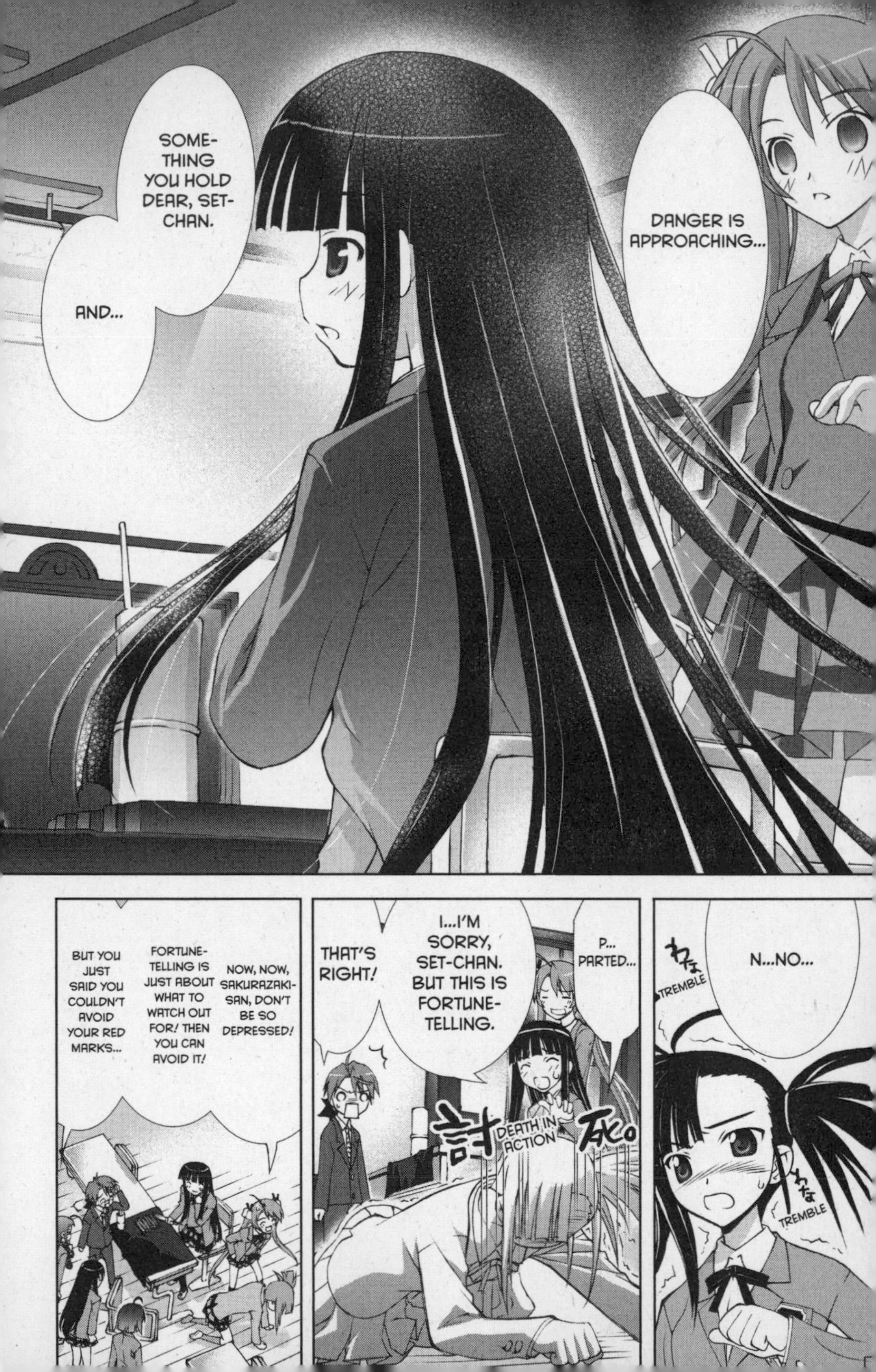
DANGER IS APPROACHING...
SOME-THING YOU HOLD DEAR, SET-CHAN.
AND...
N...NO...
TREMBLE
TREMBLE
P... PARTED...
I...I'M SORRY, SET-CHAN. BUT THIS IS FORTUNE-TELLING.
THAT'S RIGHT!
DEATH IN ACTION
NOW, NOW, SAKURAZAKI-SAN, DON'T BE SO DEPRESSED!
FORTUNE-TELLING IS JUST ABOUT WHAT TO WATCH OUT FOR! THEN YOU CAN AVOID IT!
BUT YOU JUST SAID YOU COULDN'T AVOID YOUR RED MARKS...

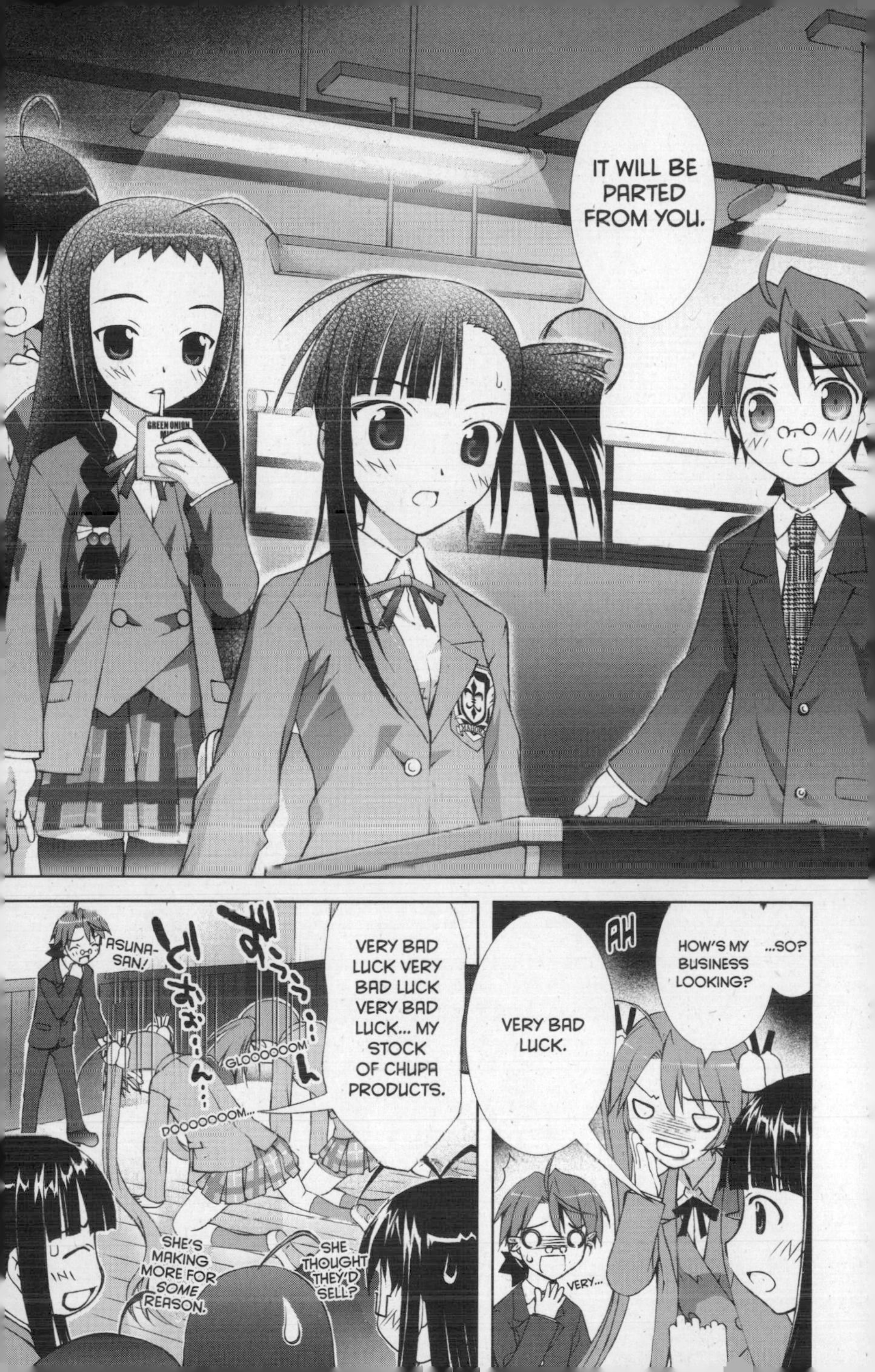
IT WILL BE PARTED FROM YOU.
...SO?
HOW'S MY BUSINESS LOOKING?
AH
VERY BAD LUCK.
VERY...
VERY BAD LUCK VERY BAD LUCK VERY BAD LUCK... MY STOCK OF CHUPA PRODUCTS.
GLOOOOOOM
ASUNA-SAN!
DOOOOOOOM...
SHE THOUGHT THEY'D SELL?
SHE'S MAKING MORE FOR SOME REASON.

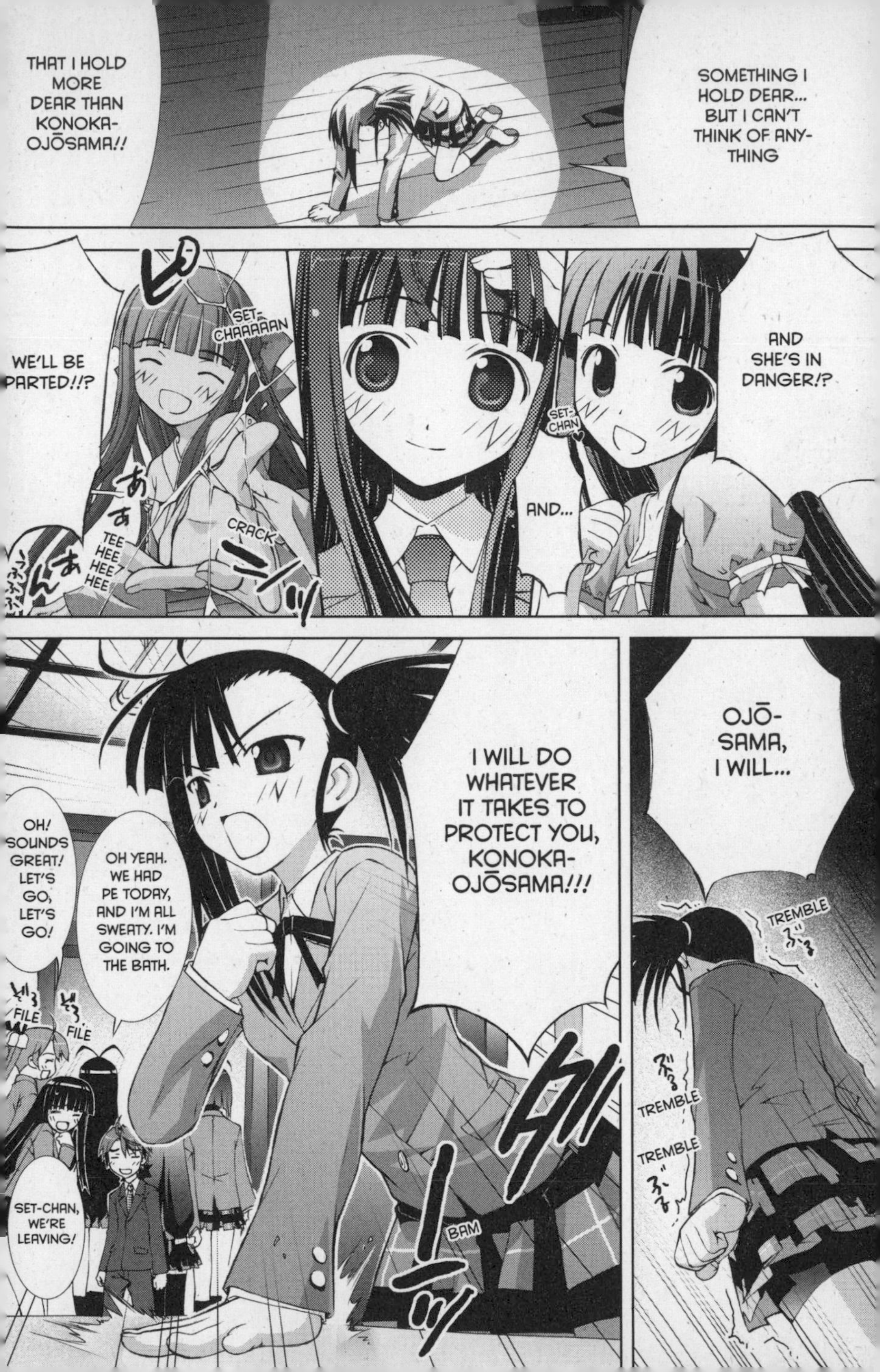
SOMETHING I HOLD DEAR... BUT I CAN'T THINK OF ANYTHING
THAT I HOLD MORE DEAR THAN KONOKA-OJŌSAMA!!
AND SHE'S IN DANGER!?
SET-CHAN♥
AND...
SET-CHAAAAAAN
WE'LL BE PARTED!!?
CRACK
TEE HEE HEE HEE
OJŌ-SAMA, I WILL...
TREMBLE
TREMBLE
TREMBLE
I WILL DO WHATEVER IT TAKES TO PROTECT YOU, KONOKA-OJŌSAMA!!!
BAM
OH YEAH. WE HAD PE TODAY, AND I'M ALL SWEATY. I'M GOING TO THE BATH.
OH! SOUNDS GREAT! LET'S GO, LET'S GO!
FILE
FILE
SET-CHAN, WE'RE LEAVING!

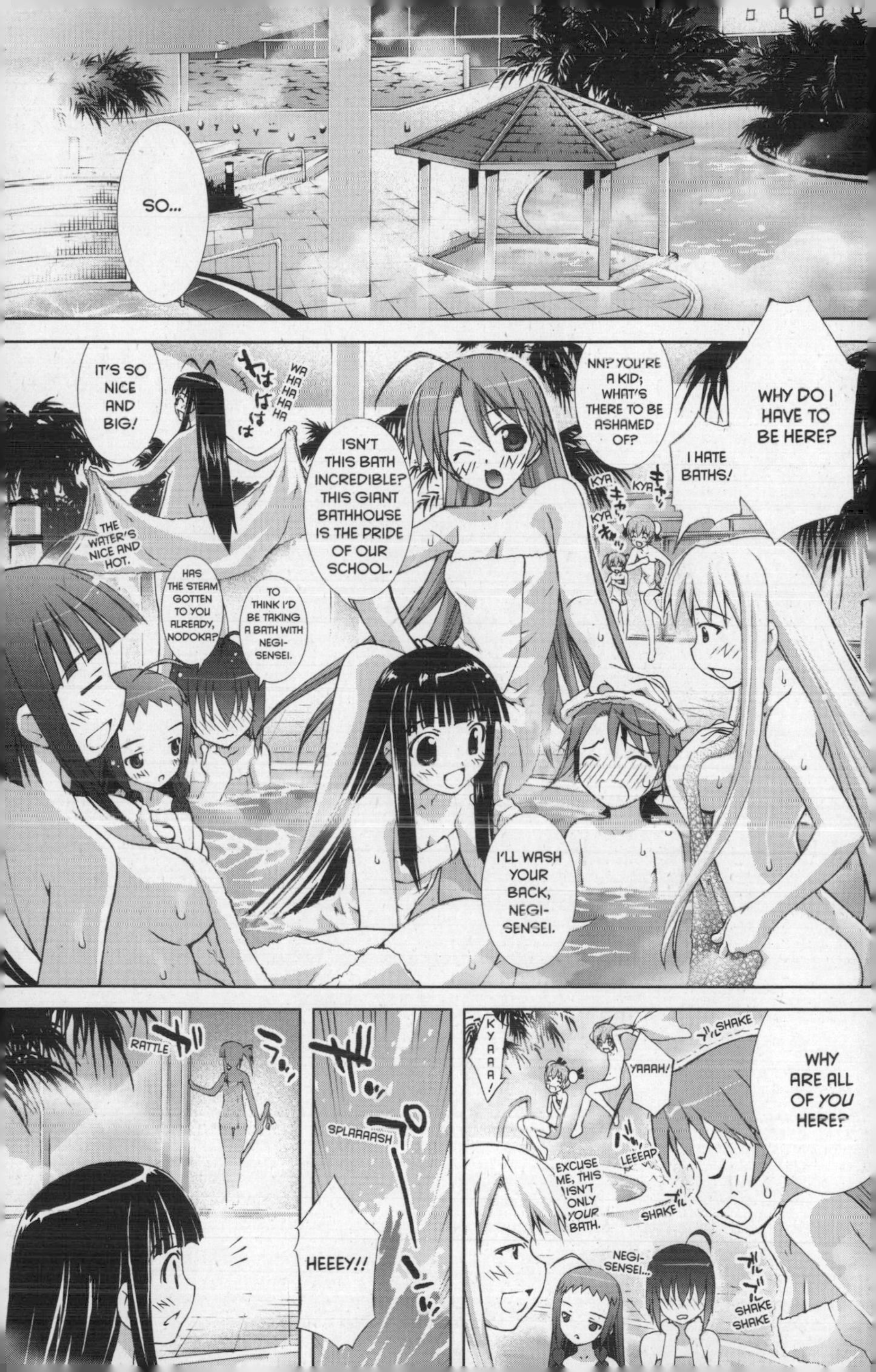
SO...
WHY DO I HAVE TO BE HERE?
I HATE BATHS!
NN? YOU'RE A KID; WHAT'S THERE TO BE ASHAMED OF?
KYA KYA KYA
ISN'T THIS BATH INCREDIBLE? THIS GIANT BATHHOUSE IS THE PRIDE OF OUR SCHOOL.
WA HA HA HA HA
IT'S SO NICE AND BIG!
THE WATER'S NICE AND HOT.
HAS THE STEAM GOTTEN TO YOU ALREADY, NODOKA?
TO THINK I'D BE TAKING A BATH WITH NEGI-SENSEI.
I'LL WASH YOUR BACK, NEGI-SENSEI.
WHY ARE ALL OF YOU HERE?
SHAKE
YAAAH!
KYAAA!
LEEEAP
EXCUSE ME, THIS ISN'T ONLY YOUR BATH.
SHAKE
NEGI-SENSEI...
SHAKE SHAKE
SPLAAAASH
HEEEY!!
RATTLE

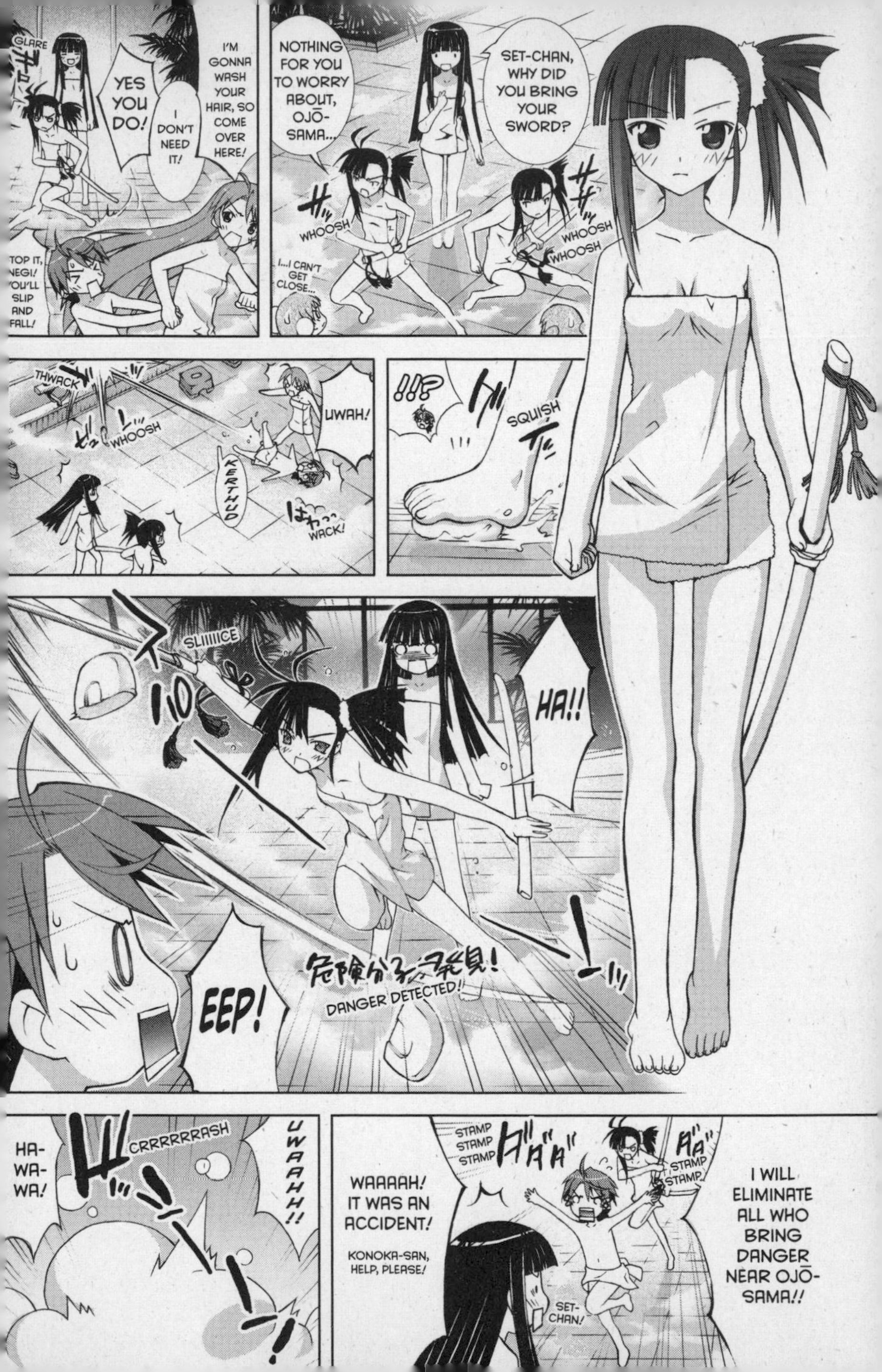
SET-CHAN, WHY DID YOU BRING YOUR SWORD?
NOTHING FOR YOU TO WORRY ABOUT, OJŌ-SAMA...
WHOOSH WHOOSH
WHOOSH
I...I CAN'T GET CLOSE...
I'M GONNA WASH YOUR HAIR, SO COME OVER HERE!
I DON'T NEED IT!
YES YOU DO!
GLARE
TOP IT, NEGI! YOU'LL SLIP AND FALL!
!!?
SQUISH
UWAH!
THWACK
WHOOSH
KERTHUD
WACK!
HA!!
SLIIIIICE
危険分子発見!
DANGER DETECTED!
EEP!
I WILL ELIMINATE ALL WHO BRING DANGER NEAR OJŌ-SAMA!!
STAMP STAMP
STAMP STAMP STAMP
WAAAAH! IT WAS AN ACCIDENT!
KONOKA-SAN, HELP, PLEASE!
SET-CHAN!
UWAAAHH!!
CRRRRRRASH
HA-WA-WA!

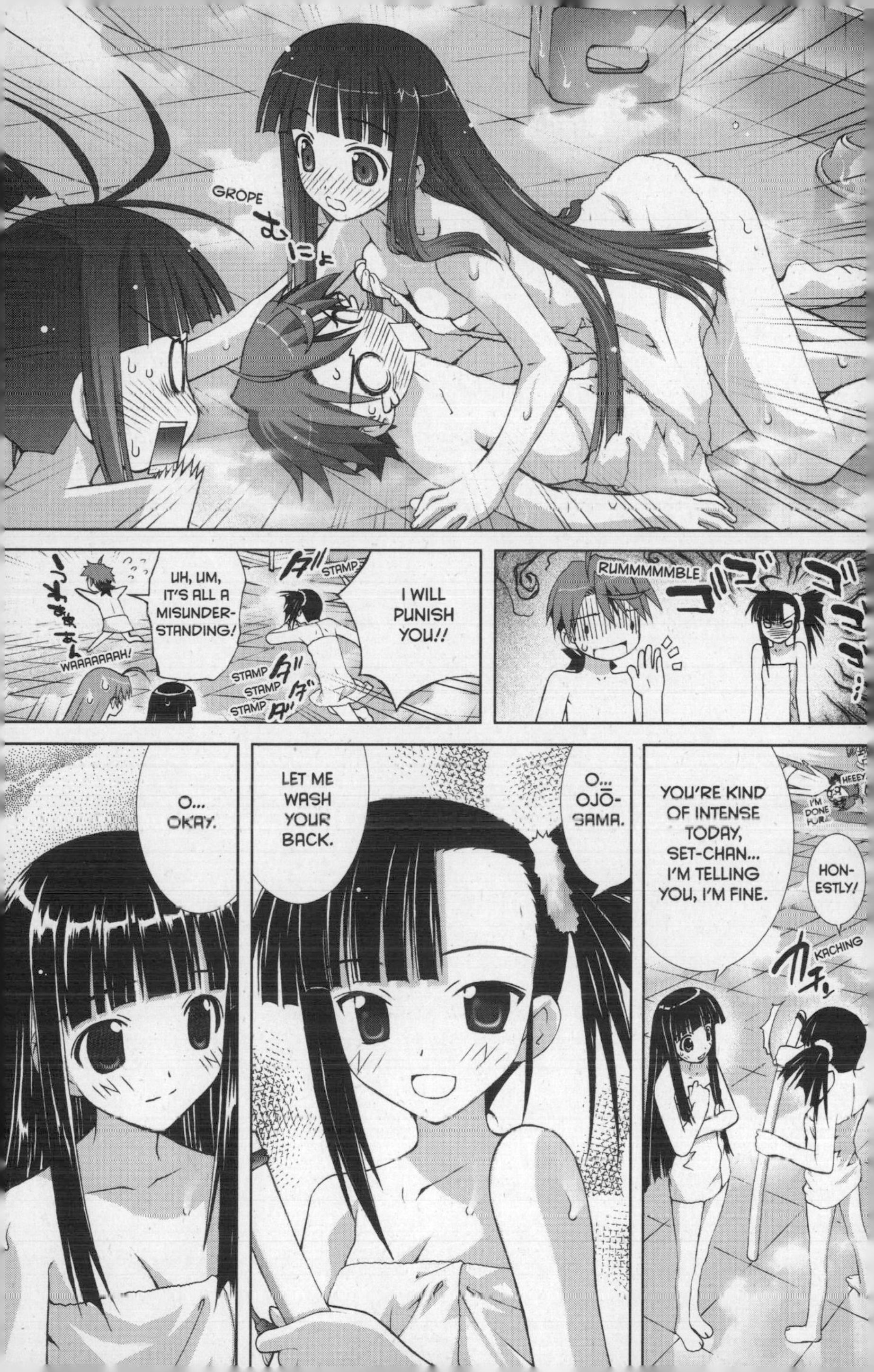
GROPE
むにょ
RUMMMMMBLE
ゴゴゴゴ…
I WILL PUNISH YOU!!
STAMP
UH, UM, IT'S ALL A MISUNDERSTANDING!
WAAAAAAAH!
STAMP STAMP STAMP
HEEEY
I'M DONE FUR...
YOU'RE KIND OF INTENSE TODAY, SET-CHAN... I'M TELLING YOU, I'M FINE.
HON-ESTLY!
KACHING
O... OJŌ-SAMA.
LET ME WASH YOUR BACK.
O... OKAY.

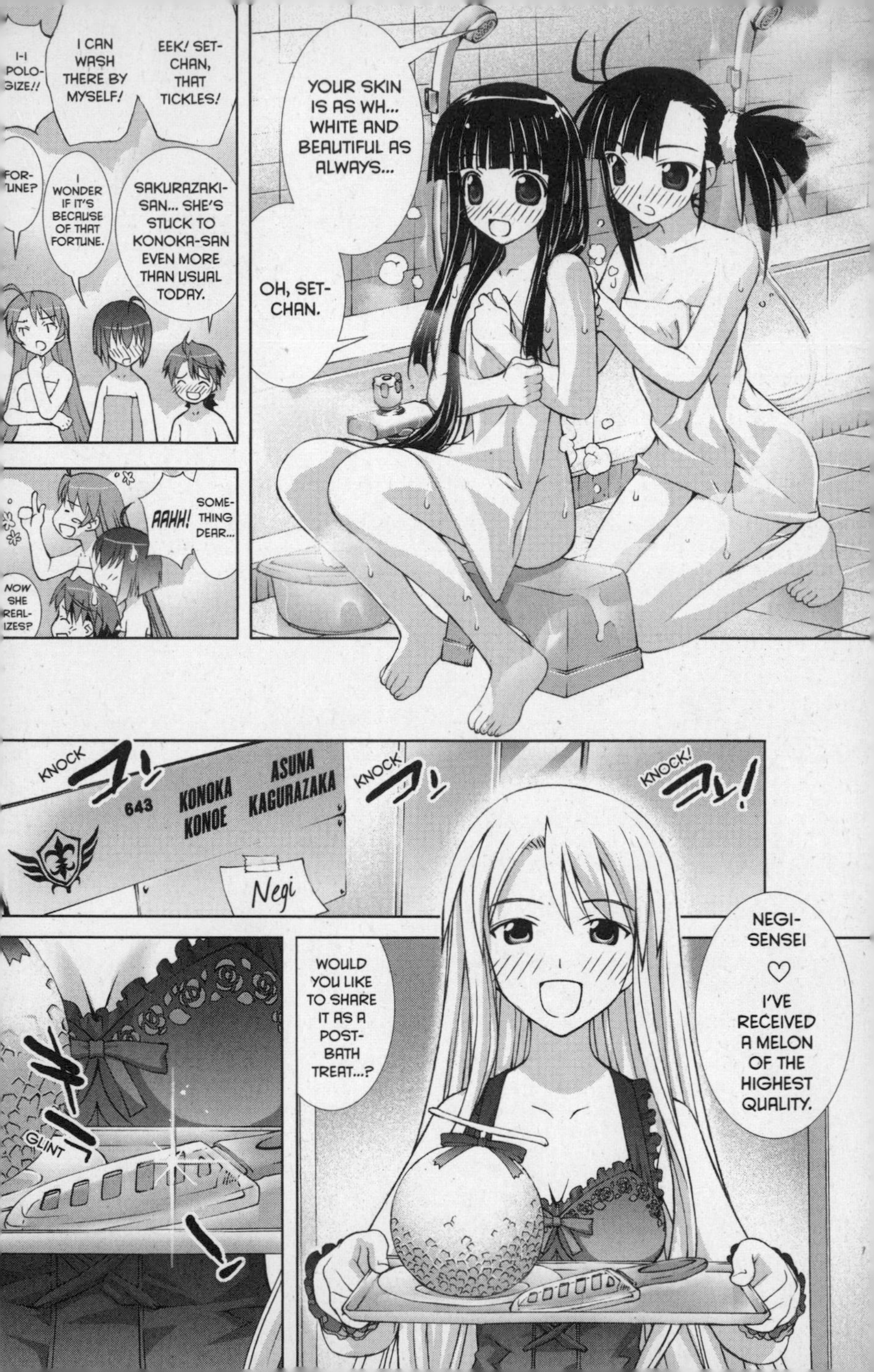
YOUR SKIN IS AS WH... WHITE AND BEAUTIFUL AS ALWAYS...
OH, SET-CHAN.
EEK! SET-CHAN, THAT TICKLES!
I CAN WASH THERE BY MYSELF!
I-I POLOGIZE!!
SAKURAZAKI-SAN... SHE'S STUCK TO KONOKA-SAN EVEN MORE THAN USUAL TODAY.
I WONDER IF IT'S BECAUSE OF THAT FORTUNE.
FORTUNE?
SOMETHING DEAR...
AAHH!
NOW SHE REALIZES?
KNOCK!
KNOCK
KNOCK
ASUNA KAGURAZAKA
KONOKA KONOE
643
Negi
NEGI-SENSEI ♡ I'VE RECEIVED A MELON OF THE HIGHEST QUALITY.
WOULD YOU LIKE TO SHARE IT AS A POST-BATH TREAT...?
GLINT

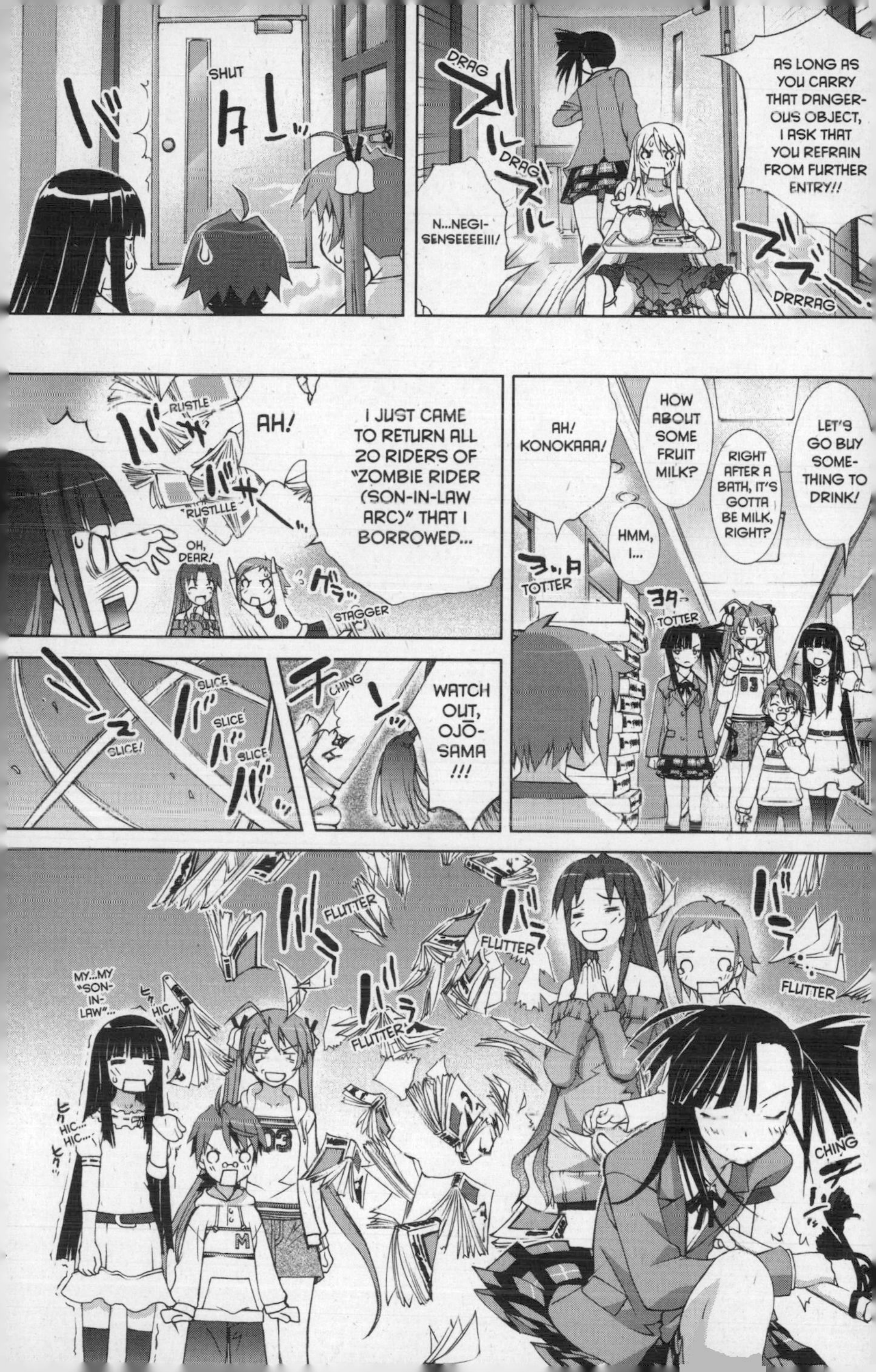
AS LONG AS YOU CARRY THAT DANGEROUS OBJECT, I ASK THAT YOU REFRAIN FROM FURTHER ENTRY!!
DRRRAG
DRAG
DRAG
N...NEGI-SENSEEEEIII!
SHUT
LET'S GO BUY SOMETHING TO DRINK!
HOW ABOUT SOME FRUIT MILK?
RIGHT AFTER A BATH, IT'S GOTTA BE MILK, RIGHT?
AH! KONOKAAA!
HMM, I...
TOTTER
TOTTER
I JUST CAME TO RETURN ALL 20 RIDERS OF "ZOMBIE RIDER (SON-IN-LAW ARC)" THAT I BORROWED...
AH!
RUSTLE
RUSTLLLE
OH, DEAR!
STAGGER
WATCH OUT, OJŌ-SAMA!!!
CHING
SLICE
SLICE
SLICE
SLICE!
FLUTTER
FLUTTER
FLUTTER
FLUTTER
CHING
MY...MY "SON-IN-LAW"...
HIC...
HIC... HIC...

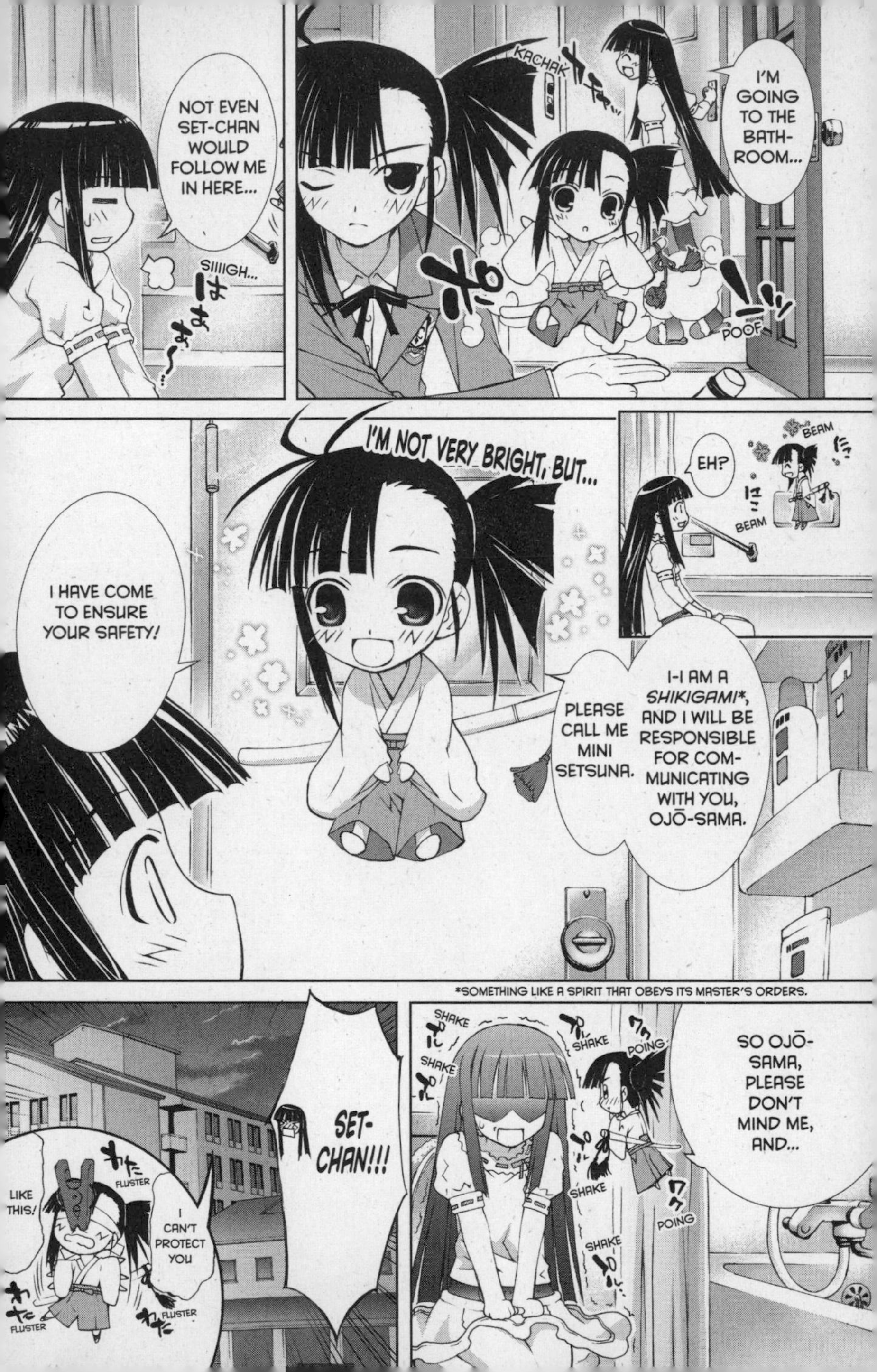
I'M GOING TO THE BATH-ROOM...
KACHAK
POOF
NOT EVEN SET-CHAN WOULD FOLLOW ME IN HERE...
SIIIGH...
EH?
BEAM
BEAM
I'M NOT VERY BRIGHT, BUT...
I-I AM A SHIKIGAMI*, AND I WILL BE RESPONSIBLE FOR COM-MUNICATING WITH YOU, OJŌ-SAMA.
PLEASE CALL ME MINI SETSUNA.
I HAVE COME TO ENSURE YOUR SAFETY!
SO OJŌ-SAMA, PLEASE DON'T MIND ME, AND...
SHAKE
POING
SHAKE
SHAKE
SHAKE
POING
SHAKE
SET-CHAN!!!
I CAN'T PROTECT YOU
FLUSTER
LIKE THIS!
FLUSTER
FLUSTER

*SOMETHING LIKE A SPIRIT THAT OBEYS ITS MASTER'S ORDERS.

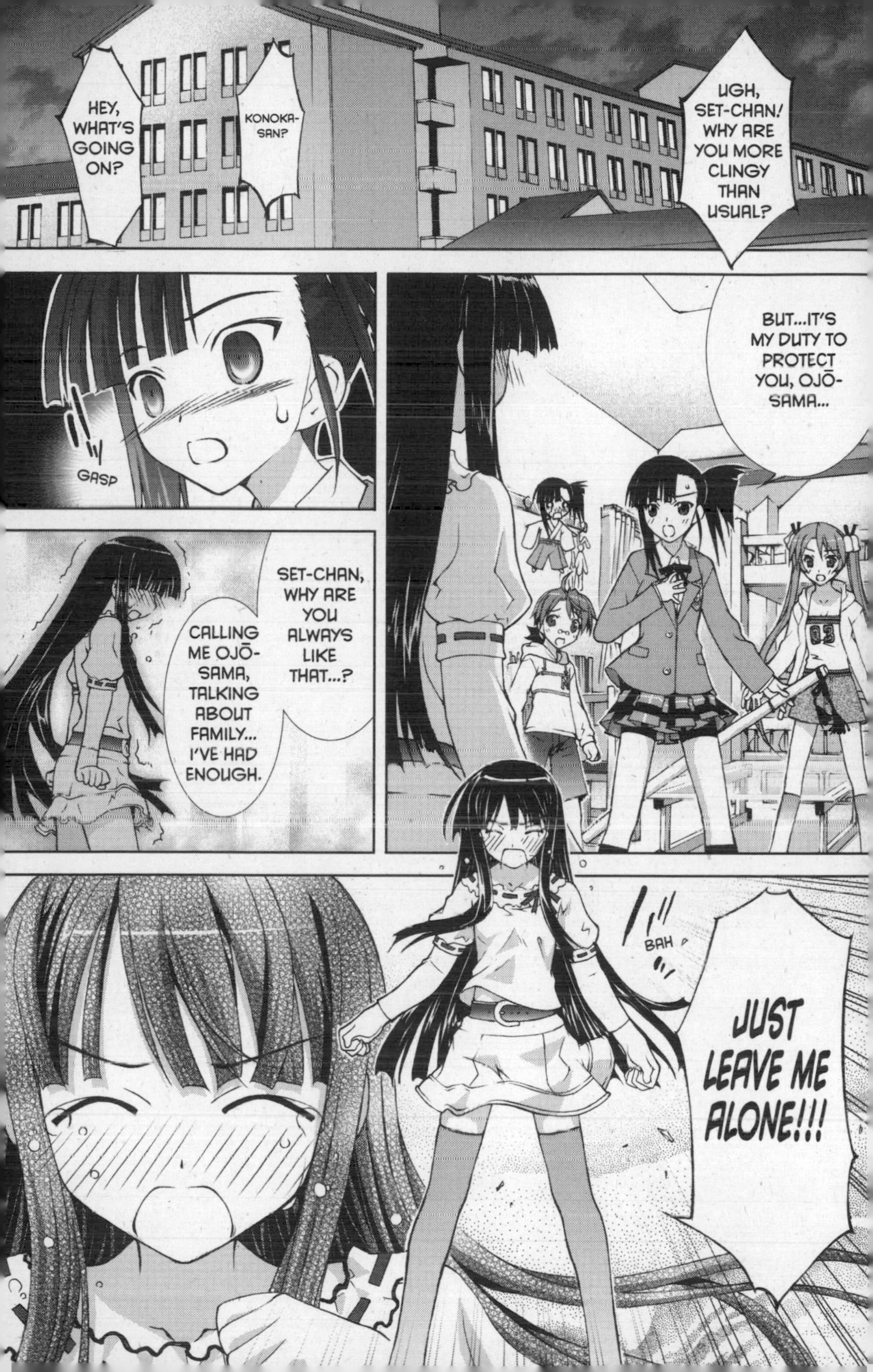
UGH, SET-CHAN! WHY ARE YOU MORE CLINGY THAN USUAL?
KONOKA-SAN?
HEY, WHAT'S GOING ON?
BUT...IT'S MY DUTY TO PROTECT YOU, OJŌ-SAMA...
GASP
SET-CHAN, WHY ARE YOU ALWAYS LIKE THAT...?
CALLING ME OJŌ-SAMA, TALKING ABOUT FAMILY... I'VE HAD ENOUGH.
BAH
JUST LEAVE ME ALONE!!!

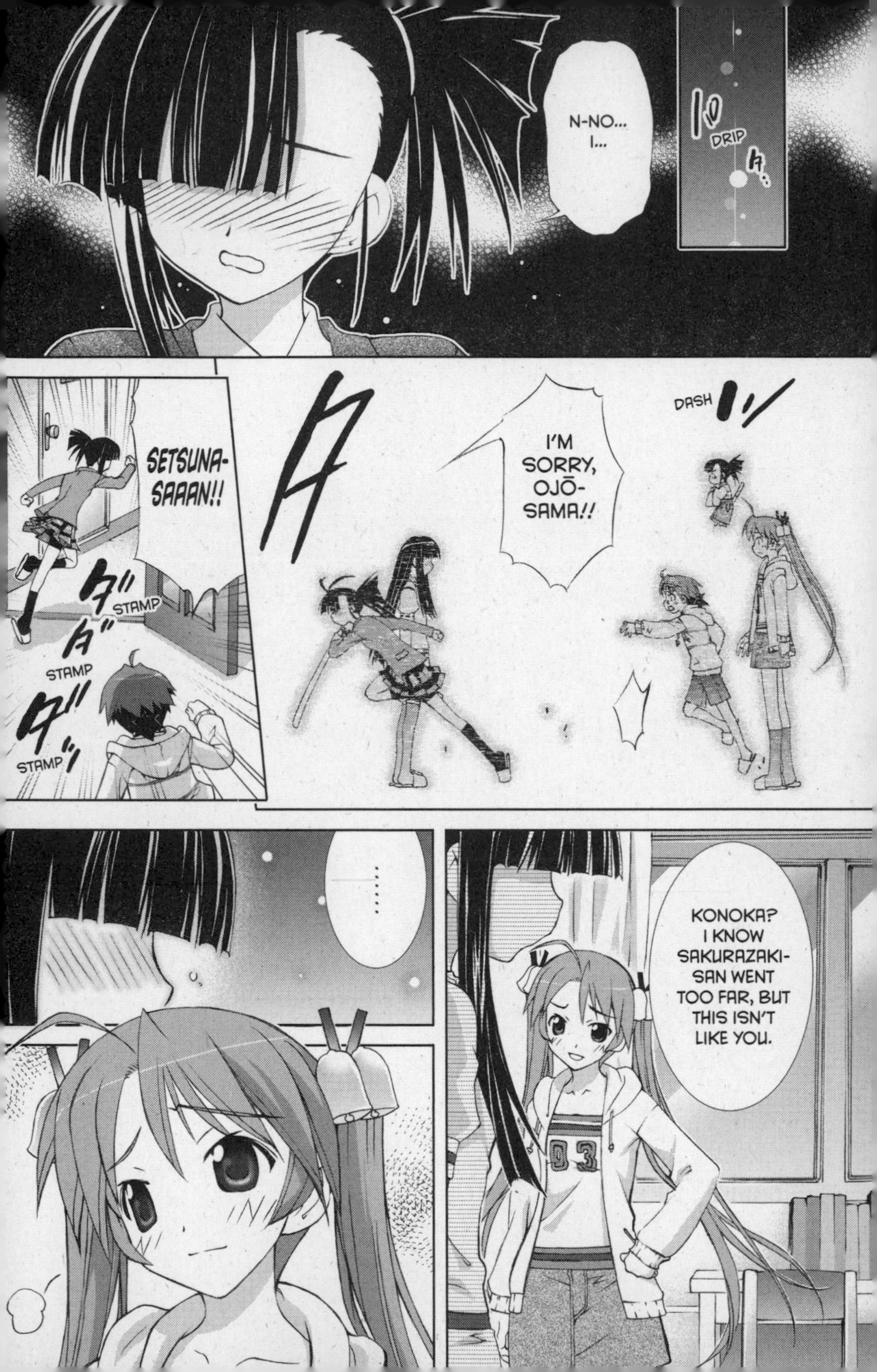
DRIP
N-NO... I...
DASH
I'M SORRY, OJŌ-SAMA!!
SETSUNA-SAAAN!!
STAMP
STAMP
STAMP
KONOKA? I KNOW SAKURAZAKI-SAN WENT TOO FAR, BUT THIS ISN'T LIKE YOU.
......

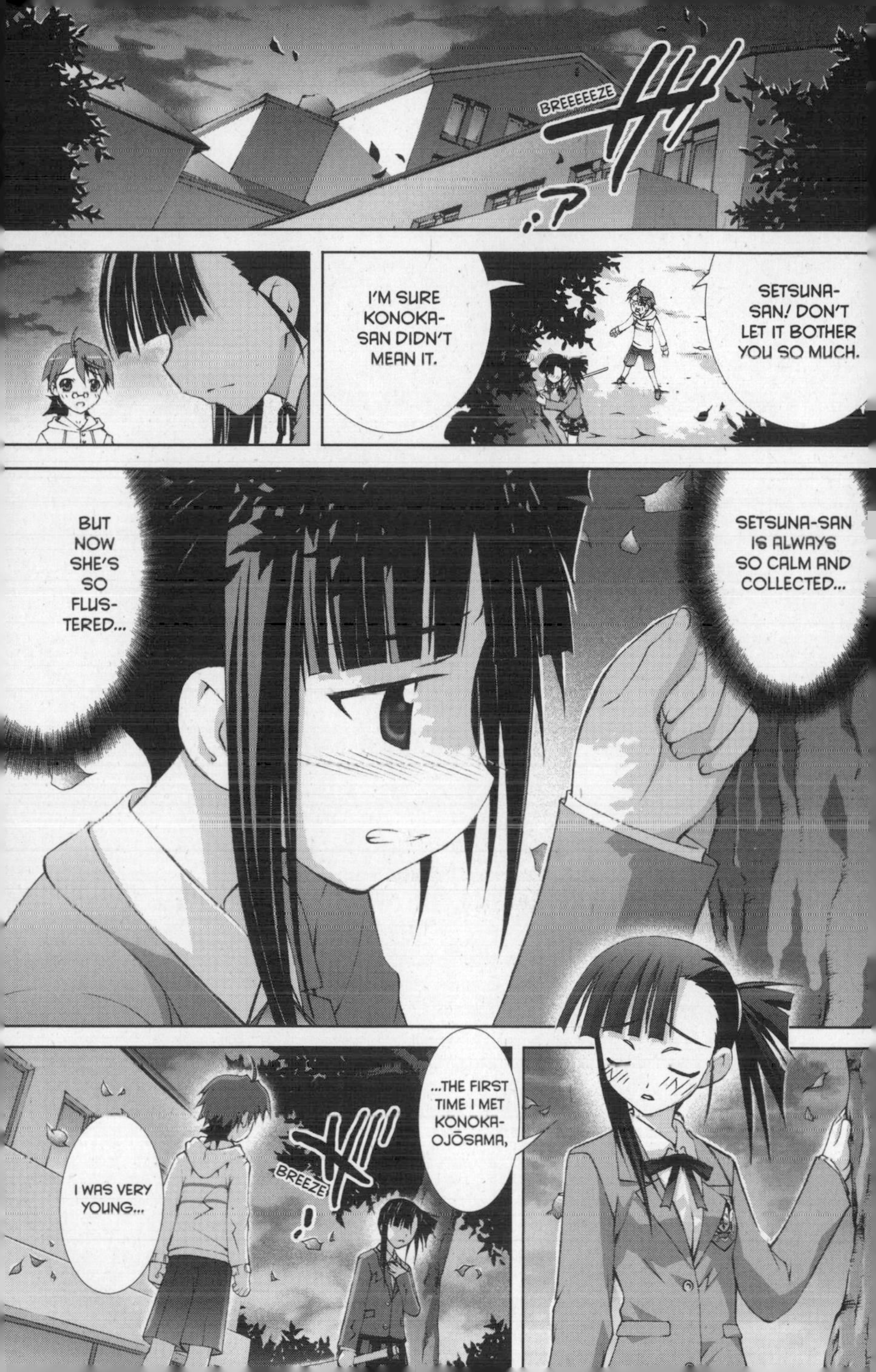
BREEEEEZE
SETSUNA-SAN! DON'T LET IT BOTHER YOU SO MUCH.
I'M SURE KONOKA-SAN DIDN'T MEAN IT.
SETSUNA-SAN IS ALWAYS SO CALM AND COLLECTED...
BUT NOW SHE'S SO FLUS-TERED...
...THE FIRST TIME I MET KONOKA-OJŌSAMA,
BREEZE
!
I WAS VERY YOUNG...

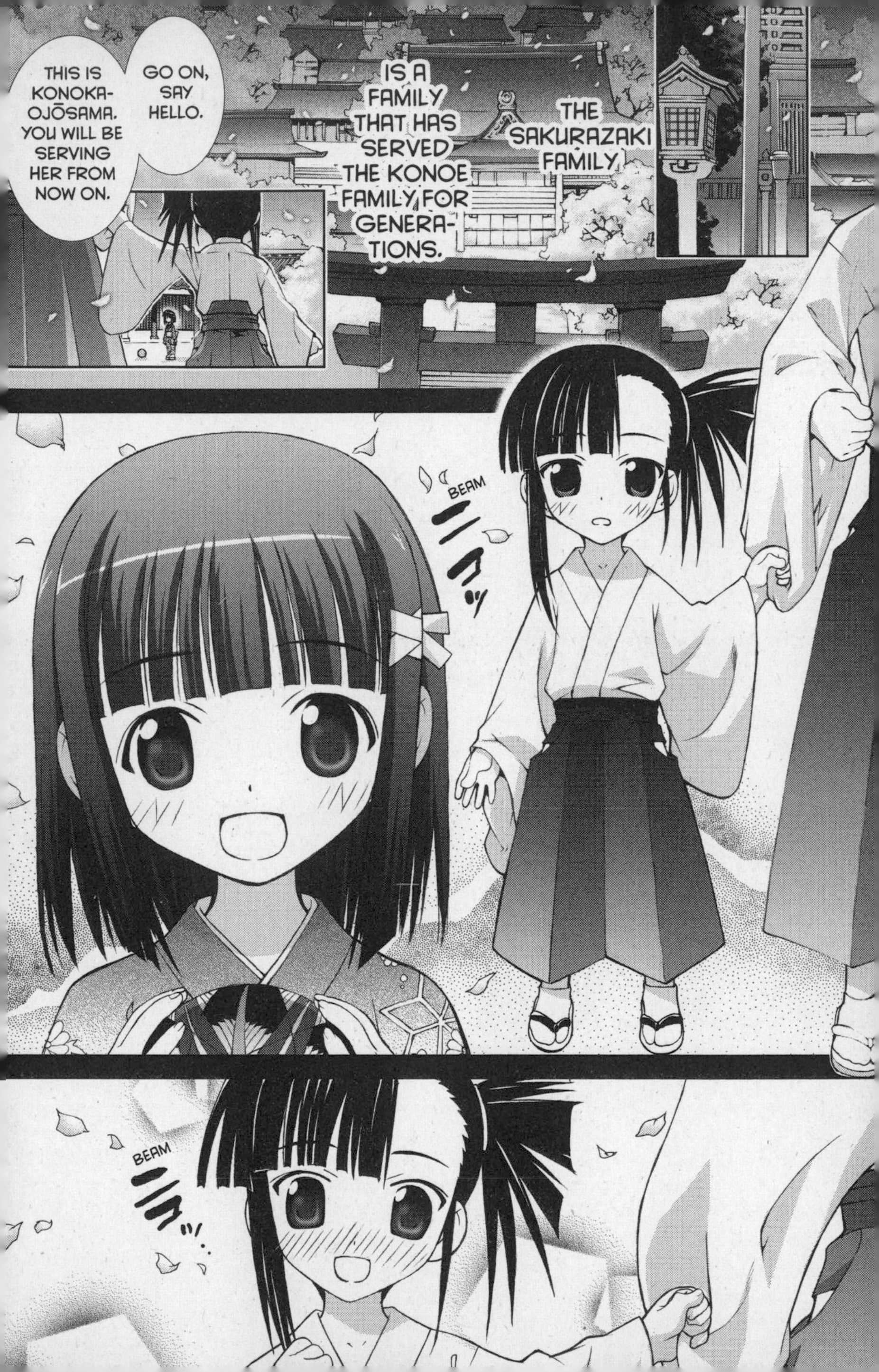
THE SAKURAZAKI FAMILY
IS A FAMILY THAT HAS SERVED THE KONOE FAMILY FOR GENERATIONS.
GO ON, SAY HELLO.
THIS IS KONOKA-OJŌSAMA. YOU WILL BE SERVING HER FROM NOW ON.
BEAM
BEAM

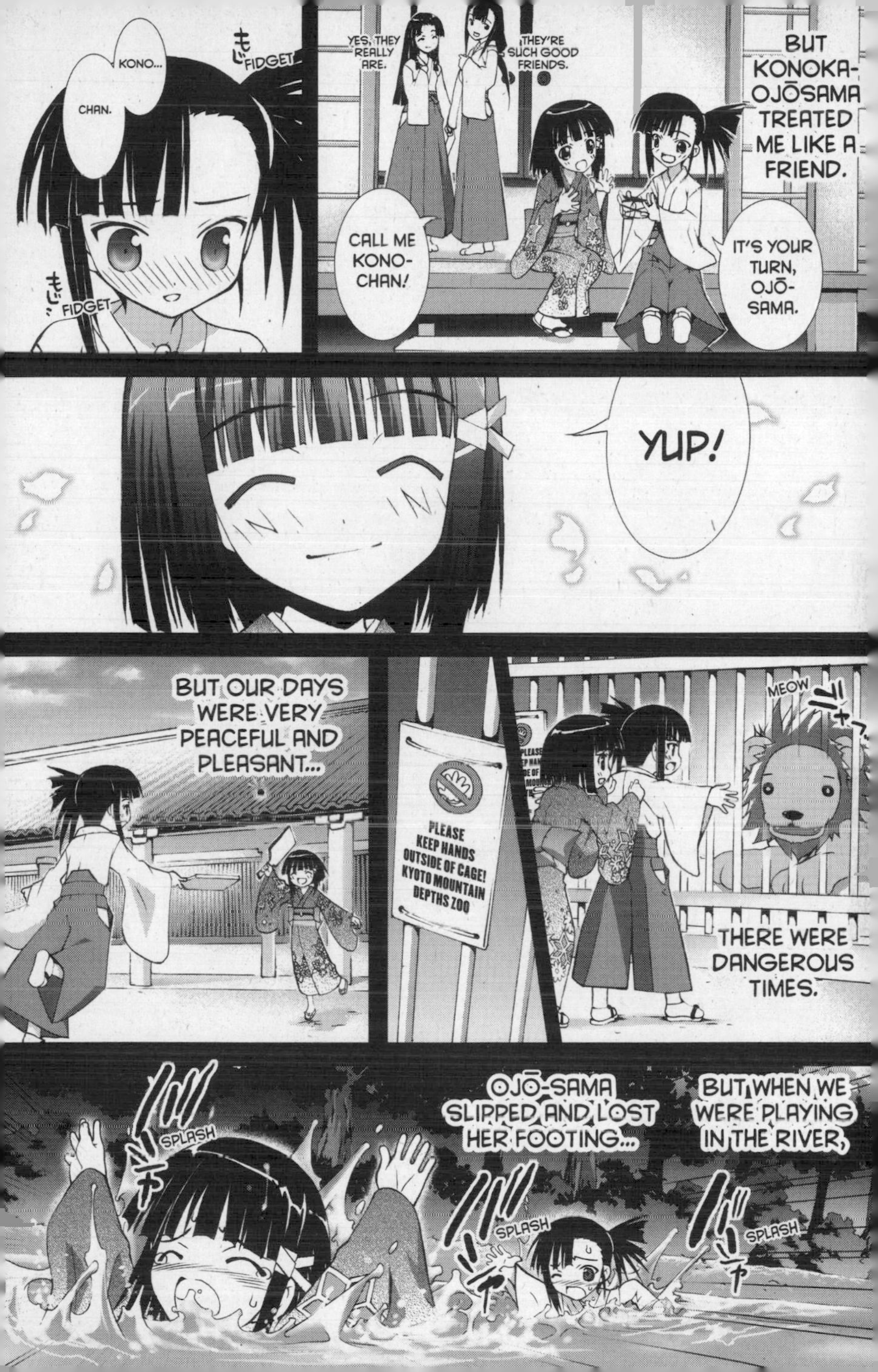
BUT KONOKA-OJŌSAMA TREATED ME LIKE A FRIEND.
IT'S YOUR TURN, OJŌ-SAMA.
CALL ME KONO-CHAN!
THEY'RE SUCH GOOD FRIENDS.
YES, THEY REALLY ARE.
FIDGET
KONO...
CHAN.
FIDGET
YUP!
MEOW
PLEASE KEEP HANDS OUTSIDE OF CAGE! KYOTO MOUNTAIN DEPTHS ZOO
THERE WERE DANGEROUS TIMES.
BUT OUR DAYS WERE VERY PEACEFUL AND PLEASANT...
BUT WHEN WE WERE PLAYING IN THE RIVER,
OJŌ-SAMA SLIPPED AND LOST HER FOOTING...
SPLASH
SPLASH
SPLASH

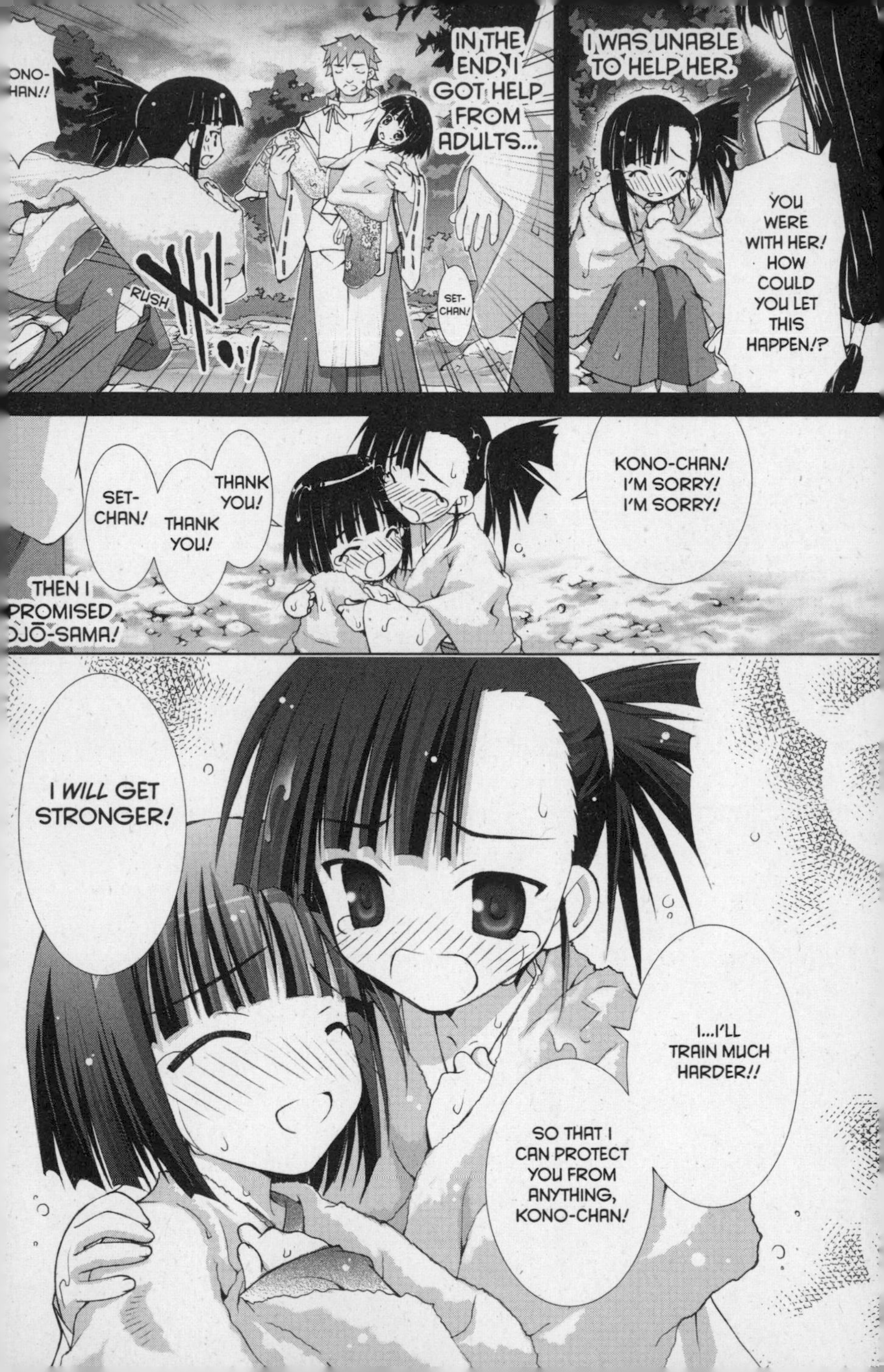
I WAS UNABLE TO HELP HER.
YOU WERE WITH HER! HOW COULD YOU LET THIS HAPPEN!?
IN THE END, I GOT HELP FROM ADULTS...
SET-CHAN!
RUSH
KONO-CHAN!!
KONO-CHAN! I'M SORRY! I'M SORRY!
SET-CHAN! THANK YOU! THANK YOU!
THEN I PROMISED OJŌ-SAMA!
I...I'LL TRAIN MUCH HARDER!!
SO THAT I CAN PROTECT YOU FROM ANYTHING, KONO-CHAN!
I *WILL* GET STRONGER!

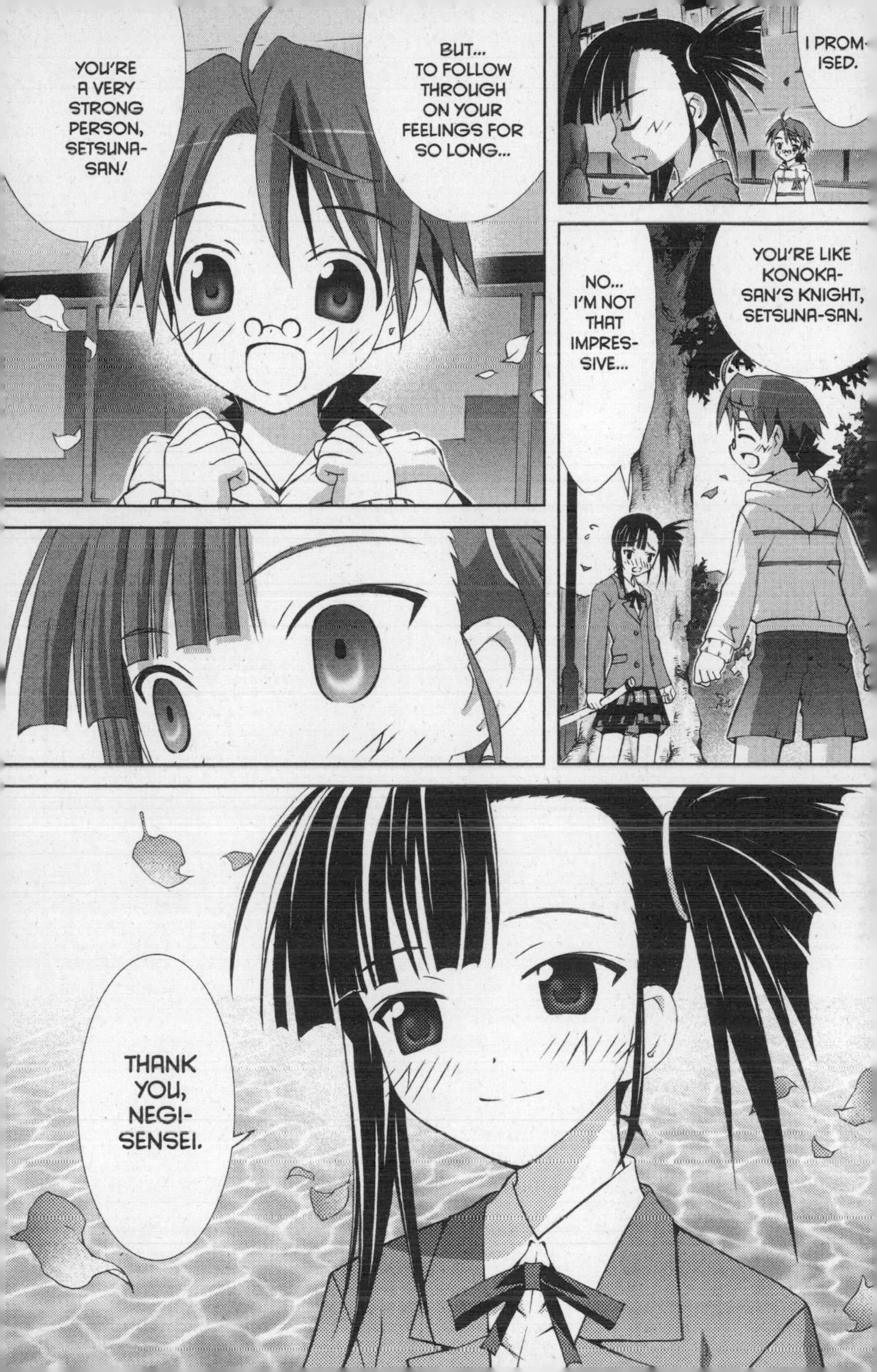
I PROMISED.
YOU'RE A VERY STRONG PERSON, SETSUNA-SAN!
BUT... TO FOLLOW THROUGH ON YOUR FEELINGS FOR SO LONG...
YOU'RE LIKE KONOKA-SAN'S KNIGHT, SETSUNA-SAN.
NO... I'M NOT THAT IMPRESSIVE...
THANK YOU, NEGI-SENSEI.

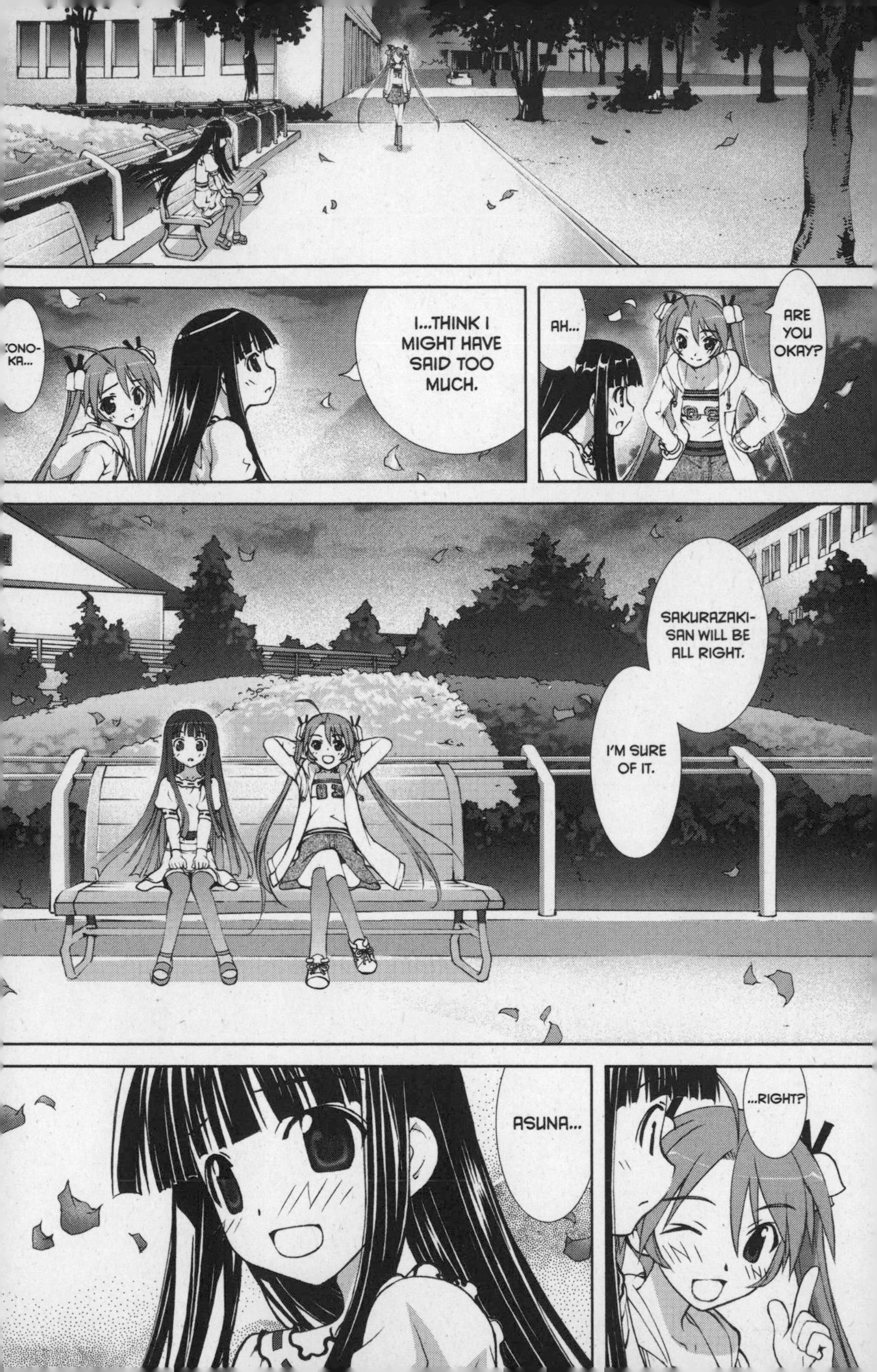
ARE YOU OKAY?
AH...
I...THINK I MIGHT HAVE SAID TOO MUCH.
KONO-KA...
SAKURAZAKI-SAN WILL BE ALL RIGHT.
I'M SURE OF IT.
...RIGHT?
ASUNA...

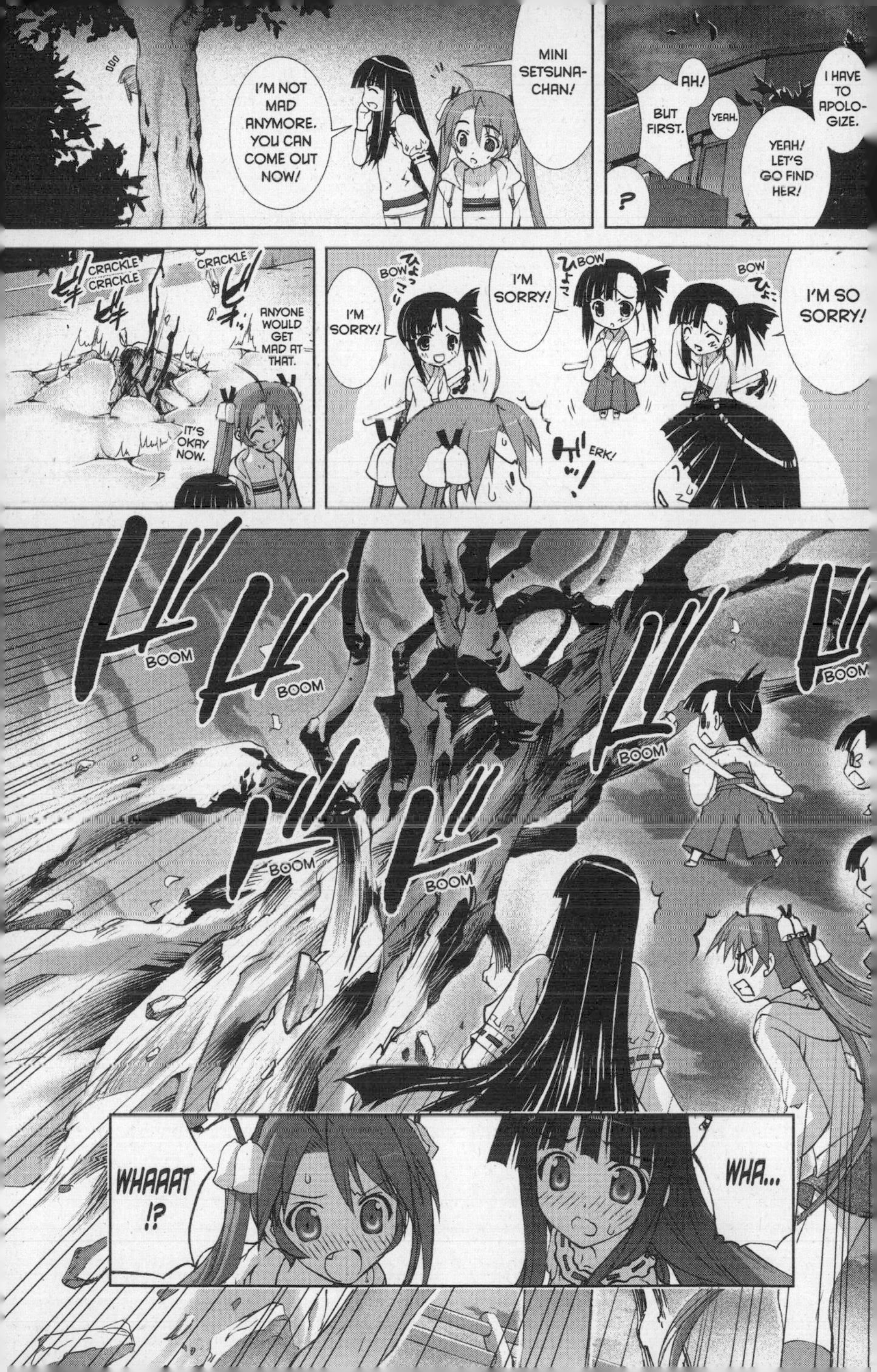
I HAVE TO APOLOGIZE.
YEAH.
AH!
YEAH! LET'S GO FIND HER!
BUT FIRST.
?
MINI SETSUNA-CHAN!
I'M NOT MAD ANYMORE. YOU CAN COME OUT NOW!
BOW
I'M SO SORRY!
BOW
I'M SORRY!
BOW
I'M SORRY!
ERK!
CRACKLE
ANYONE WOULD GET MAD AT THAT.
CRACKLE
CRACKLE
IT'S OKAY NOW.
BOOM
BOOM
BOOM
BOOM
BOOM
BOOM
WHA...
WHAAAT !?

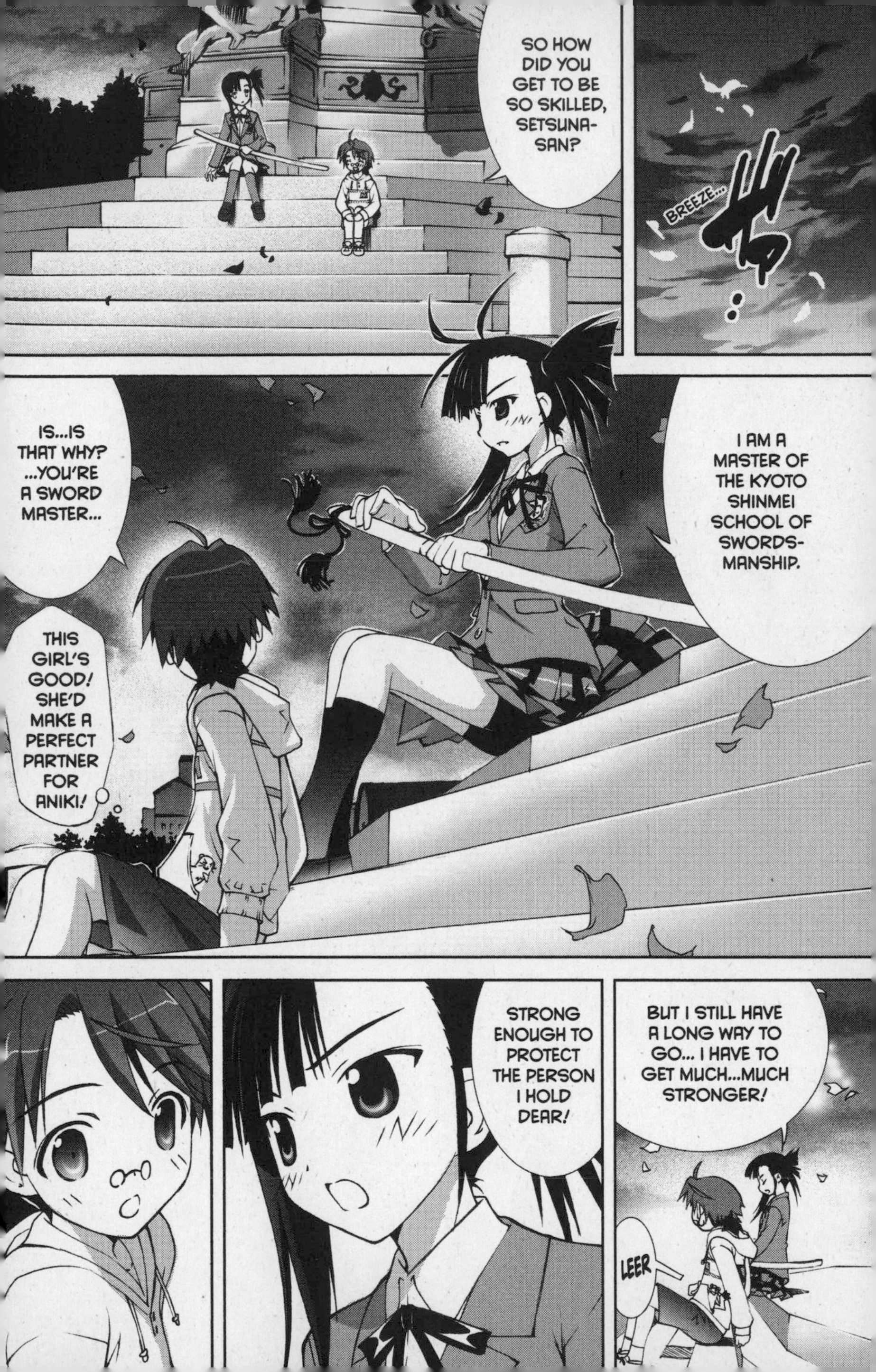
BREEZE...
SO HOW DID YOU GET TO BE SO SKILLED, SETSUNA-SAN?
I AM A MASTER OF THE KYOTO SHINMEI SCHOOL OF SWORDS-MANSHIP.
IS...IS THAT WHY? ...YOU'RE A SWORD MASTER...
THIS GIRL'S GOOD! SHE'D MAKE A PERFECT PARTNER FOR ANIKI!
BUT I STILL HAVE A LONG WAY TO GO... I HAVE TO GET MUCH...MUCH STRONGER!
LEER
STRONG ENOUGH TO PROTECT THE PERSON I HOLD DEAR!

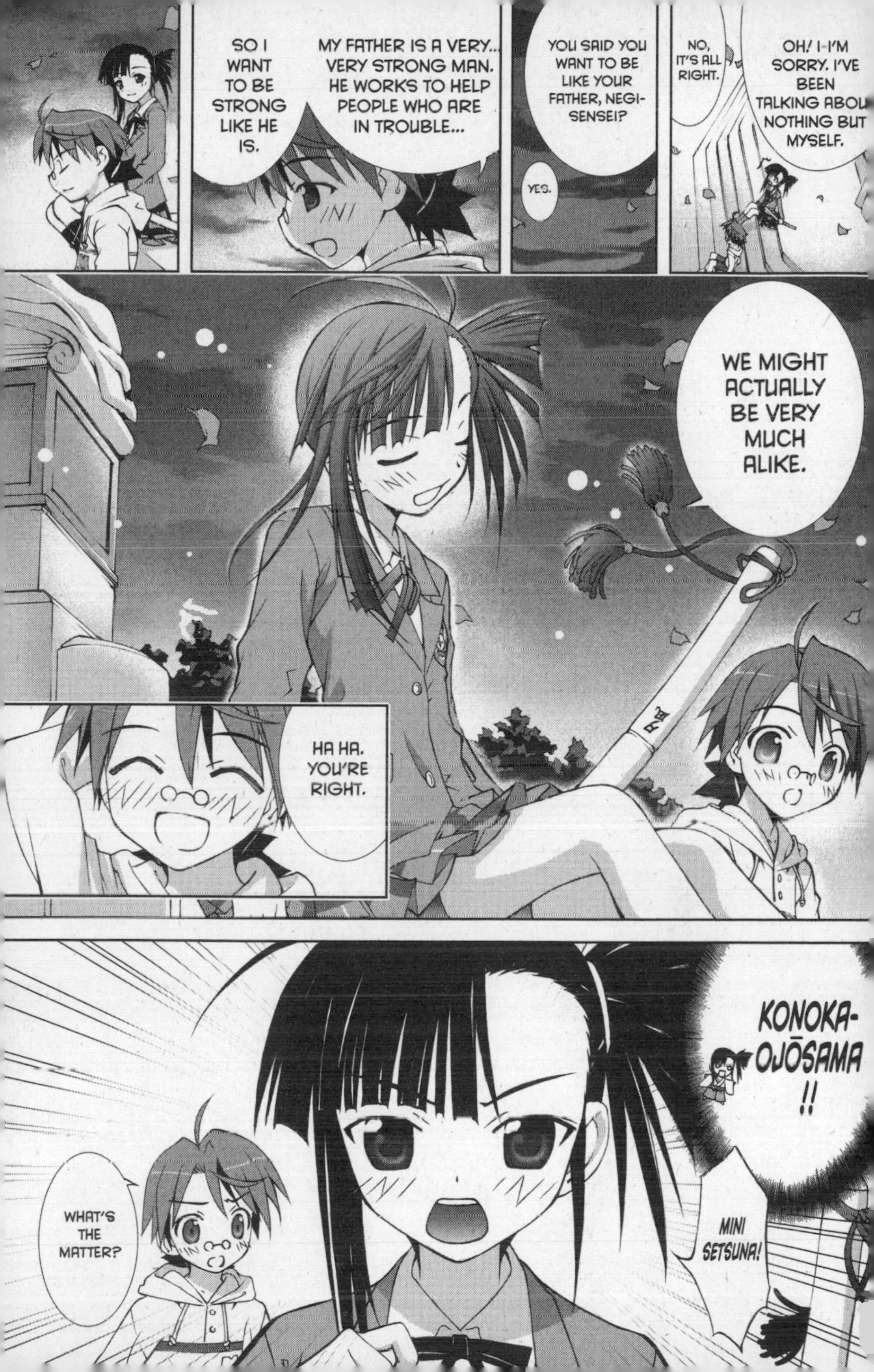
OH! I-I'M SORRY. I'VE BEEN TALKING ABOU NOTHING BUT MYSELF.
NO, IT'S ALL RIGHT.
YOU SAID YOU WANT TO BE LIKE YOUR FATHER, NEGI-SENSEI?
YES.
MY FATHER IS A VERY... VERY STRONG MAN. HE WORKS TO HELP PEOPLE WHO ARE IN TROUBLE...
SO I WANT TO BE STRONG LIKE HE IS.
WE MIGHT ACTUALLY BE VERY MUCH ALIKE.
HA HA. YOU'RE RIGHT.
KONOKA-OJŌSAMA !!
MINI SETSUNA!
WHAT'S THE MATTER?

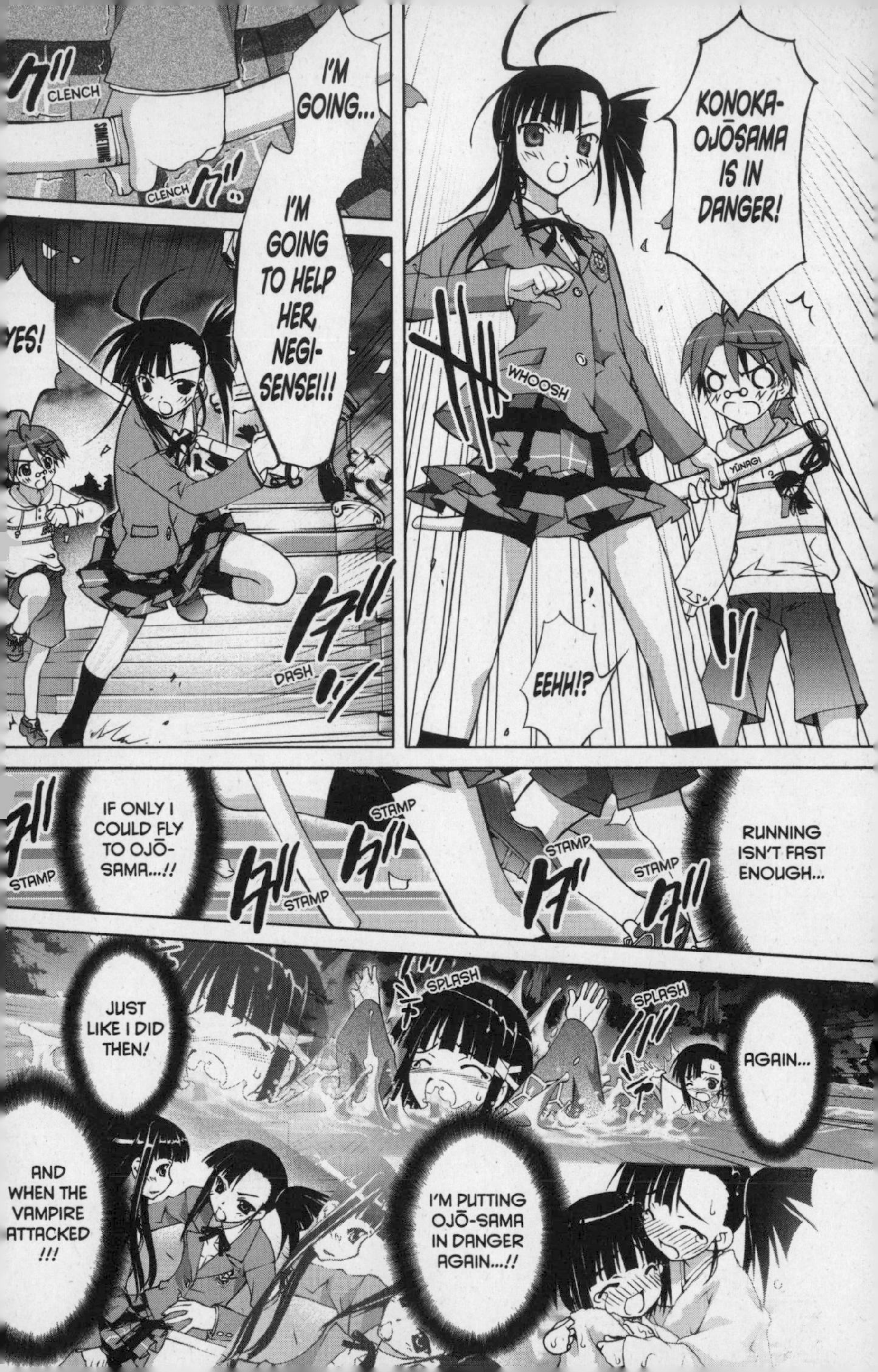
KONOKA-OJŌSAMA IS IN DANGER!
WHOOSH
YŪNAGI
EEHH!?
I'M GOING...
CLENCH
SOMETHING
CLENCH
I'M GOING TO HELP HER, NEGI-SENSEI!!
YES!
DASH
RUNNING ISN'T FAST ENOUGH...
STAMP
STAMP
STAMP
STAMP
IF ONLY I COULD FLY TO OJŌ-SAMA...!!
STAMP
AGAIN...
SPLASH
SPLASH
JUST LIKE I DID THEN!
I'M PUTTING OJŌ-SAMA IN DANGER AGAIN...!!
AND WHEN THE VAMPIRE ATTACKED!!!

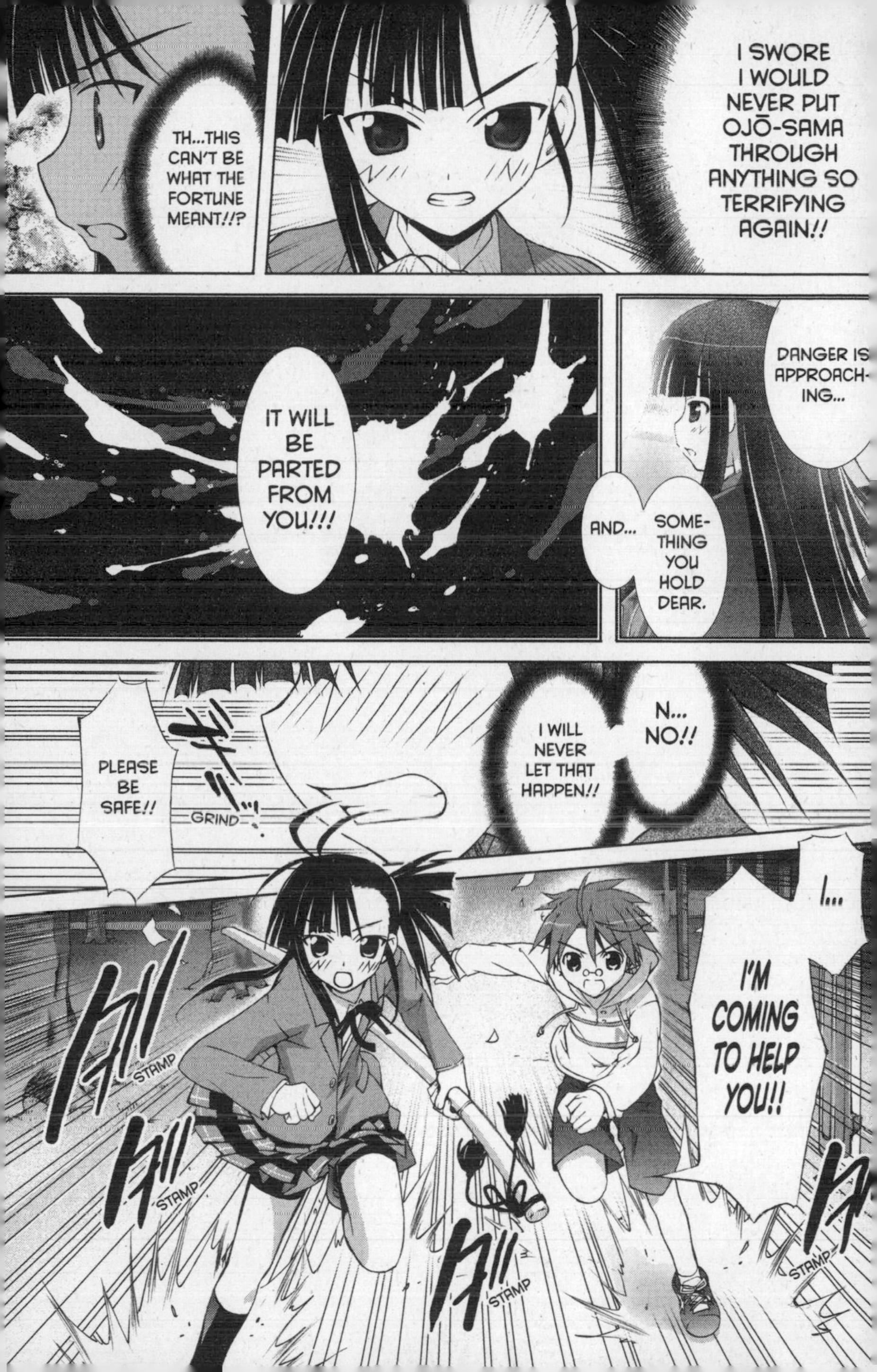
I SWORE I WOULD NEVER PUT OJŌ-SAMA THROUGH ANYTHING SO TERRIFYING AGAIN!!
TH...THIS CAN'T BE WHAT THE FORTUNE MEANT!!?
DANGER IS APPROACHING...
AND...
SOMETHING YOU HOLD DEAR.
IT WILL BE PARTED FROM YOU!!!
N... NO!!
I WILL NEVER LET THAT HAPPEN!!
GRIND
PLEASE BE SAFE!!
I...
I'M COMING TO HELP YOU!!
STAMP
STAMP
STAMP
STAMP

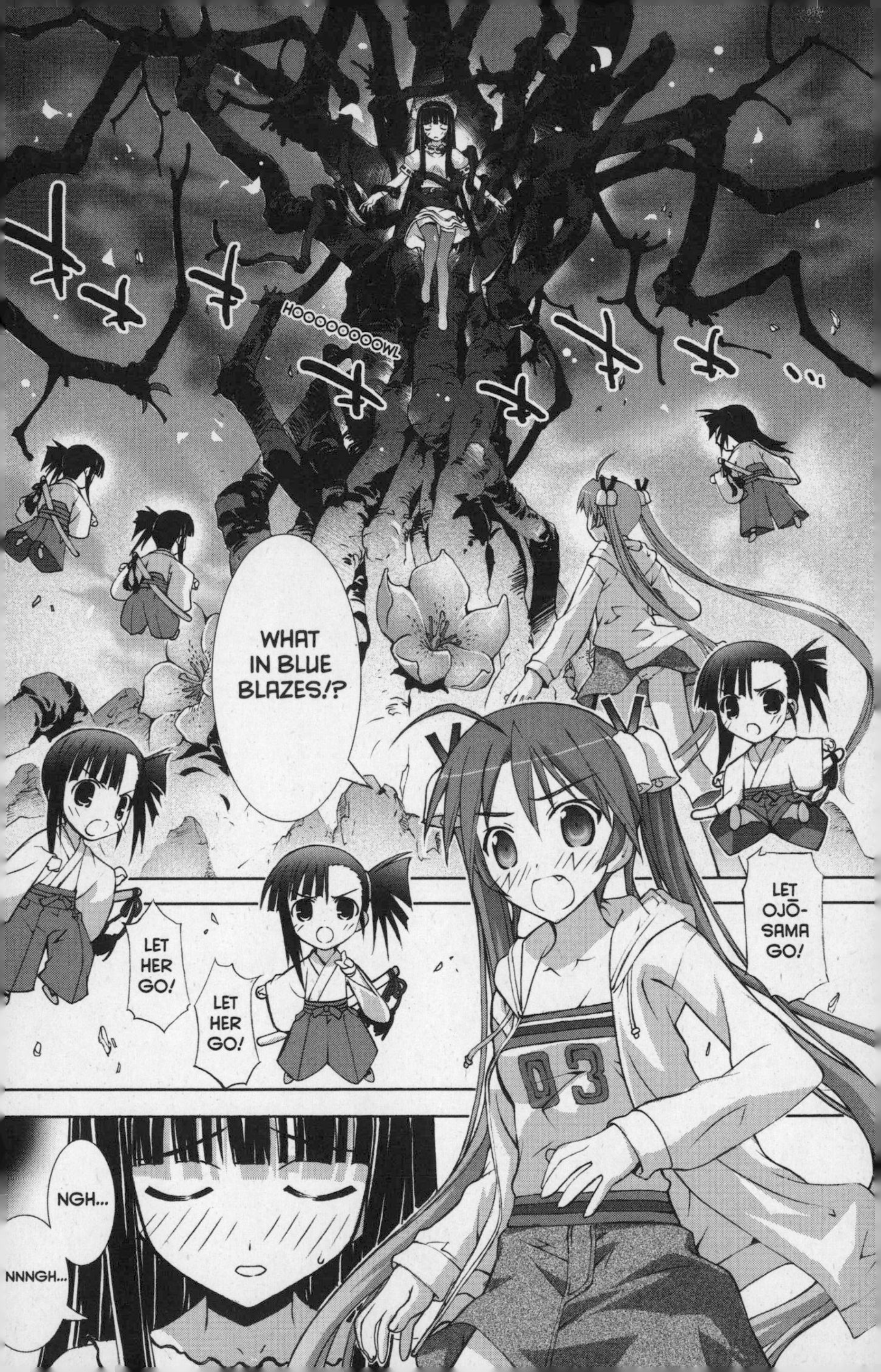
HOOOOOOOOOWL
WHAT IN BLUE BLAZES!?
LET OJŌ-SAMA GO!
LET HER GO!
LET HER GO!
NGH...
NNNGH...

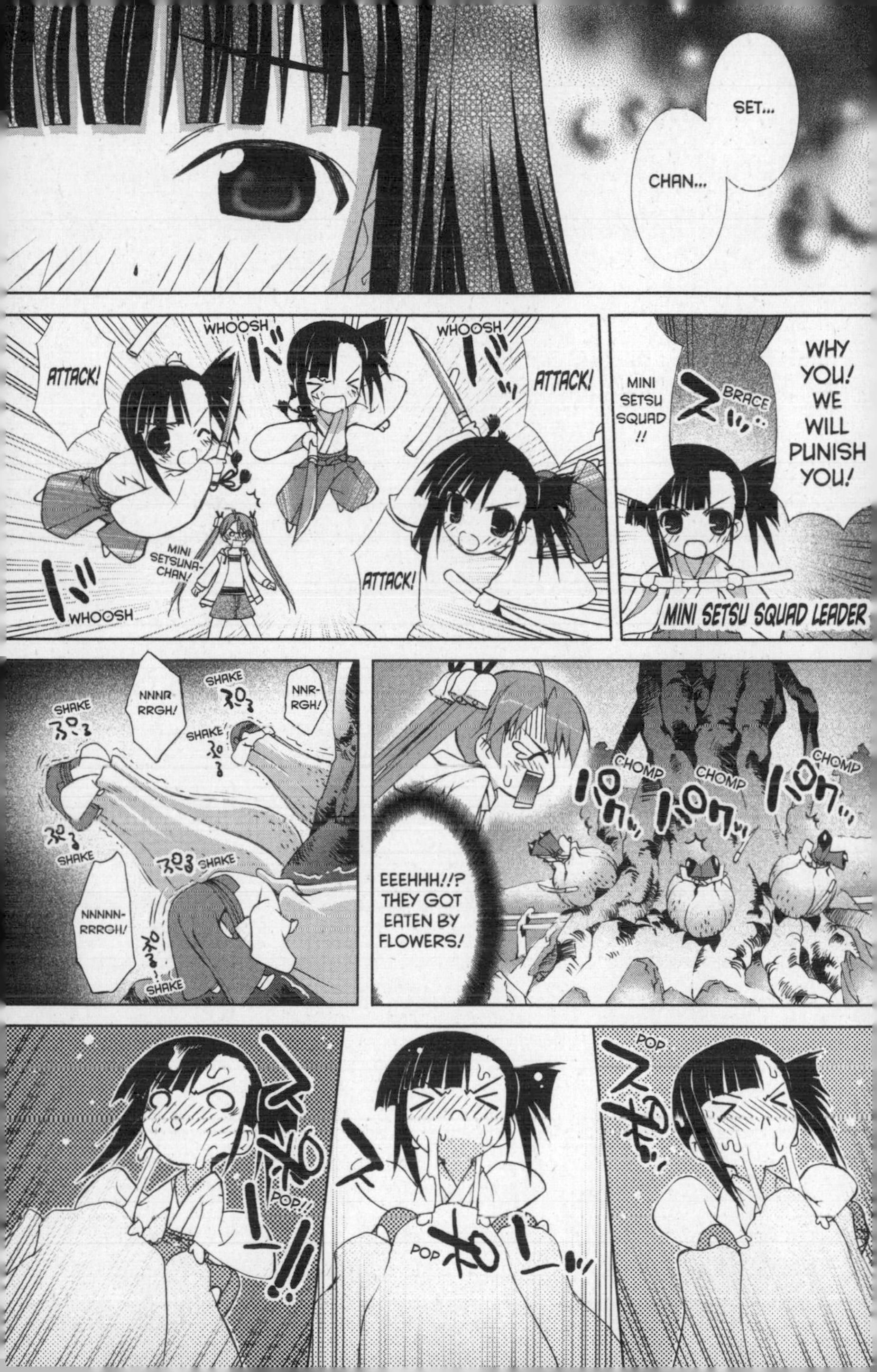
SET...
CHAN...
WHY YOU! WE WILL PUNISH YOU!
BRACE
MINI SETSU SQUAD !!
MINI SETSU SQUAD LEADER
WHOOSH
ATTACK!
WHOOSH
ATTACK!
MINI SETSUNA-CHAN!
ATTACK!
WHOOSH
CHOMP
CHOMP
CHOMP
EEEHHH!!? THEY GOT EATEN BY FLOWERS!
NNR-RGH!
SHAKE
NNNR RRGH!
SHAKE
SHAKE
SHAKE
SHAKE
NNNNN-RRRGH!
SHAKE
POP
POP
POP!!

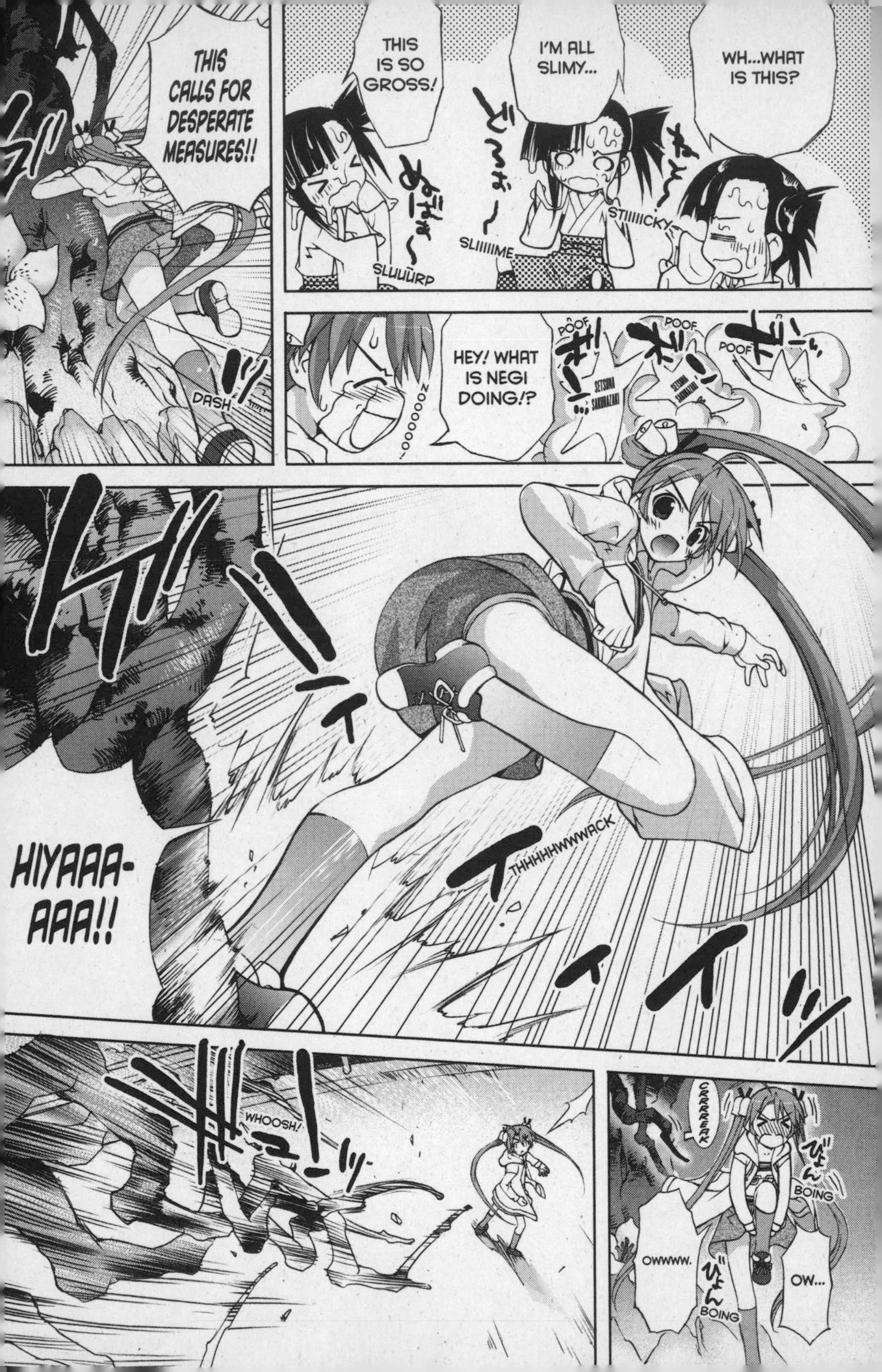

WH...WHAT IS THIS?
STIIIICKY
I'M ALL SLIMY...
SLIIIIME
THIS IS SO GROSS!
SLUUURP
POOF
POOF
POOF
SETSUNA SAKURAZAKI
SETSUNA SAKURAZAKI
HEY! WHAT IS NEGI DOING!?
NOOOOOOO!
THIS CALLS FOR DESPERATE MEASURES!!
DASH
THHHHHWWWACK
HIYAAAA-AAA!!
CRRRRERK
BOING
OW...
BOING
OWWWW.
WHOOSH!

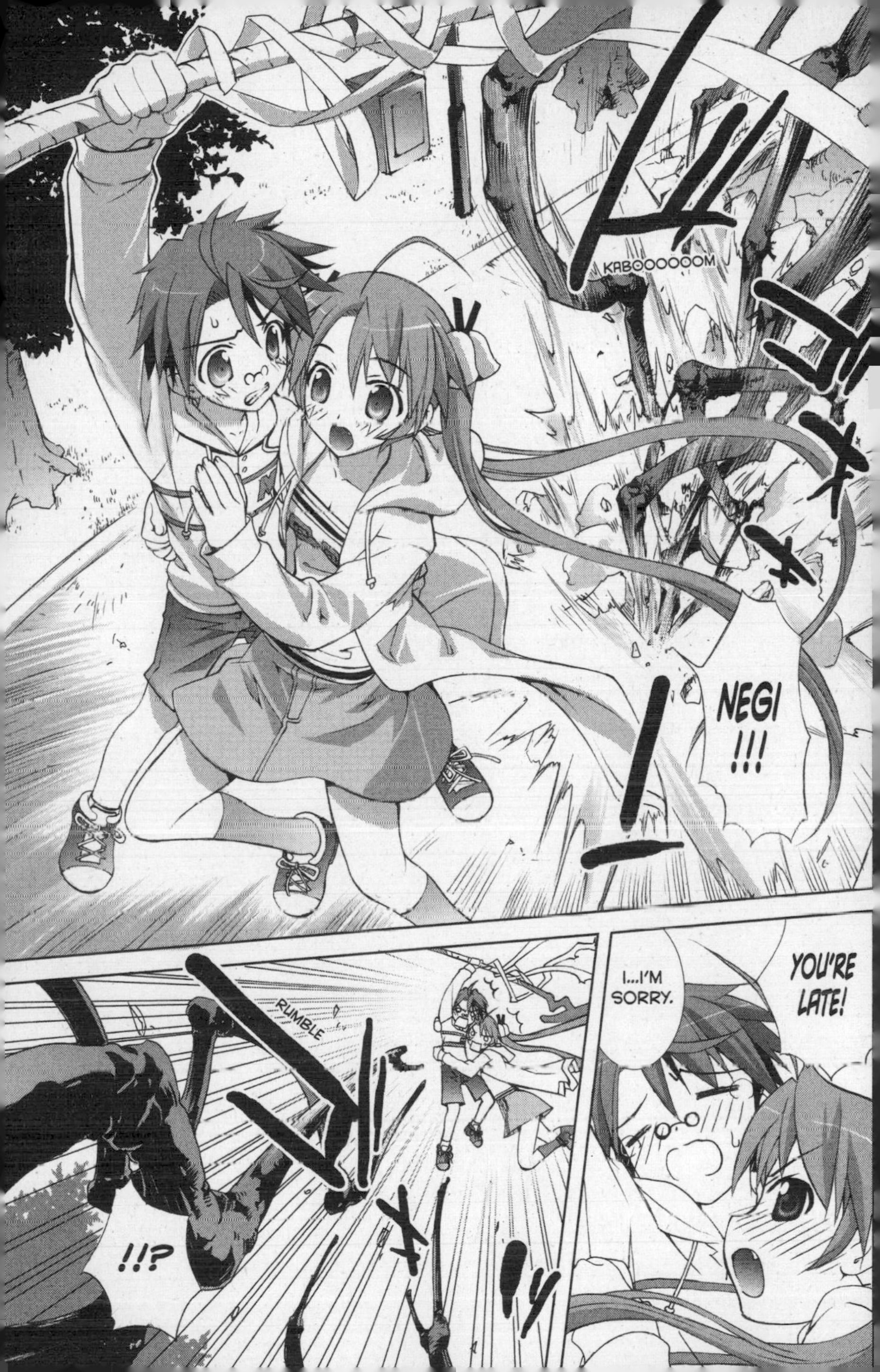
KABOOOOOOM
NEGI !!!
YOU'RE LATE!
I...I'M SORRY.
RUMBLE
!!?

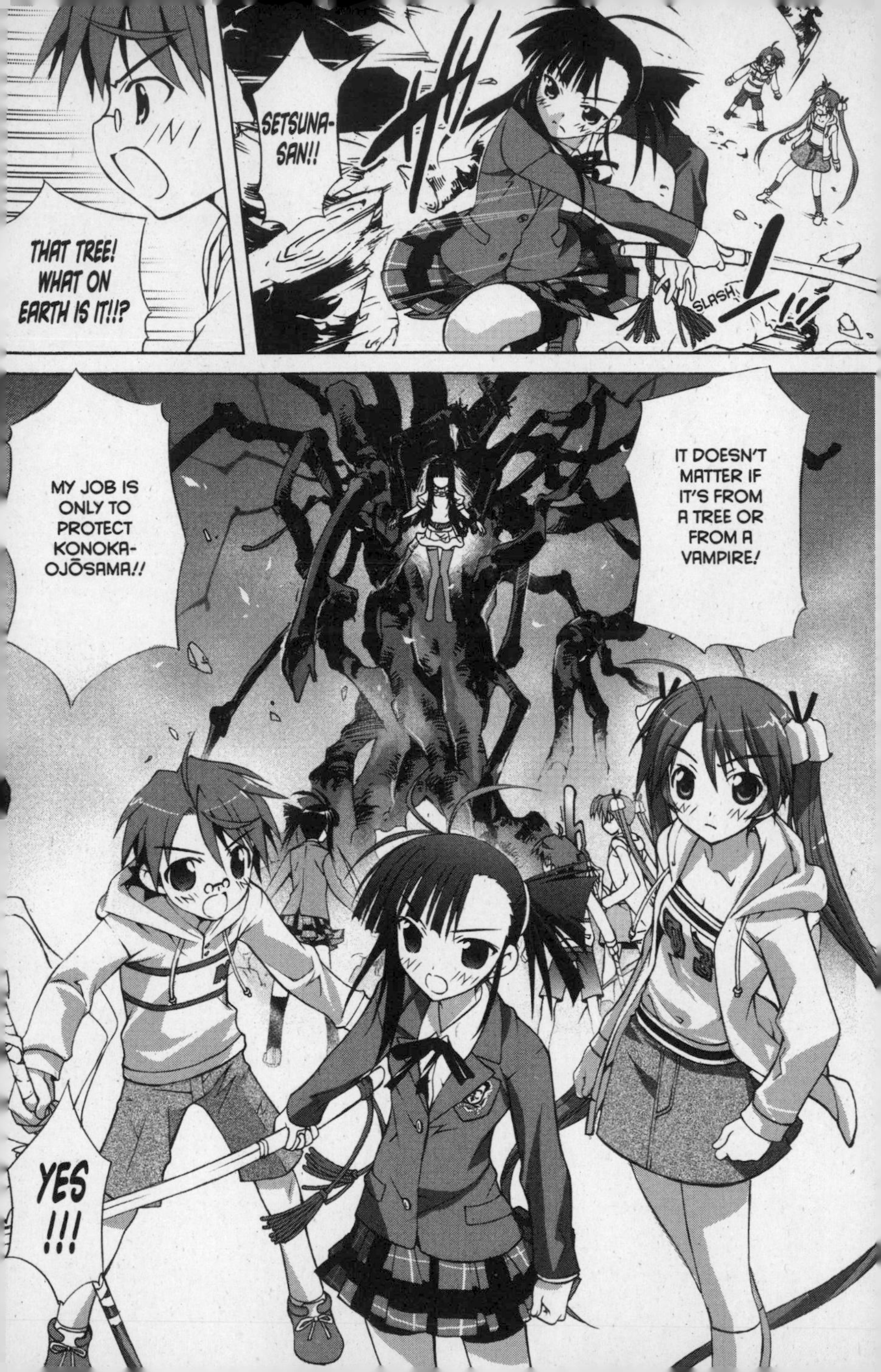
SETSUNA-SAN!!
SLASH
THAT TREE! WHAT ON EARTH IS IT!!?
IT DOESN'T MATTER IF IT'S FROM A TREE OR FROM A VAMPIRE!
MY JOB IS ONLY TO PROTECT KONOKA-OJŌSAMA!!
YES!!!

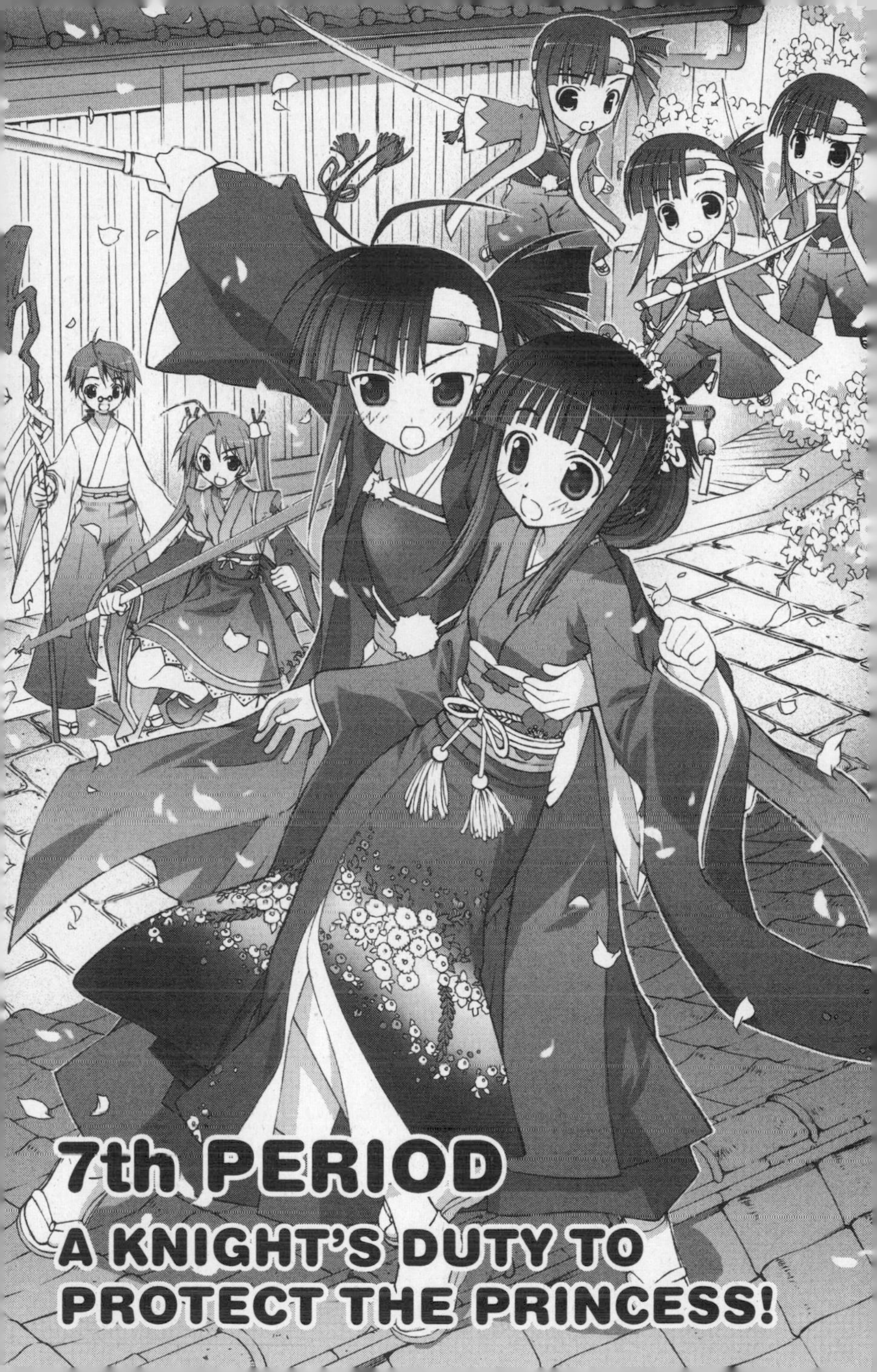

7th PERIOD
A KNIGHT'S DUTY TO PROTECT THE PRINCESS!

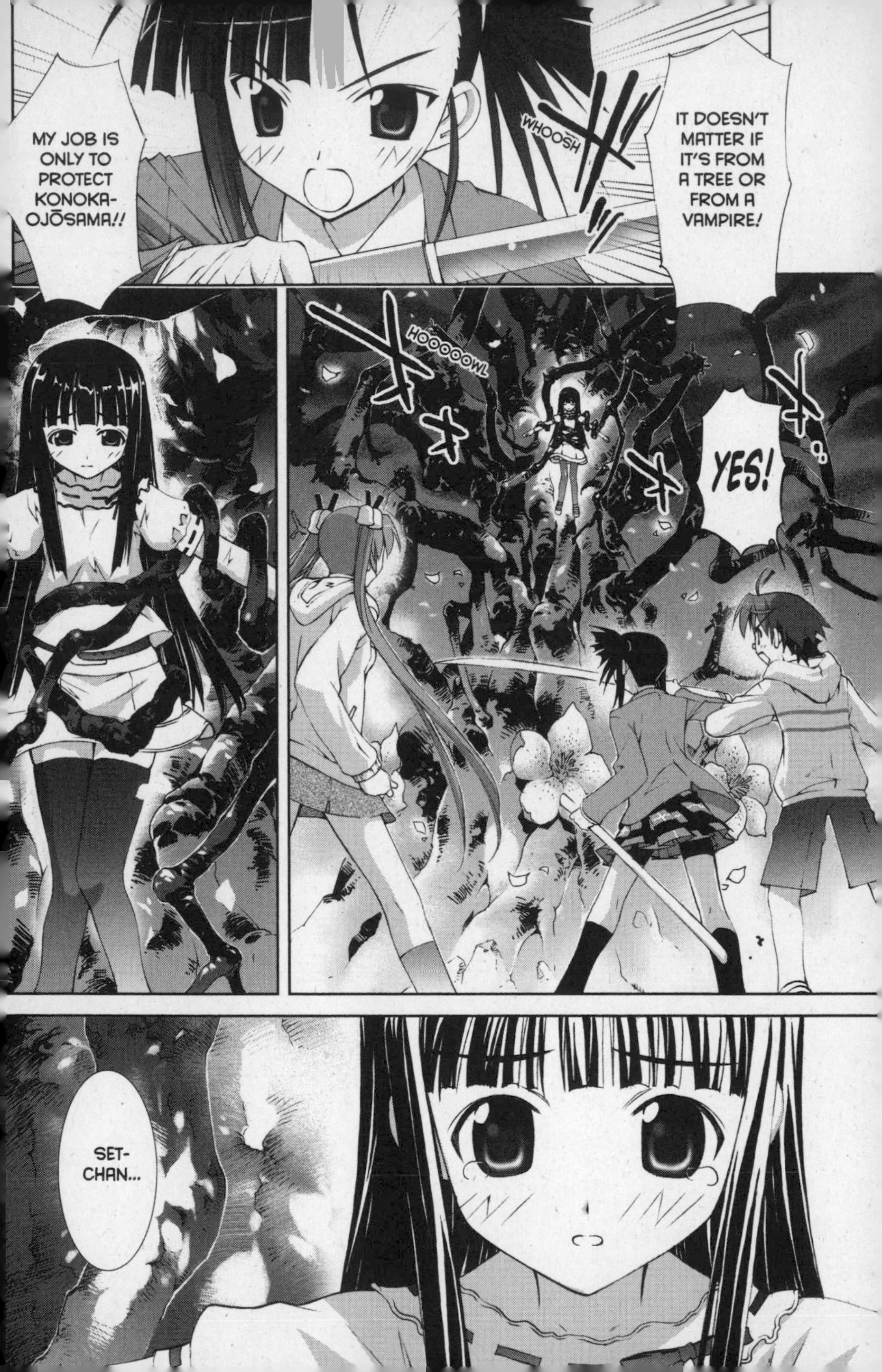
IT DOESN'T MATTER IF IT'S FROM A TREE OR FROM A VAMPIRE!
WHOOSH
MY JOB IS ONLY TO PROTECT KONOKA-OJŌSAMA!!
YES!
HOOOOOWL
SET-CHAN...

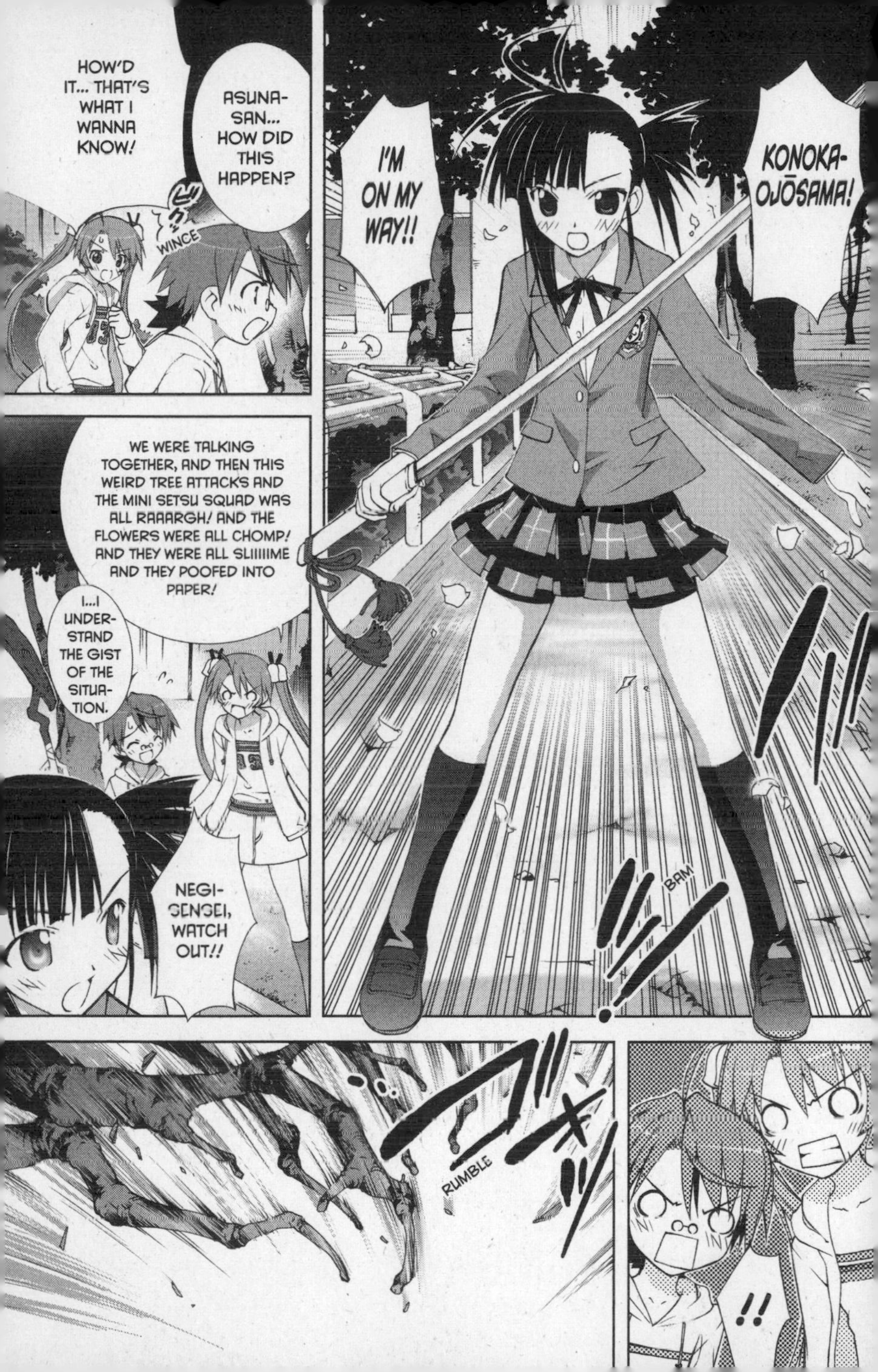
KONOKA-OJŌSAMA!
I'M ON MY WAY!!
BAM
ASUNA-SAN... HOW DID THIS HAPPEN?
WINCE
HOW'D IT... THAT'S WHAT I WANNA KNOW!
WE WERE TALKING TOGETHER, AND THEN THIS WEIRD TREE ATTACKS AND THE MINI SETSU SQUAD WAS ALL RAAARGH! AND THE FLOWERS WERE ALL CHOMP! AND THEY WERE ALL SLIIIIIME AND THEY POOFED INTO PAPER!
I...I UNDERSTAND THE GIST OF THE SITUATION.
NEGI-SENSEI, WATCH OUT!!
!!
RUMBLE

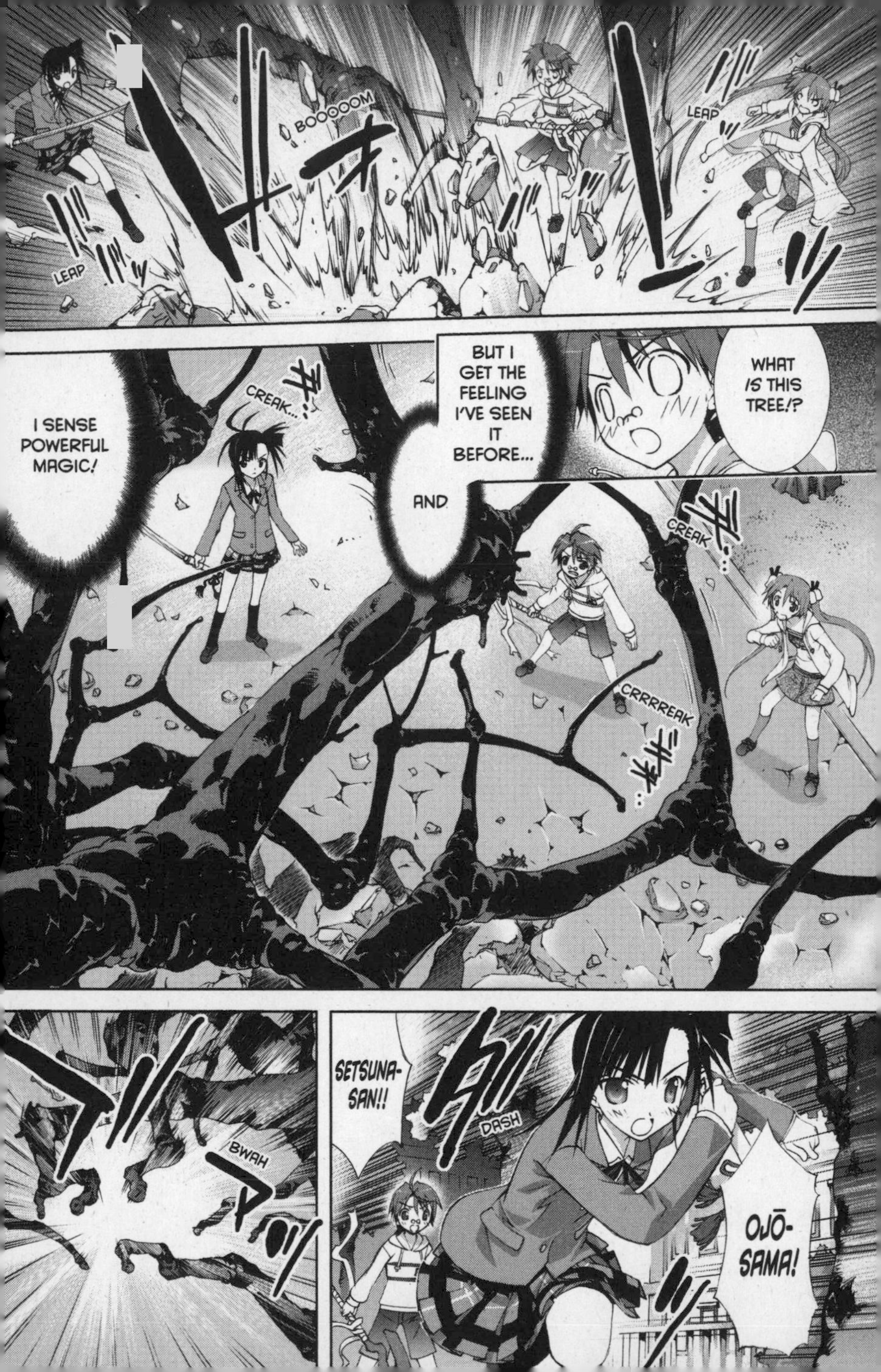
LEAP
BOOOOOM
LEAP
WHAT IS THIS TREE!?
BUT I GET THE FEELING I'VE SEEN IT BEFORE...
AND.
CREAK
CRRRREAK
CREAK...
I SENSE POWERFUL MAGIC!
OJŌ-SAMA!
DASH
SETSUNA-SAN!!
BWAH

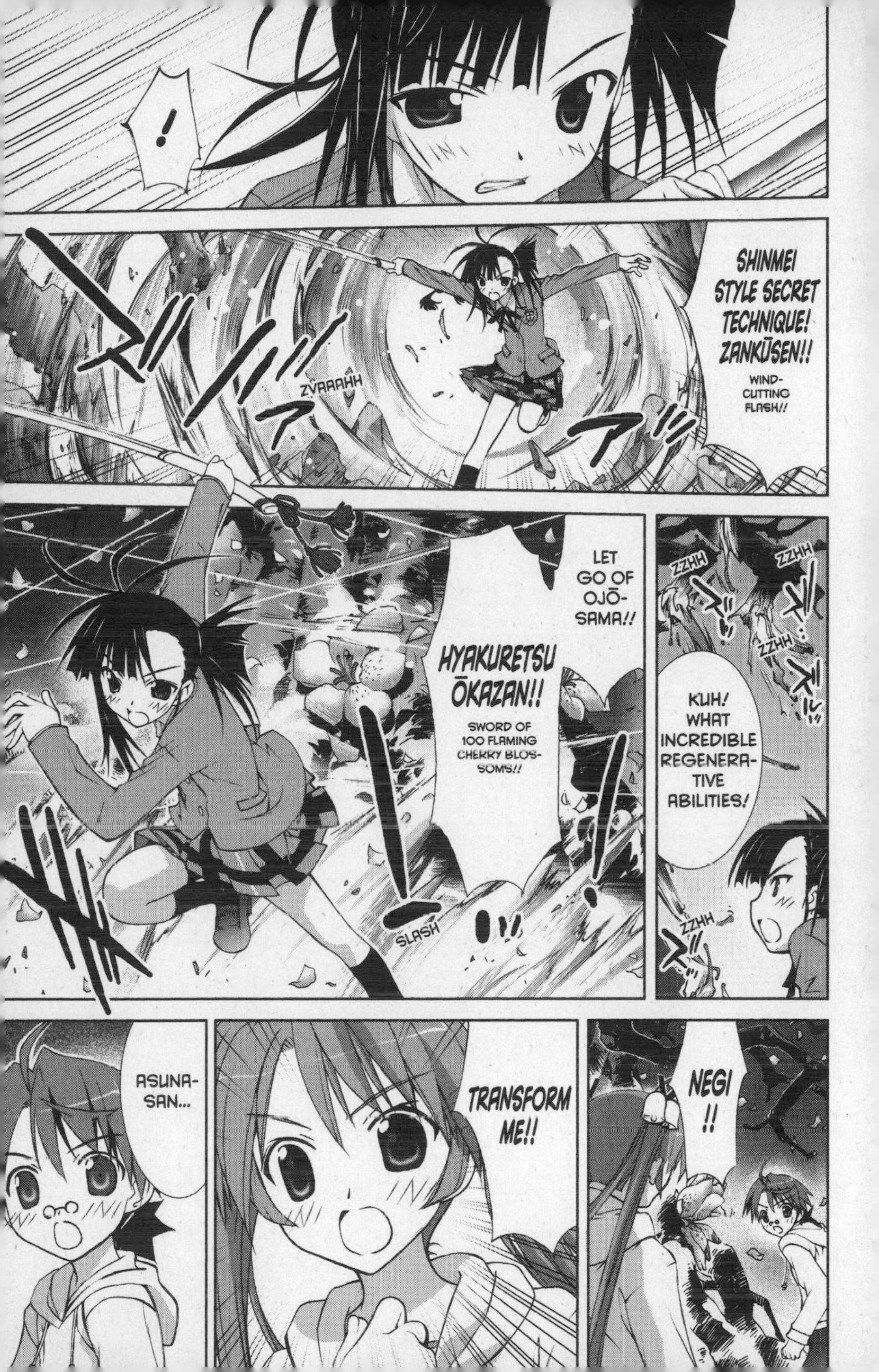
!
SHINMEI STYLE SECRET TECHNIQUE! ZANKŪSEN!!
WIND-CUTTING FLASH!!
ZVAAAHH
ZZHH
ZZHH
ZZHH
KUH! WHAT INCREDIBLE REGENERA-TIVE ABILITIES!
ZZHH
LET GO OF OJŌ-SAMA!!
HYAKURETSU ŌKAZAN!!
SWORD OF 100 FLAMING CHERRY BLOS-SOMS!!
SLASH
NEGI !!
TRANSFORM ME!!
ASUNA-SAN...

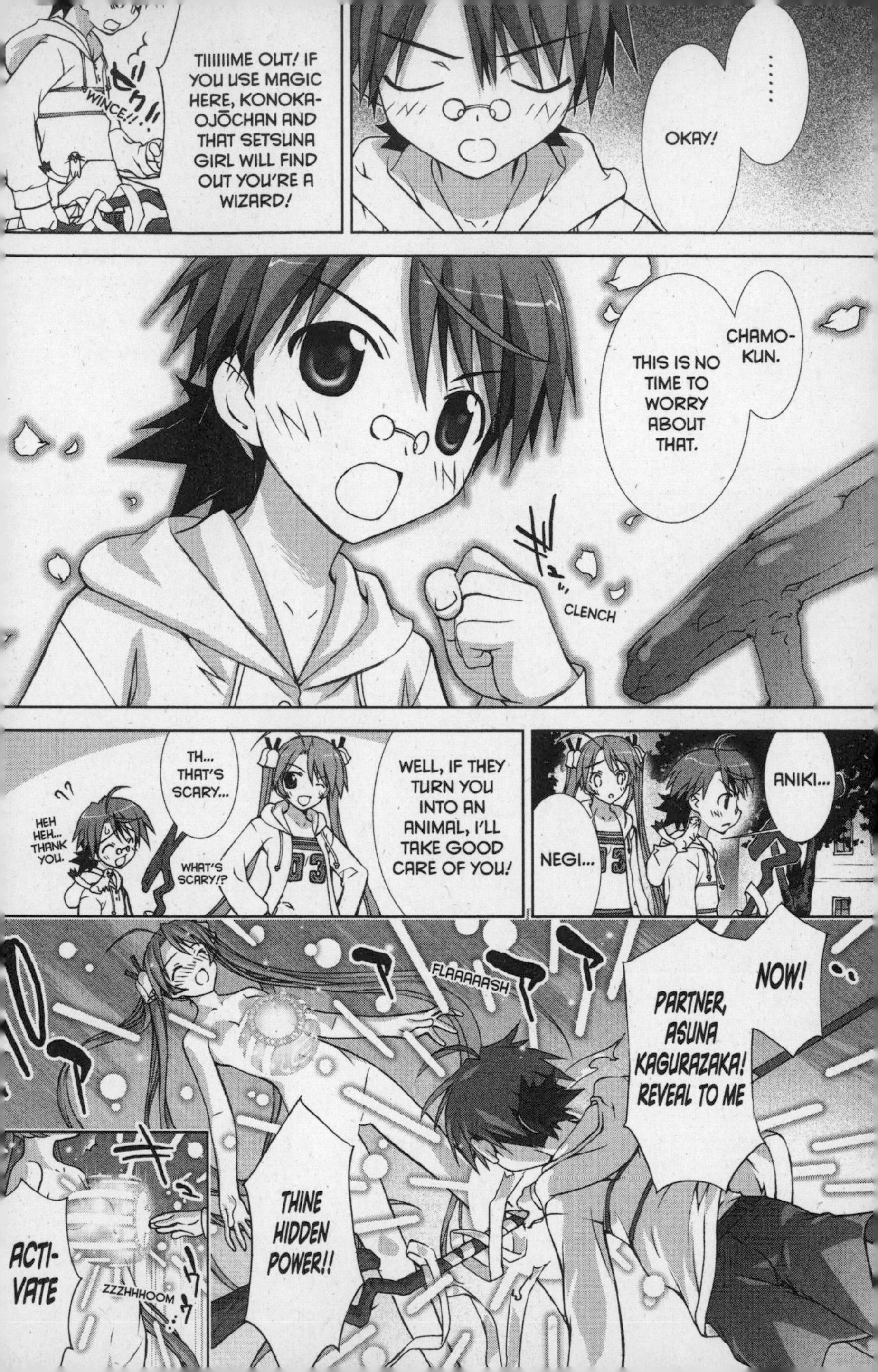
......
OKAY!
TIIIIIIME OUT! IF YOU USE MAGIC HERE, KONOKA-OJŌCHAN AND THAT SETSUNA GIRL WILL FIND OUT YOU'RE A WIZARD!
WINCE!!
CHAMO-KUN.
THIS IS NO TIME TO WORRY ABOUT THAT.
CLENCH
ANIKI...
NEGI...
WELL, IF THEY TURN YOU INTO AN ANIMAL, I'LL TAKE GOOD CARE OF YOU!
TH... THAT'S SCARY...
WHAT'S SCARY!?
HEH HEH... THANK YOU.
??
NOW!
PARTNER, ASUNA KAGURAZAKA! REVEAL TO ME
THINE HIDDEN POWER!!
FLAAAAASH
ACTI-VATE
ZZZHHHOOM

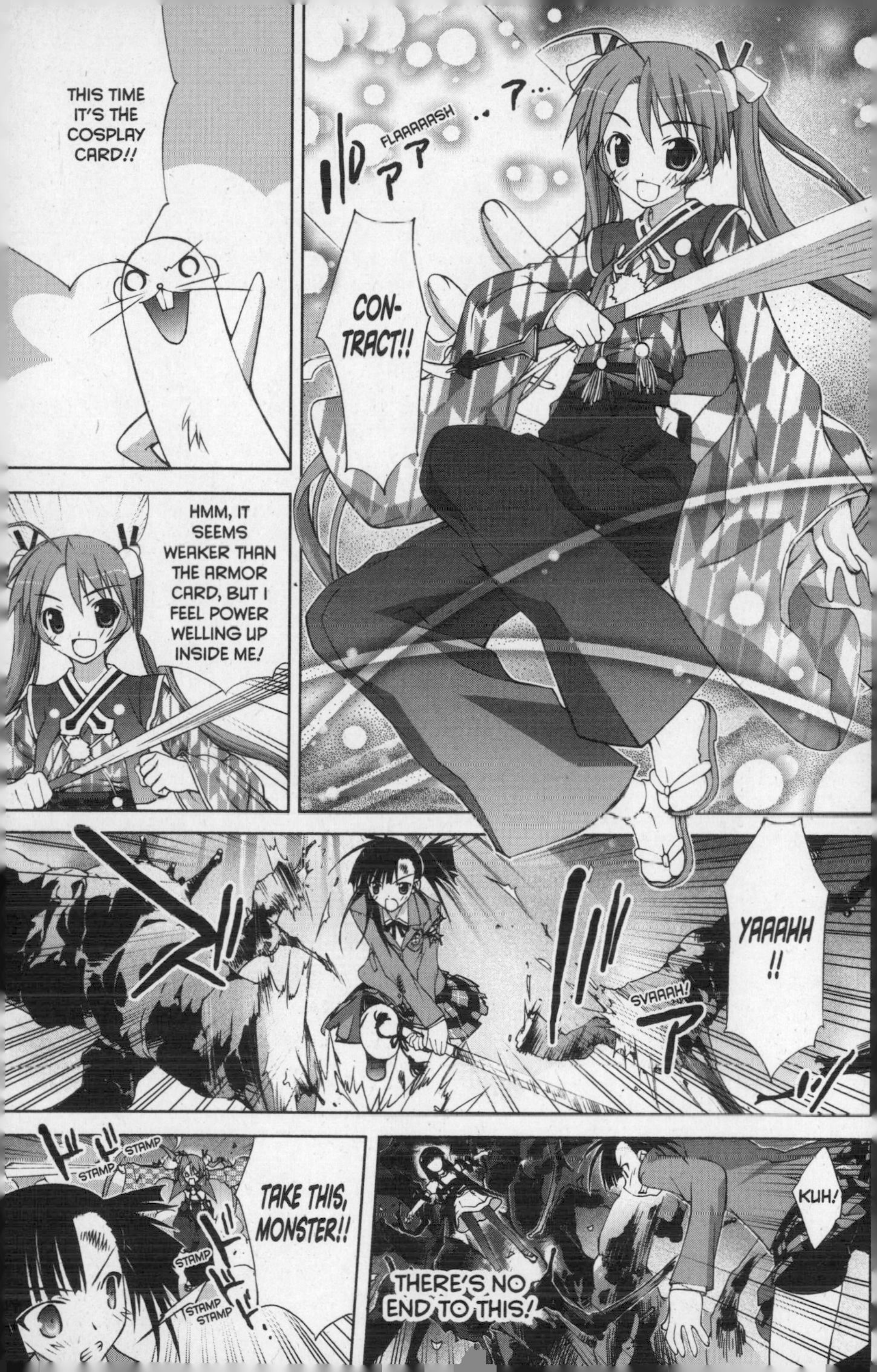
FLAAAAASH
CONTRACT!!
THIS TIME IT'S THE COSPLAY CARD!!
HMM, IT SEEMS WEAKER THAN THE ARMOR CARD, BUT I FEEL POWER WELLING UP INSIDE ME!
YAAAHH!!
SVAAAH!
KUH!
THERE'S NO END TO THIS!
STAMP
STAMP
TAKE THIS, MONSTER!!
STAMP
STAMP
STAMP

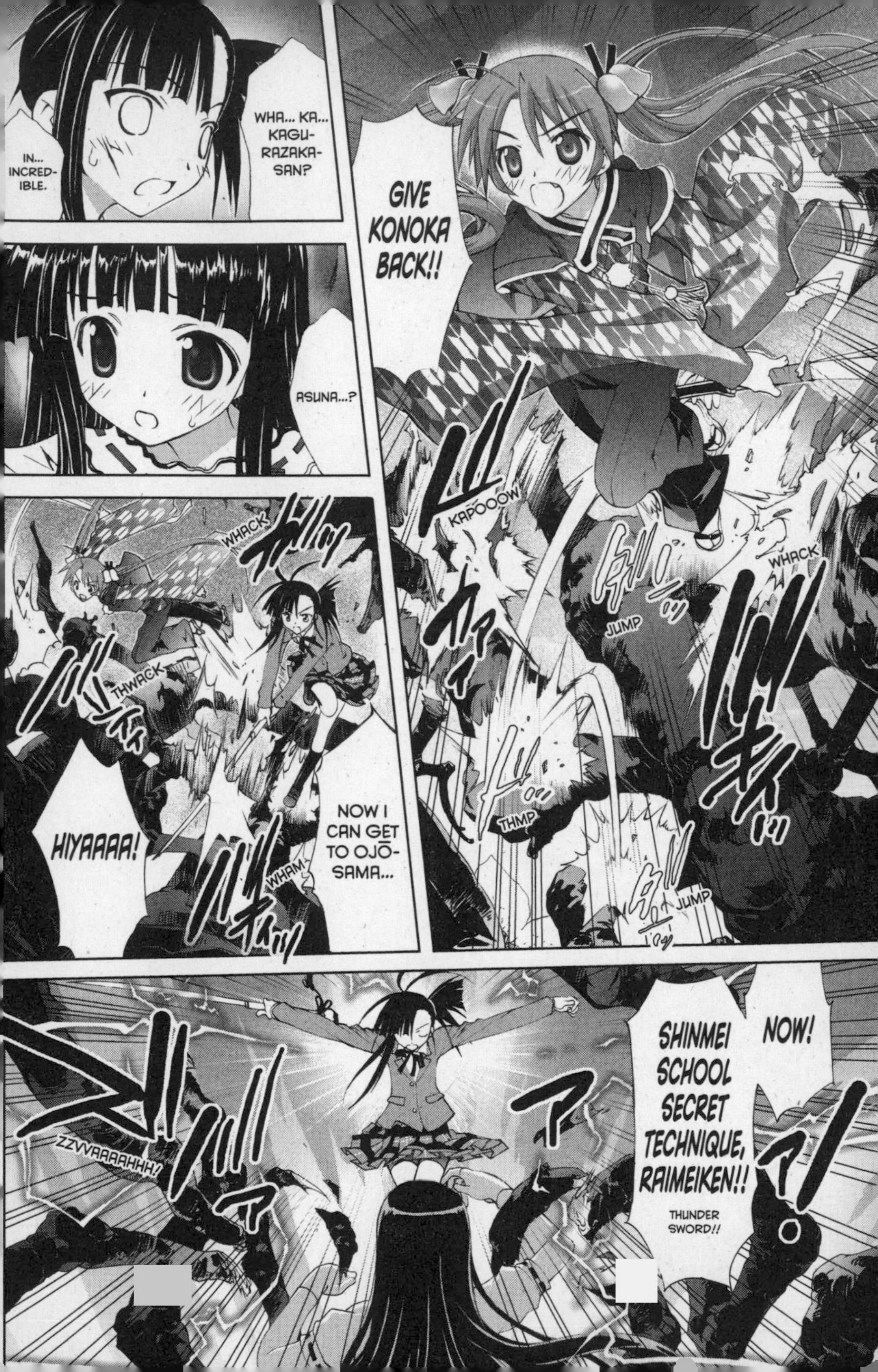
GIVE KONOKA BACK!!
KAPOOOW
WHACK
JUMP
THMP
JUMP
WHA... KA... KAGURAZAKA-SAN?
IN... INCREDIBLE.
ASUNA...?
WHACK
NOW I CAN GET TO OJŌ-SAMA...
THWACK
WHAM
HIYAAAA!
NOW!
SHINMEI SCHOOL SECRET TECHNIQUE, RAIMEIKEN!!
THUNDER SWORD!!
ZZVVAAAAAHHH!

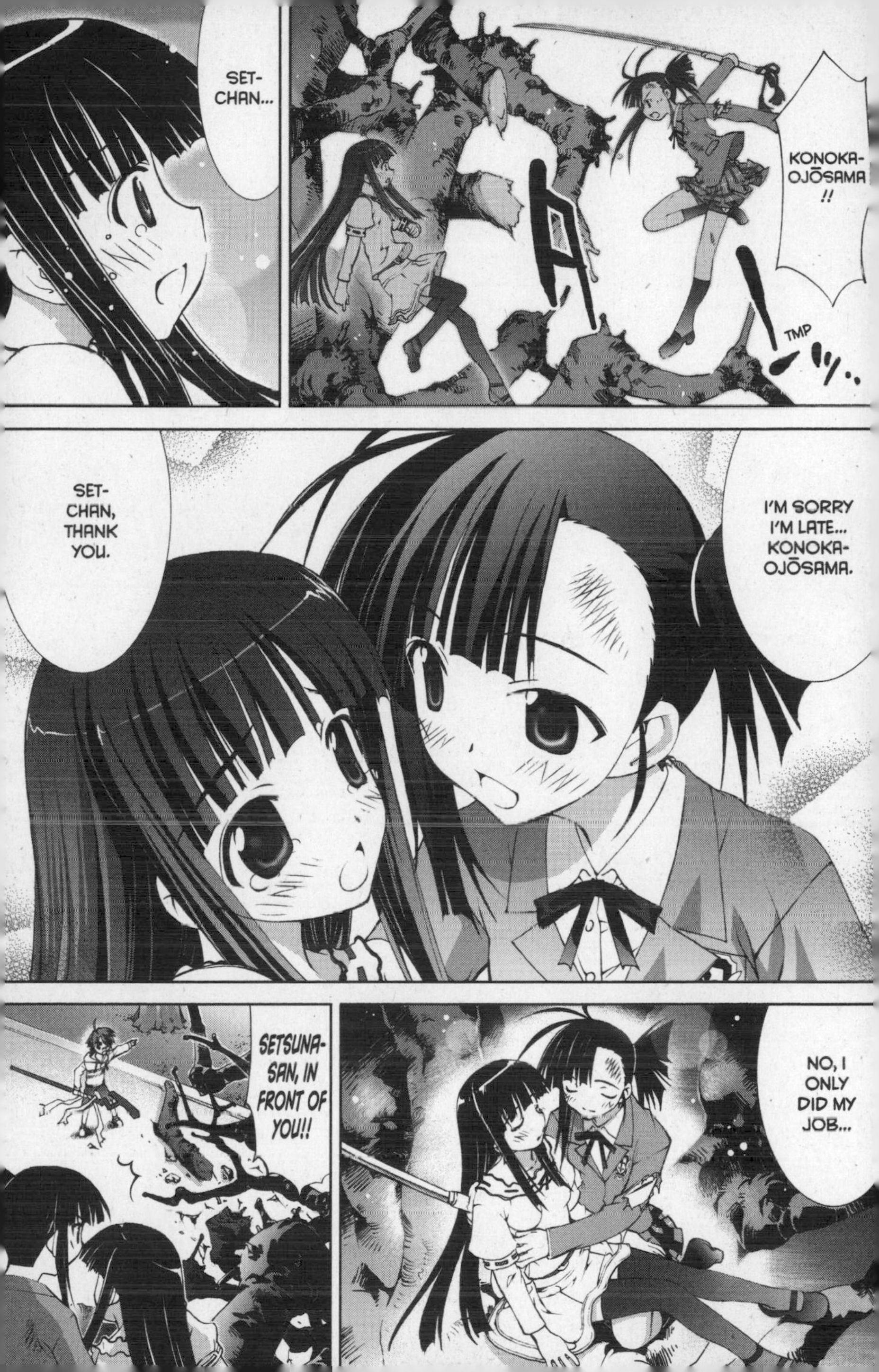
KONOKA-OJŌSAMA !!
TMP
SET-CHAN...
I'M SORRY I'M LATE... KONOKA-OJŌSAMA.
SET-CHAN, THANK YOU.
NO, I ONLY DID MY JOB...
SETSUNA-SAN, IN FRONT OF YOU!!

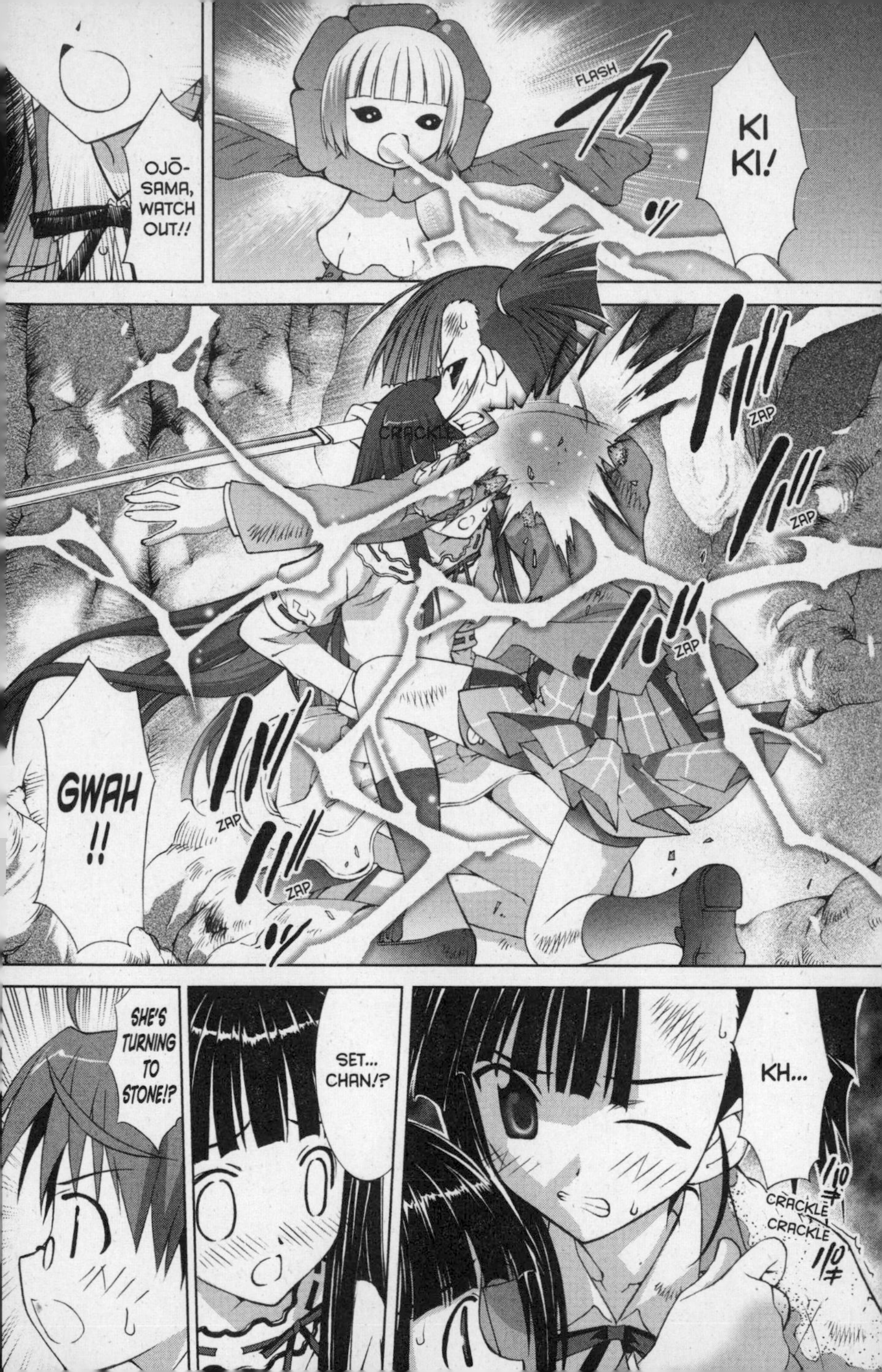
FLASH
KI KI!
OJŌ-SAMA, WATCH OUT!!
ZAP
ZAP
CRACKLE
ZAP
GWAH!!
ZAP
ZAP
KH...
CRACKLE
CRACKLE
SET... CHAN!?
SHE'S TURNING TO STONE!?

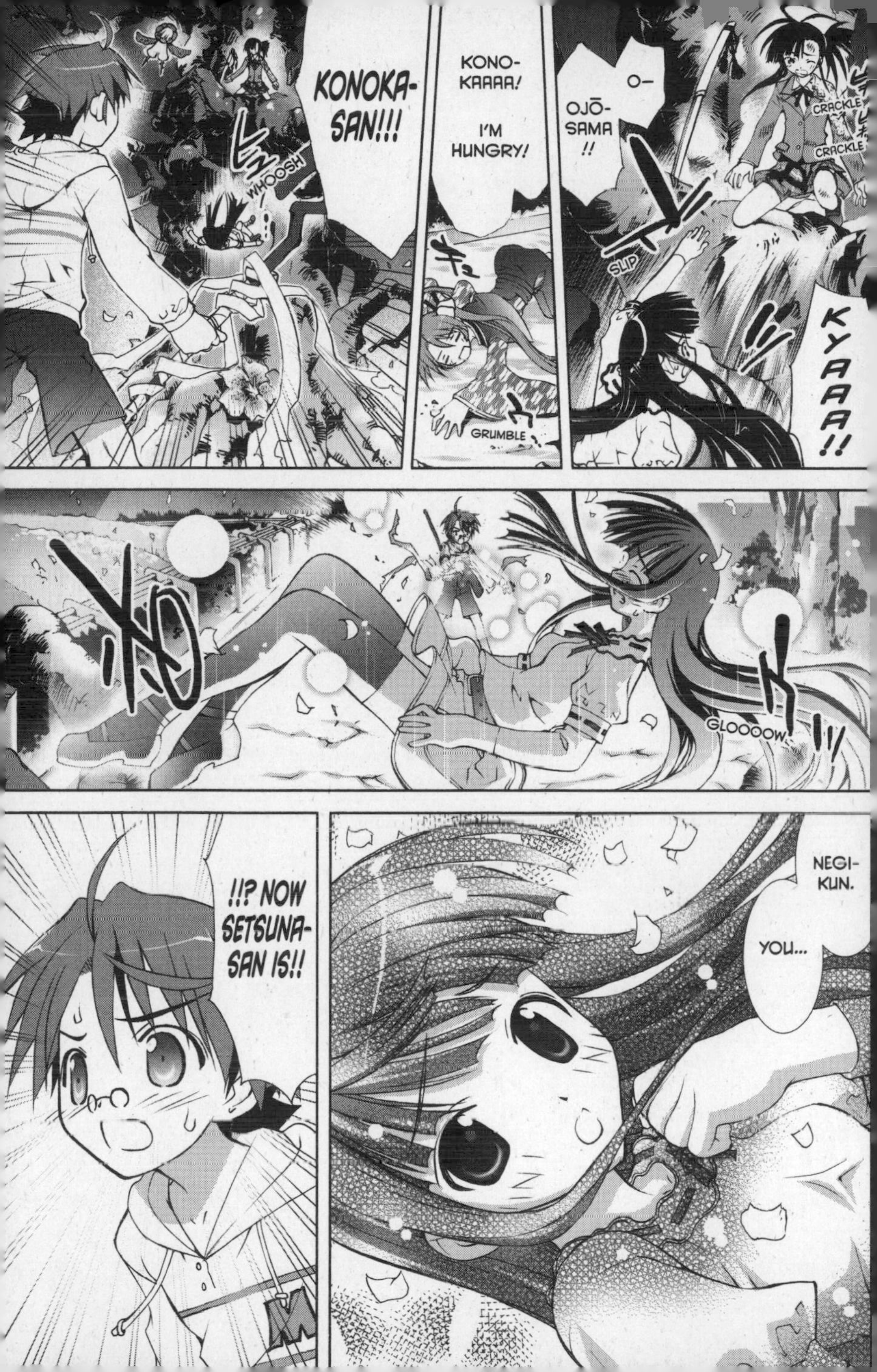
CRACKLE
CRACKLE
O–
OJŌ-SAMA !!
SLIP
KYAAAA!!
KONO-KAAAA!
I'M HUNGRY!
GRUMBLE
KONOKA-SAN!!!
WHOOSH
GLOOOOW
NEGI-KUN.
YOU...
!!? NOW SETSUNA-SAN IS!!

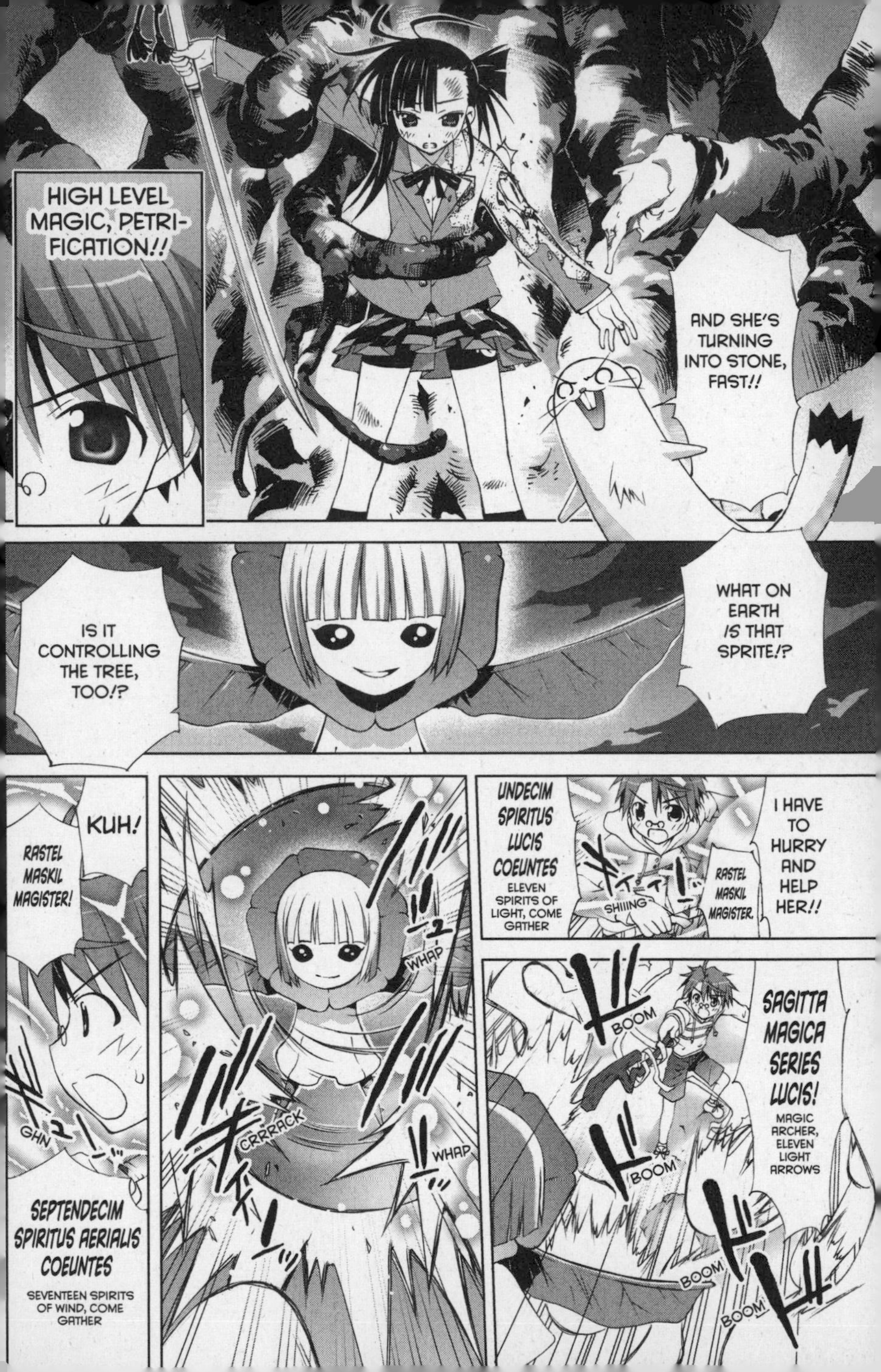
HIGH LEVEL MAGIC, PETRIFICATION!!
AND SHE'S TURNING INTO STONE, FAST!!
WHAT ON EARTH IS THAT SPRITE!?
IS IT CONTROLLING THE TREE, TOO!?
I HAVE TO HURRY AND HELP HER!!
RASTEL MASKIL MAGISTER.
UNDECIM SPIRITUS LUCIS COEUNTES
ELEVEN SPIRITS OF LIGHT, COME GATHER
SHIIING
SAGITTA MAGICA SERIES LUCIS!
MAGIC ARCHER, ELEVEN LIGHT ARROWS
BOOM
BOOM
BOOM
BOOM
WHAP
CRRRACK
WHAP
KUH!
RASTEL MASKIL MAGISTER!
GHN
SEPTENDECIM SPIRITUS AERIALIS COEUNTES
SEVENTEEN SPIRITS OF WIND, COME GATHER

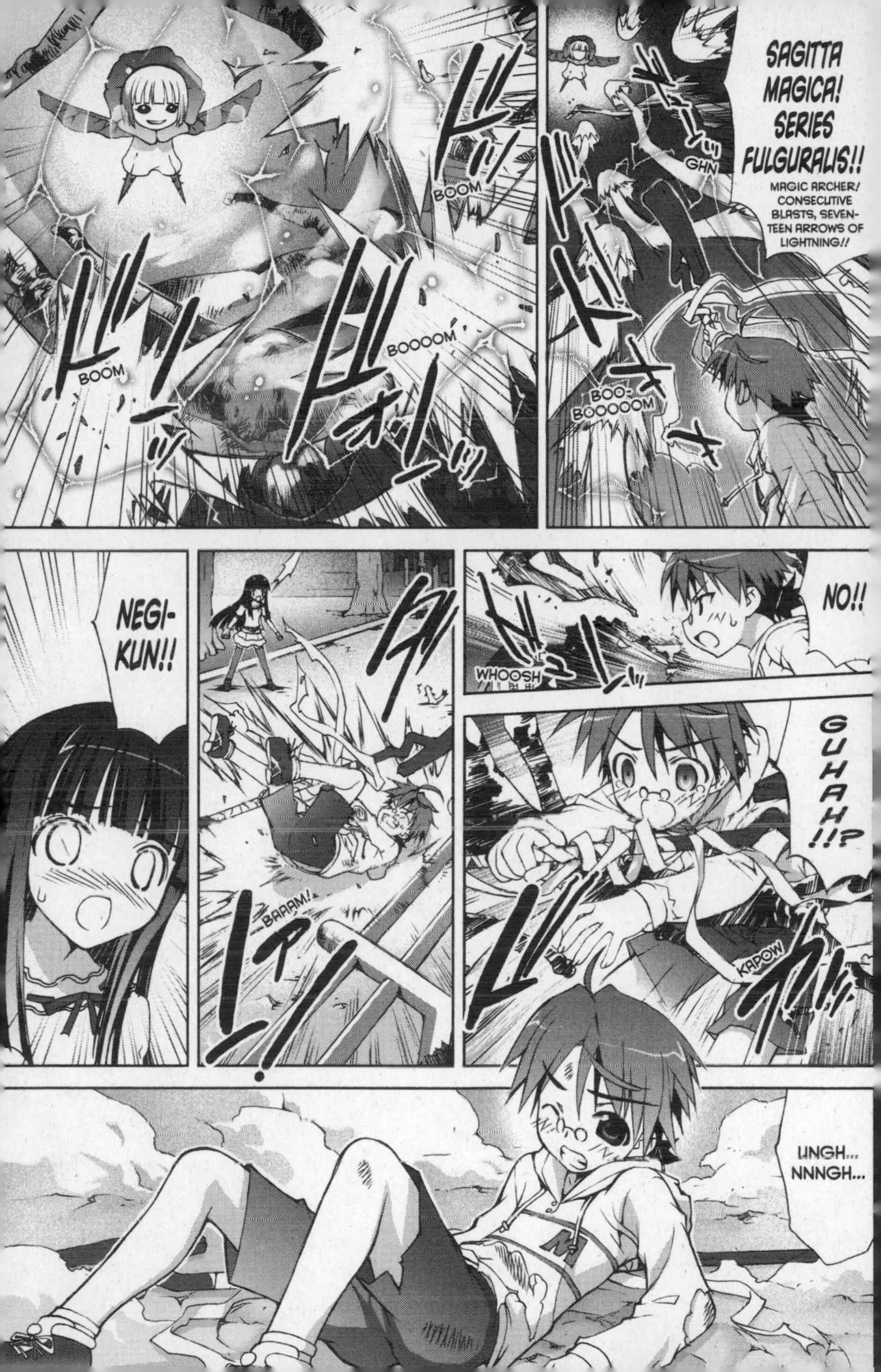
SAGITTA MAGICA! SERIES FULGURALIS!!
MAGIC ARCHER! CONSECUTIVE BLASTS, SEVEN-TEEN ARROWS OF LIGHTNING!!
GHN
BOO-BOOOOOM
BOOM
BOOOOM
BOOM
NO!!
WHOOSH
GUHAH!!?
KAPOW
BAAAM!
NEGI-KUN!!
UNGH... NNNGH...

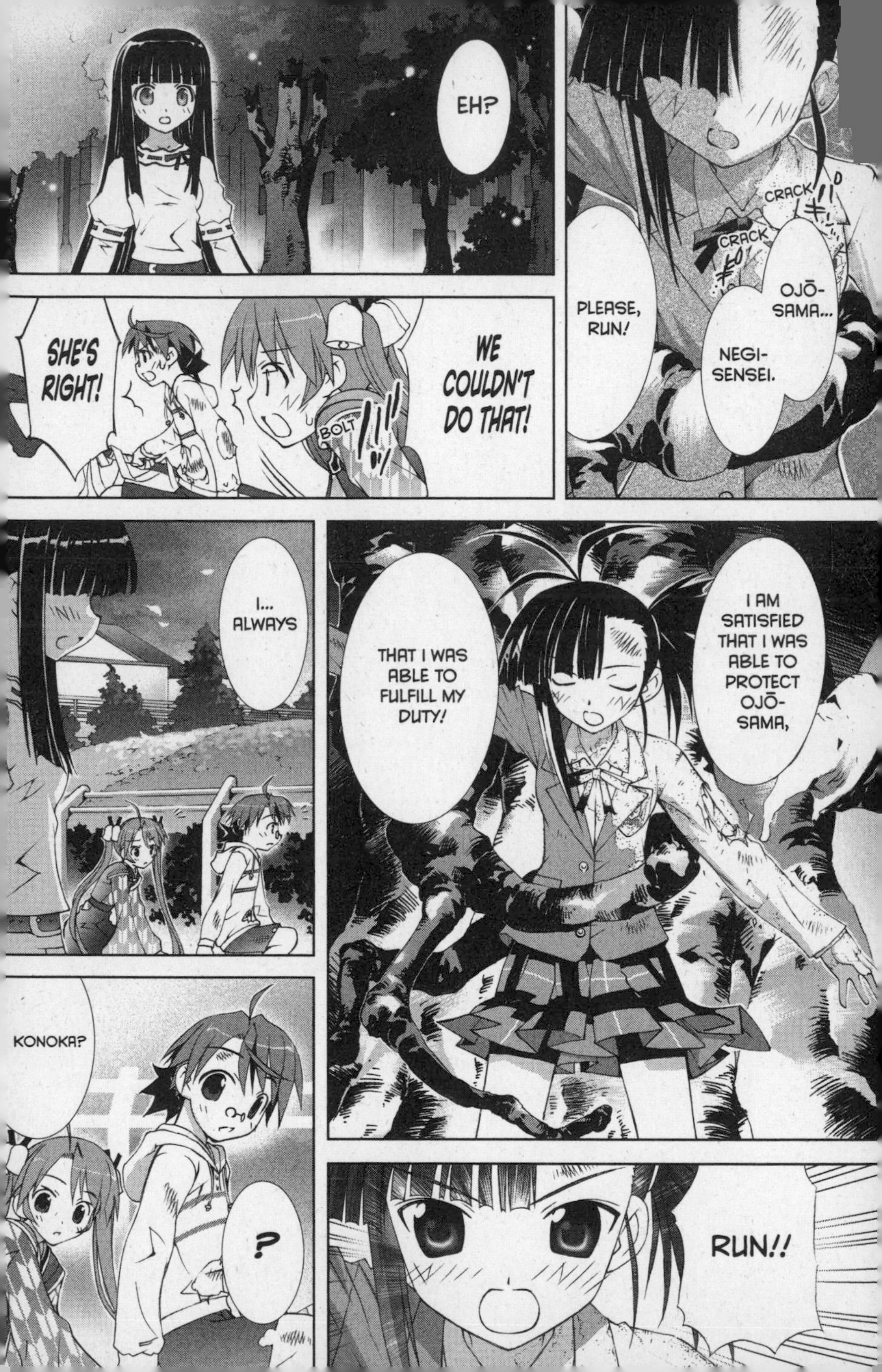
CRACK
CRACK
OJŌ-SAMA...
NEGI-SENSEI.
PLEASE, RUN!
EH?
WE COULDN'T DO THAT!
BOLT
SHE'S RIGHT!
I AM SATISFIED THAT I WAS ABLE TO PROTECT OJŌ-SAMA,
THAT I WAS ABLE TO FULFILL MY DUTY!
RUN!!
I... ALWAYS
KONOKA?
?

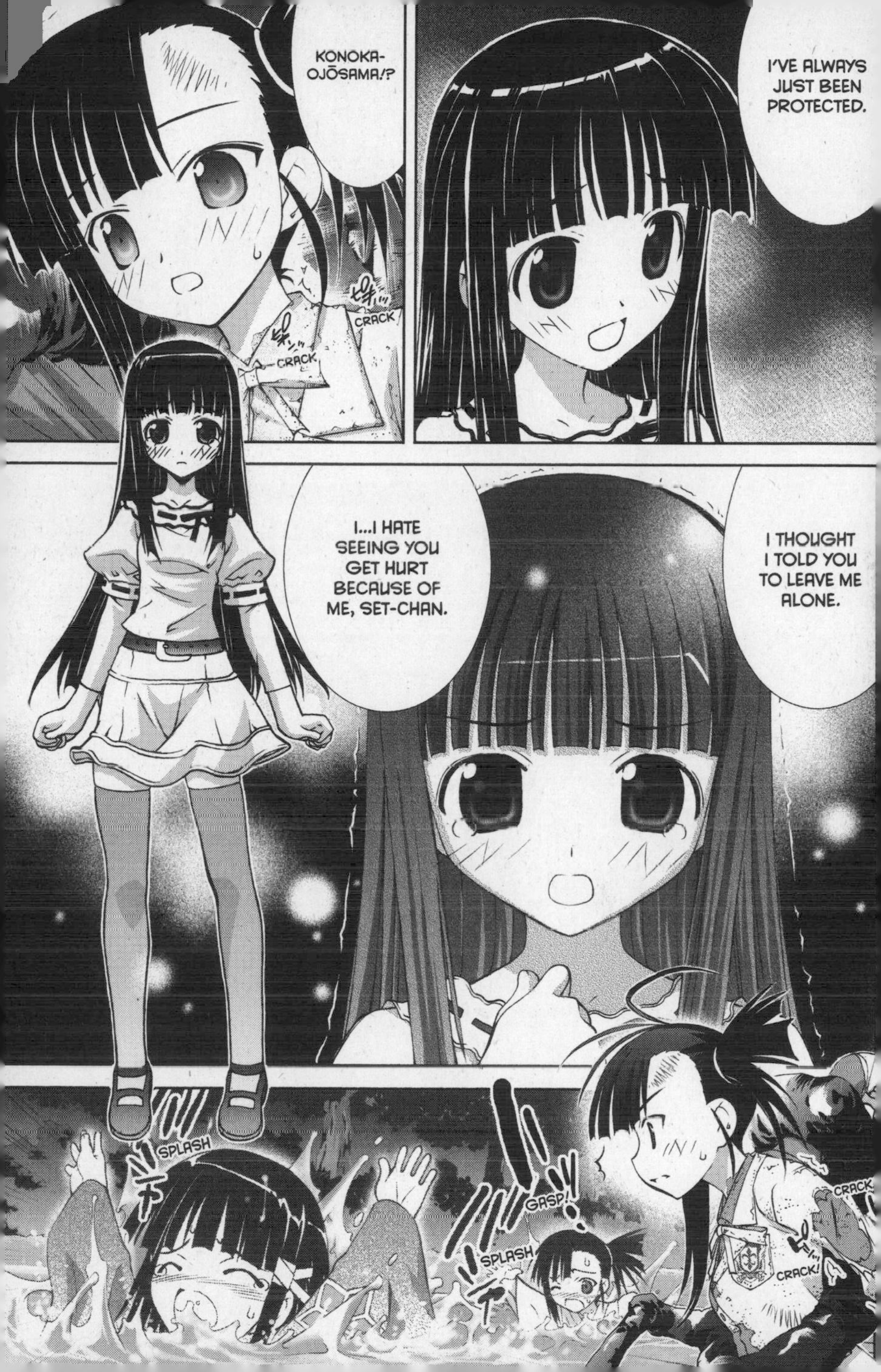
I'VE ALWAYS JUST BEEN PROTECTED.
KONOKA-OJŌSAMA!?
CRACK
CRACK
I THOUGHT I TOLD YOU TO LEAVE ME ALONE.
I...I HATE SEEING YOU GET HURT BECAUSE OF ME, SET-CHAN.
CRACK
CRACK!
GASP!
SPLASH
SPLASH

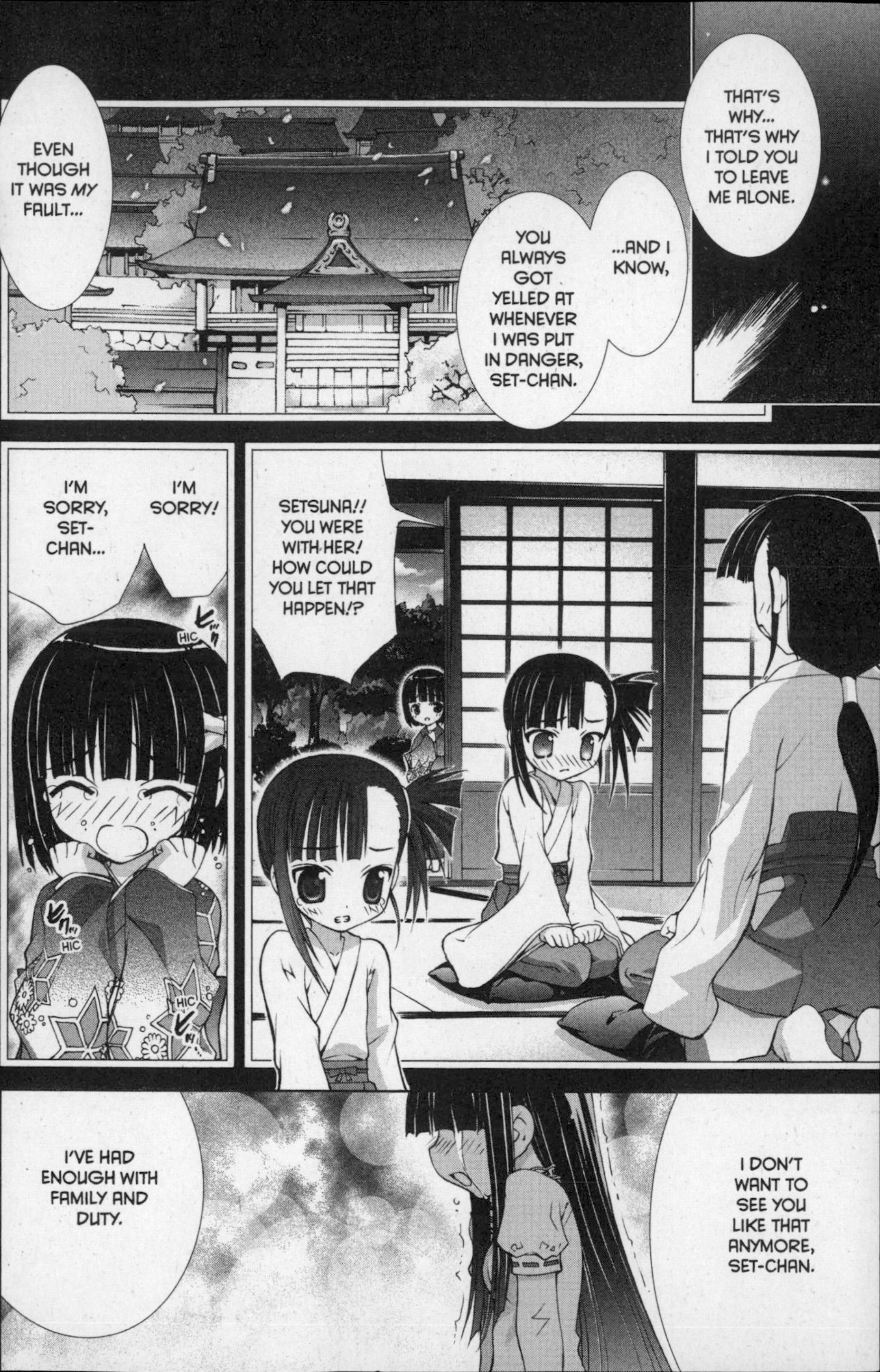

THAT'S WHY... THAT'S WHY I TOLD YOU TO LEAVE ME ALONE.
...AND I KNOW,
YOU ALWAYS GOT YELLED AT WHENEVER I WAS PUT IN DANGER, SET-CHAN.
EVEN THOUGH IT WAS *MY* FAULT...
SETSUNA!! YOU WERE WITH HER! HOW COULD YOU LET THAT HAPPEN!?
I'M SORRY!
I'M SORRY, SET-CHAN...
HIC
HIC
HIC
I DON'T WANT TO SEE YOU LIKE THAT ANYMORE, SET-CHAN.
I'VE HAD ENOUGH WITH FAMILY AND DUTY.

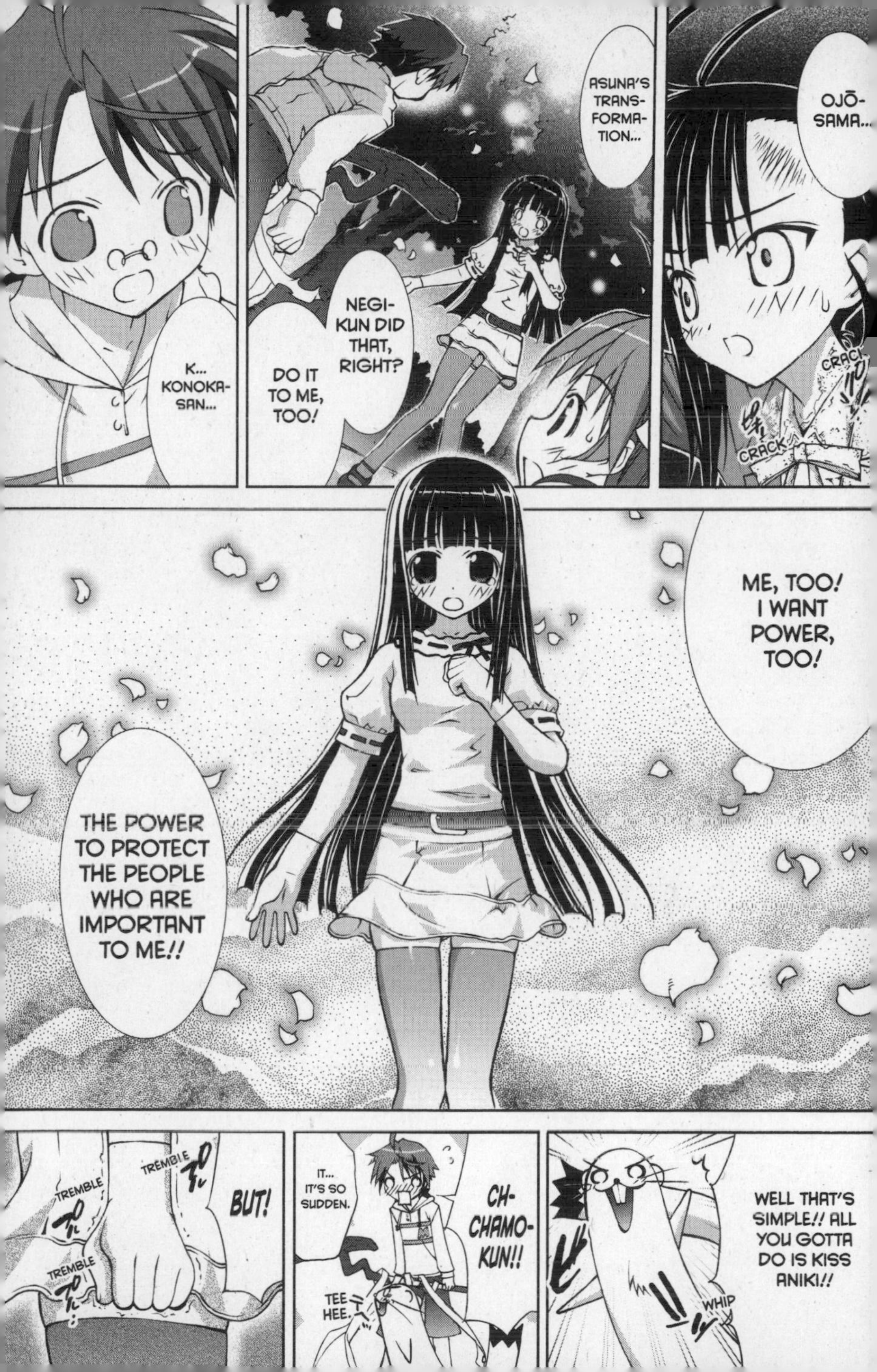
OJŌ-SAMA...
CRAC
CRACK
ASUNA'S TRANS-FORMA-TION...
NEGI-KUN DID THAT, RIGHT?
DO IT TO ME, TOO!
K... KONOKA-SAN...
ME, TOO! I WANT POWER, TOO!
THE POWER TO PROTECT THE PEOPLE WHO ARE IMPORTANT TO ME!!
WELL THAT'S SIMPLE!! ALL YOU GOTTA DO IS KISS ANIKI!!
WHIP
CH-CHAMO-KUN!!
IT... IT'S SO SUDDEN.
TEE HEE.
BUT!
TREMBLE
TREMBLE
TREMBLE

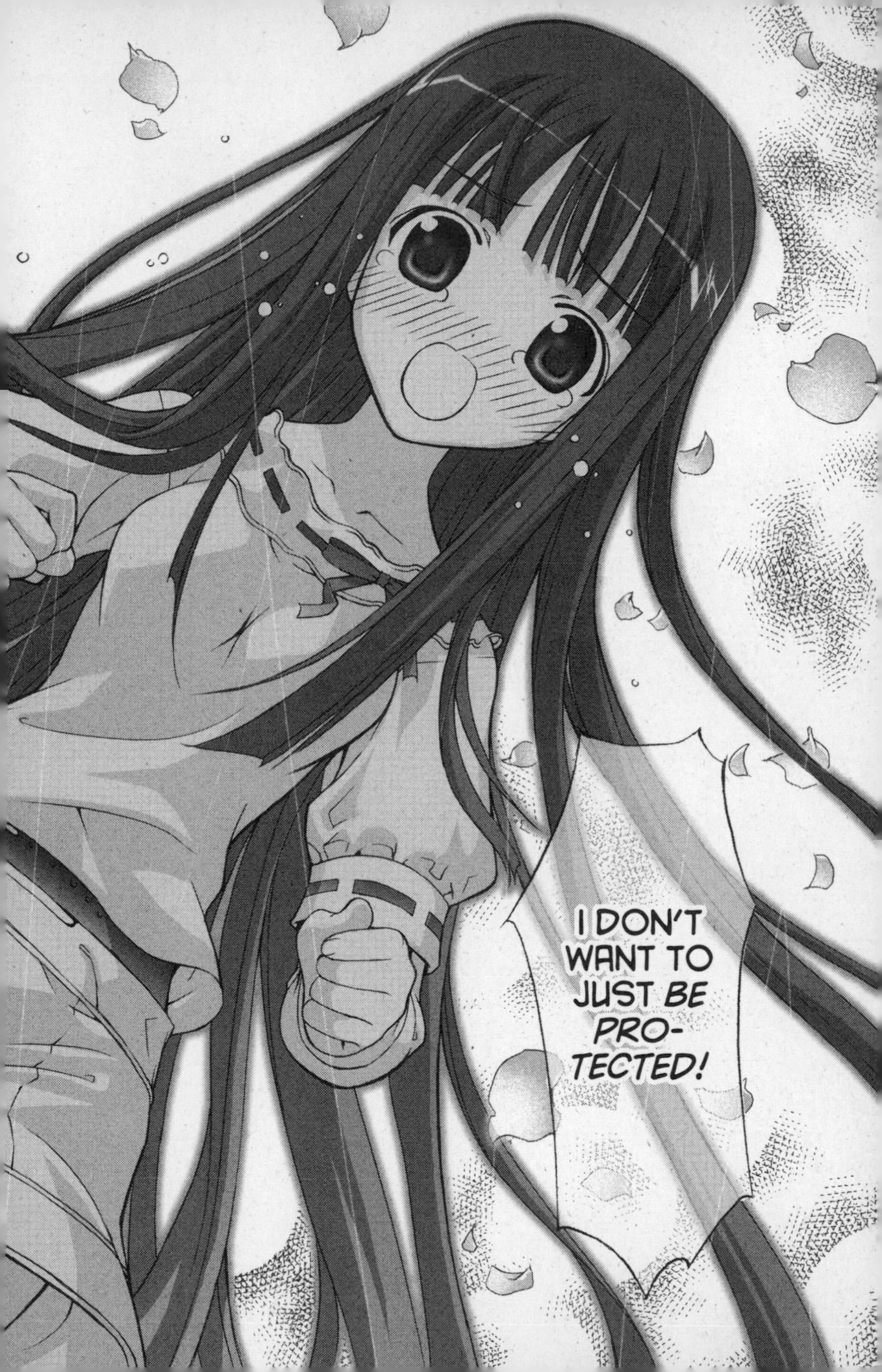
I DON'T WANT TO JUST BE PRO-TECTED!

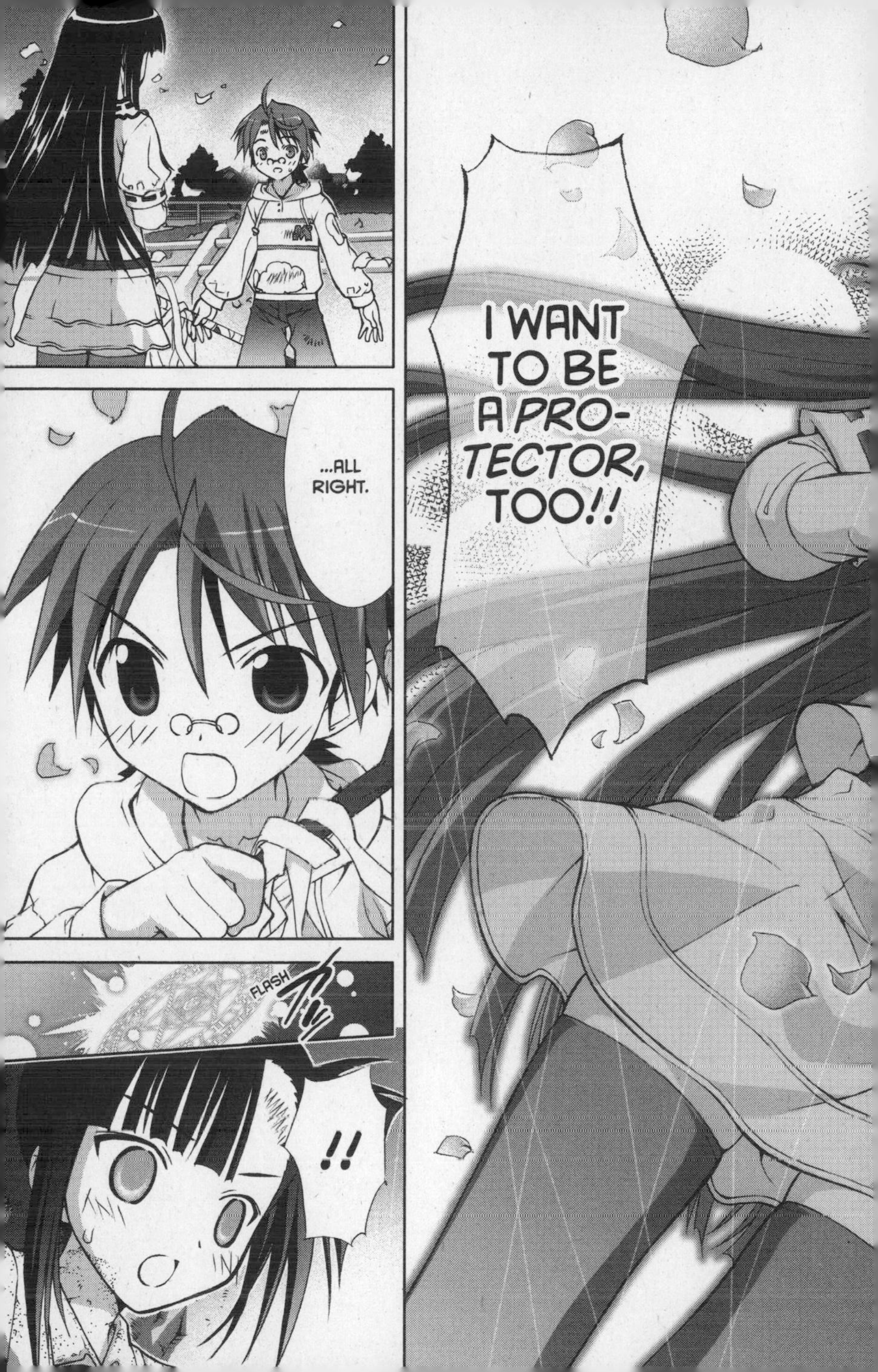
I WANT TO BE A PRO-TECTOR, TOO!!
...ALL RIGHT.
FLASH
!!

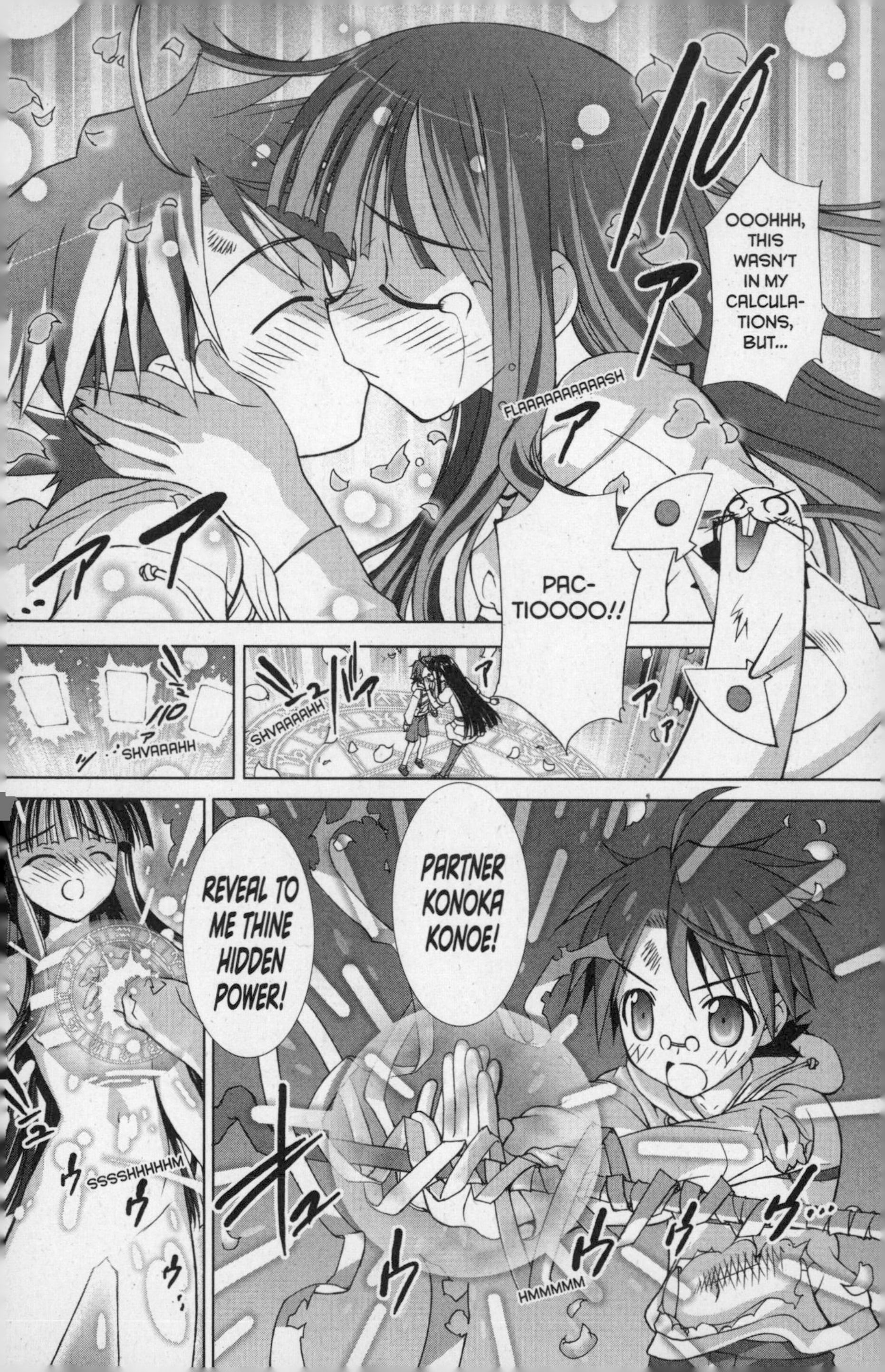
OOOHHH, THIS WASN'T IN MY CALCULATIONS, BUT...
FLAAAAAAAAAASH
PAC-TIOOOO!!
SHVAAAAHH
SHVAAAHH
PARTNER KONOKA KONOE!
REVEAL TO ME THINE HIDDEN POWER!
HMMMMM
SSSSHHHHHM

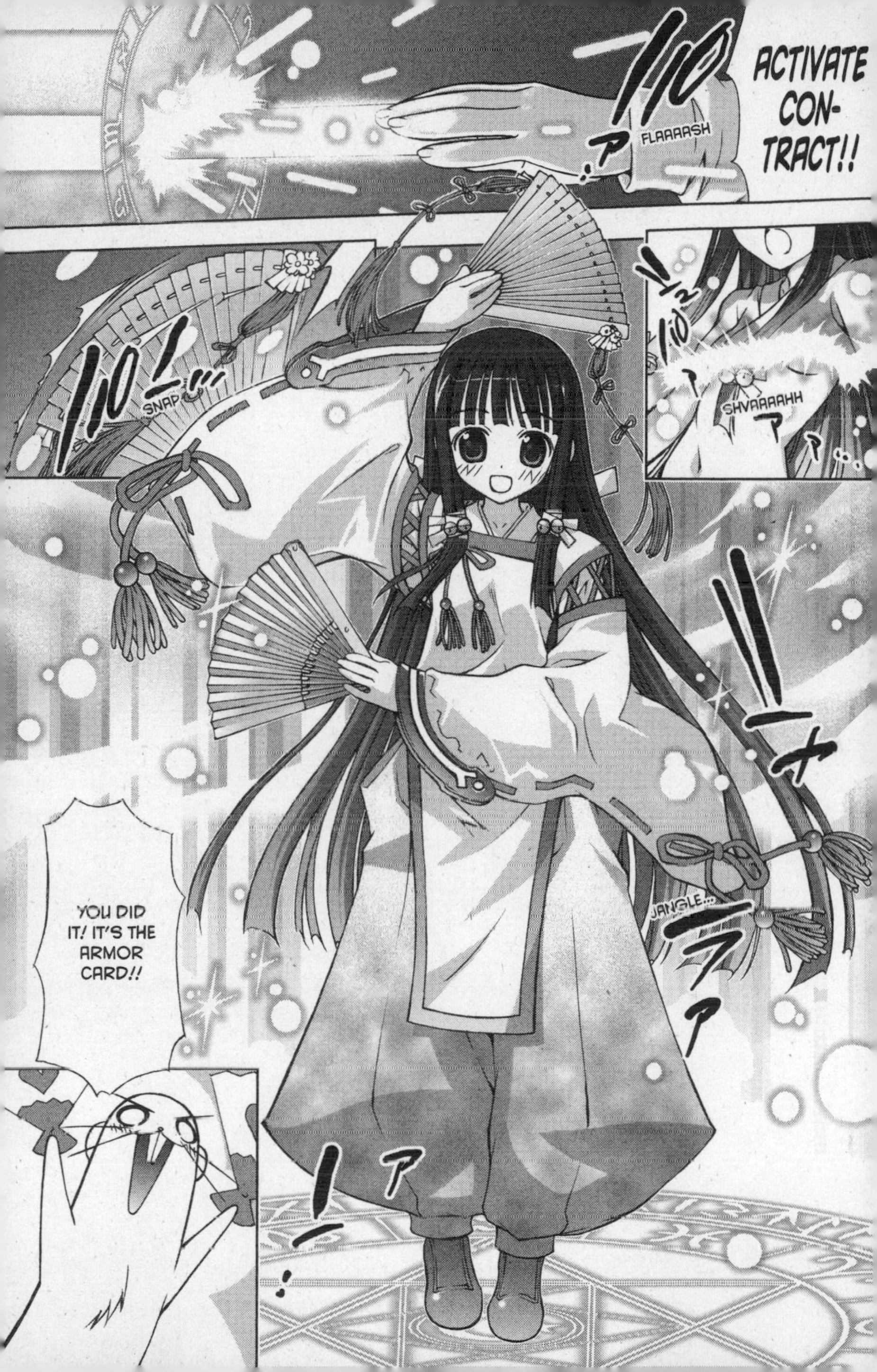
ACTIVATE CON-TRACT!!
FLAAAASH
SHVAAAAHH
SNAP
JANGLE...
YOU DID IT! IT'S THE ARMOR CARD!!

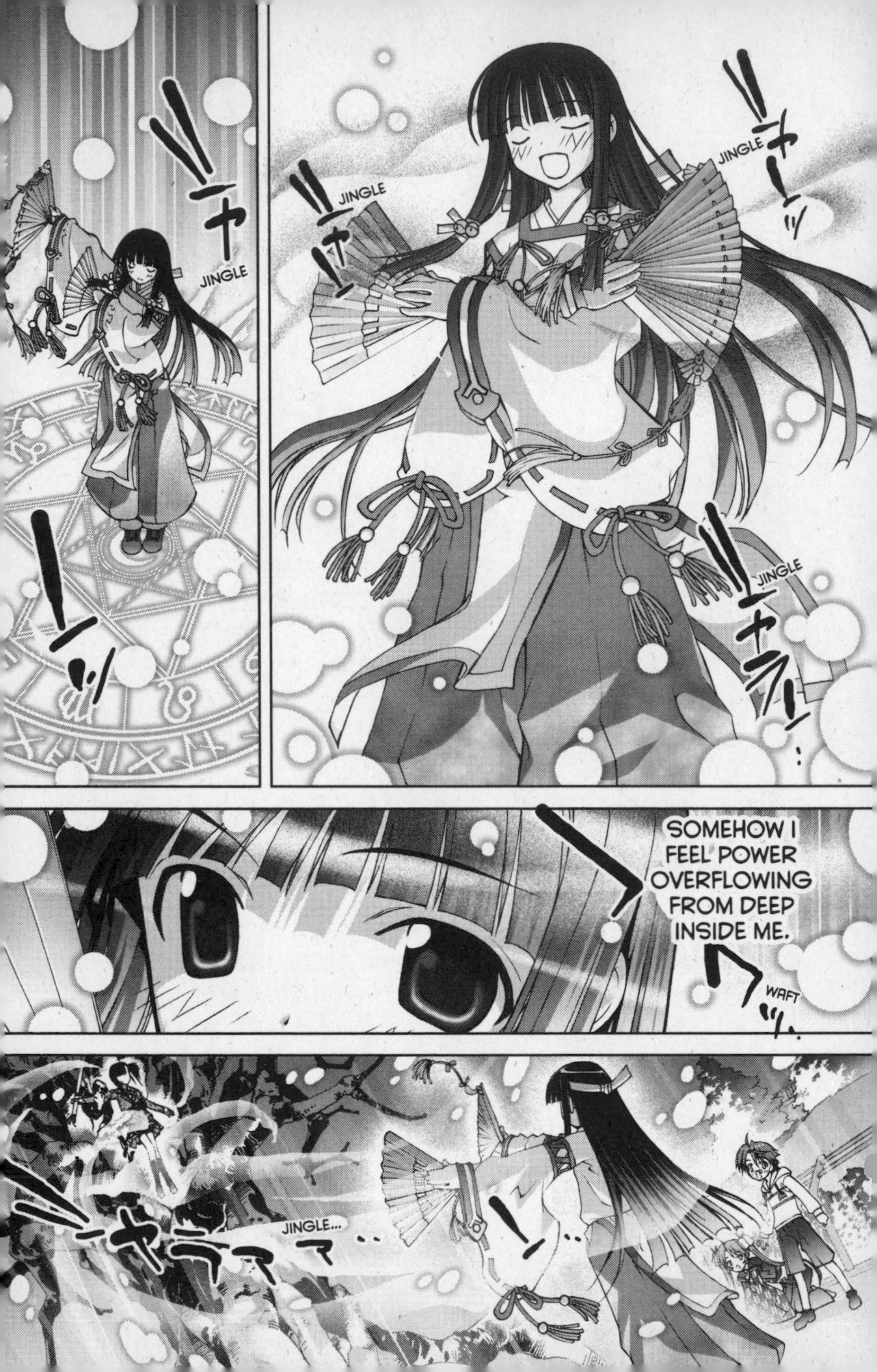
JINGLE
JINGLE
JINGLE
JINGLE
SOMEHOW I FEEL POWER OVERFLOWING FROM DEEP INSIDE ME.
WAFT
JINGLE...

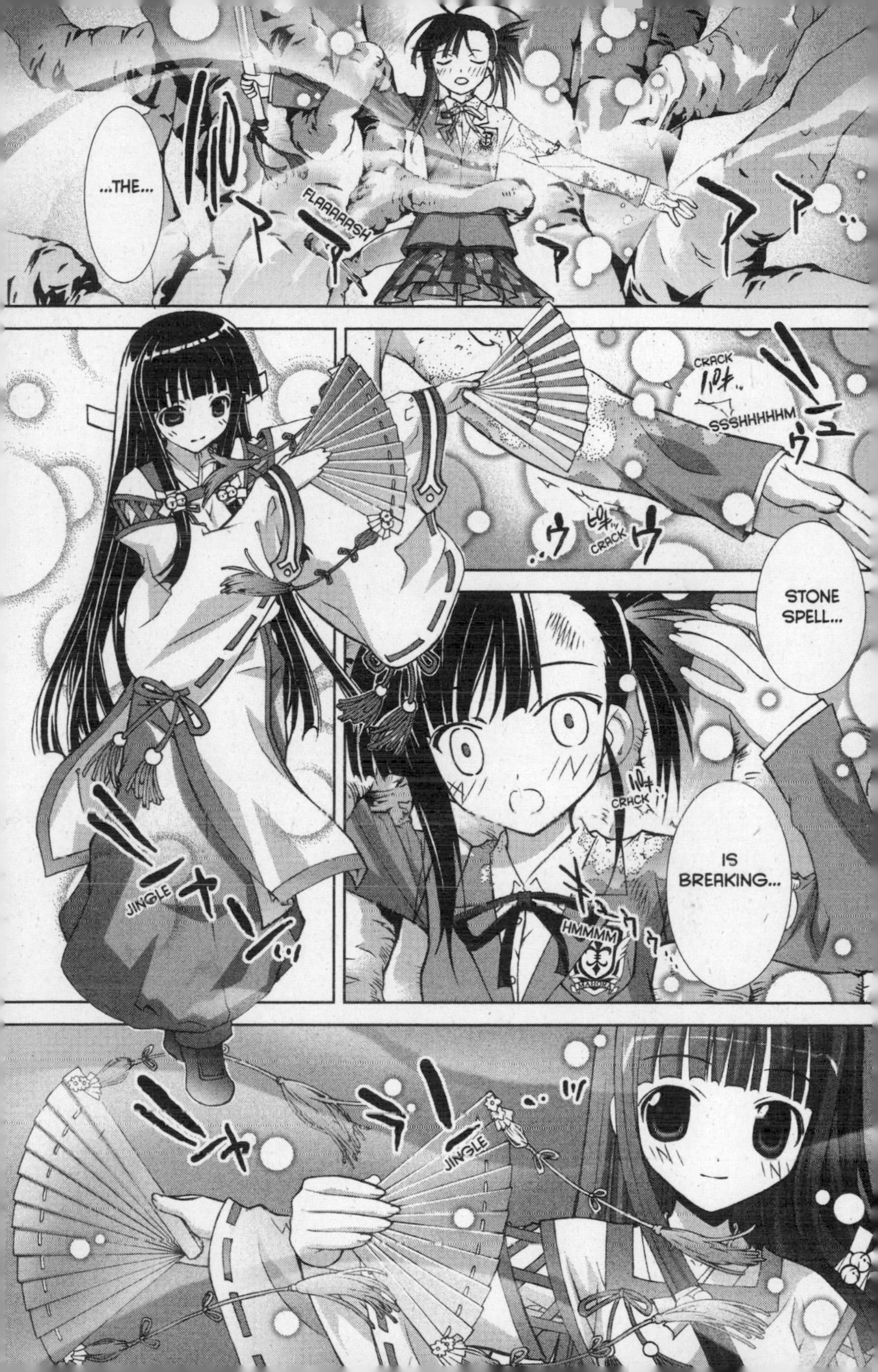
FLAAAAASH
...THE...
CRACK
SSSHHHHHM
CRACK
STONE SPELL...
CRACK
IS BREAKING...
HMMMM
JINGLE
JINGLE

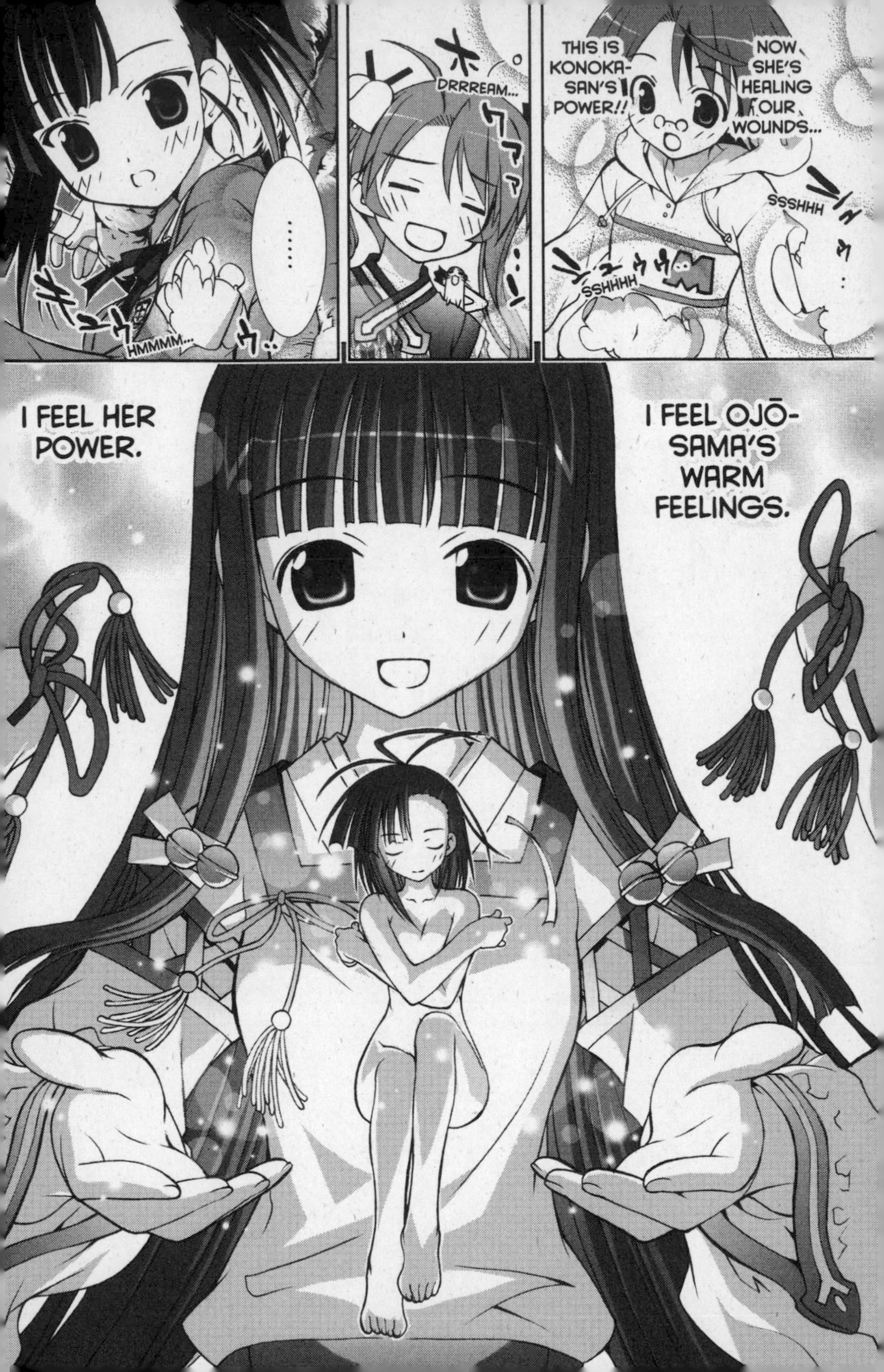
THIS IS KONOKA-SAN'S POWER!!
NOW SHE'S HEALING OUR WOUNDS...
SSSHHH
SSHHHH
DRRREAM...
......
HMMMM...
I FEEL OJŌ-SAMA'S WARM FEELINGS.
I FEEL HER POWER.

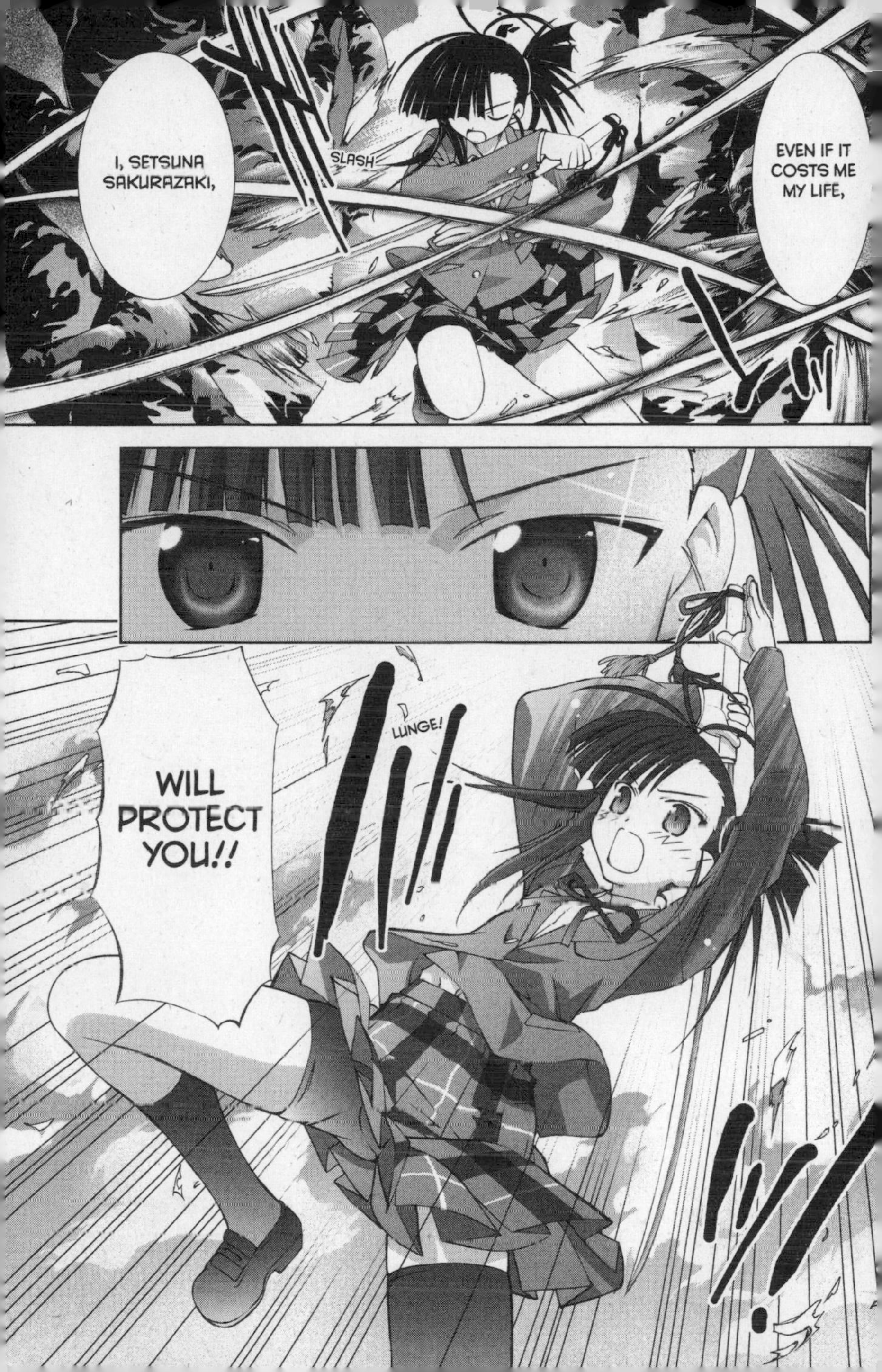
EVEN IF IT COSTS ME MY LIFE,
SLASH
I, SETSUNA SAKURAZAKI,
LUNGE!
WILL PROTECT YOU!!

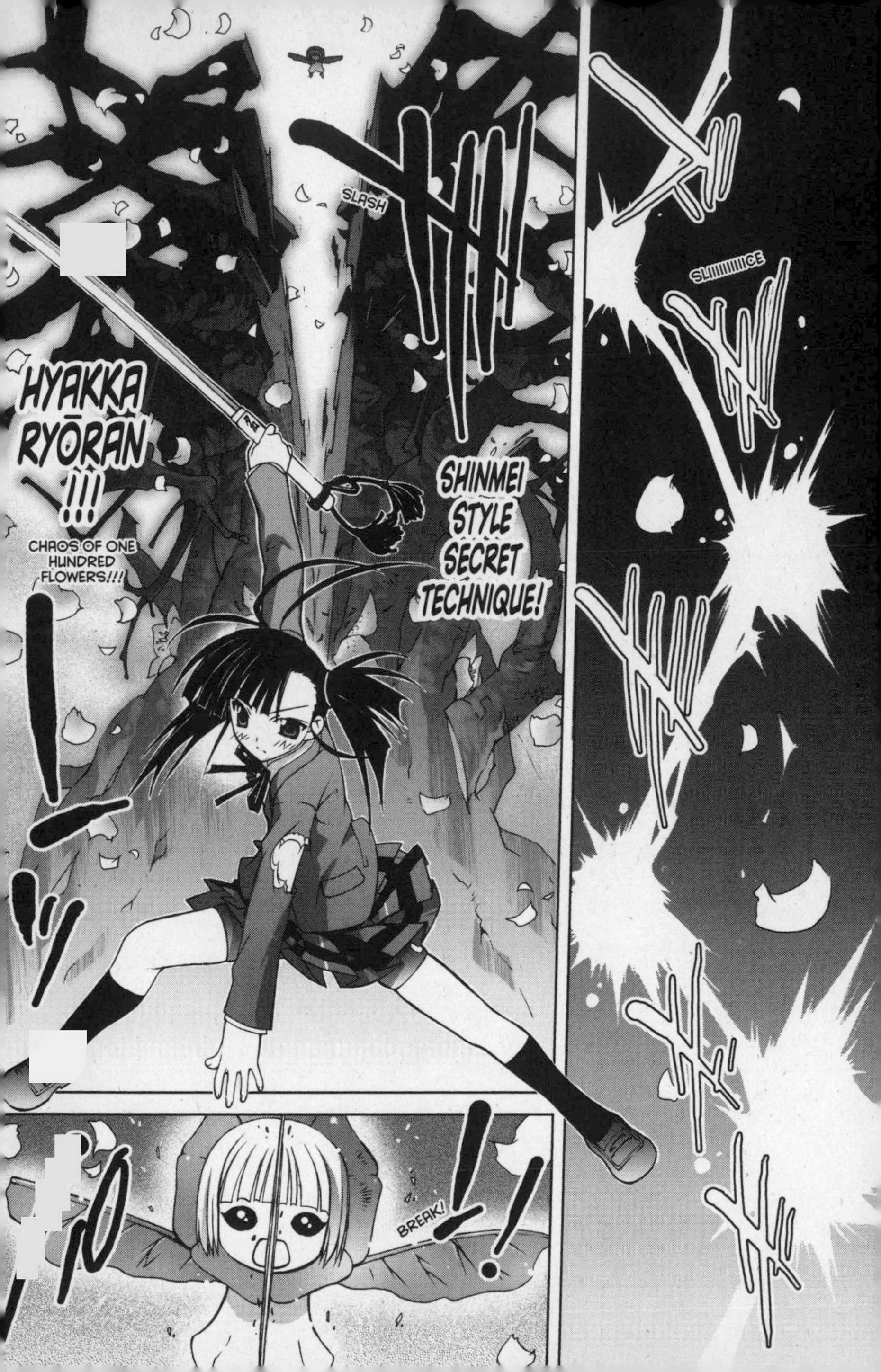
SLIIIIIIIICE
SLASH
SHINMEI STYLE SECRET TECHNIQUE!
HYAKKA RYŌRAN!!!
CHAOS OF ONE HUNDRED FLOWERS!!!
BREAK!

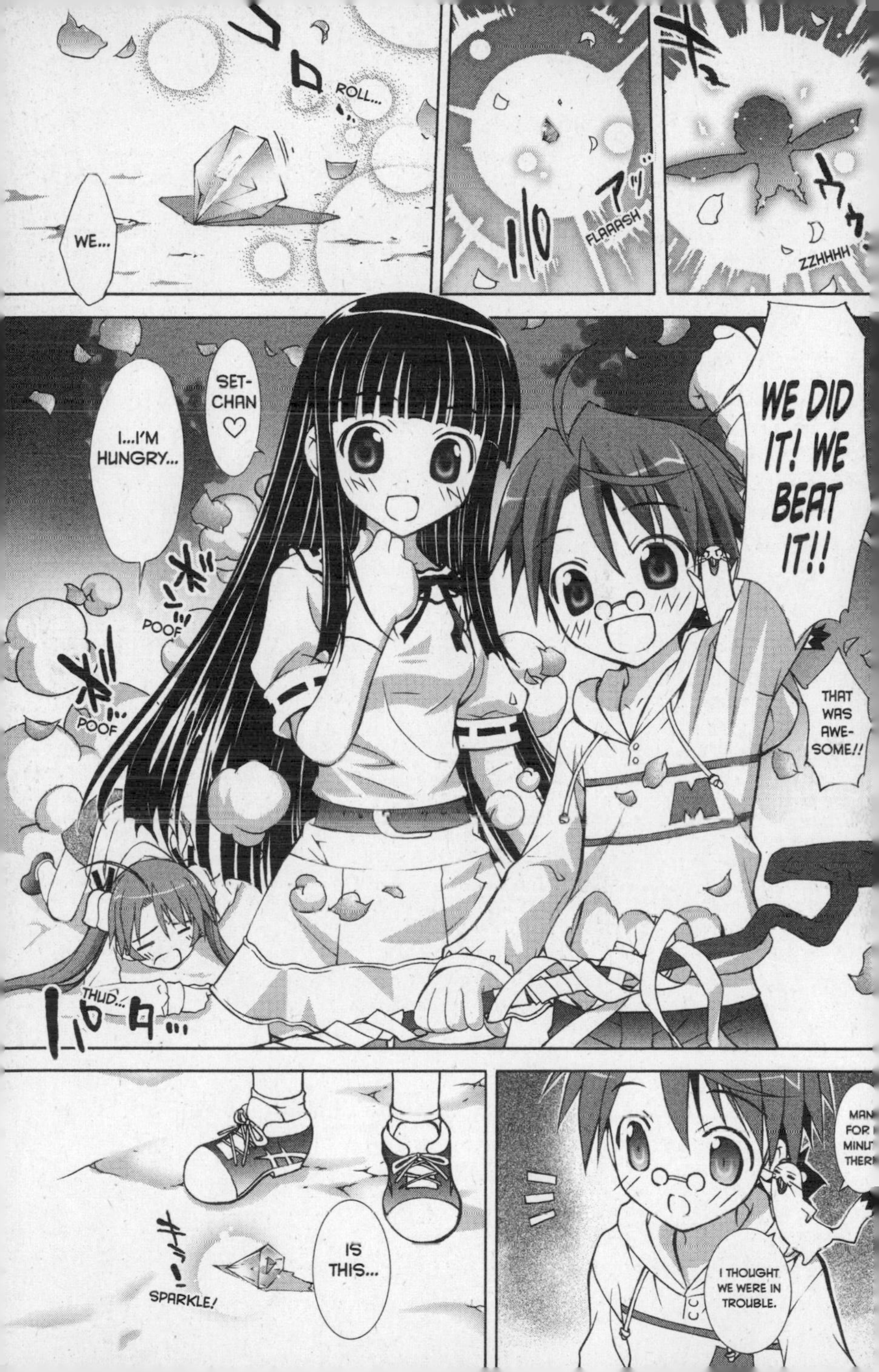
ZZHHHH
FLAAARSH
ROLL...
WE...
WE DID IT! WE BEAT IT!!
THAT WAS AWESOME!!
SET-CHAN ♡
I...I'M HUNGRY...
POOF
POOF
THUD...
MAN
FOR
MINUT
THER
I THOUGHT WE WERE IN TROUBLE.
IS THIS...
SPARKLE!

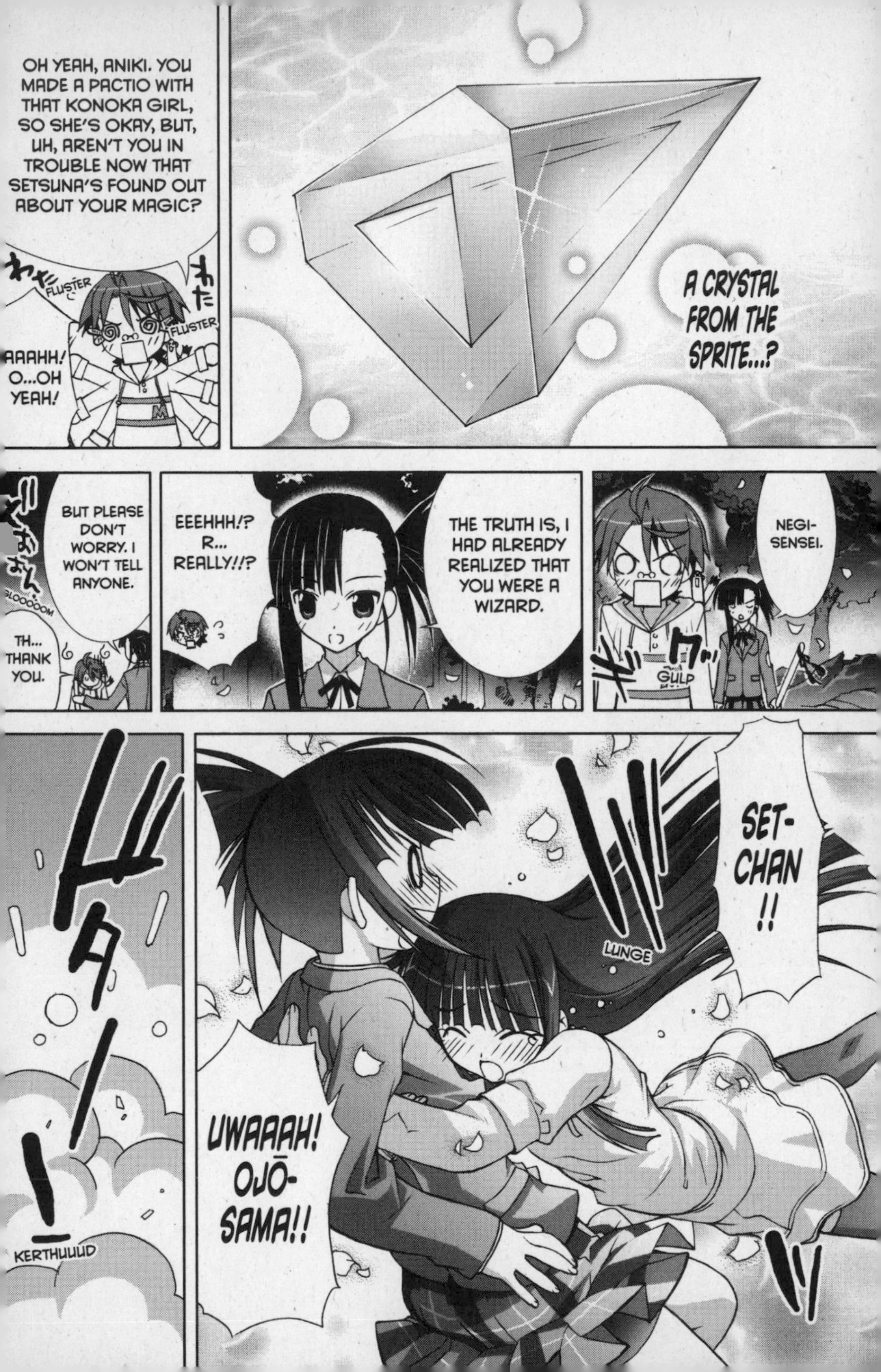
A CRYSTAL FROM THE SPRITE...?
OH YEAH, ANIKI. YOU MADE A PACTIO WITH THAT KONOKA GIRL, SO SHE'S OKAY, BUT, UH, AREN'T YOU IN TROUBLE NOW THAT SETSUNA'S FOUND OUT ABOUT YOUR MAGIC?
FLUSTER
FLUSTER
AAAHH! O...OH YEAH!
NEGI-SENSEI.
GULP
THE TRUTH IS, I HAD ALREADY REALIZED THAT YOU WERE A WIZARD.
EEEHHH!? R... REALLY!!?
BUT PLEASE DON'T WORRY. I WON'T TELL ANYONE.
SLOOOOOM
TH... THANK YOU.
SET-CHAN!!
LUNGE
UWAAAH! OJŌ-SAMA!!
KERTHUUUD

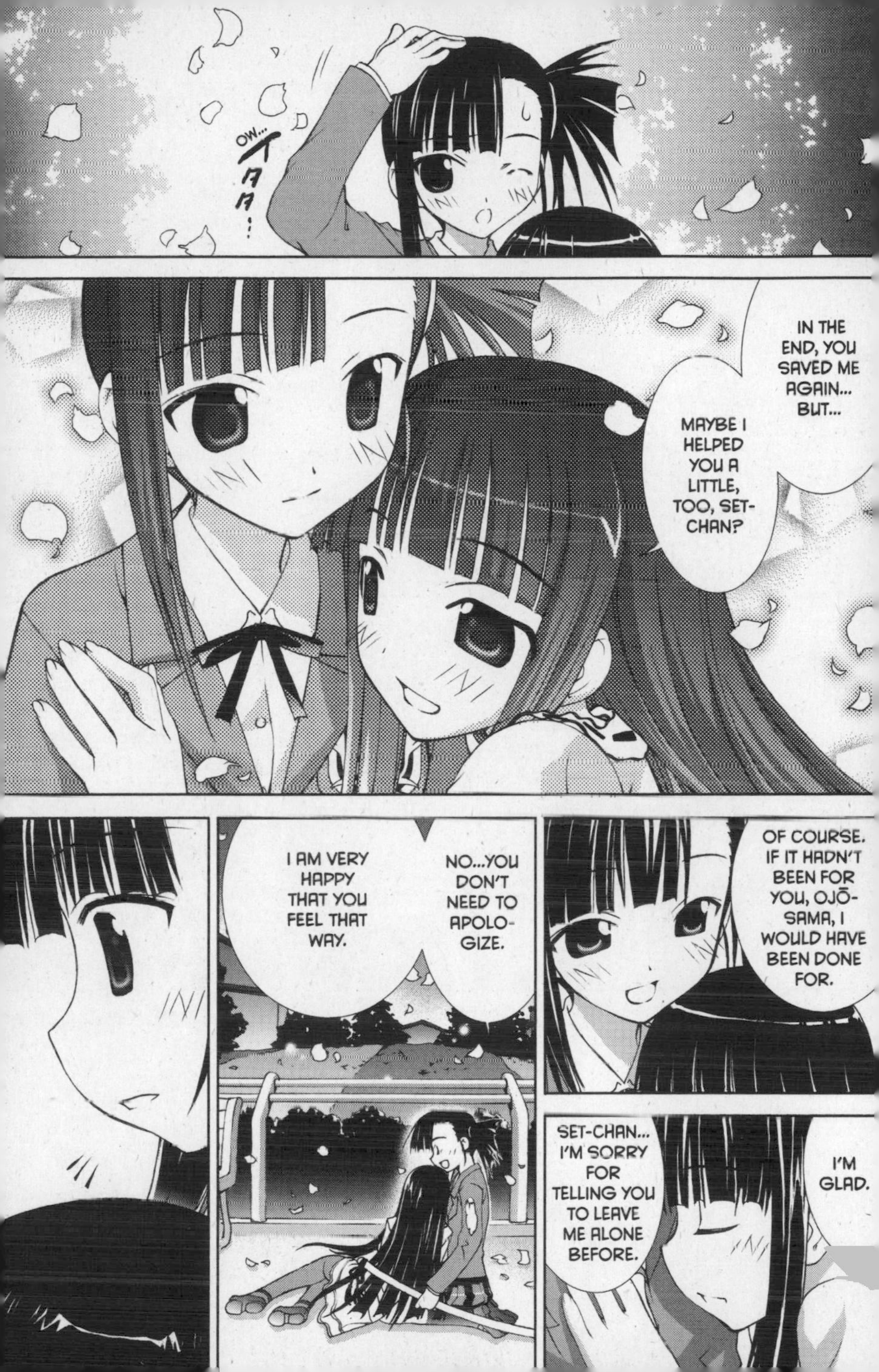
OW... イタタ‥
IN THE END, YOU SAVED ME AGAIN... BUT...
MAYBE I HELPED YOU A LITTLE, TOO, SET-CHAN?
OF COURSE. IF IT HADN'T BEEN FOR YOU, OJŌ-SAMA, I WOULD HAVE BEEN DONE FOR.
I'M GLAD.
SET-CHAN... I'M SORRY FOR TELLING YOU TO LEAVE ME ALONE BEFORE.
NO...YOU DON'T NEED TO APOLOGIZE.
I AM VERY HAPPY THAT YOU FEEL THAT WAY.

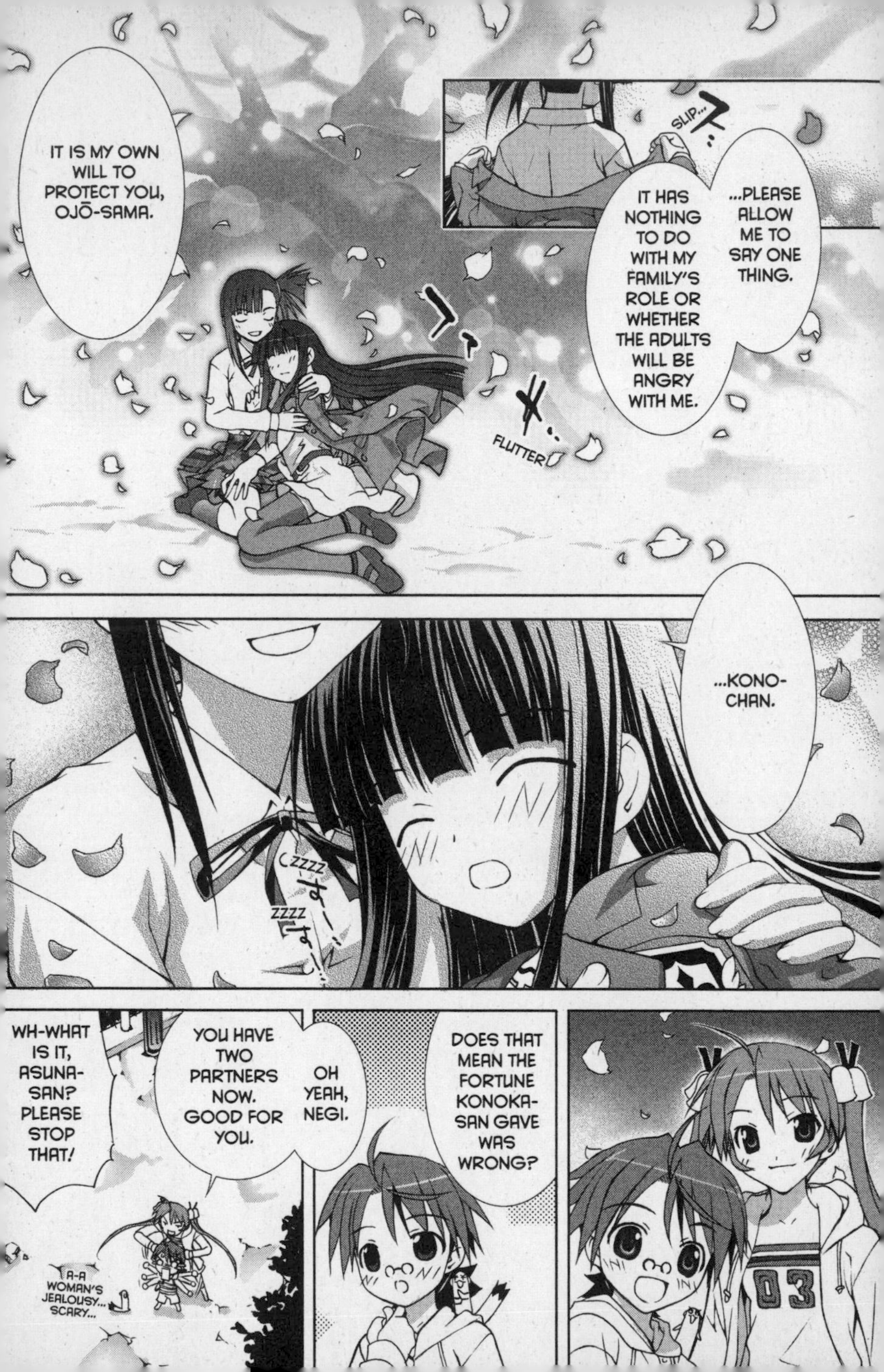
SLIP...
...PLEASE ALLOW ME TO SAY ONE THING.
IT HAS NOTHING TO DO WITH MY FAMILY'S ROLE OR WHETHER THE ADULTS WILL BE ANGRY WITH ME.
FLUTTER
IT IS MY OWN WILL TO PROTECT YOU, OJŌ-SAMA.
...KONO-CHAN.
ZZZZ
ZZZZ
DOES THAT MEAN THE FORTUNE KONOKA-SAN GAVE WAS WRONG?
OH YEAH, NEGI.
YOU HAVE TWO PARTNERS NOW. GOOD FOR YOU.
WH-WHAT IS IT, ASUNA-SAN? PLEASE STOP THAT!
A-A WOMAN'S JEALOUSY... SCARY...

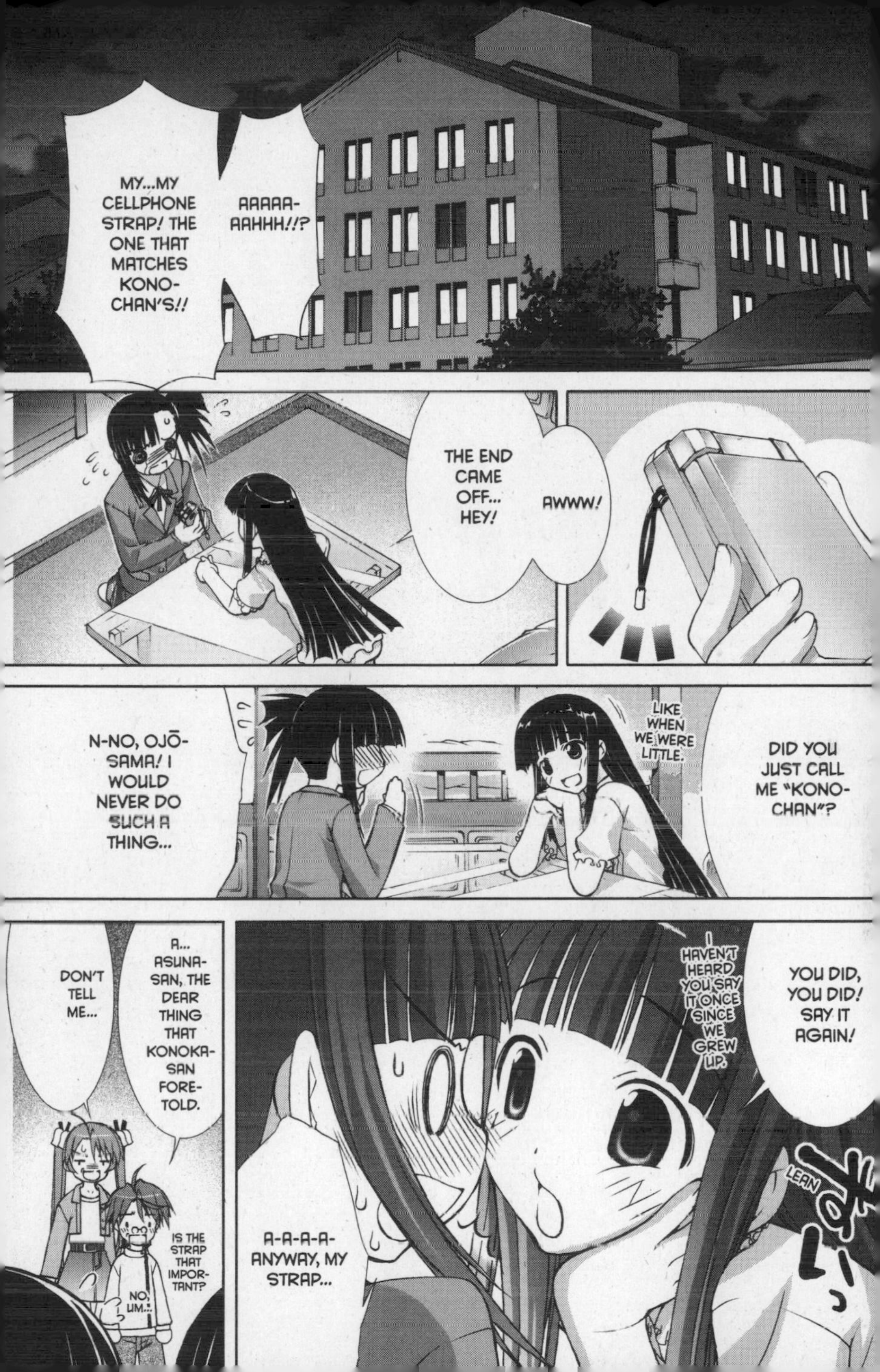
AAAAA-AAHHH!!?
MY...MY CELLPHONE STRAP! THE ONE THAT MATCHES KONO-CHAN'S!!
AWWW!
THE END CAME OFF... HEY!
DID YOU JUST CALL ME "KONO-CHAN"?
LIKE WHEN WE WERE LITTLE.
N-NO, OJŌ-SAMA! I WOULD NEVER DO SUCH A THING...
YOU DID, YOU DID! SAY IT AGAIN!
I HAVEN'T HEARD YOU SAY IT ONCE SINCE WE GREW UP.
LEAN
A-A-A-A-ANYWAY, MY STRAP...
A... ASUNA-SAN, THE DEAR THING THAT KONOKA-SAN FORETOLD.
DON'T TELL ME...
IS THE STRAP THAT IMPORTANT?
NO, UM...

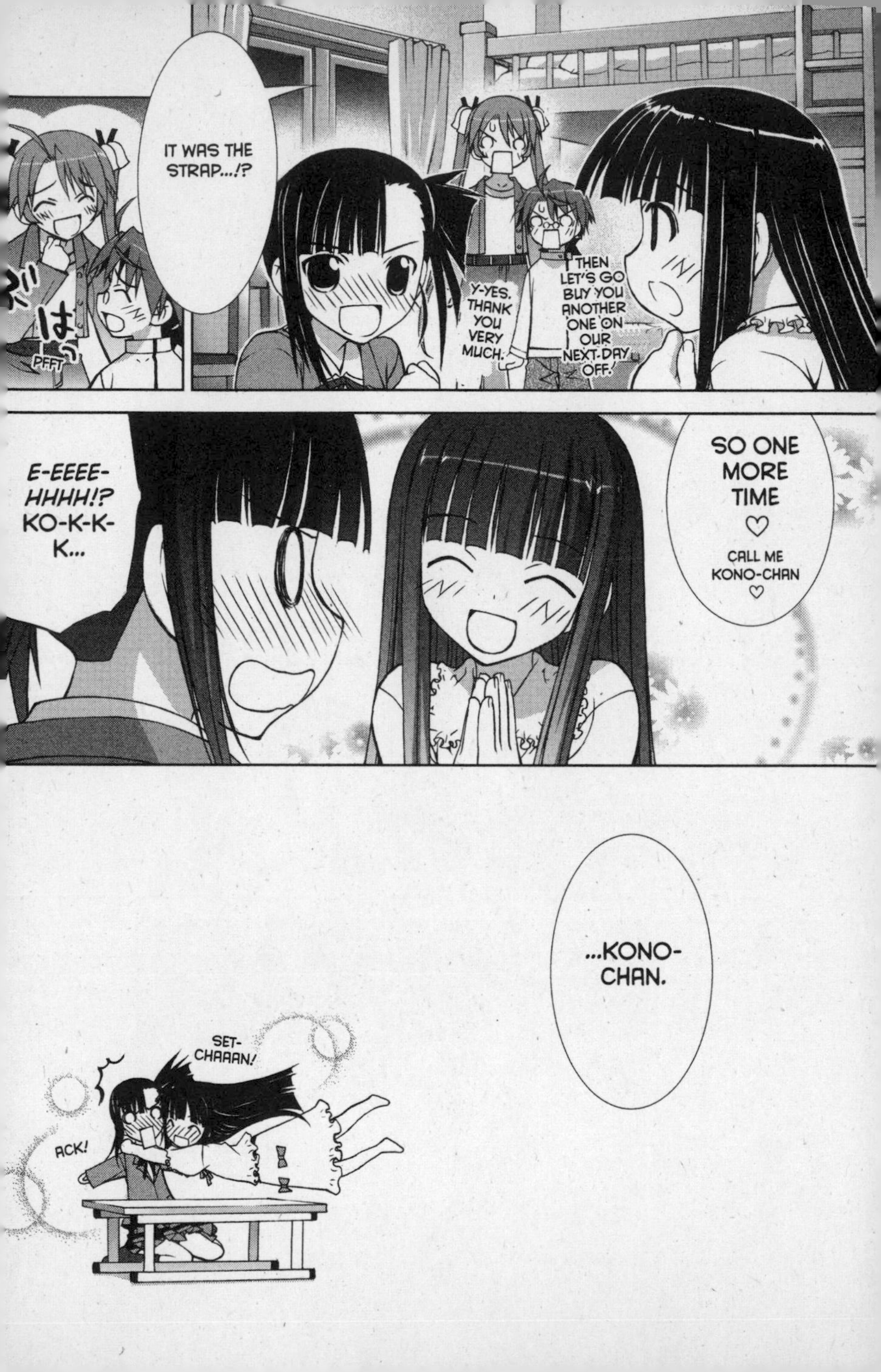
THEN LET'S GO BUY YOU ANOTHER ONE ON OUR NEXT-DAY OFF!
Y-YES. THANK YOU VERY MUCH.
IT WAS THE STRAP...!?
ぶは
PFFT
SO ONE MORE TIME ♡
CALL ME KONO-CHAN ♡
E-EEEE-HHHH!? KO-K-K-K...
...KONO-CHAN.
SET-CHAAAN!
ACK!

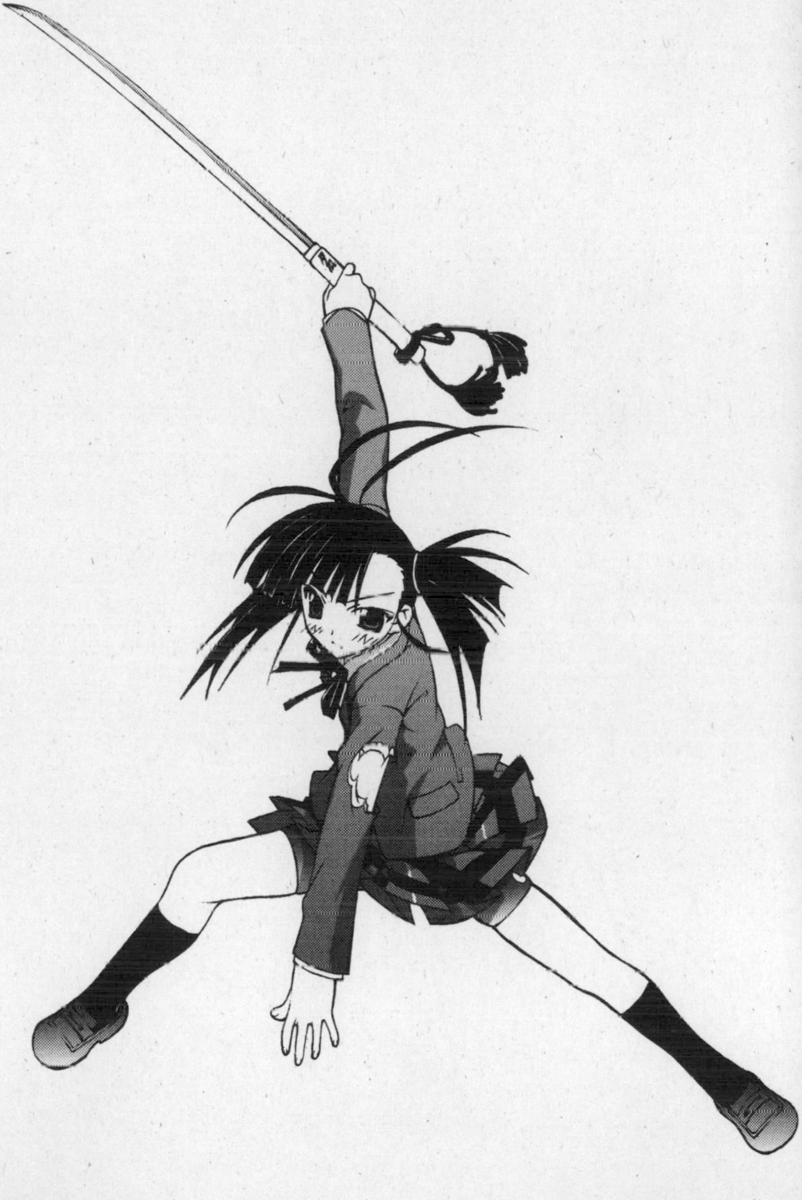

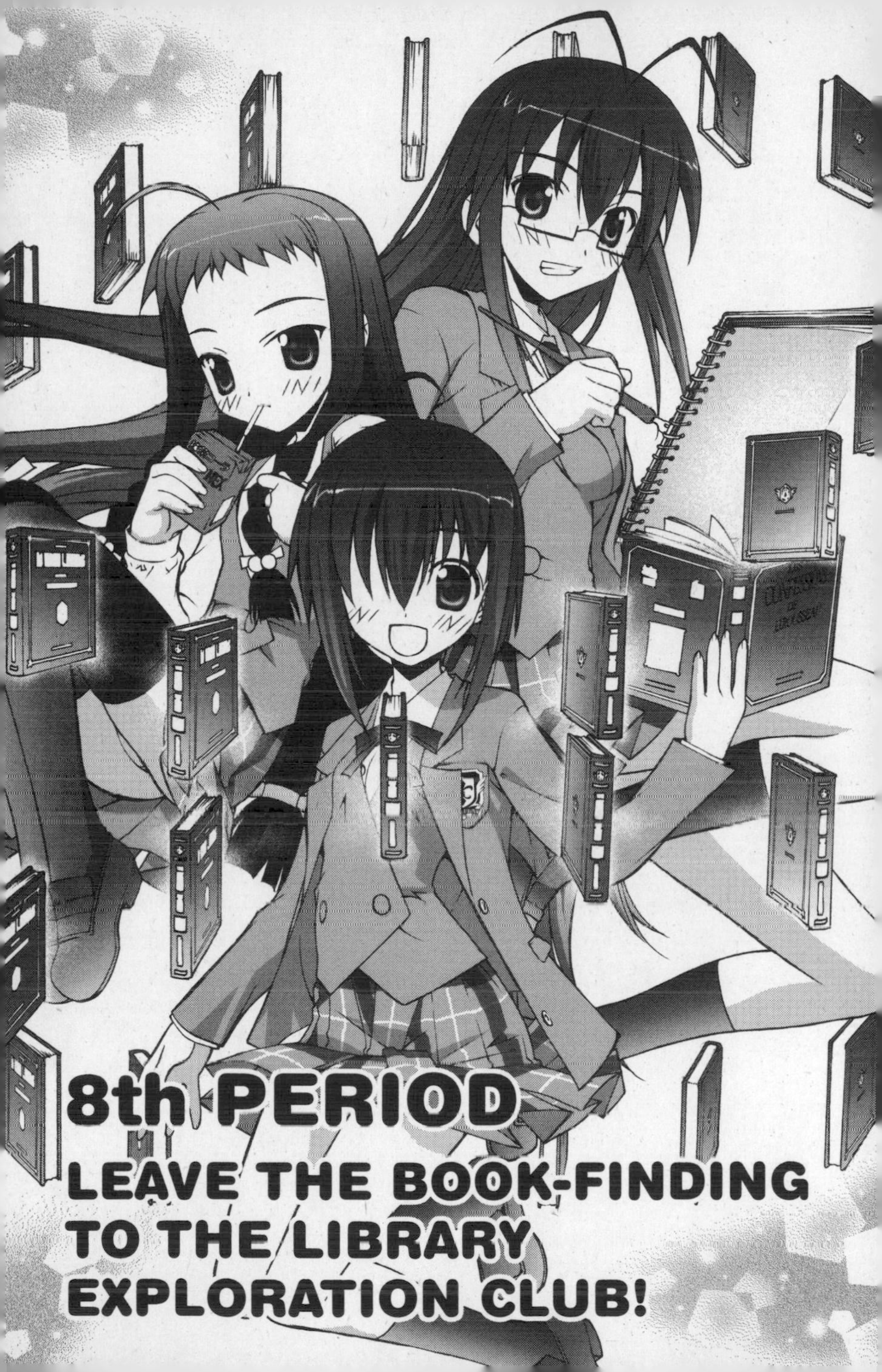
8th PERIOD
LEAVE THE BOOK-FINDING
TO THE LIBRARY
EXPLORATION CLUB!

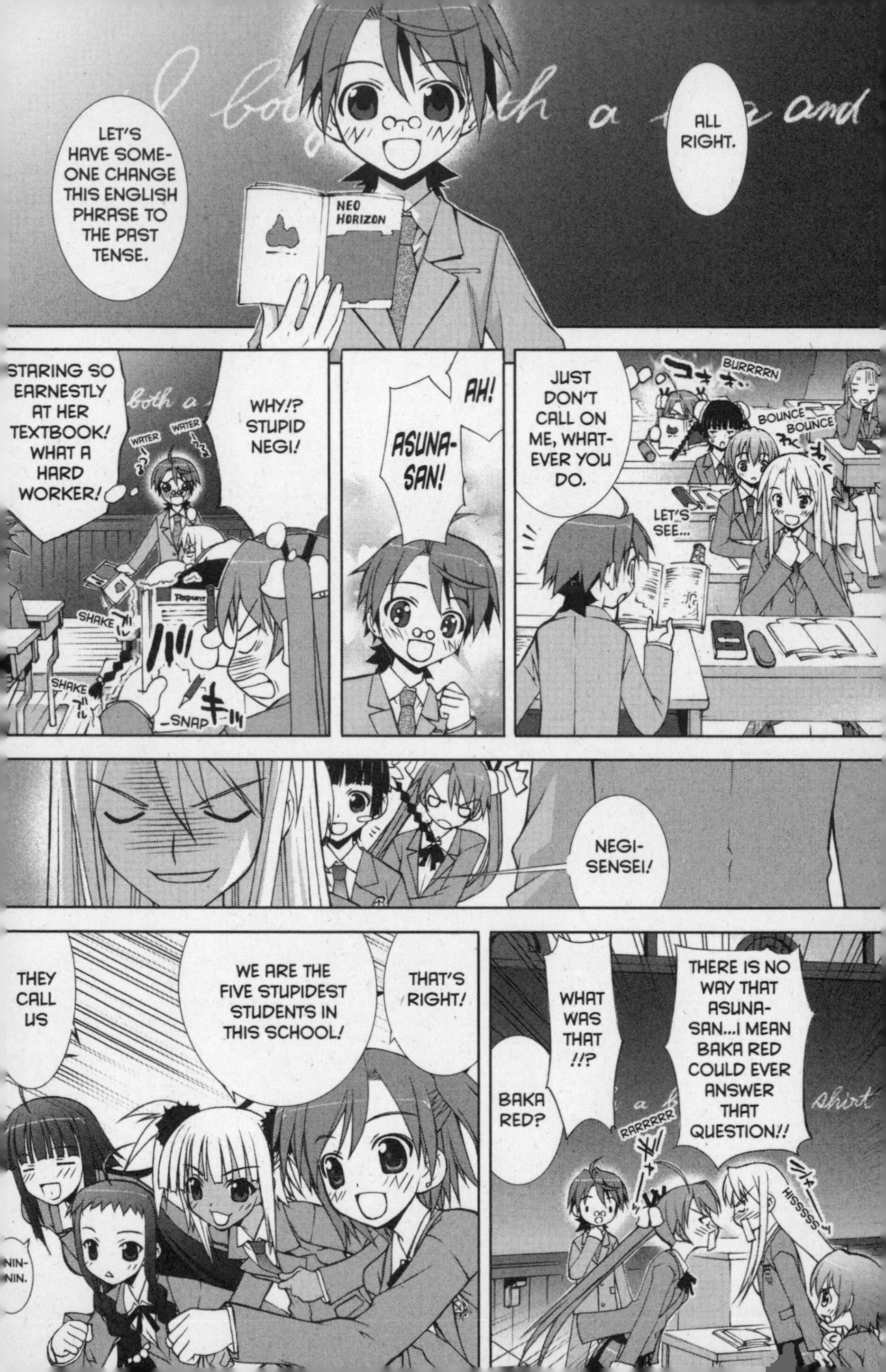

ALL RIGHT.
LET'S HAVE SOME-ONE CHANGE THIS ENGLISH PHRASE TO THE PAST TENSE.
NEO HORIZON
BURRRRN
BOUNCE
BOUNCE
JUST DON'T CALL ON ME, WHAT-EVER YOU DO.
LET'S SEE...
AH!
ASUNA-SAN!
WHY!? STUPID NEGI!
STARING SO EARNESTLY AT HER TEXTBOOK! WHAT A HARD WORKER!
WATER
WATER
SHAKE
SHAKE
SNAP
NEGI-SENSEI!
THERE IS NO WAY THAT ASUNA-SAN...I MEAN BAKA RED COULD EVER ANSWER THAT QUESTION!!
WHAT WAS THAT !!?
BAKA RED?
RARRRRR
HISSSSS
THAT'S RIGHT!
WE ARE THE FIVE STUPIDEST STUDENTS IN THIS SCHOOL!
THEY CALL US
NIN-NIN.

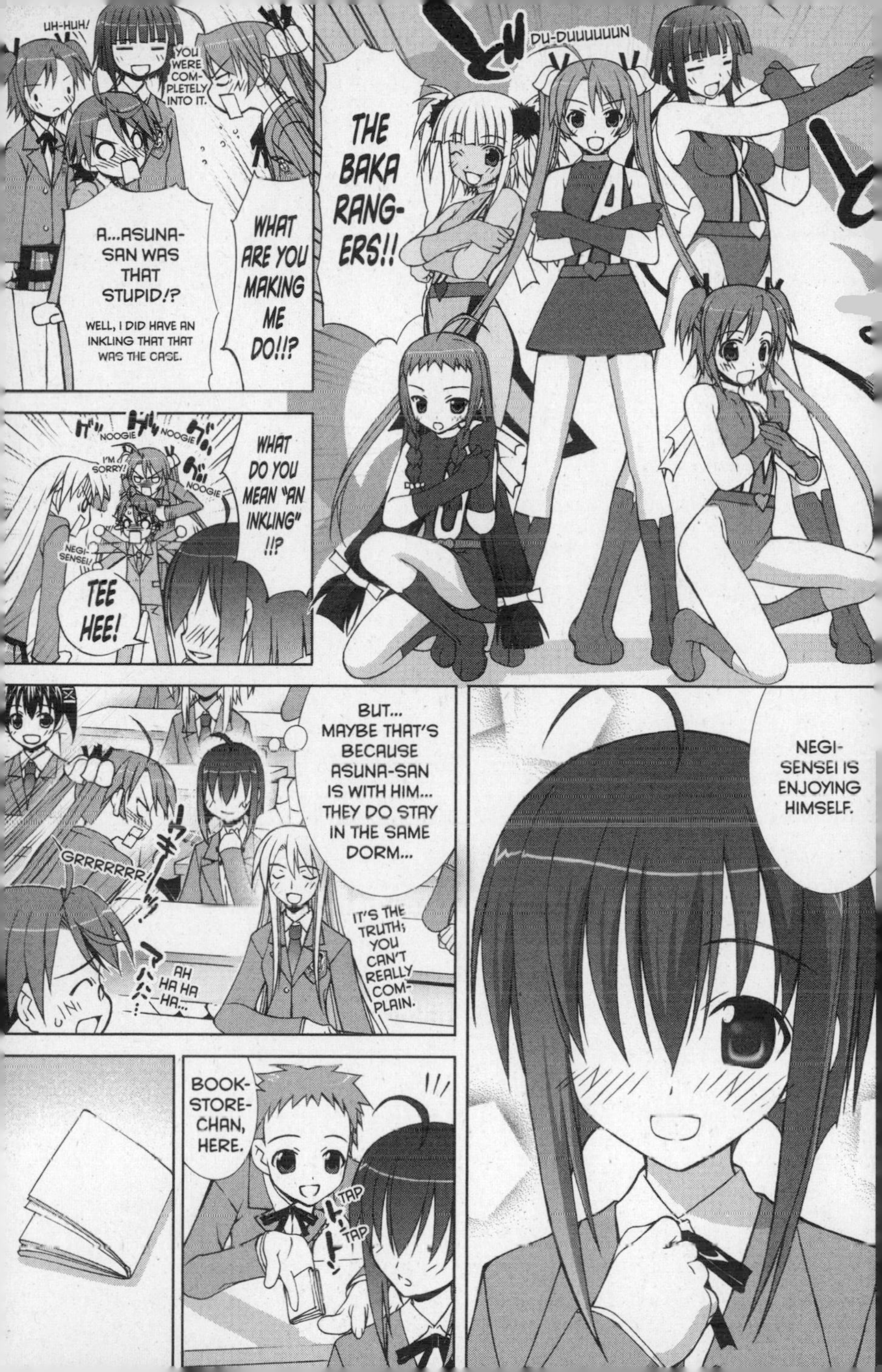
DU-DUUUUUUN
THE BAKA RANGERS!!
YOU WERE COMPLETELY INTO IT.
UH-HUH!
WHAT ARE YOU MAKING ME DO!!?
A...ASUNA-SAN WAS THAT STUPID!?
WELL, I DID HAVE AN INKLING THAT THAT WAS THE CASE.
WHAT DO YOU MEAN "AN INKLING" !!?
NOOGIE
NOOGIE
NOOGIE
I'M SORRY!
NEGI-SENSEI!
TEE HEE!
NEGI-SENSEI IS ENJOYING HIMSELF.
BUT... MAYBE THAT'S BECAUSE ASUNA-SAN IS WITH HIM... THEY DO STAY IN THE SAME DORM...
IT'S THE TRUTH; YOU CAN'T REALLY COMPLAIN.
GRRRRRRR!
AH HA HA HA...
BOOK-STORE-CHAN, HERE.
TAP
TAP

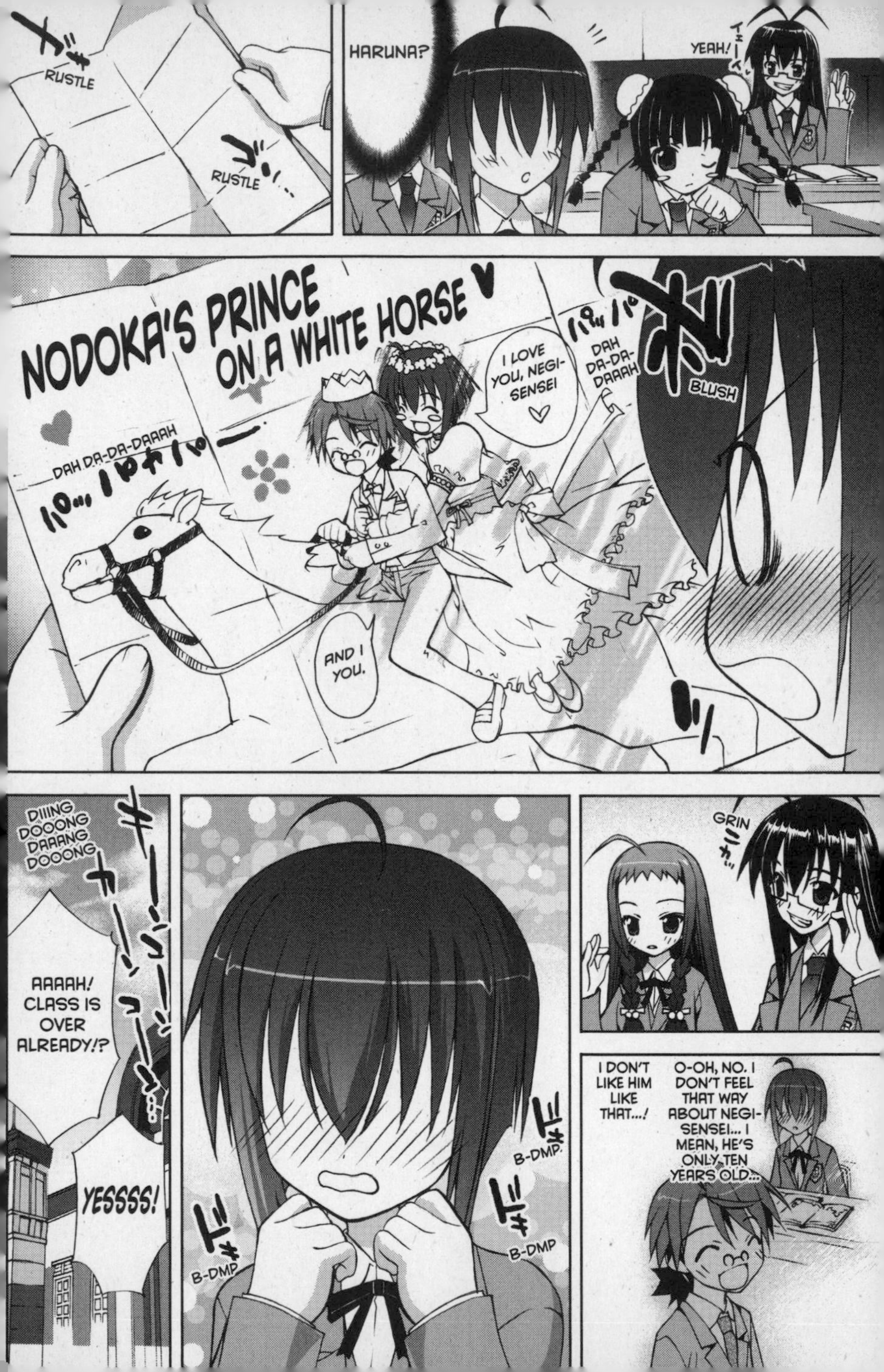
YEAH!
HARUNA?
RUSTLE
RUSTLE
BLUSH
DAH DA-DA-DAAAH
I LOVE YOU, NEGI-SENSEI
NODOKA'S PRINCE ON A WHITE HORSE
DAH DA-DA-DAAAH
AND I YOU.
GRIN
O-OH, NO. I DON'T FEEL THAT WAY ABOUT NEGI-SENSEI... I MEAN, HE'S ONLY TEN YEARS OLD...
I DON'T LIKE HIM LIKE THAT...!
B-DMP
B-DMP
B-DMP
DIIING DOOONG DAAANG DOOONG
AAAAH! CLASS IS OVER ALREADY!?
YESSSS!

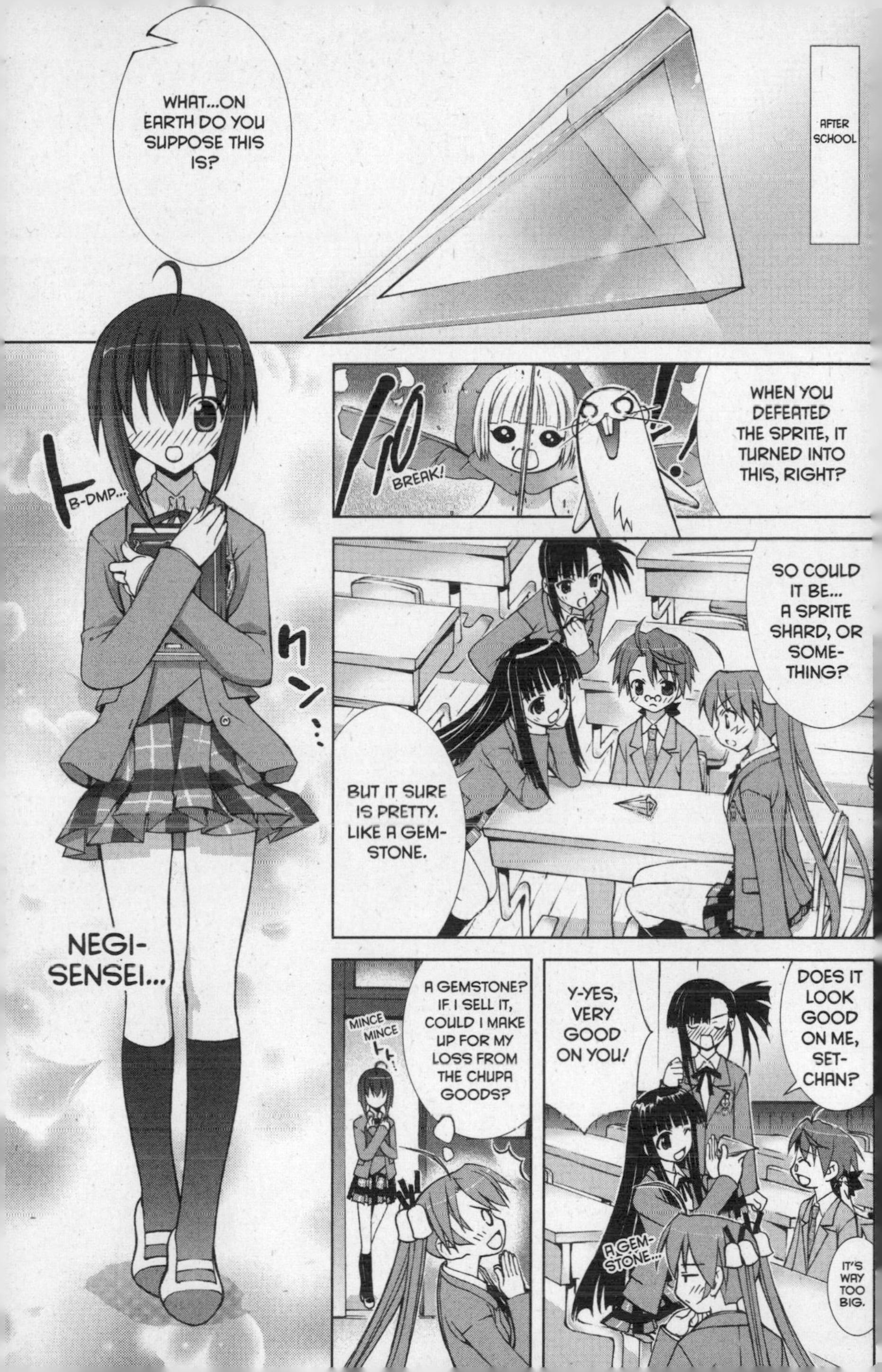
AFTER SCHOOL
WHAT...ON EARTH DO YOU SUPPOSE THIS IS?
WHEN YOU DEFEATED THE SPRITE, IT TURNED INTO THIS, RIGHT?
BREAK!
SO COULD IT BE... A SPRITE SHARD, OR SOME-THING?
BUT IT SURE IS PRETTY. LIKE A GEM-STONE.
DOES IT LOOK GOOD ON ME, SET-CHAN?
Y-YES, VERY GOOD ON YOU!
A GEM-STONE...
IT'S WAY TOO BIG.
A GEMSTONE? IF I SELL IT, COULD I MAKE UP FOR MY LOSS FROM THE CHUPA GOODS?
MINCE MINCE
B-DMP...
NEGI-SENSEI...

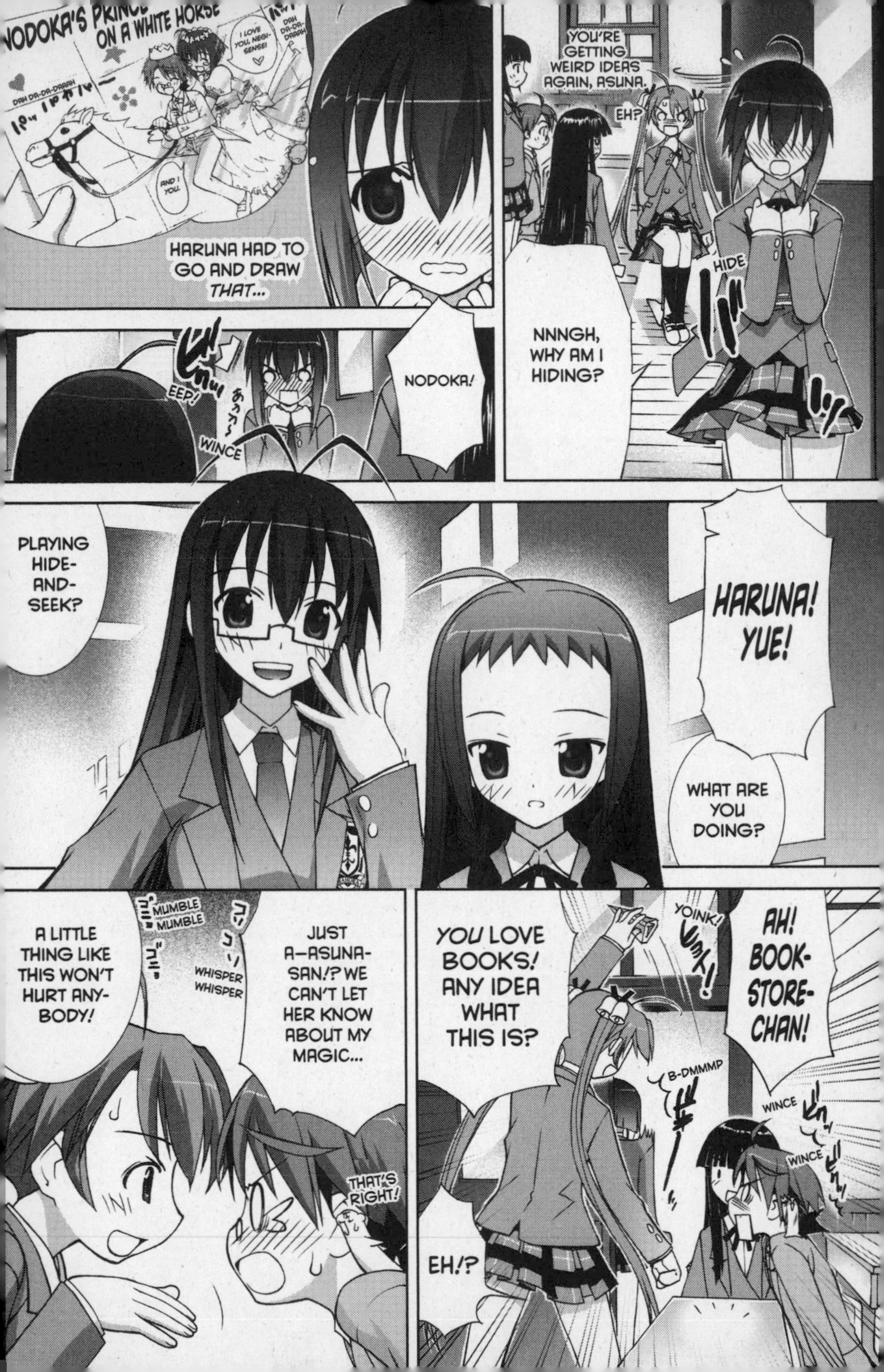

YOU'RE GETTING WEIRD IDEAS AGAIN, ASUNA.
EH?
HIDE
NNNGH, WHY AM I HIDING?
NODOKA'S PRINCE ON A WHITE HORSE
I LOVE YOU, NEGI-SENSEI!
DAH DA-DA-DAAAH
DAH DA-DA-DARAH
AND I YOU.
HARUNA HAD TO GO AND DRAW THAT...
NODOKA!
EEP!
WINCE
HARUNA! YUE!
WHAT ARE YOU DOING?
PLAYING HIDE-AND-SEEK?
AH! BOOK-STORE-CHAN!
YOINK!
WINCE
WINCE
B-DMMMP
YOU LOVE BOOKS! ANY IDEA WHAT THIS IS?
EH!?
JUST A—ASUNA-SAN!? WE CAN'T LET HER KNOW ABOUT MY MAGIC...
WHISPER WHISPER
THAT'S RIGHT!
MUMBLE MUMBLE
A LITTLE THING LIKE THIS WON'T HURT ANYBODY!

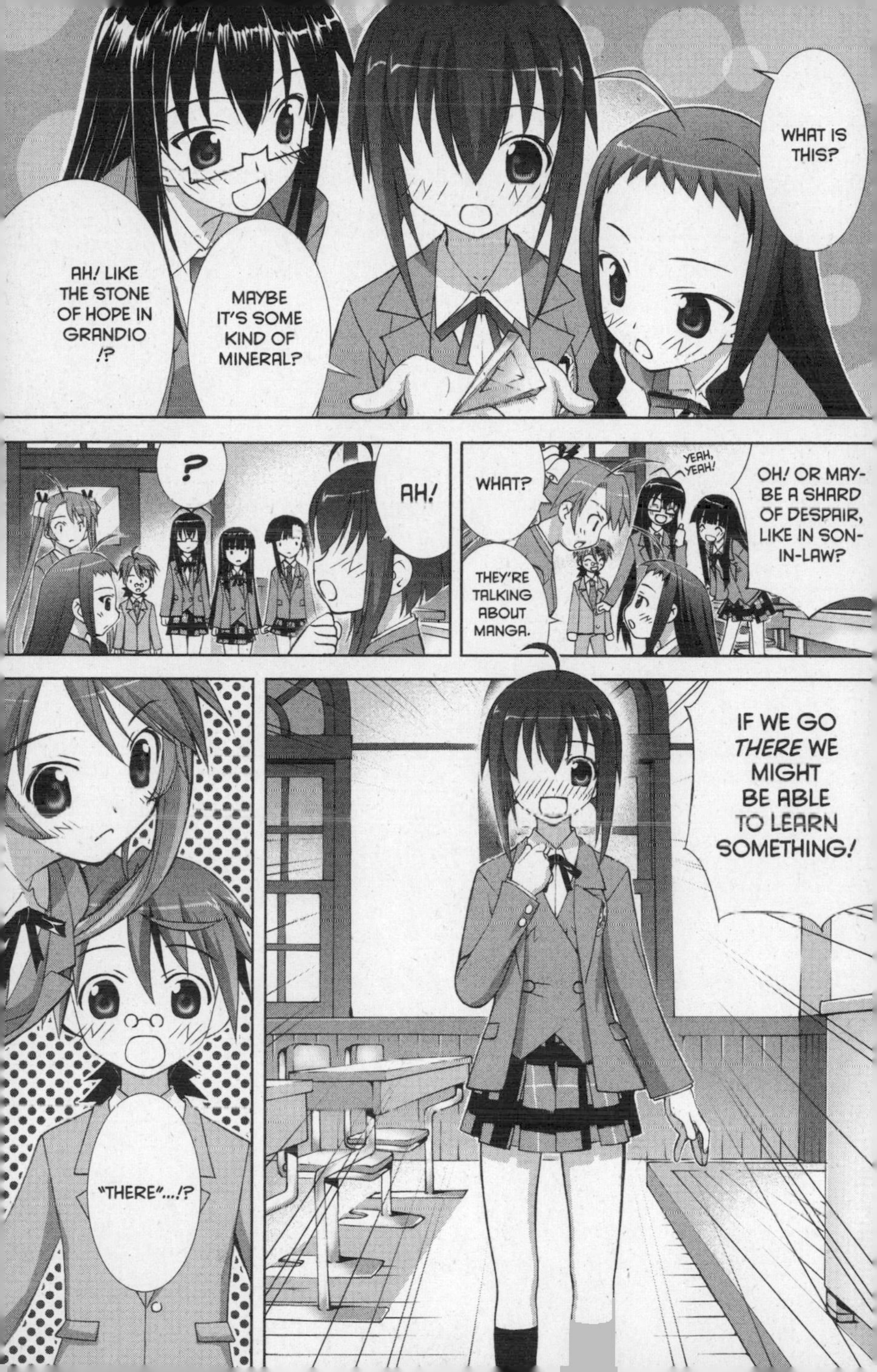
WHAT IS THIS?
MAYBE IT'S SOME KIND OF MINERAL?
AH! LIKE THE STONE OF HOPE IN GRANDIO !?
OH! OR MAY-BE A SHARD OF DESPAIR, LIKE IN SON-IN-LAW?
YEAH, YEAH!
WHAT?
THEY'RE TALKING ABOUT MANGA.
AH!
?
IF WE GO *THERE* WE MIGHT BE ABLE TO LEARN SOMETHING!
"THERE"...!?

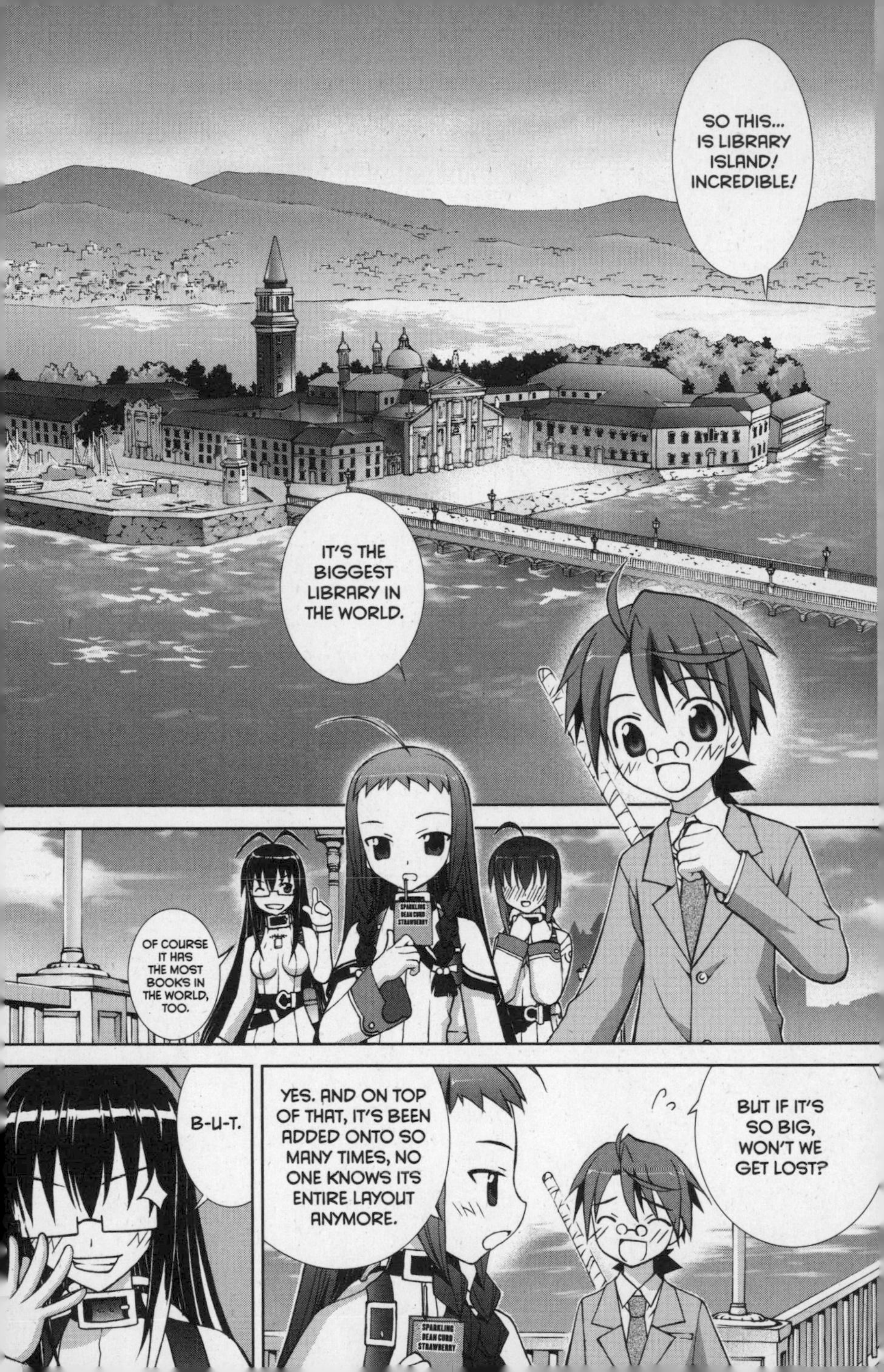
SO THIS... IS LIBRARY ISLAND! INCREDIBLE!
IT'S THE BIGGEST LIBRARY IN THE WORLD.
SPARKLING BEAN CURD STRAWBERRY
OF COURSE IT HAS THE MOST BOOKS IN THE WORLD, TOO.
BUT IF IT'S SO BIG, WON'T WE GET LOST?
YES. AND ON TOP OF THAT, IT'S BEEN ADDED ONTO SO MANY TIMES, NO ONE KNOWS ITS ENTIRE LAYOUT ANYMORE.
B-U-T.

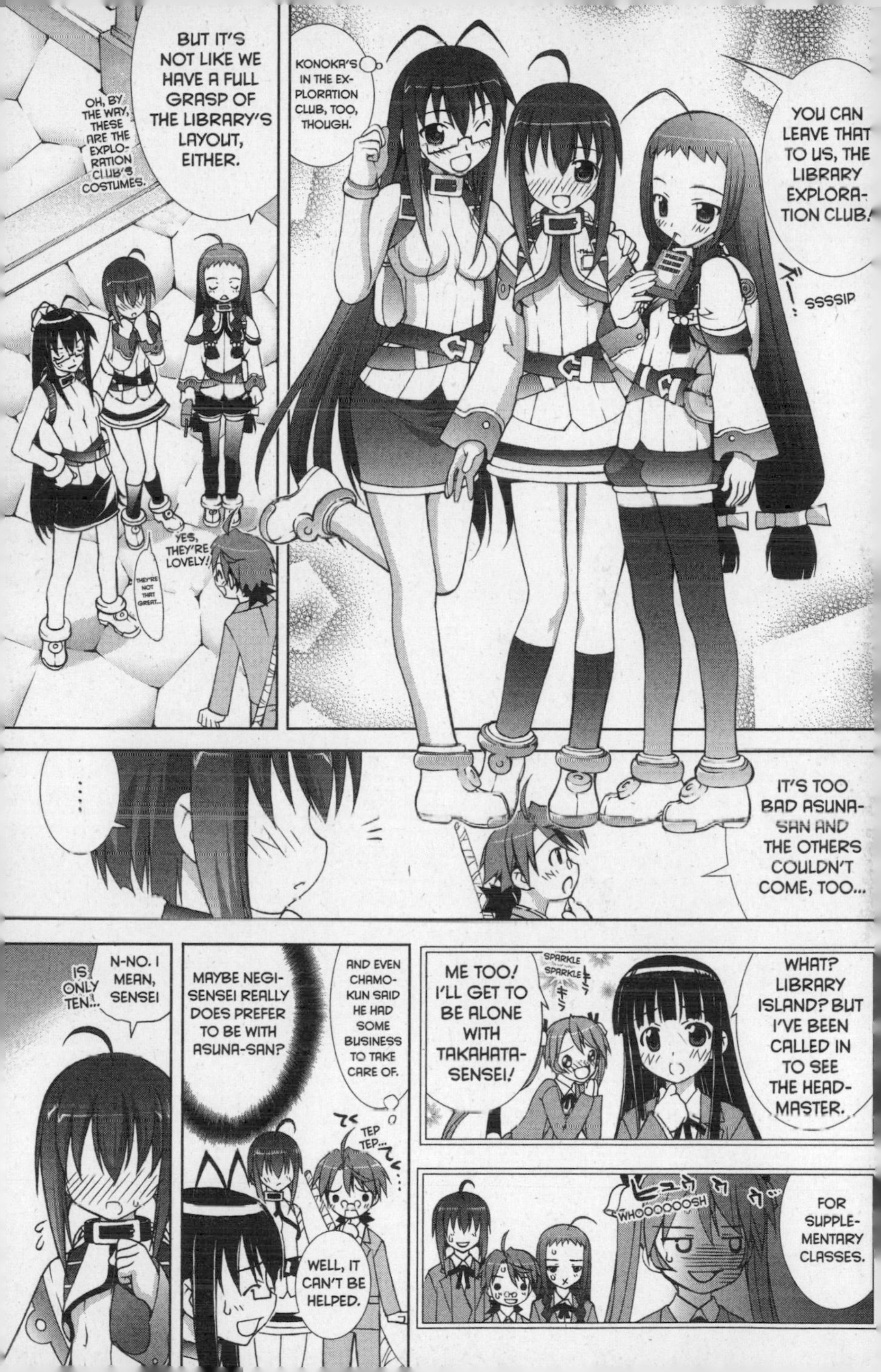
YOU CAN LEAVE THAT TO US, THE LIBRARY EXPLORATION CLUB!
SSSSIP
KONOKA'S IN THE EXPLORATION CLUB, TOO, THOUGH.
BUT IT'S NOT LIKE WE HAVE A FULL GRASP OF THE LIBRARY'S LAYOUT, EITHER.
OH, BY THE WAY, THESE ARE THE EXPLORATION CLUB'S COSTUMES.
YES, THEY'RE LOVELY!
THEY'RE NOT THAT GREAT...
IT'S TOO BAD ASUNA-SAN AND THE OTHERS COULDN'T COME, TOO...
.....
WHAT? LIBRARY ISLAND? BUT I'VE BEEN CALLED IN TO SEE THE HEADMASTER.
SPARKLE SPARKLE
ME TOO! I'LL GET TO BE ALONE WITH TAKAHATA-SENSEI!
FOR SUPPLEMENTARY CLASSES.
WHOOOOOOSH
AND EVEN CHAMO-KUN SAID HE HAD SOME BUSINESS TO TAKE CARE OF.
TEP TEP...
WELL, IT CAN'T BE HELPED.
MAYBE NEGI-SENSEI REALLY DOES PREFER TO BE WITH ASUNA-SAN?
N-NO. I MEAN, SENSEI
IS ONLY TEN...

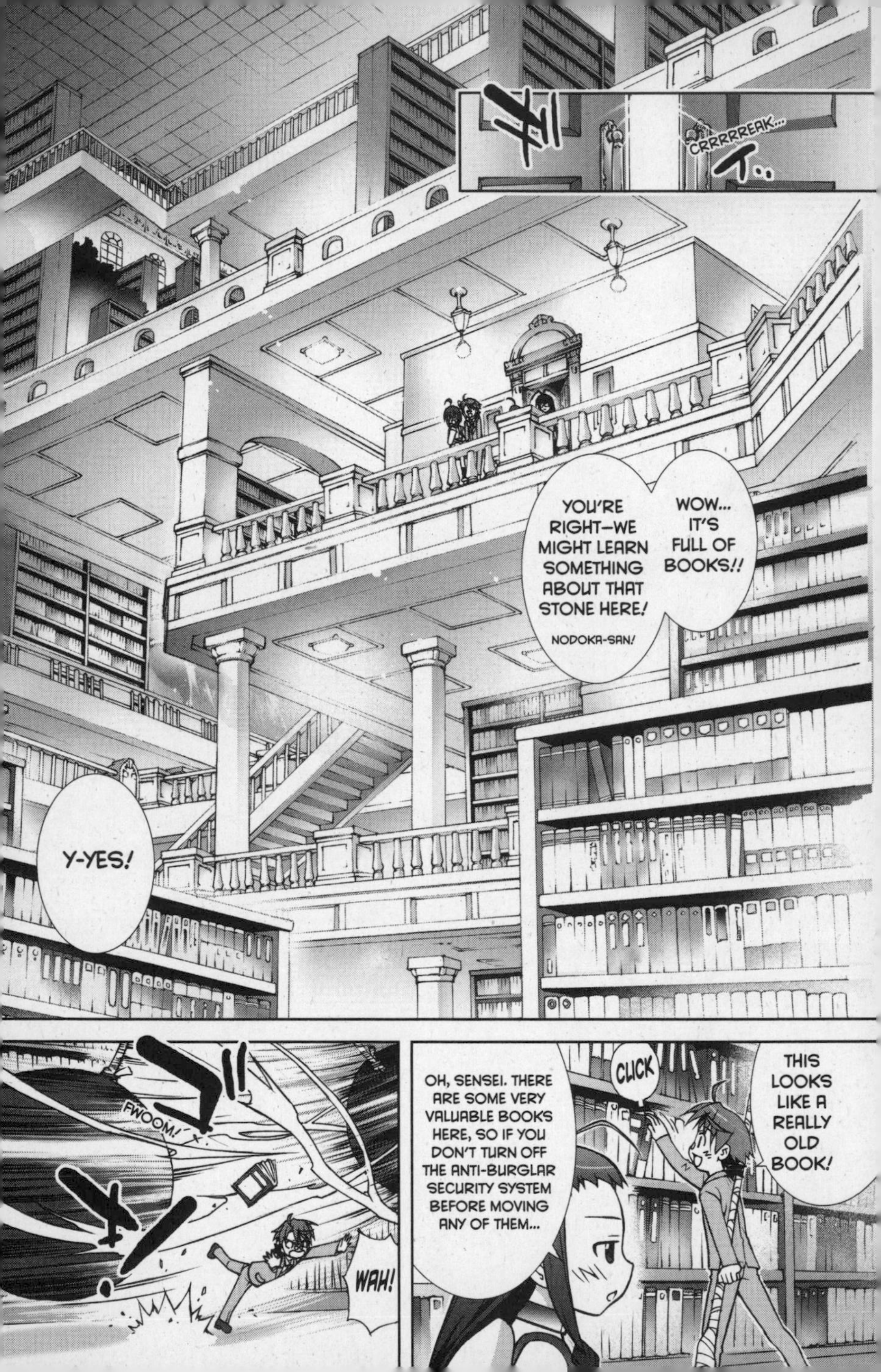
CRRRRREAK...
WOW... IT'S FULL OF BOOKS!!
YOU'RE RIGHT—WE MIGHT LEARN SOMETHING ABOUT THAT STONE HERE! NODOKA-SAN!
Y-YES!
THIS LOOKS LIKE A REALLY OLD BOOK!
CLICK
OH, SENSEI. THERE ARE SOME VERY VALUABLE BOOKS HERE, SO IF YOU DON'T TURN OFF THE ANTI-BURGLAR SECURITY SYSTEM BEFORE MOVING ANY OF THEM...
FWOOM!
WAH!

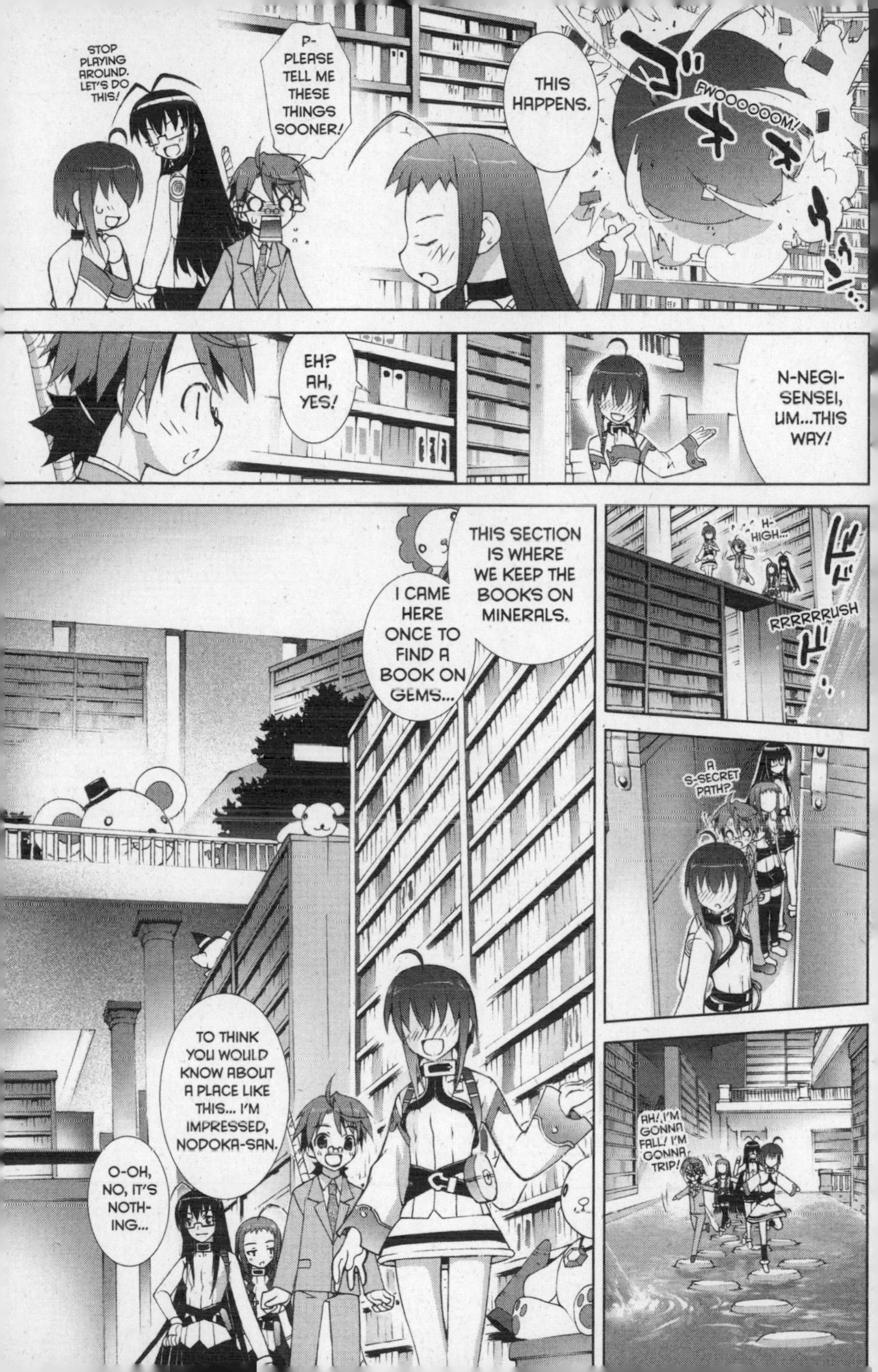
FWOOOOOOOM!
THIS HAPPENS.
P- PLEASE TELL ME THESE THINGS SOONER!
STOP PLAYING AROUND. LET'S DO THIS!
N-NEGI-SENSEI, UM...THIS WAY!
EH? AH, YES!
RRRRRRUSH
H- HIGH...
A S-SECRET PATH?
AH! I'M GONNA FALL! I'M GONNA TRIP!
THIS SECTION IS WHERE WE KEEP THE BOOKS ON MINERALS.
I CAME HERE ONCE TO FIND A BOOK ON GEMS...
TO THINK YOU WOULD KNOW ABOUT A PLACE LIKE THIS... I'M IMPRESSED, NODOKA-SAN.
O-OH, NO, IT'S NOTHING...

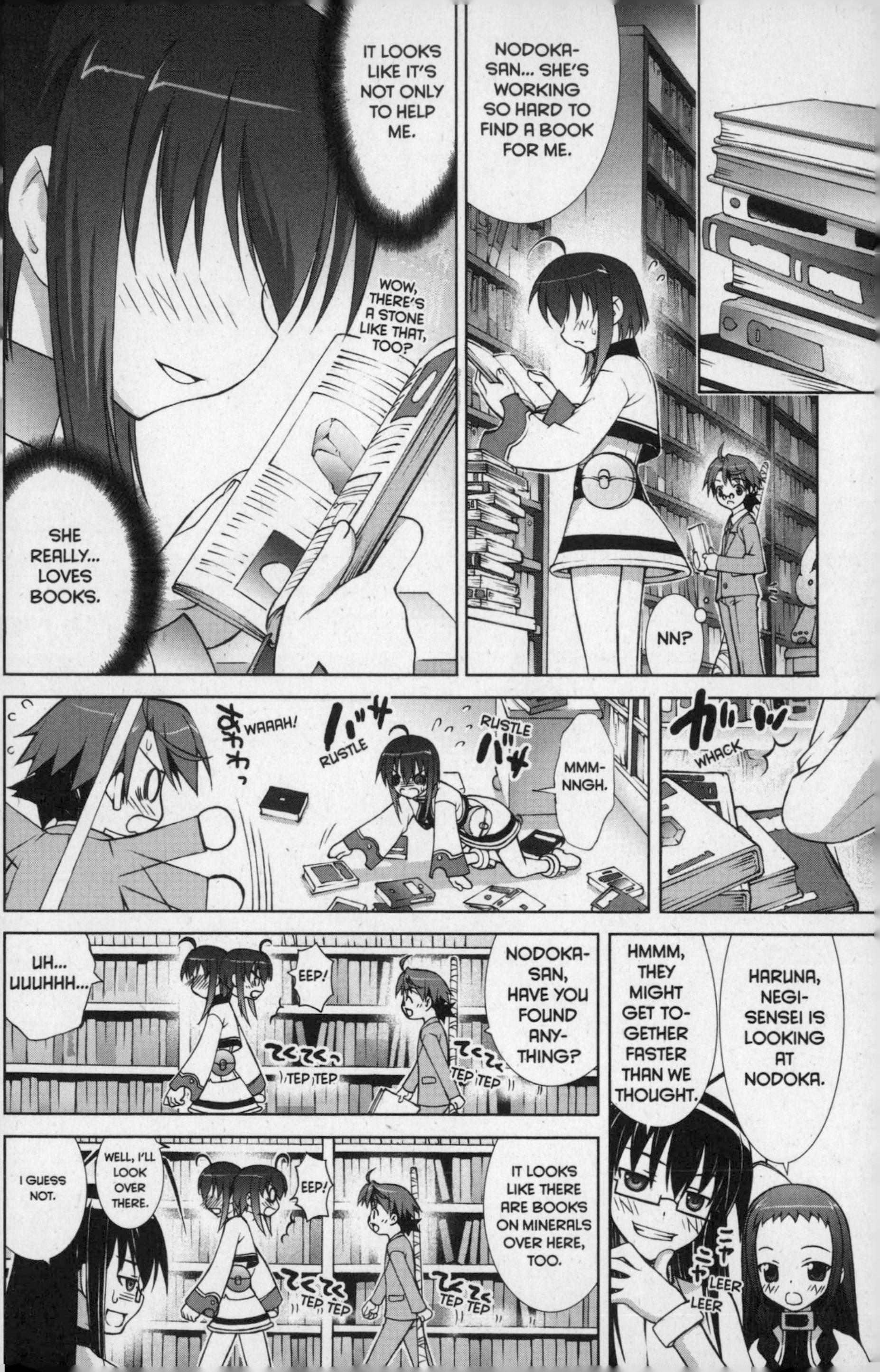
NODOKA-SAN... SHE'S WORKING SO HARD TO FIND A BOOK FOR ME.
NN?
IT LOOKS LIKE IT'S NOT ONLY TO HELP ME.
WOW, THERE'S A STONE LIKE THAT, TOO?
SHE REALLY... LOVES BOOKS.
WHACK
RUSTLE
RUSTLE
MMM-NNGH.
WAAAH!
HARUNA, NEGI-SENSEI IS LOOKING AT NODOKA.
HMMM, THEY MIGHT GET TO-GETHER FASTER THAN WE THOUGHT.
LEER LEER
NODOKA-SAN, HAVE YOU FOUND ANY-THING?
TEP TEP
EEP!
TEP TEP
UH... UUUHHH...
IT LOOKS LIKE THERE ARE BOOKS ON MINERALS OVER HERE, TOO.
TEP TEP
EEP!
TEP TEP
WELL, I'LL LOOK OVER THERE.
I GUESS NOT.

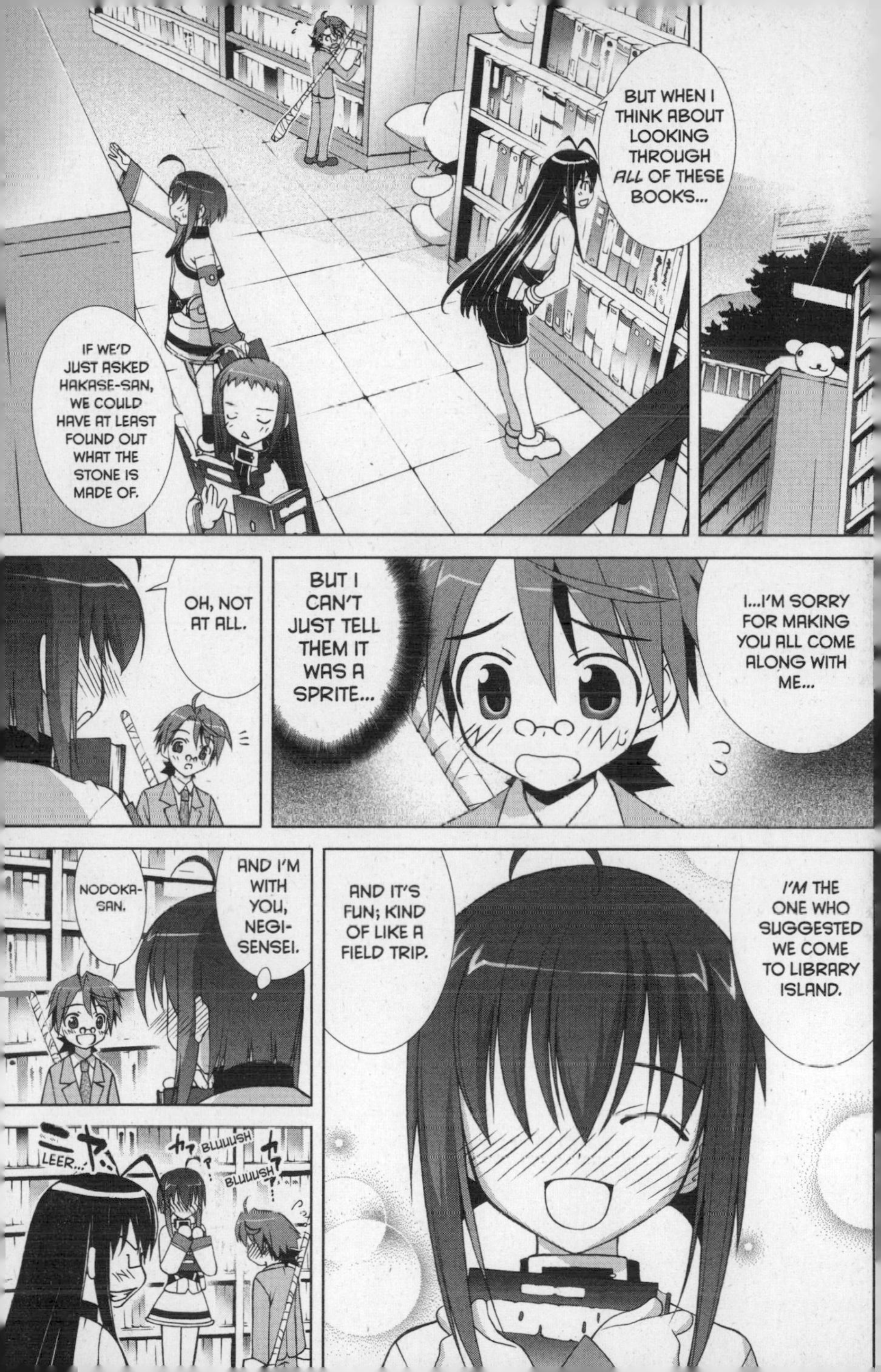
BUT WHEN I THINK ABOUT LOOKING THROUGH *ALL* OF THESE BOOKS...
IF WE'D JUST ASKED HAKASE-SAN, WE COULD HAVE AT LEAST FOUND OUT WHAT THE STONE IS MADE OF.
I...I'M SORRY FOR MAKING YOU ALL COME ALONG WITH ME...
BUT I CAN'T JUST TELL THEM IT WAS A SPRITE...
OH, NOT AT ALL.
I'M THE ONE WHO SUGGESTED WE COME TO LIBRARY ISLAND.
AND IT'S FUN; KIND OF LIKE A FIELD TRIP.
AND I'M WITH YOU, NEGI-SENSEI.
NODOKA-SAN.
LEER...
BLUUUSH
BLUUUSH

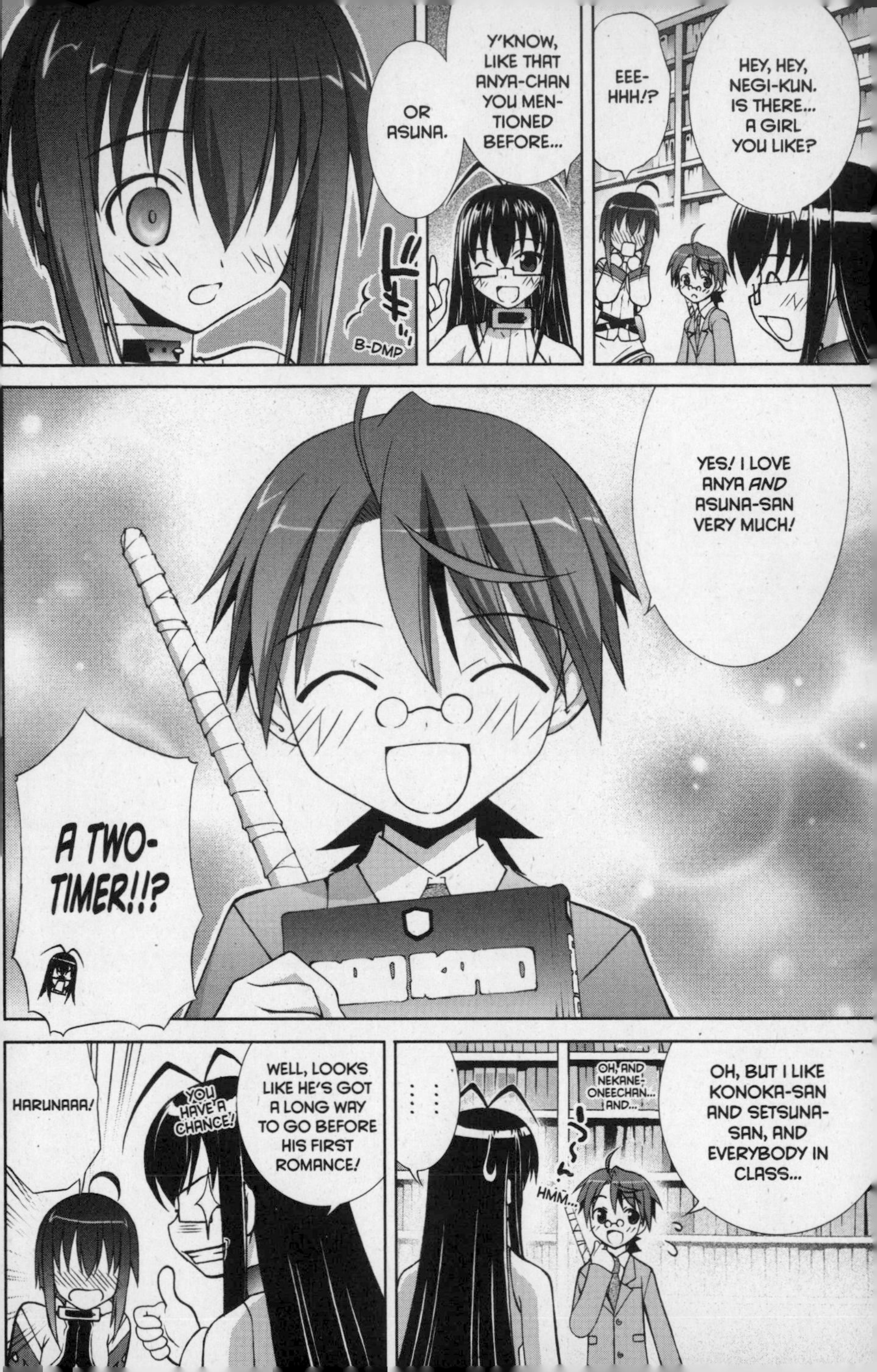
HEY, HEY, NEGI-KUN. IS THERE... A GIRL YOU LIKE?
EEE-HHH!?
Y'KNOW, LIKE THAT ANYA-CHAN YOU MEN-TIONED BEFORE...
OR ASUNA.
B-DMP
YES! I LOVE ANYA *AND* ASUNA-SAN VERY MUCH!
A TWO-TIMER!!?
OH, BUT I LIKE KONOKA-SAN AND SETSUNA-SAN, AND EVERYBODY IN CLASS...
OH, AND NEKANE-ONEECHAN... AND...
HMM...
......
WELL, LOOKS LIKE HE'S GOT A LONG WAY TO GO BEFORE HIS FIRST ROMANCE!
YOU HAVE A CHANCE!
HARUNAAA!

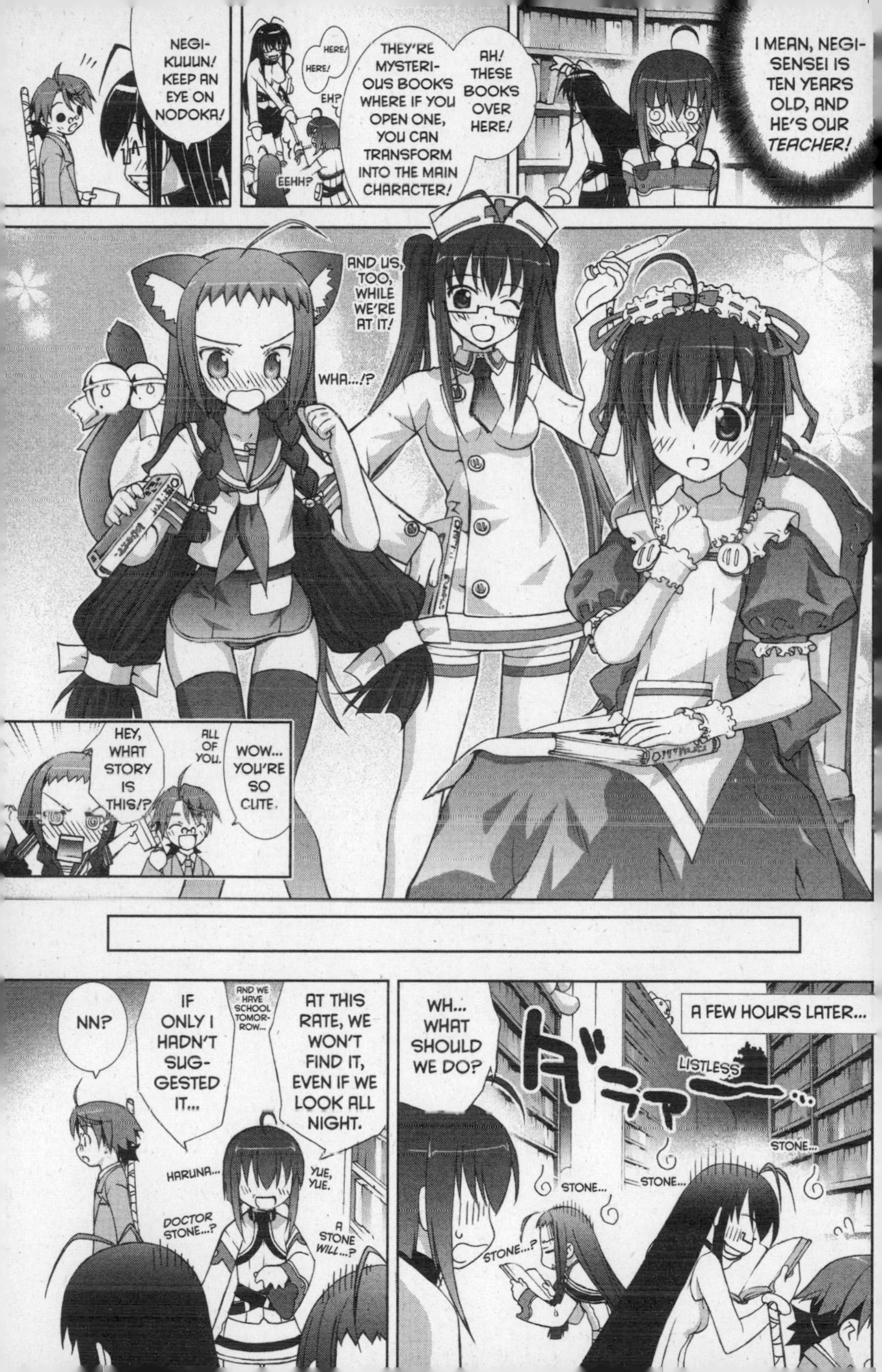
I MEAN, NEGI-SENSEI IS TEN YEARS OLD, AND HE'S OUR *TEACHER*!
AH! THESE BOOKS OVER HERE!
THEY'RE MYSTERIOUS BOOKS WHERE IF YOU OPEN ONE, YOU CAN TRANSFORM INTO THE MAIN CHARACTER!
HERE!
HERE!
EH?
EEHH?
NEGI-KUUUN! KEEP AN EYE ON NODOKA!
AND US, TOO, WHILE WE'RE AT IT!
WHA...!?
WOW... YOU'RE SO CUTE.
ALL OF YOU.
HEY, WHAT STORY IS THIS!?
A FEW HOURS LATER...
LISTLESS
STONE...
STONE...
STONE...
STONE...?
WH... WHAT SHOULD WE DO?
AT THIS RATE, WE WON'T FIND IT, EVEN IF WE LOOK ALL NIGHT.
AND WE HAVE SCHOOL TOMORROW...
IF ONLY I HADN'T SUGGESTED IT...
NN?
YUE, YUE.
HARUNA...
A STONE *WILL*...?
DOCTOR STONE...?

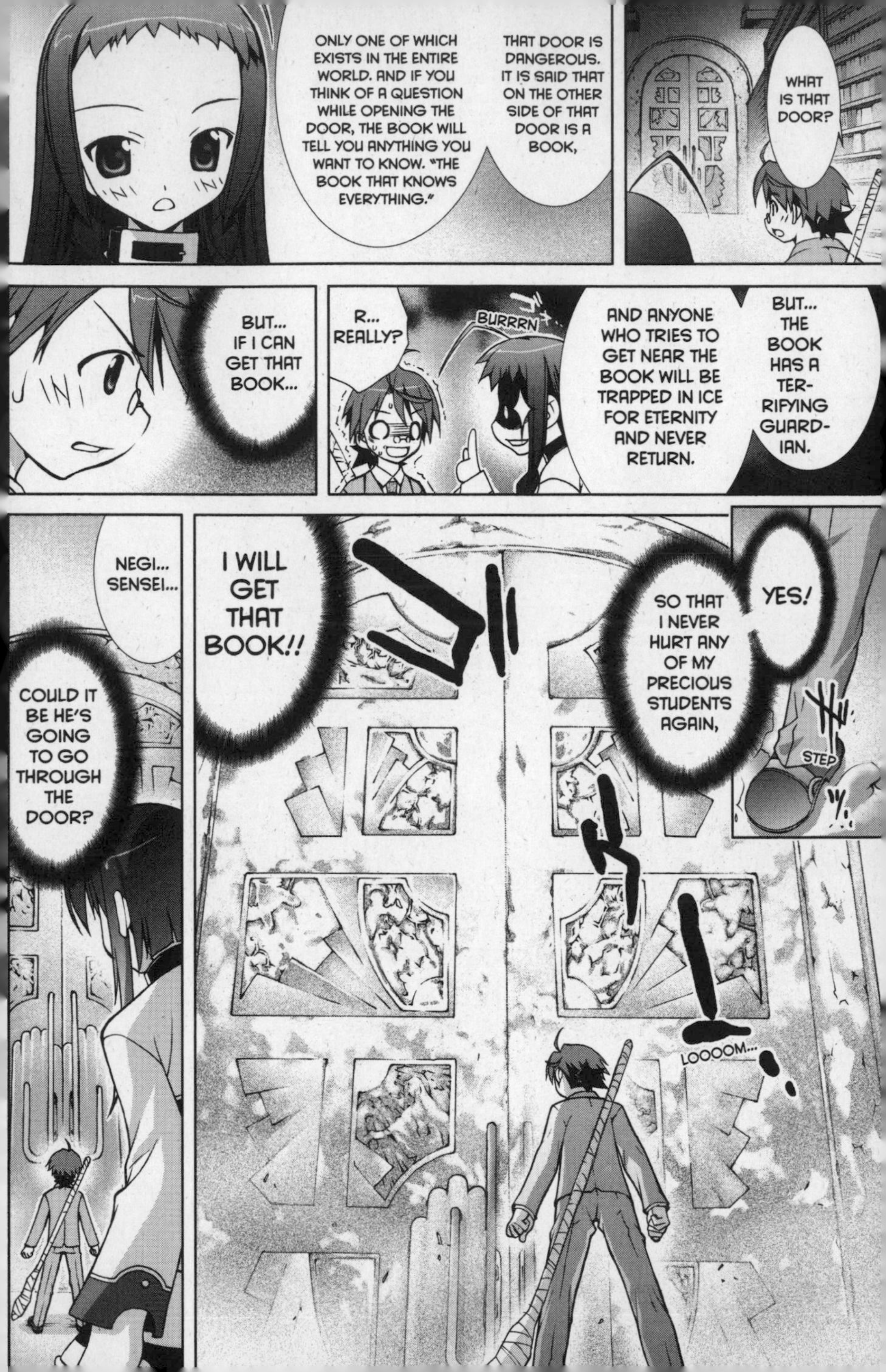
WHAT IS THAT DOOR?
THAT DOOR IS DANGEROUS. IT IS SAID THAT ON THE OTHER SIDE OF THAT DOOR IS A BOOK,
ONLY ONE OF WHICH EXISTS IN THE ENTIRE WORLD. AND IF YOU THINK OF A QUESTION WHILE OPENING THE DOOR, THE BOOK WILL TELL YOU ANYTHING YOU WANT TO KNOW. "THE BOOK THAT KNOWS EVERYTHING."
BUT... THE BOOK HAS A TER-RIFYING GUARD-IAN.
AND ANYONE WHO TRIES TO GET NEAR THE BOOK WILL BE TRAPPED IN ICE FOR ETERNITY AND NEVER RETURN.
BURRRN
R... REALLY?
BUT... IF I CAN GET THAT BOOK...
YES!
SO THAT I NEVER HURT ANY OF MY PRECIOUS STUDENTS AGAIN,
STEP
I WILL GET THAT BOOK!!
LOOOOM...
NEGI... SENSEI...
COULD IT BE HE'S GOING TO GO THROUGH THE DOOR?

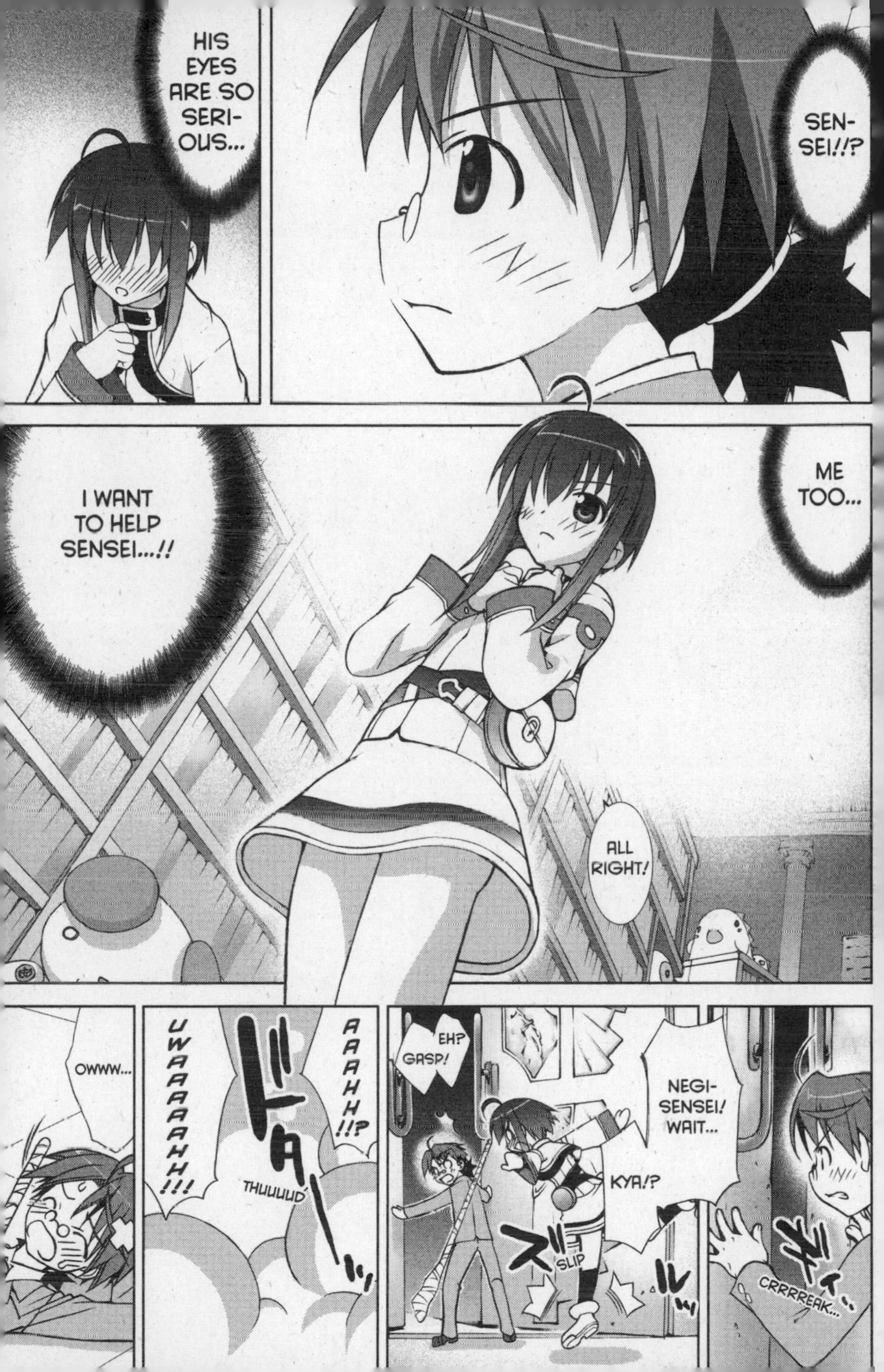
SEN-SEI!!?
HIS EYES ARE SO SERI-OUS...
ME TOO...
I WANT TO HELP SENSEI...!!
ALL RIGHT!
CRRRREAK...
NEGI-SENSEI! WAIT...
EH? GASP!
KYA!?
SLIP
AAAAHH!!?
UWAAAAAAAHH!!!
THUUUUD
OWWW...

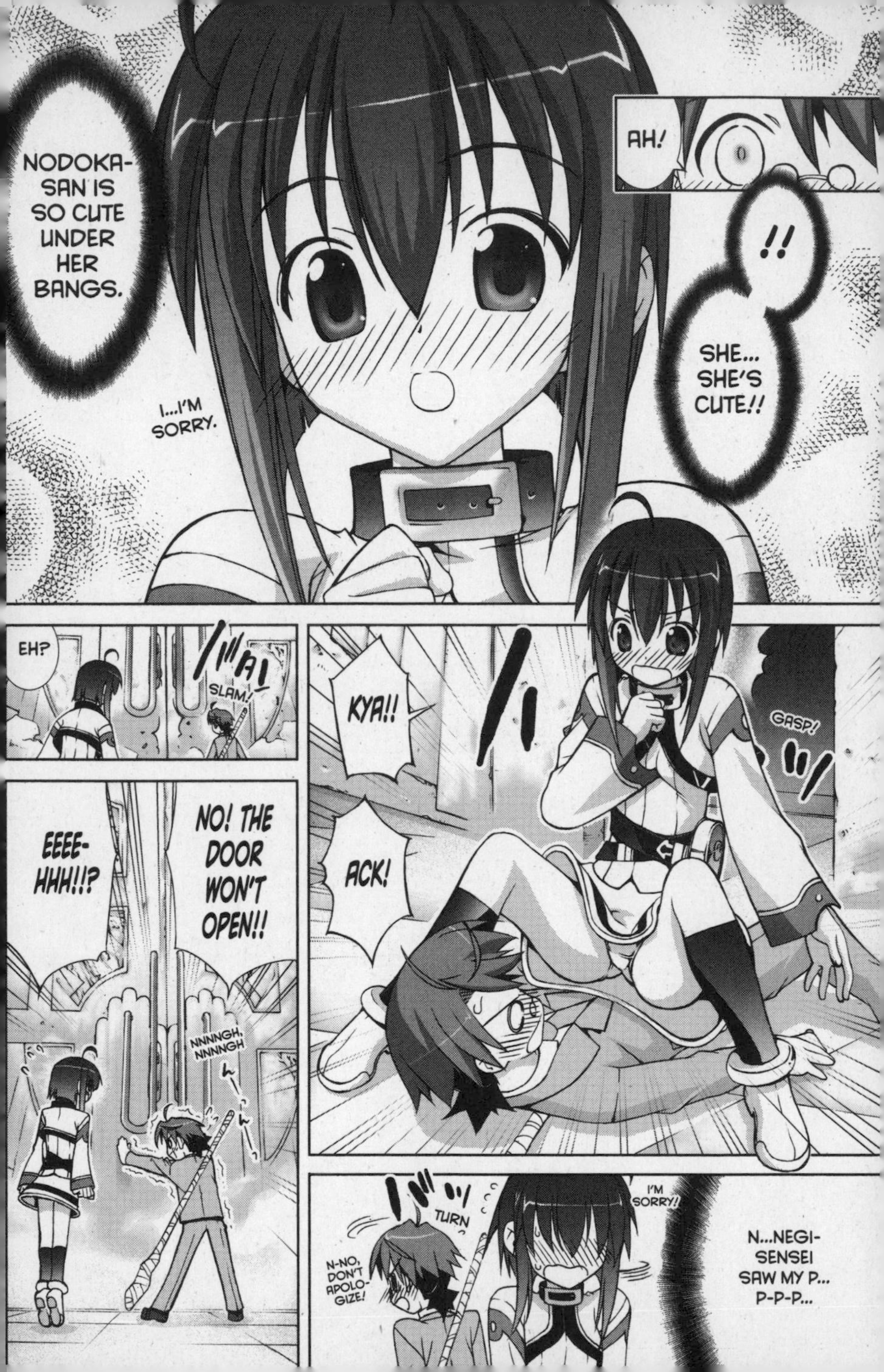

AH!
!!
SHE... SHE'S CUTE!!
NODOKA-SAN IS SO CUTE UNDER HER BANGS.
I...I'M SORRY.
KYA!!
GASP!
ACK!
I'M SORRY!
N...NEGI-SENSEI SAW MY P... P-P-P...
TURN
N-NO, DON'T APOLOGIZE!
EH?
SLAM!
NO! THE DOOR WON'T OPEN!!
EEEE-HHH!!?
NNNNGH, NNNNGH

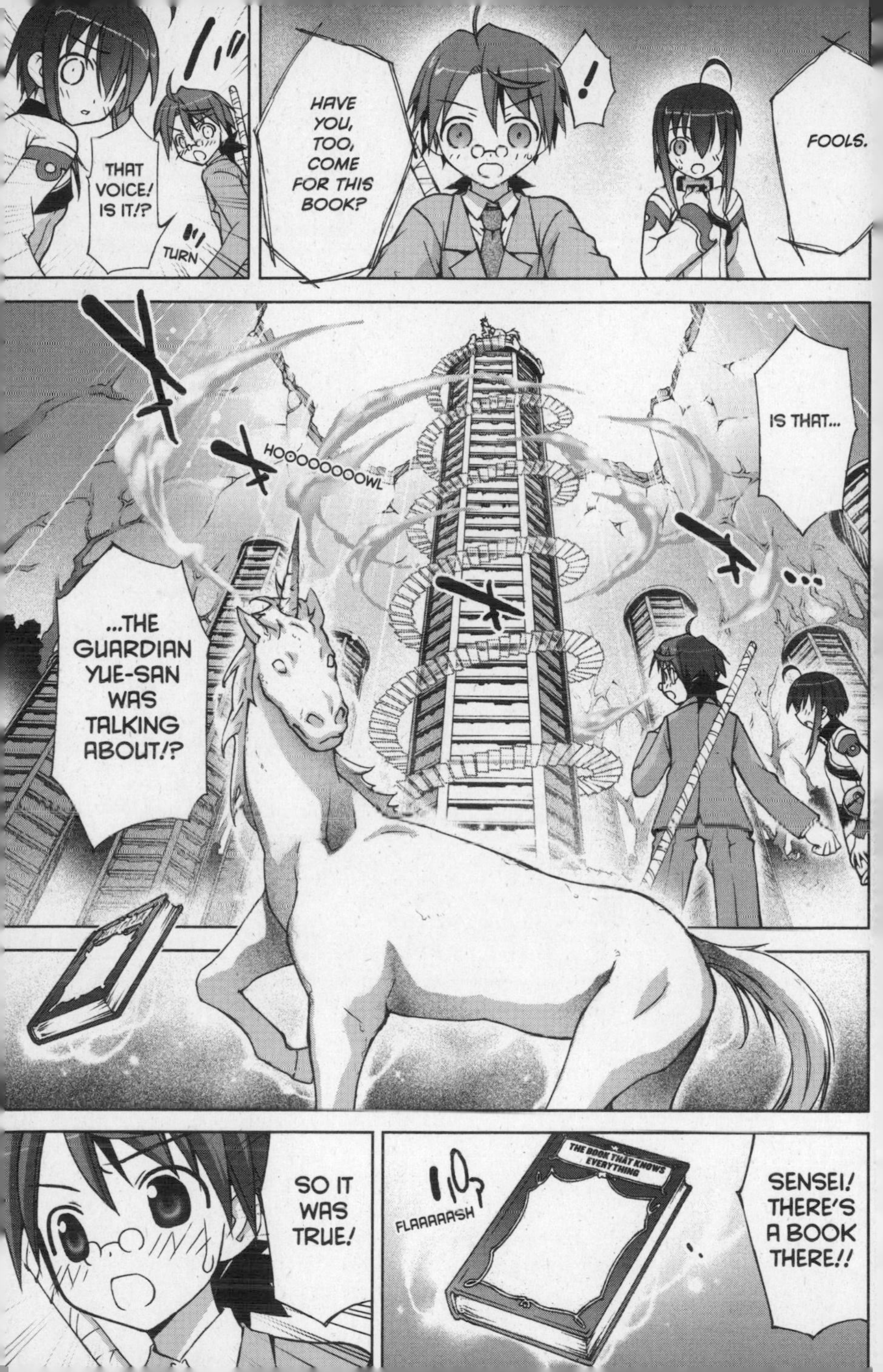
FOOLS.
!
HAVE YOU, TOO, COME FOR THIS BOOK?
THAT VOICE! IS IT!?
TURN
IS THAT...
...
HOOOOOOOOWL
...THE GUARDIAN YUE-SAN WAS TALKING ABOUT!?
SENSEI! THERE'S A BOOK THERE!!
THE BOOK THAT KNOWS EVERYTHING
FLAAAAAASH
SO IT WAS TRUE!

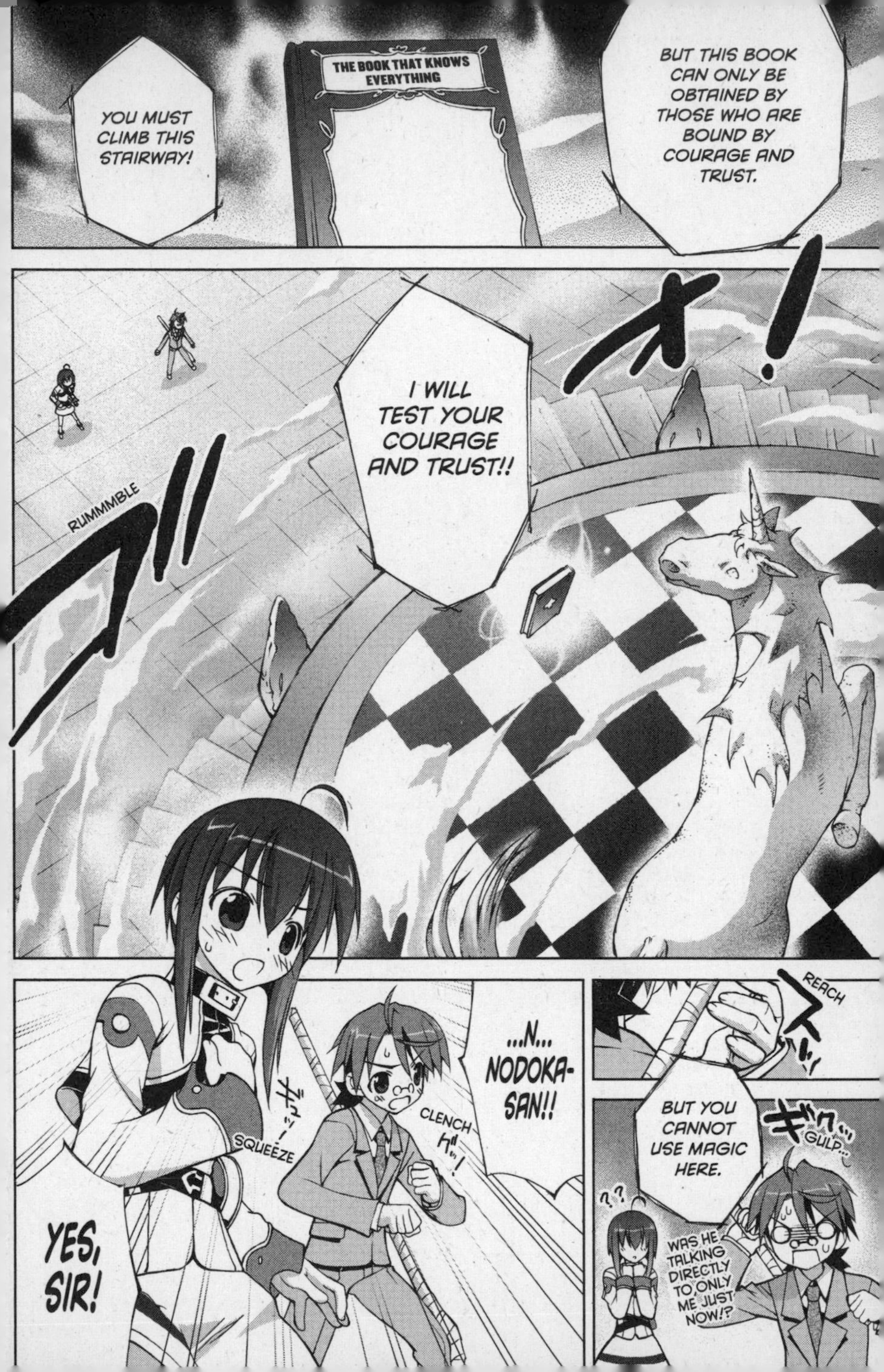
BUT THIS BOOK CAN ONLY BE OBTAINED BY THOSE WHO ARE BOUND BY COURAGE AND TRUST.
THE BOOK THAT KNOWS EVERYTHING
YOU MUST CLIMB THIS STAIRWAY!
I WILL TEST YOUR COURAGE AND TRUST!!
RUMMMBLE
REACH
BUT YOU CANNOT USE MAGIC HERE.
GULP...
??
WAS HE TALKING DIRECTLY TO ONLY ME JUST NOW!?
...N... NODOKA-SAN!!
CLENCH
SQUEEZE
YES, SIR!

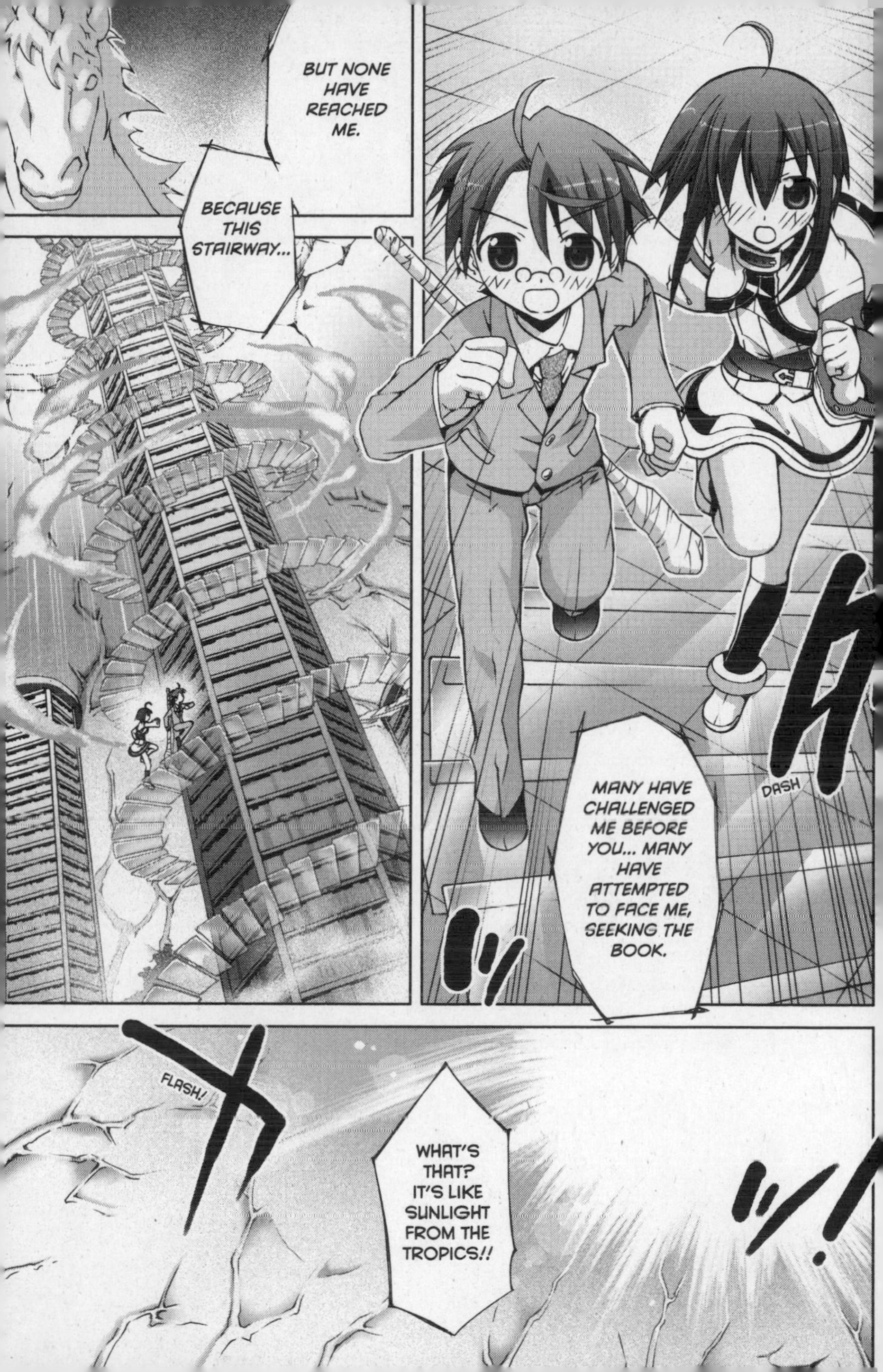
MANY HAVE CHALLENGED ME BEFORE YOU... MANY HAVE ATTEMPTED TO FACE ME, SEEKING THE BOOK.
DASH
BUT NONE HAVE REACHED ME.
BECAUSE THIS STAIRWAY...
FLASH!
WHAT'S THAT? IT'S LIKE SUNLIGHT FROM THE TROPICS!!

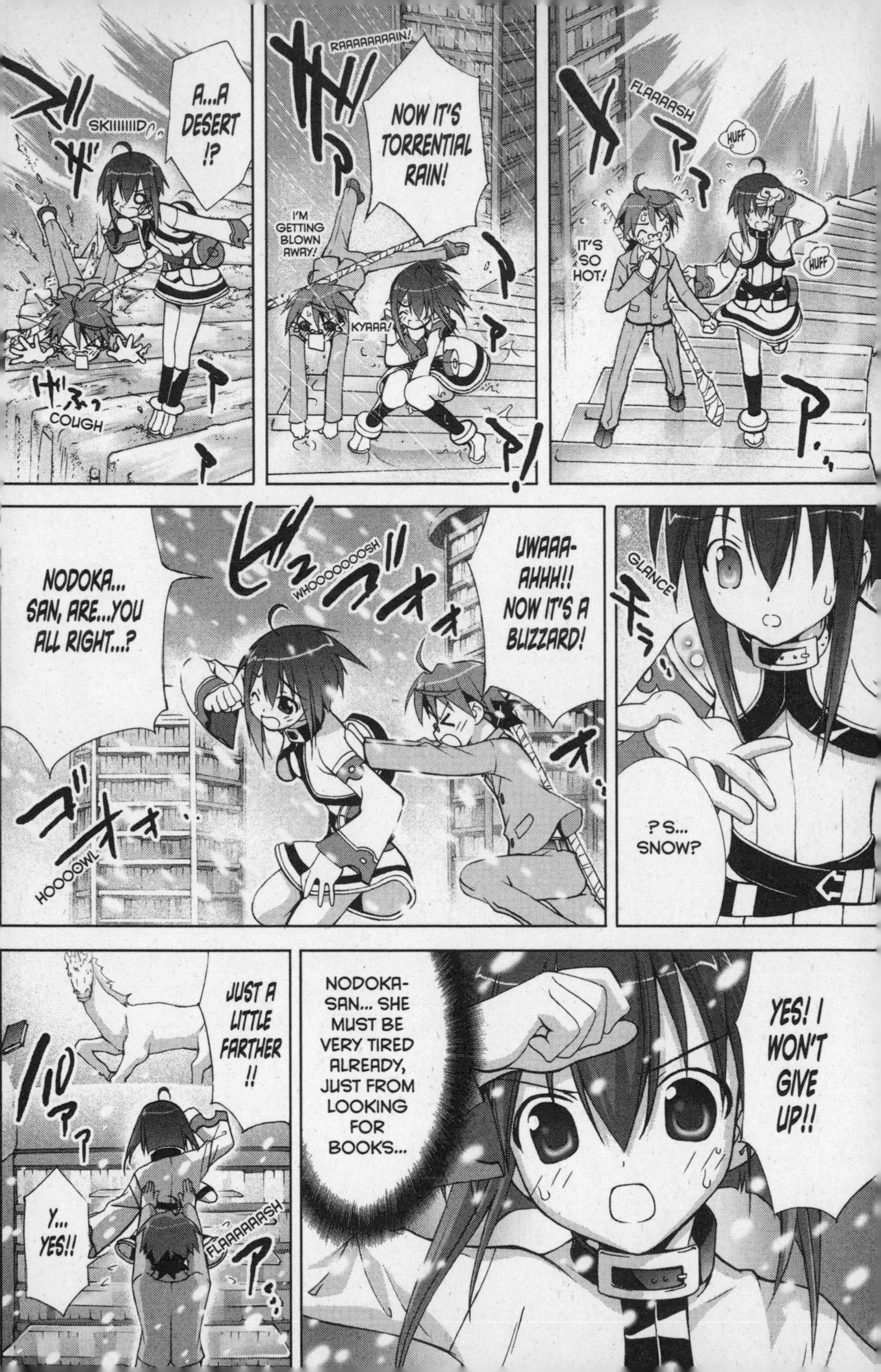
FLAAAAASH
HUFF
HUFF
IT'S SO HOT!
RAAAAAAAAIN!
NOW IT'S TORRENTIAL RAIN!
I'M GETTING BLOWN AWAY!
KYAAA!
SKIIIIIID
A...A DESERT !?
COUGH
GLANCE
?S... SNOW?
WHOOOOOOOOSH
UWAAA-AHHH!! NOW IT'S A BLIZZARD!
NODOKA... SAN, ARE...YOU ALL RIGHT...?
HOOOOWL
YES! I WON'T GIVE UP!!
NODOKA-SAN... SHE MUST BE VERY TIRED ALREADY, JUST FROM LOOKING FOR BOOKS...
JUST A LITTLE FARTHER !!
Y... YES!!
FLAAAAAASH

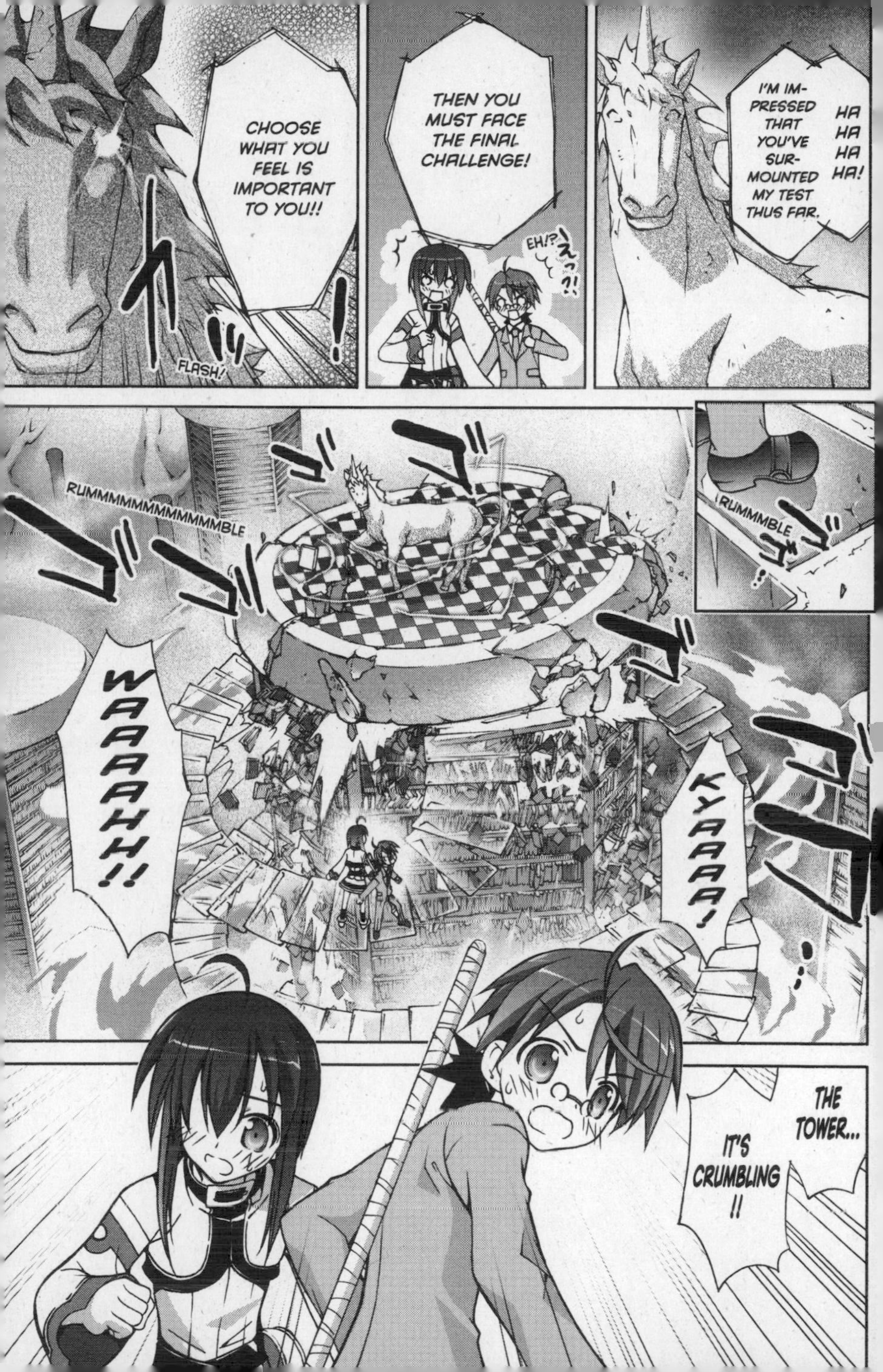
HA HA HA HA!
I'M IMPRESSED THAT YOU'VE SURMOUNTED MY TEST THUS FAR.
THEN YOU MUST FACE THE FINAL CHALLENGE!
EH!?
えっ?!
CHOOSE WHAT YOU FEEL IS IMPORTANT TO YOU!!
FLASH!
RUMMMBLE
RUMMMMMMMMMMMMBLE
KYAAAAA!
WAAAAAHH!!
THE TOWER...
IT'S CRUMBLING!!

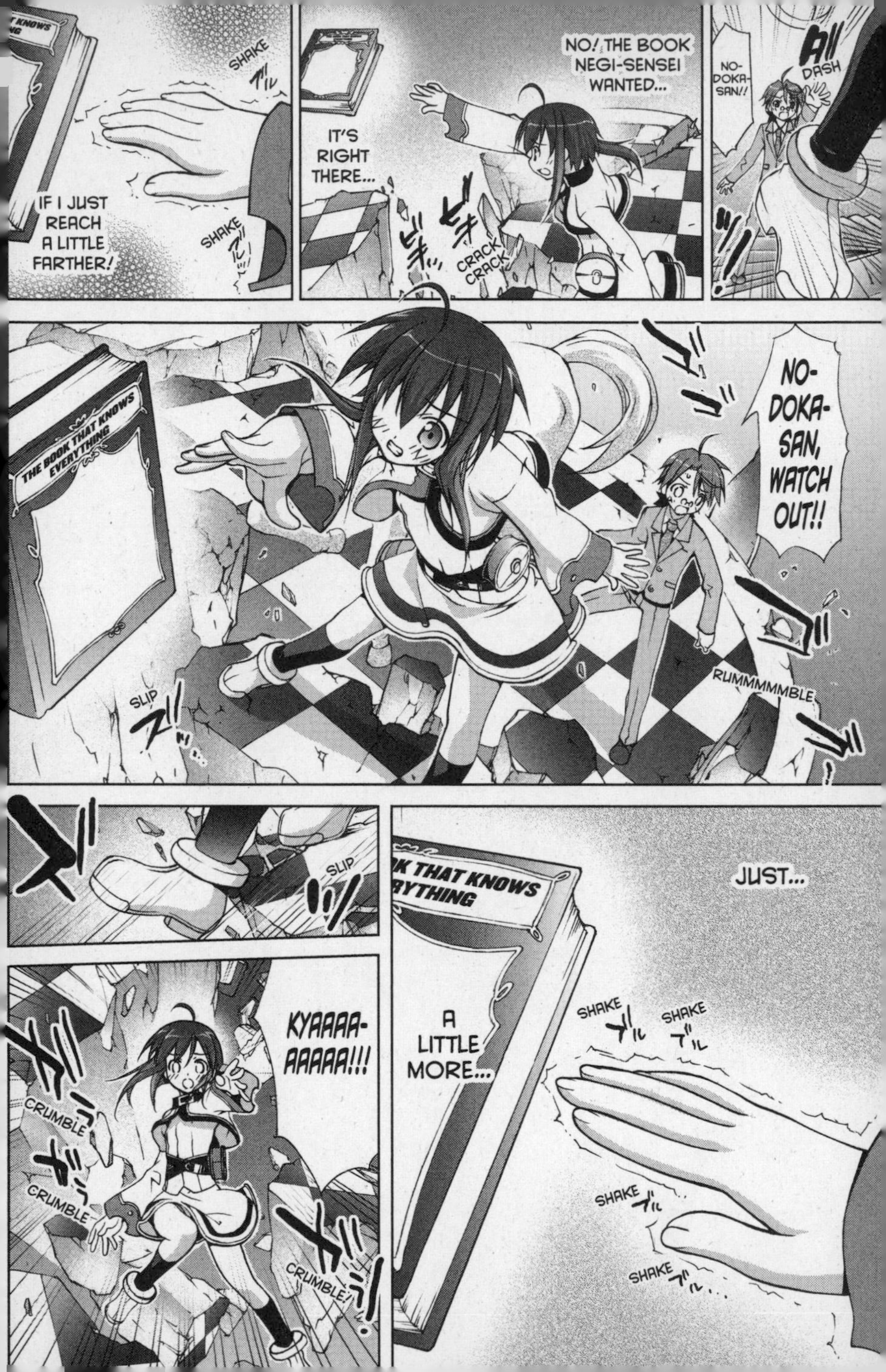
NO-DOKA-SAN!!
DASH
NO! THE BOOK NEGI-SENSEI WANTED...
IT'S RIGHT THERE...
CRACK CRACK
SHAKE
IF I JUST REACH A LITTLE FARTHER!
SHAKE
NO-DOKA-SAN, WATCH OUT!!
THE BOOK THAT KNOWS EVERYTHING
RUMMMMMBLE
SLIP
JUST...
A LITTLE MORE...
SHAKE
SHAKE
SHAKE
SHAKE
SLIP
KYAAAA-AAAAA!!!
CRUMBLE
CRUMBLE
CRUMBLE!

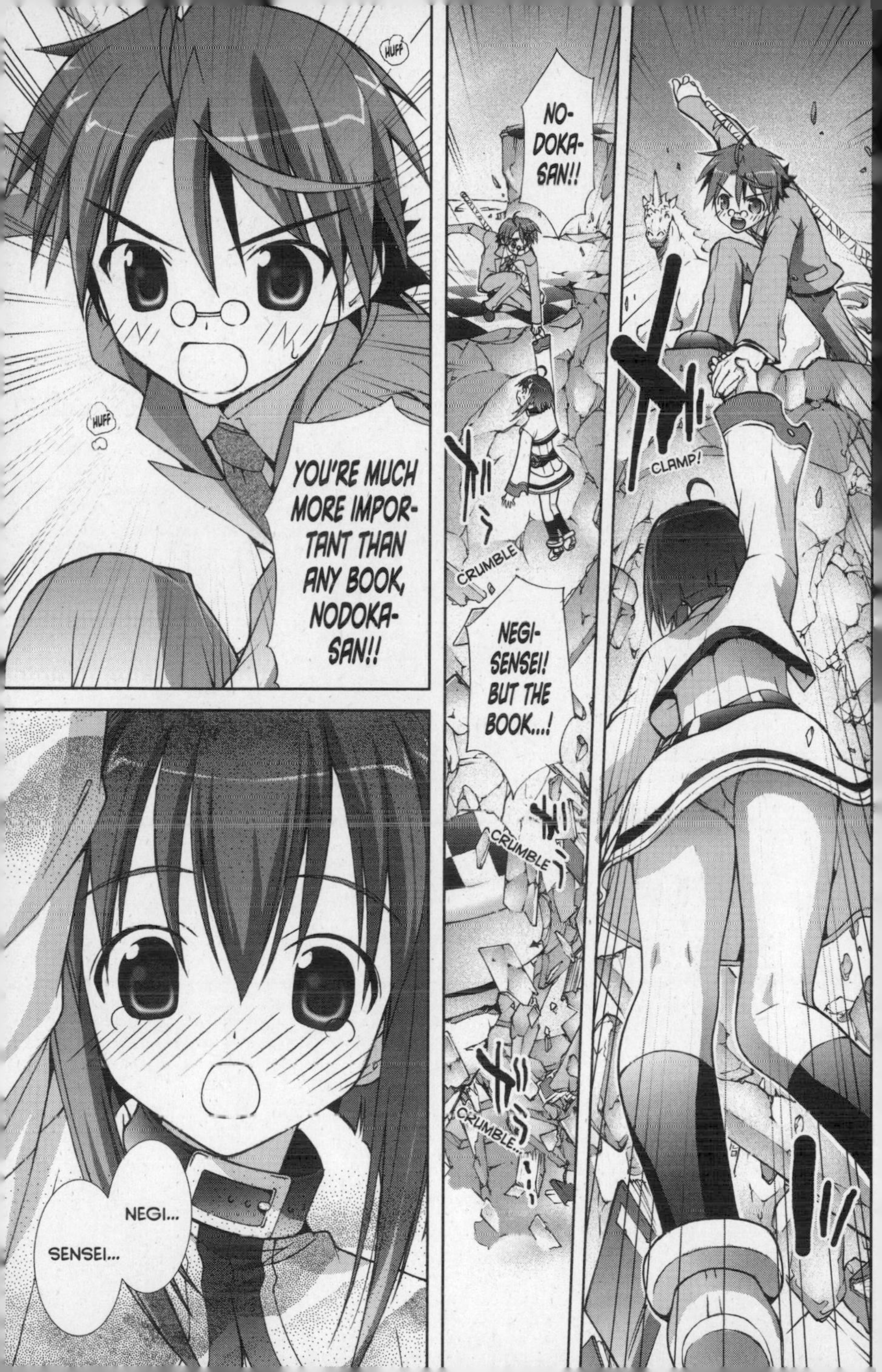
CLAMP!
NO-DOKA-SAN!!
CRUMBLE
NEGI-SENSEI! BUT THE BOOK...!
CRUMBLE
CRUMBLE...
HUFF
HUFF
YOU'RE MUCH MORE IMPOR-TANT THAN ANY BOOK, NODOKA-SAN!!
NEGI... SENSEI...

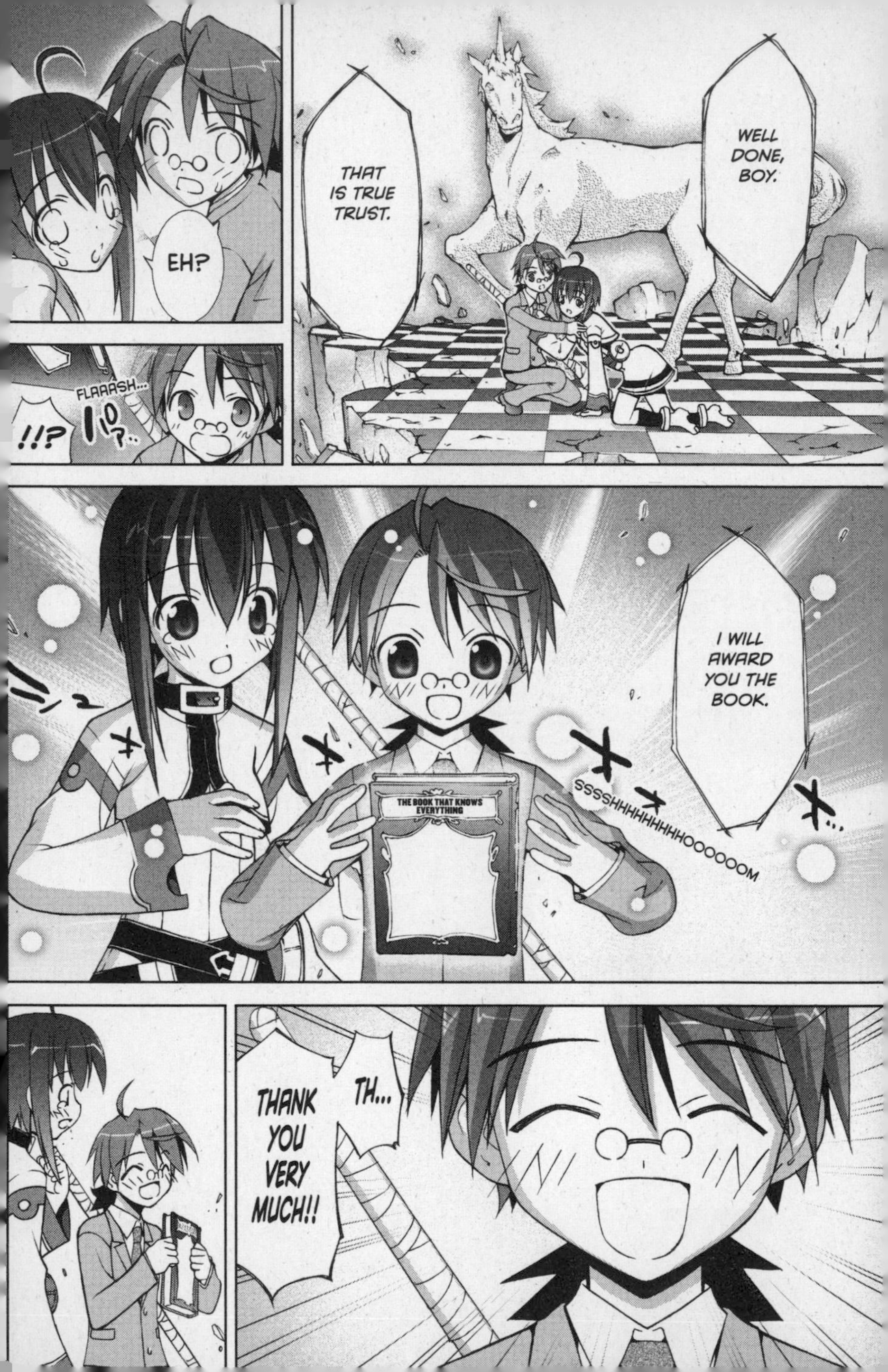
WELL DONE, BOY.
THAT IS TRUE TRUST.
EH?
FLAAASH...
!!?
I WILL AWARD YOU THE BOOK.
SSSSHHHHHHHHHHOOOOOOOM
THE BOOK THAT KNOWS EVERYTHING
TH...
THANK YOU VERY MUCH!!

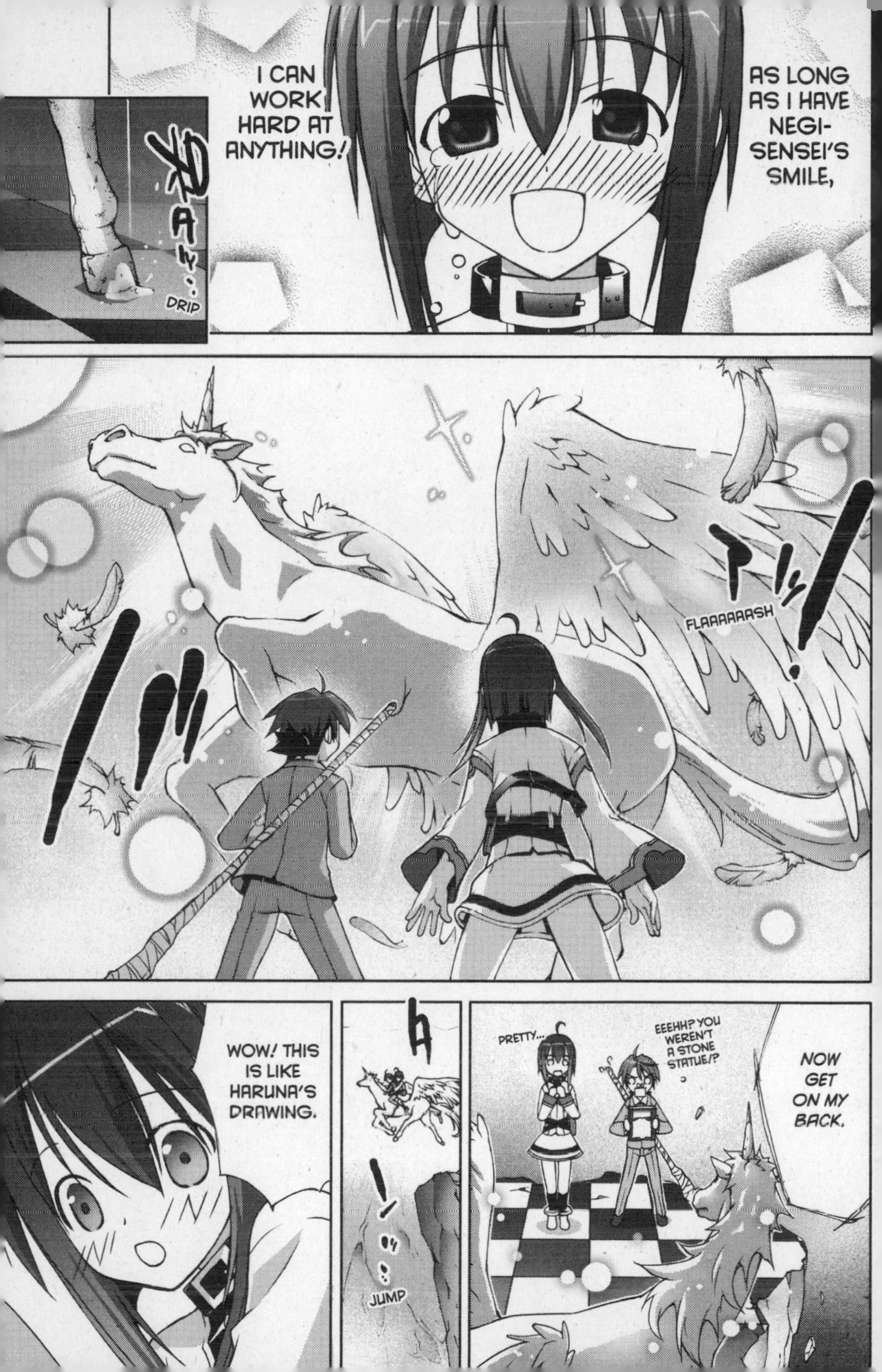
AS LONG AS I HAVE NEGI-SENSEI'S SMILE,
I CAN WORK HARD AT ANYTHING!
DRIP
FLAAAAAAASH
NOW GET ON MY BACK.
EEEHH? YOU WEREN'T A STONE STATUE!?
PRETTY...
JUMP
WOW! THIS IS LIKE HARUNA'S DRAWING.

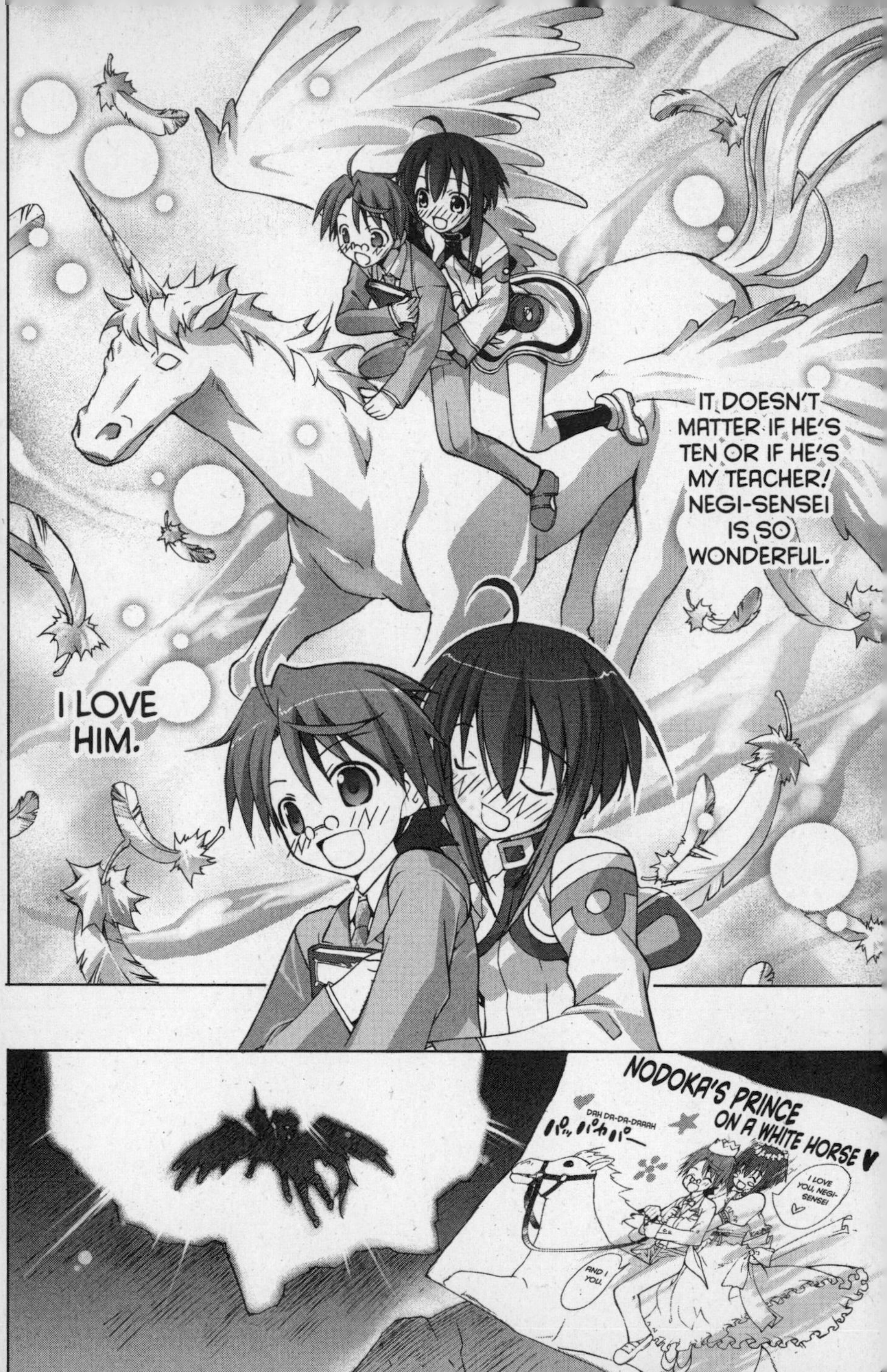
IT DOESN'T MATTER IF HE'S TEN OR IF HE'S MY TEACHER! NEGI-SENSEI IS SO WONDERFUL.
I LOVE HIM.
NODOKA'S PRINCE ON A WHITE HORSE ♥
DAH DA-DA-DAAAH
パッパカパー
I LOVE YOU, NEGI-SENSEI
AND I YOU.

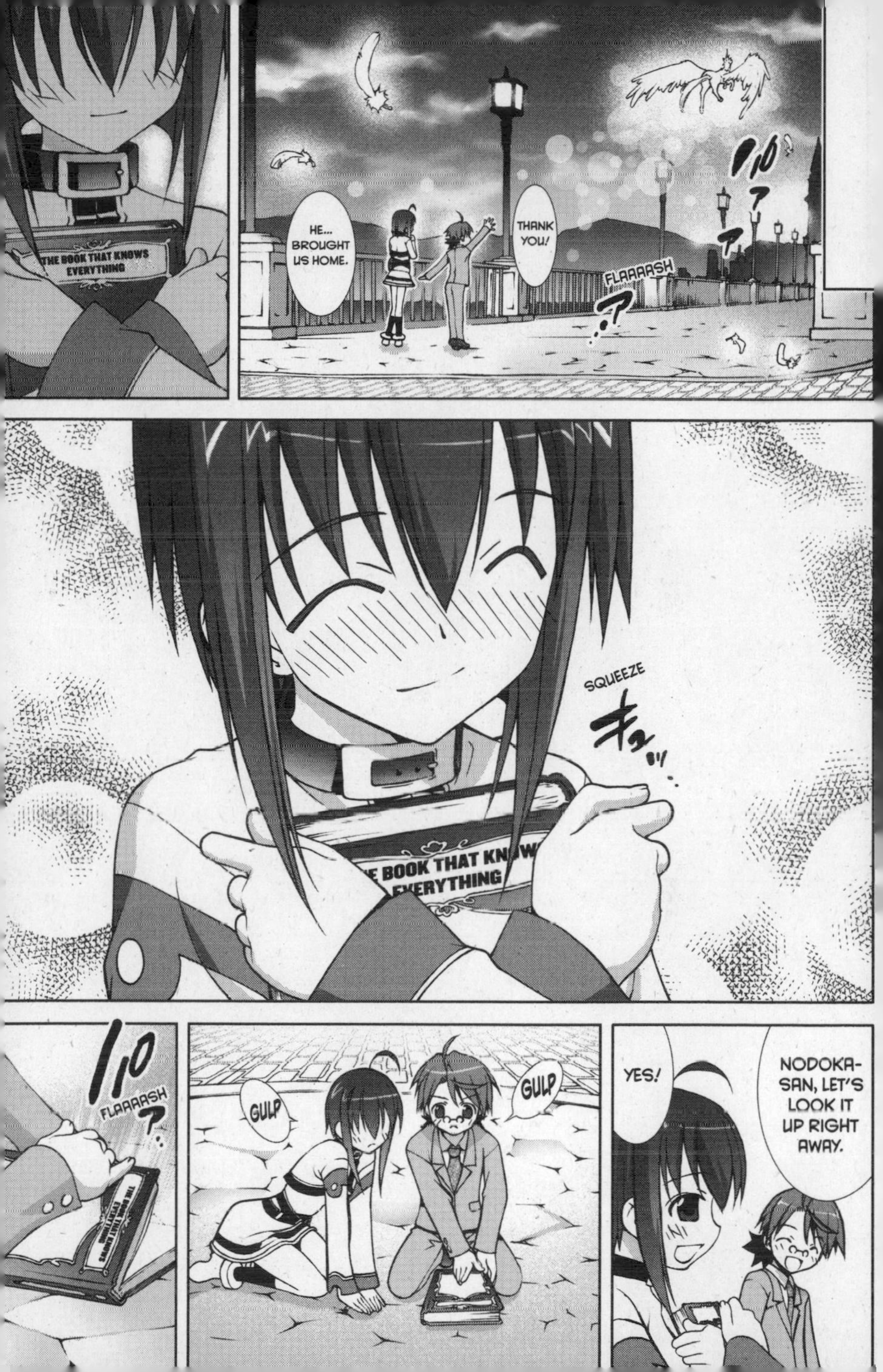
THANK YOU!
HE... BROUGHT US HOME.
FLAAAASH
THE BOOK THAT KNOWS EVERYTHING
SQUEEZE
E BOOK THAT KNOW
EVERYTHING
NODOKA-SAN, LET'S LOOK IT UP RIGHT AWAY.
YES!
GULP
GULP
FLAAAASH

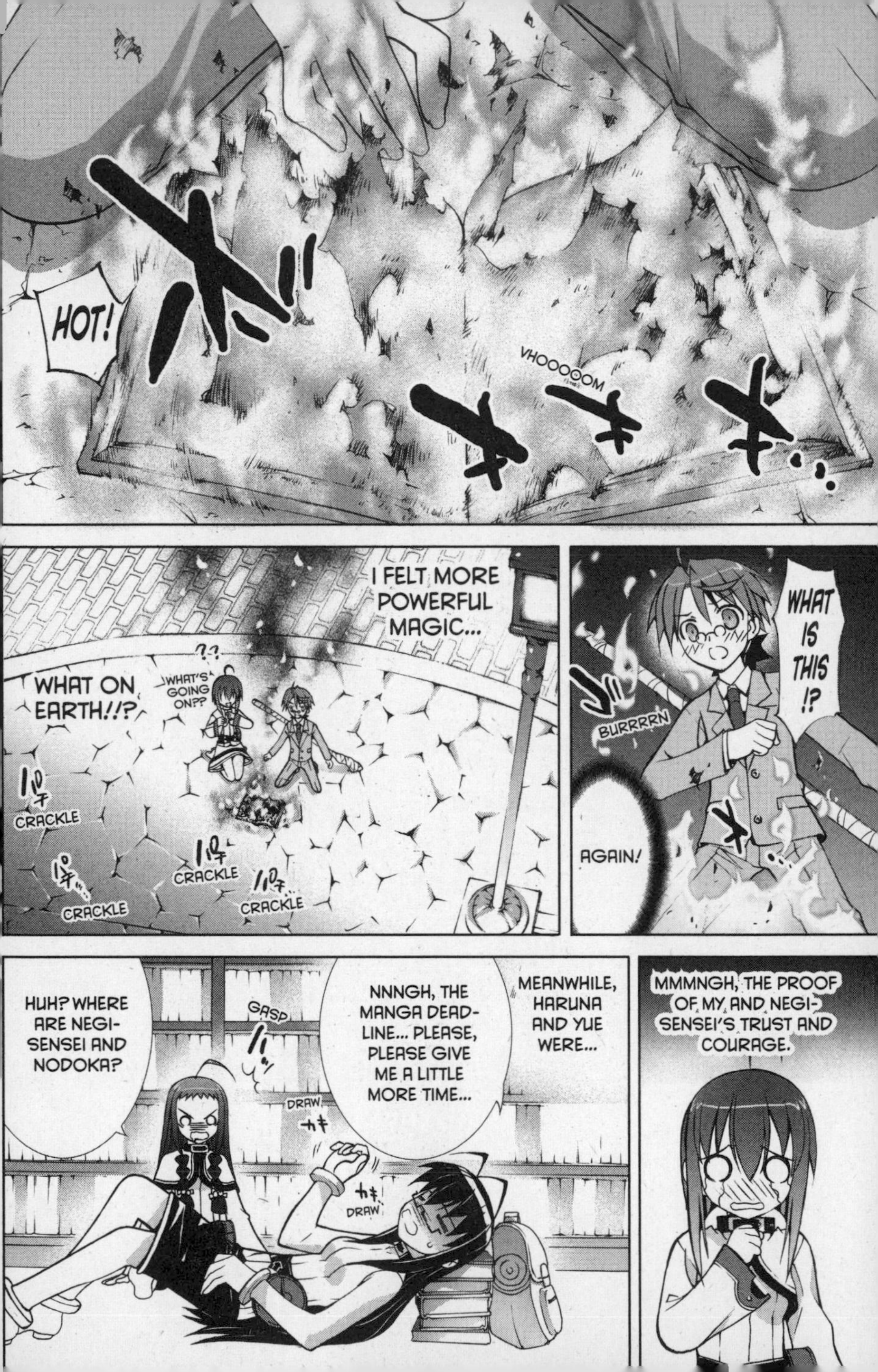
HOT!
VHOOOOOM
WHAT IS THIS !?
BURRRRN
AGAIN!
I FELT MORE POWERFUL MAGIC...
??
WHAT'S GOING ON??
WHAT ON EARTH!!?
CRACKLE
CRACKLE
CRACKLE
CRACKLE
MMMNGH, THE PROOF OF MY AND NEGI-SENSEI'S TRUST AND COURAGE.
MEANWHILE, HARUNA AND YUE WERE...
NNNGH, THE MANGA DEAD-LINE... PLEASE, PLEASE GIVE ME A LITTLE MORE TIME...
GASP
DRAW
DRAW
HUH? WHERE ARE NEGI-SENSEI AND NODOKA?

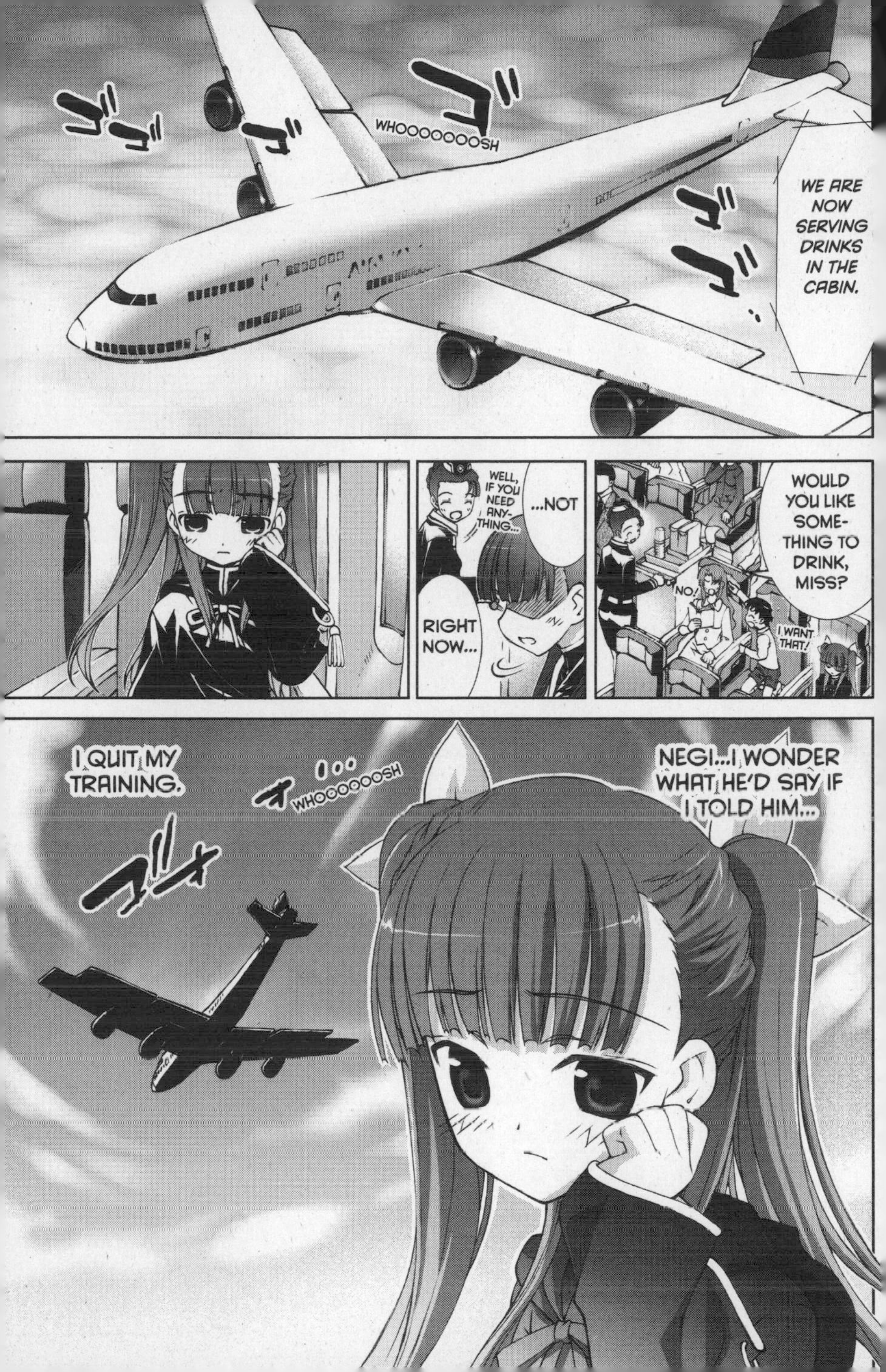
WHOOOOOOOOSH
WE ARE NOW SERVING DRINKS IN THE CABIN.
WOULD YOU LIKE SOME-THING TO DRINK, MISS?
NO!
I WANT THAT!
...NOT RIGHT NOW...
WELL, IF YOU NEED ANY-THING...
NEGI...I WONDER WHAT HE'D SAY IF I TOLD HIM...
I QUIT MY TRAINING.
WHOOOOOOOSH

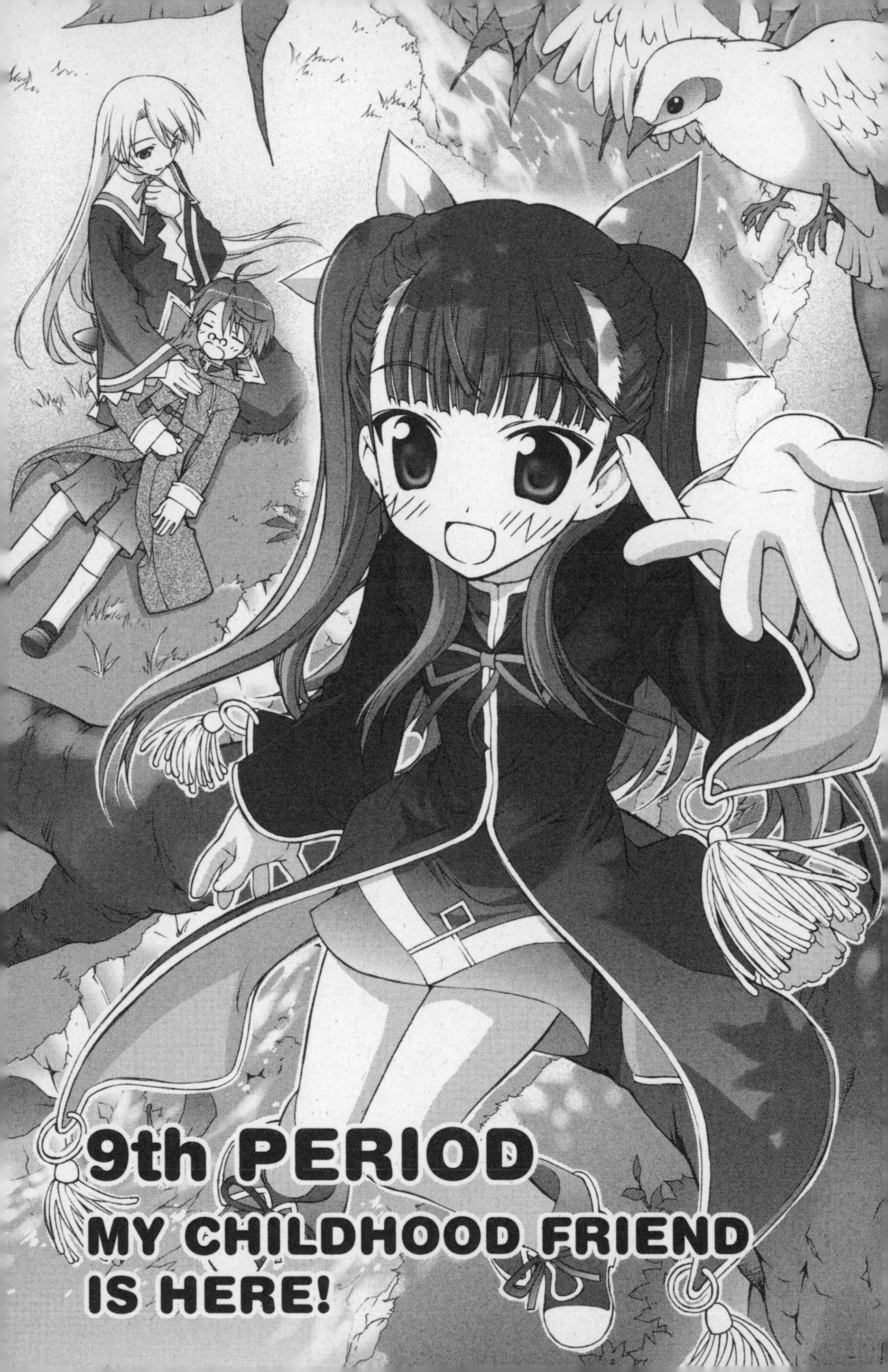
9th PERIOD
MY CHILDHOOD FRIEND IS HERE!

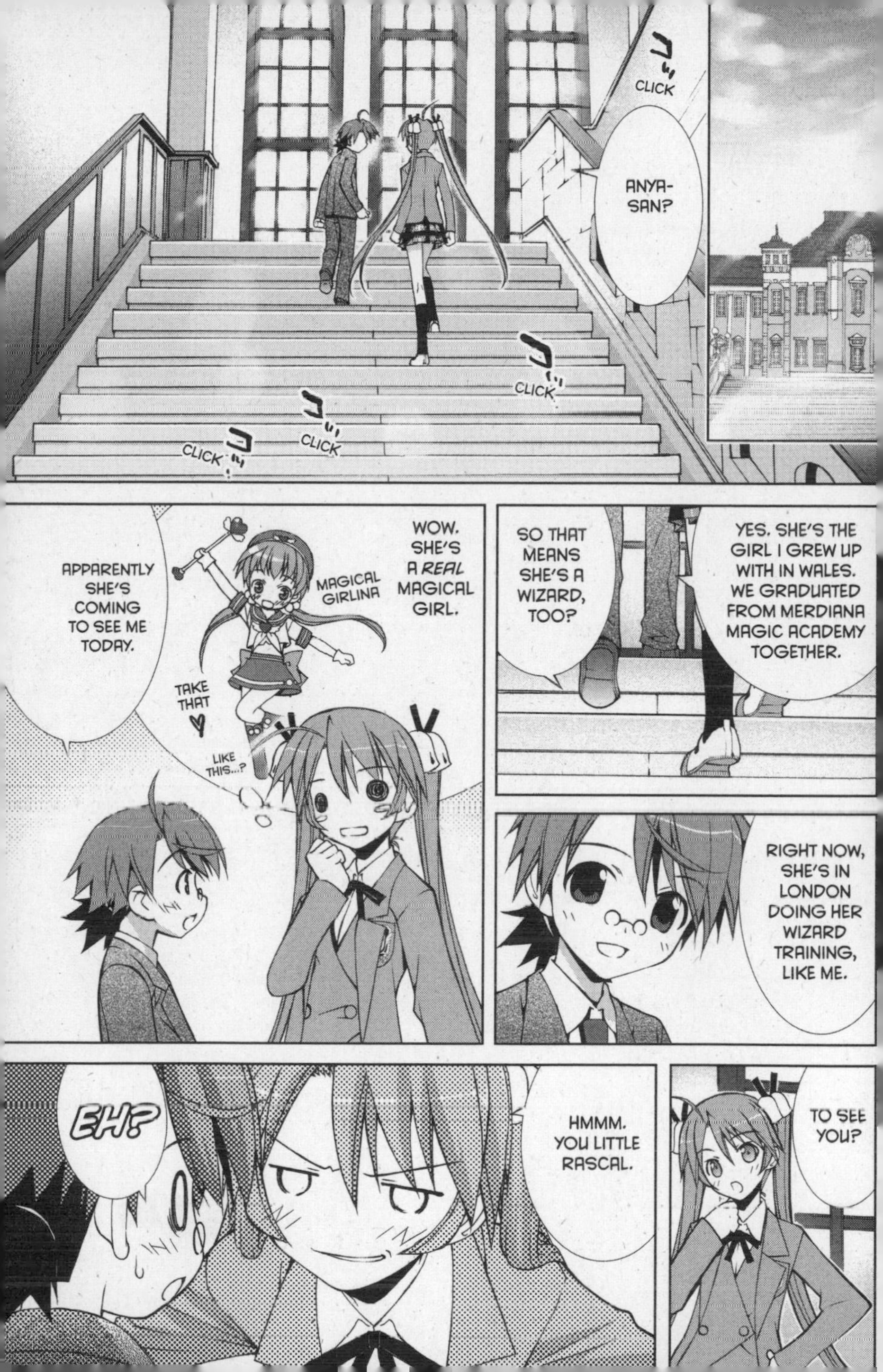
CLICK
ANYA-SAN?
CLICK
CLICK
CLICK
YES. SHE'S THE GIRL I GREW UP WITH IN WALES. WE GRADUATED FROM MERDIANA MAGIC ACADEMY TOGETHER.
SO THAT MEANS SHE'S A WIZARD, TOO?
RIGHT NOW, SHE'S IN LONDON DOING HER WIZARD TRAINING, LIKE ME.
WOW. SHE'S A *REAL* MAGICAL GIRL.
MAGICAL GIRLINA
APPARENTLY SHE'S COMING TO SEE ME TODAY.
TAKE THAT ♥
LIKE THIS...?
TO SEE YOU?
HMMM. YOU LITTLE RASCAL.
EH?

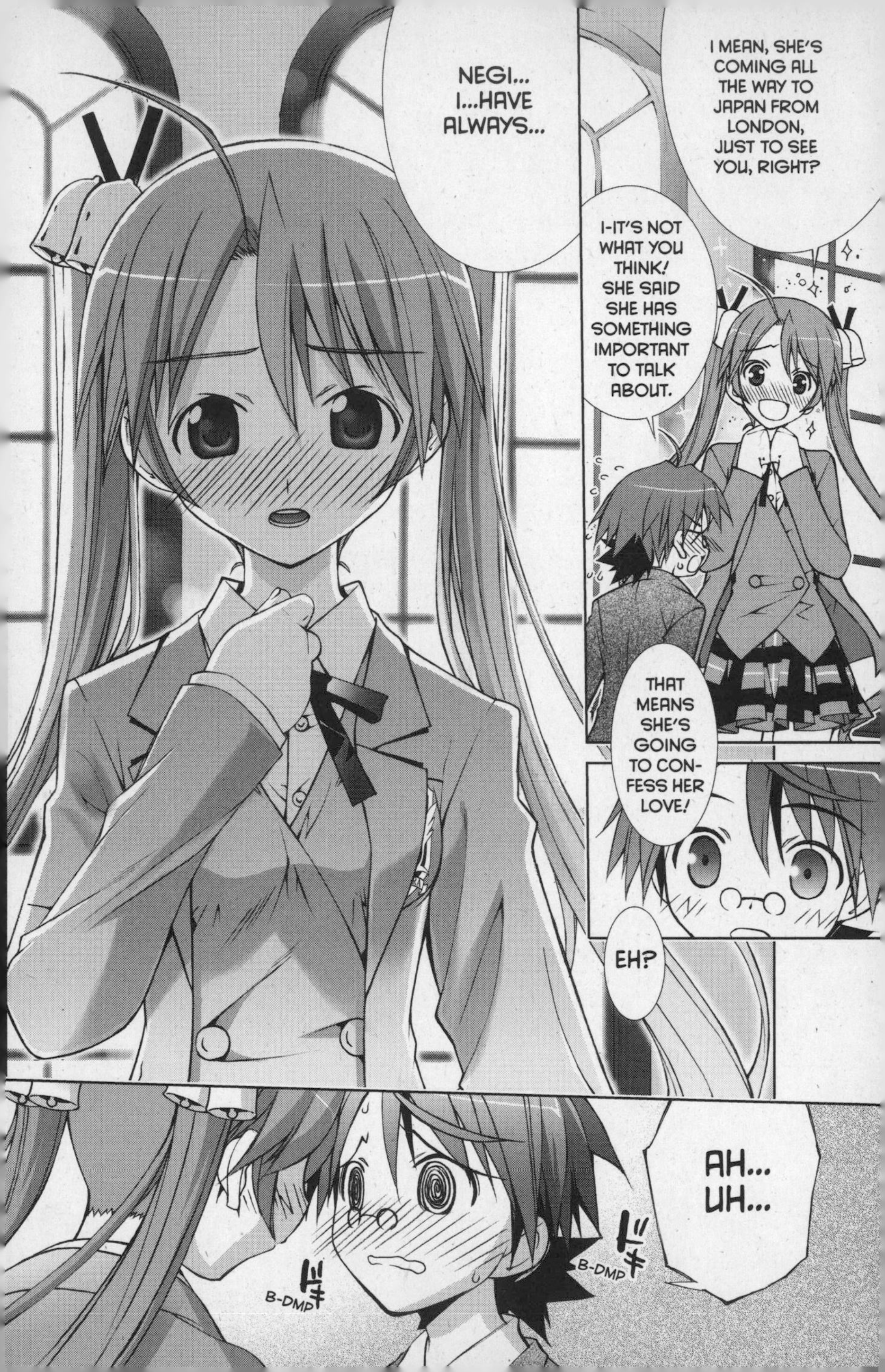
I MEAN, SHE'S COMING ALL THE WAY TO JAPAN FROM LONDON, JUST TO SEE YOU, RIGHT?
I-IT'S NOT WHAT YOU THINK! SHE SAID SHE HAS SOMETHING IMPORTANT TO TALK ABOUT.
THAT MEANS SHE'S GOING TO CON-FESS HER LOVE!
EH?
NEGI... I...HAVE ALWAYS...
AH... UH...
B-DMP
B-DMP

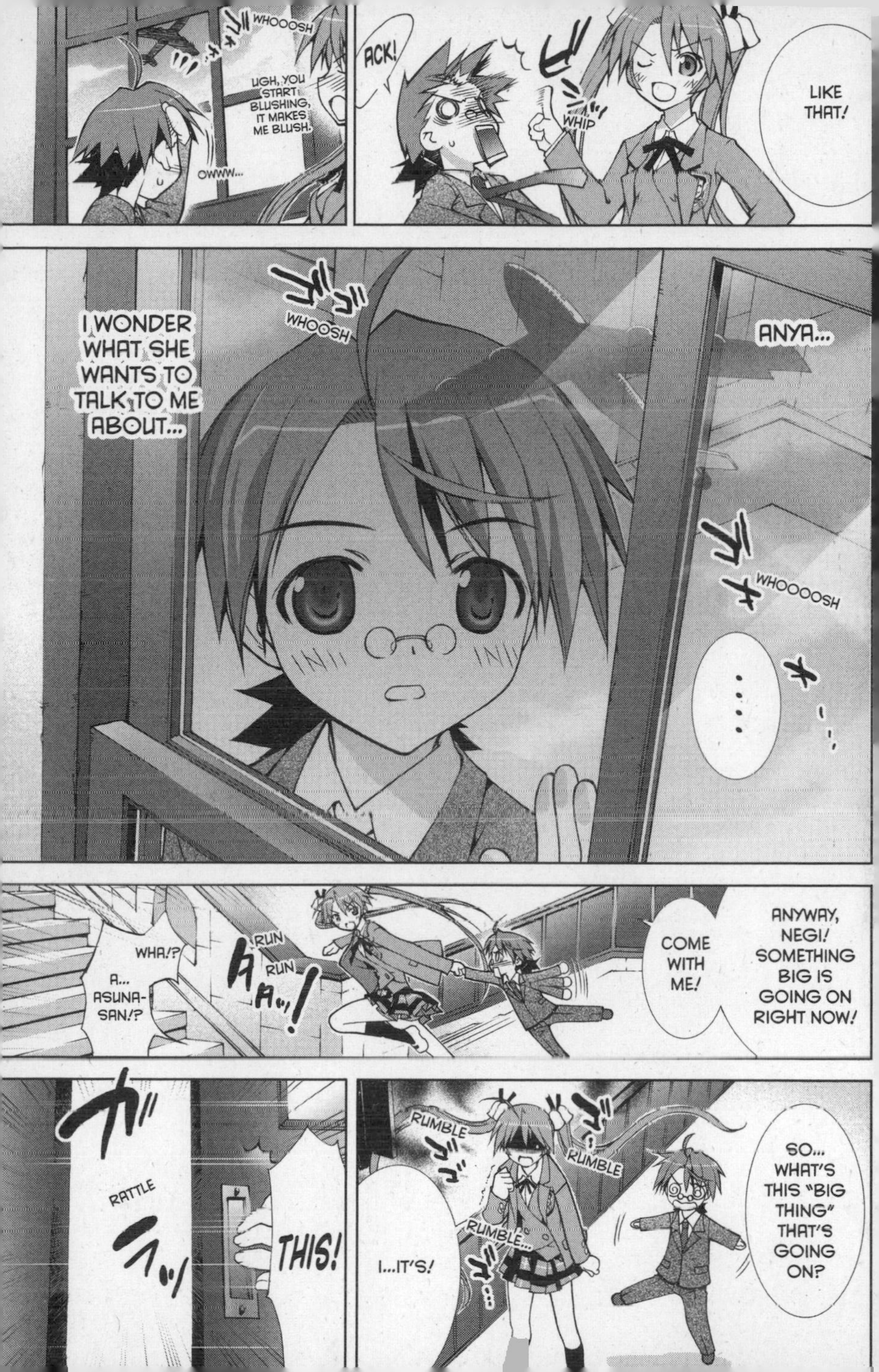
LIKE THAT!
ACK!
WHIP
WHOOOSH
UGH, YOU START BLUSHING, IT MAKES ME BLUSH.
OWWW...
ANYA...
WHOOOOSH
....
I WONDER WHAT SHE WANTS TO TALK TO ME ABOUT...
WHOOSH
ANYWAY, NEGI! SOMETHING BIG IS GOING ON RIGHT NOW!
COME WITH ME!
RUN
RUN
WHA!?
A... ASUNA-SAN!?
SO... WHAT'S THIS "BIG THING" THAT'S GOING ON?
RUMBLE
RUMBLE
RUMBLE...
I...IT'S!
THIS!
RATTLE

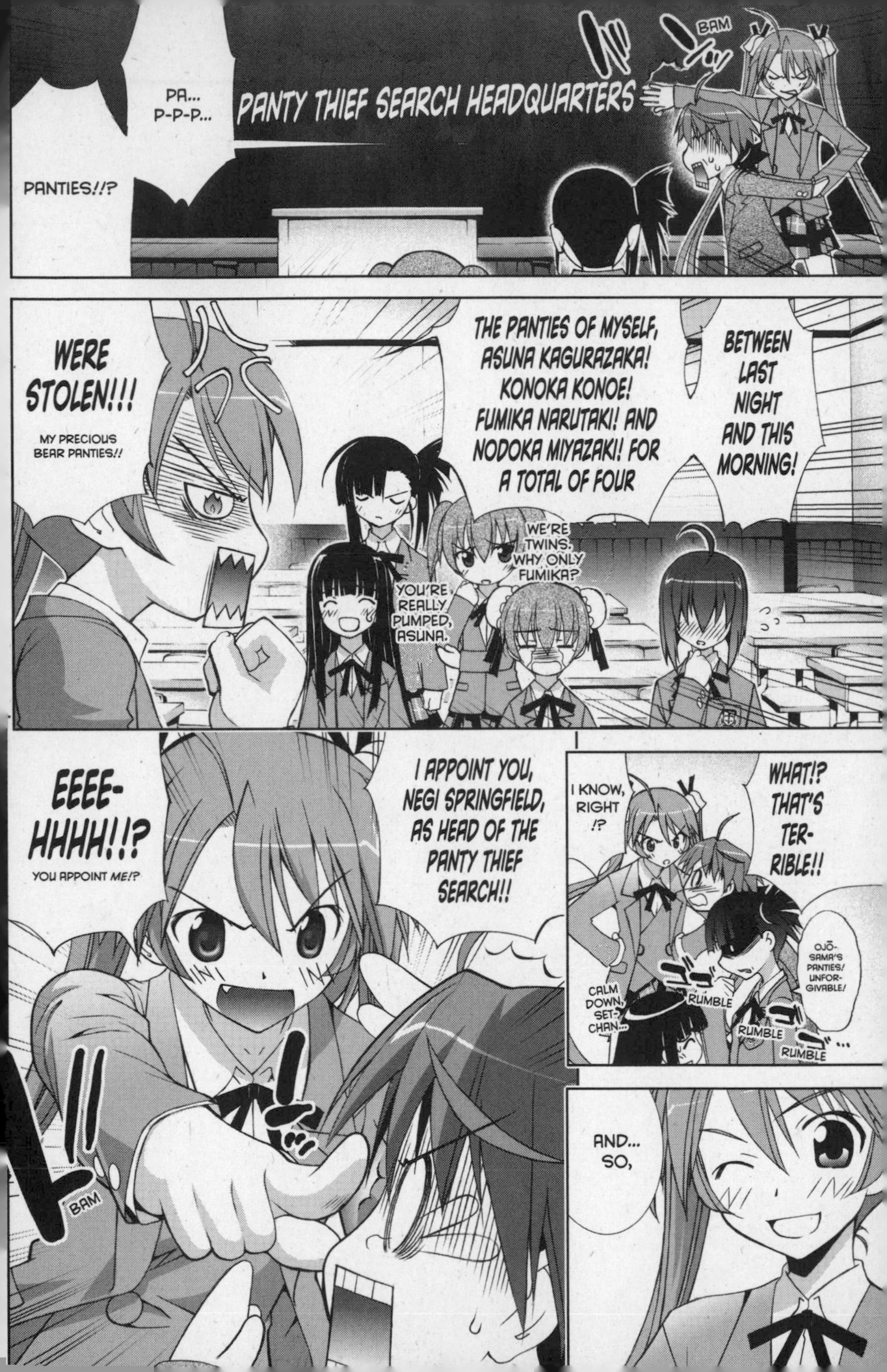
BAM
PANTY THIEF SEARCH HEADQUARTERS
PA... P-P-P...
PANTIES!!?
BETWEEN LAST NIGHT AND THIS MORNING!
THE PANTIES OF MYSELF, ASUNA KAGURAZAKA! KONOKA KONOE! FUMIKA NARUTAKI! AND NODOKA MIYAZAKI! FOR A TOTAL OF FOUR
WERE STOLEN!!!
MY PRECIOUS BEAR PANTIES!!
WE'RE TWINS. WHY ONLY FUMIKA?
YOU'RE REALLY PUMPED, ASUNA.
WHAT!? THAT'S TER-RIBLE!!
I KNOW, RIGHT!?
OJŌ-SAMA'S PANTIES! UNFORGIVABLE!
RUMBLE
RUMBLE
RUMBLE
CALM DOWN, SET-CHAN...
AND... SO,
I APPOINT YOU, NEGI SPRINGFIELD, AS HEAD OF THE PANTY THIEF SEARCH!!
EEEE-HHHH!!?
YOU APPOINT ME!?
BAM

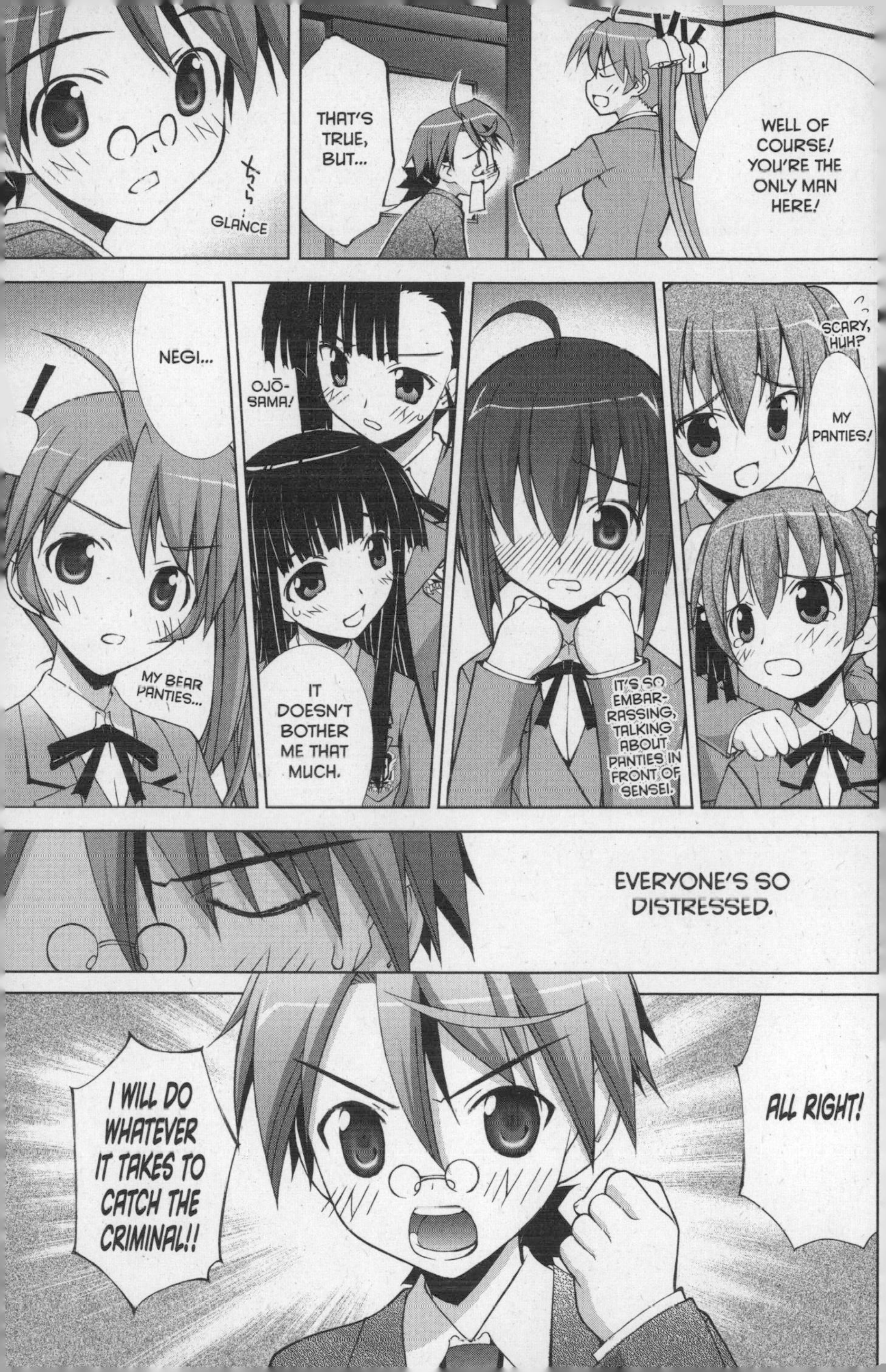
WELL OF COURSE! YOU'RE THE ONLY MAN HERE!
THAT'S TRUE, BUT...
GLANCE
SCARY, HUH?
MY PANTIES!
IT'S SO EMBARRASSING, TALKING ABOUT PANTIES IN FRONT OF SENSEI.
OJŌ-SAMA!
IT DOESN'T BOTHER ME THAT MUCH.
NEGI...
MY BEAR PANTIES...
EVERYONE'S SO DISTRESSED.
ALL RIGHT!
I WILL DO WHATEVER IT TAKES TO CATCH THE CRIMINAL!!

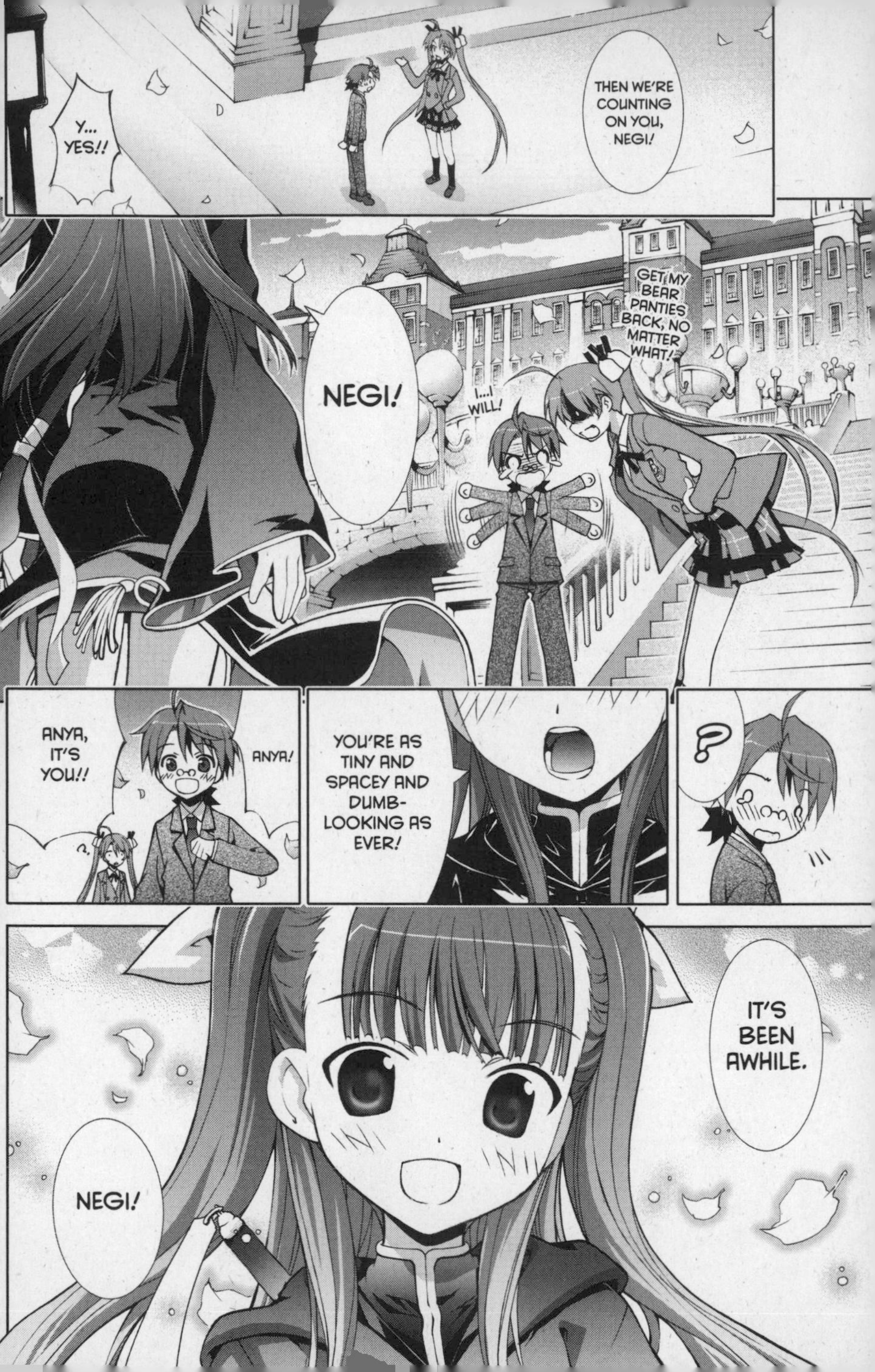
THEN WE'RE COUNTING ON YOU, NEGI!
Y... YES!!
GET MY BEAR PANTIES BACK, NO MATTER WHAT!
I...I WILL!
NEGI!
?
YOU'RE AS TINY AND SPACEY AND DUMB-LOOKING AS EVER!
ANYA!
ANYA, IT'S YOU!!
IT'S BEEN AWHILE.
NEGI!

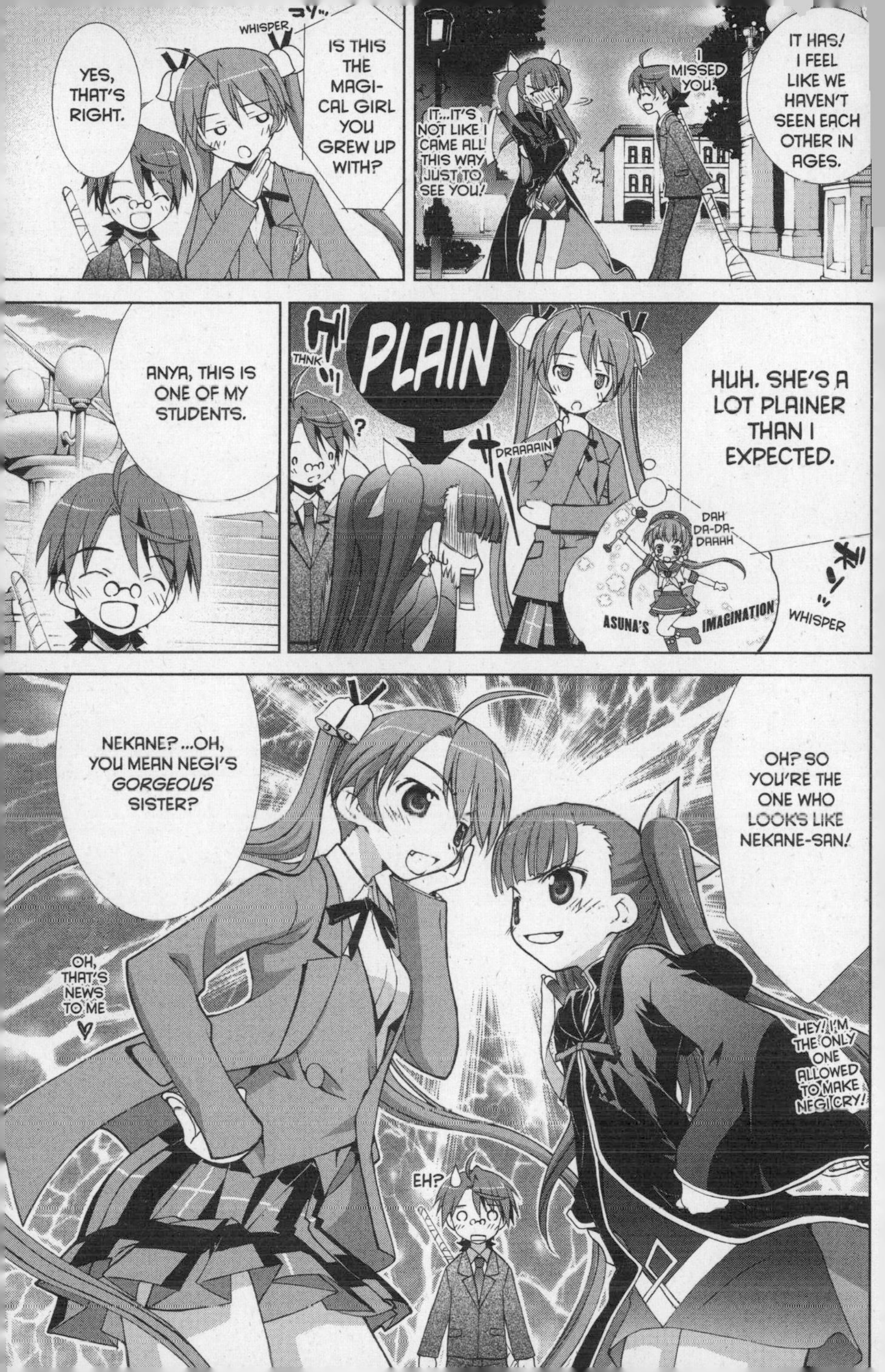
IT HAS! I FEEL LIKE WE HAVEN'T SEEN EACH OTHER IN AGES.
I MISSED YOU.
IT...IT'S NOT LIKE I CAME ALL THIS WAY JUST TO SEE YOU!
IS THIS THE MAGI-CAL GIRL YOU GREW UP WITH?
WHISPER
YES, THAT'S RIGHT.
HUH. SHE'S A LOT PLAINER THAN I EXPECTED.
PLAIN
THNK
?
DRAAAAIN
DAH DA-DA-DAAHH
ASUNA'S IMAGINATION
WHISPER
ANYA, THIS IS ONE OF MY STUDENTS.
OH? SO YOU'RE THE ONE WHO LOOKS LIKE NEKANE-SAN!
NEKANE? ...OH, YOU MEAN NEGI'S *GORGEOUS* SISTER?
HEY! I'M THE ONLY ONE ALLOWED TO MAKE NEGI CRY!
OH, THAT'S NEWS TO ME ♥
EH?

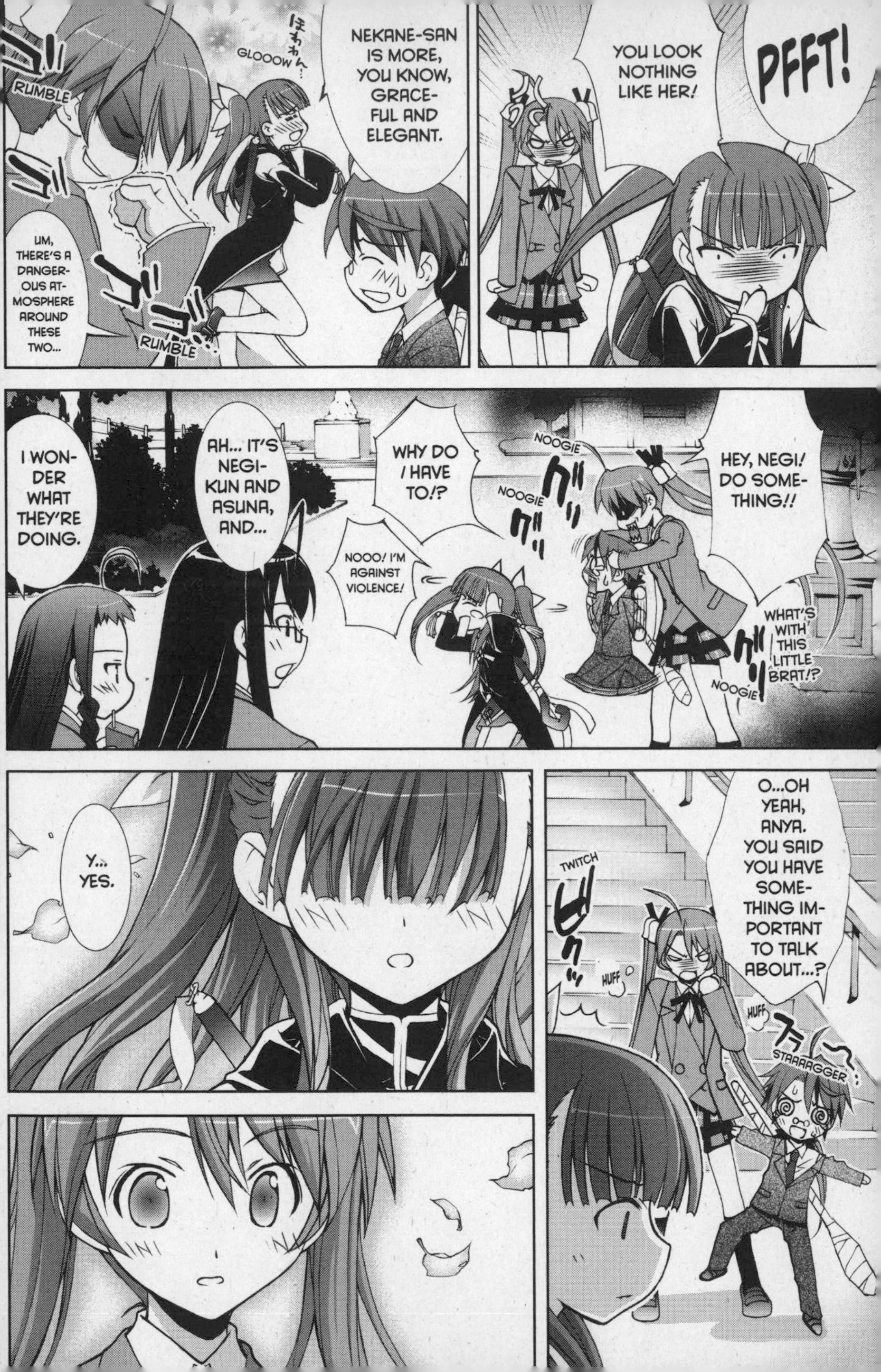
PFFT!
YOU LOOK NOTHING LIKE HER!
ほわわん…
GLOOOW
NEKANE-SAN IS MORE, YOU KNOW, GRACE-FUL AND ELEGANT.
RUMBLE
UM, THERE'S A DANGER-OUS AT-MOSPHERE AROUND THESE TWO...
RUMBLE
HEY, NEGI! DO SOME-THING!!
WHAT'S WITH THIS LITTLE BRAT!?
NOOGIE
NOOGIE
NOOGIE
WHY DO I HAVE TO!?
NOOO! I'M AGAINST VIOLENCE!
AH... IT'S NEGI-KUN AND ASUNA, AND...
I WON-DER WHAT THEY'RE DOING.
O...OH YEAH, ANYA. YOU SAID YOU HAVE SOME-THING IM-PORTANT TO TALK ABOUT...?
TWITCH
HUFF
HUFF
STAAAAGGER
Y... YES.

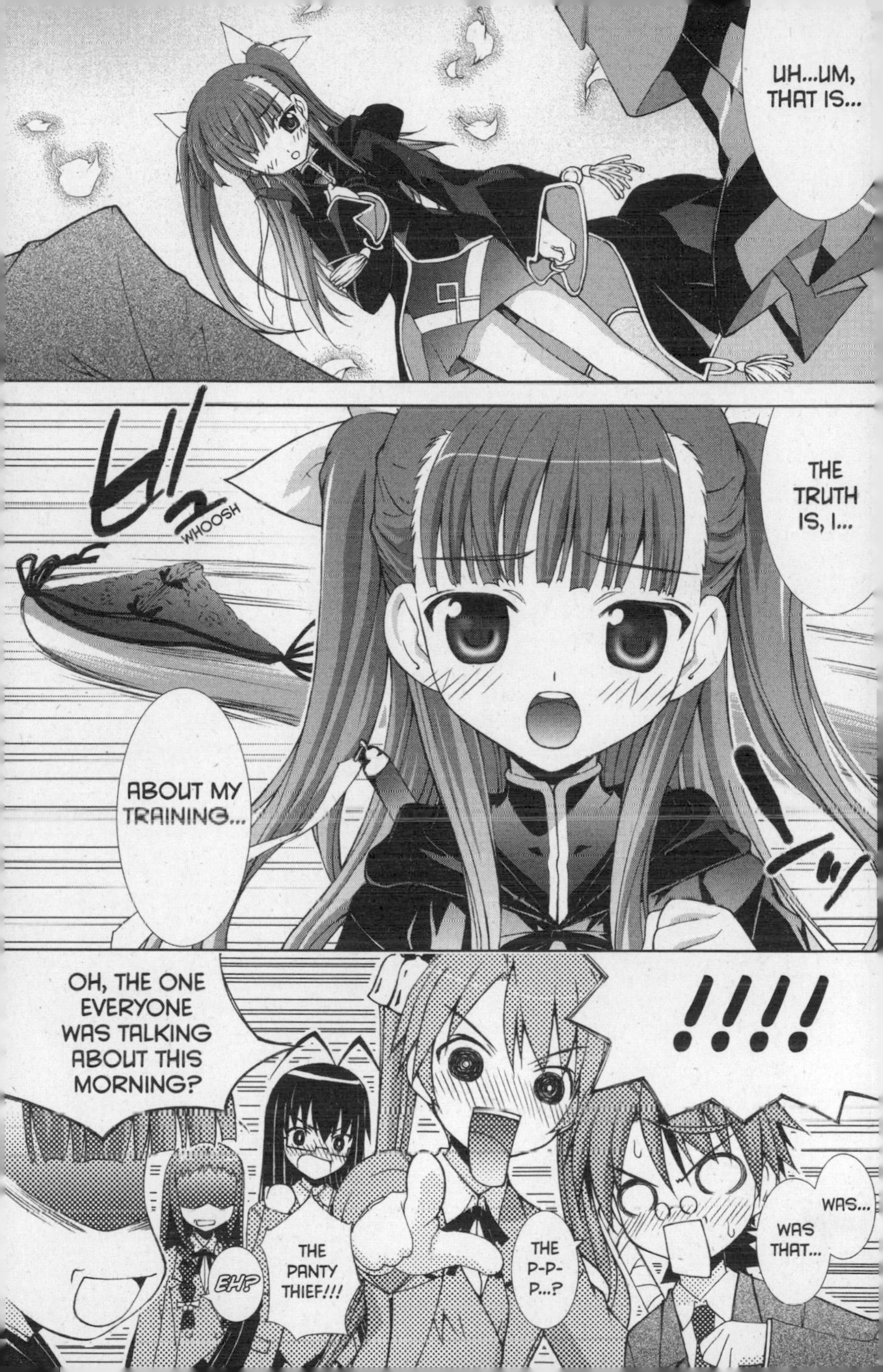
UH...UM, THAT IS...
THE TRUTH IS, I...
WHOOSH
ABOUT MY TRAINING...
OH, THE ONE EVERYONE WAS TALKING ABOUT THIS MORNING?
!!!!
WAS... WAS THAT...
THE P-P-P...?
THE PANTY THIEF!!!
EH?

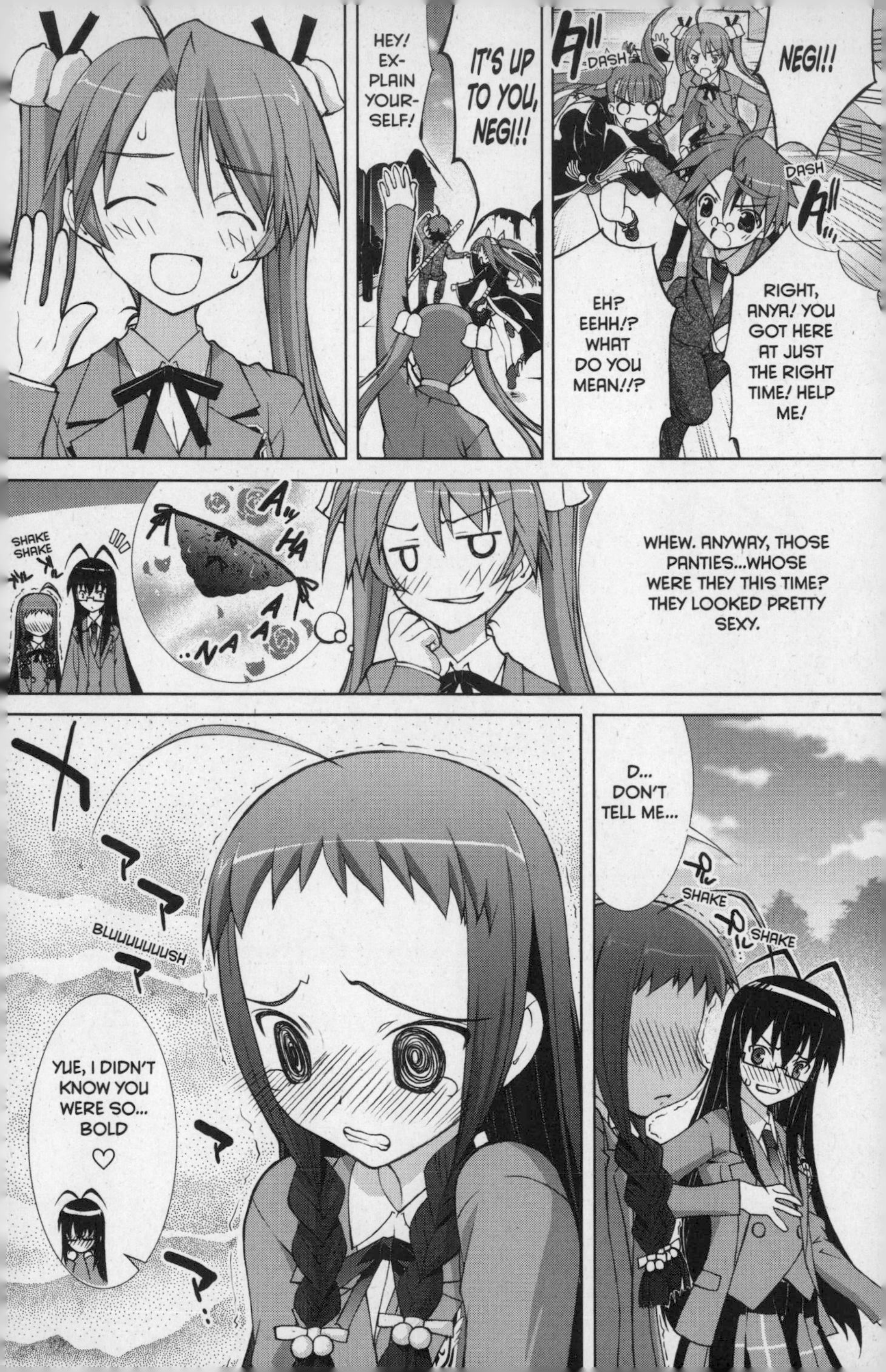

NEGI!!
DASH
DASH
RIGHT, ANYA! YOU GOT HERE AT JUST THE RIGHT TIME! HELP ME!
EH? EEHH!? WHAT DO YOU MEAN!!?
IT'S UP TO YOU, NEGI!!
HEY! EX-PLAIN YOUR-SELF!
WHEW. ANYWAY, THOSE PANTIES...WHOSE WERE THEY THIS TIME? THEY LOOKED PRETTY SEXY.
SHAKE SHAKE
D... DON'T TELL ME...
SHAKE
SHAKE
BLUUUUUUUSH
YUE, I DIDN'T KNOW YOU WERE SO... BOLD ♡

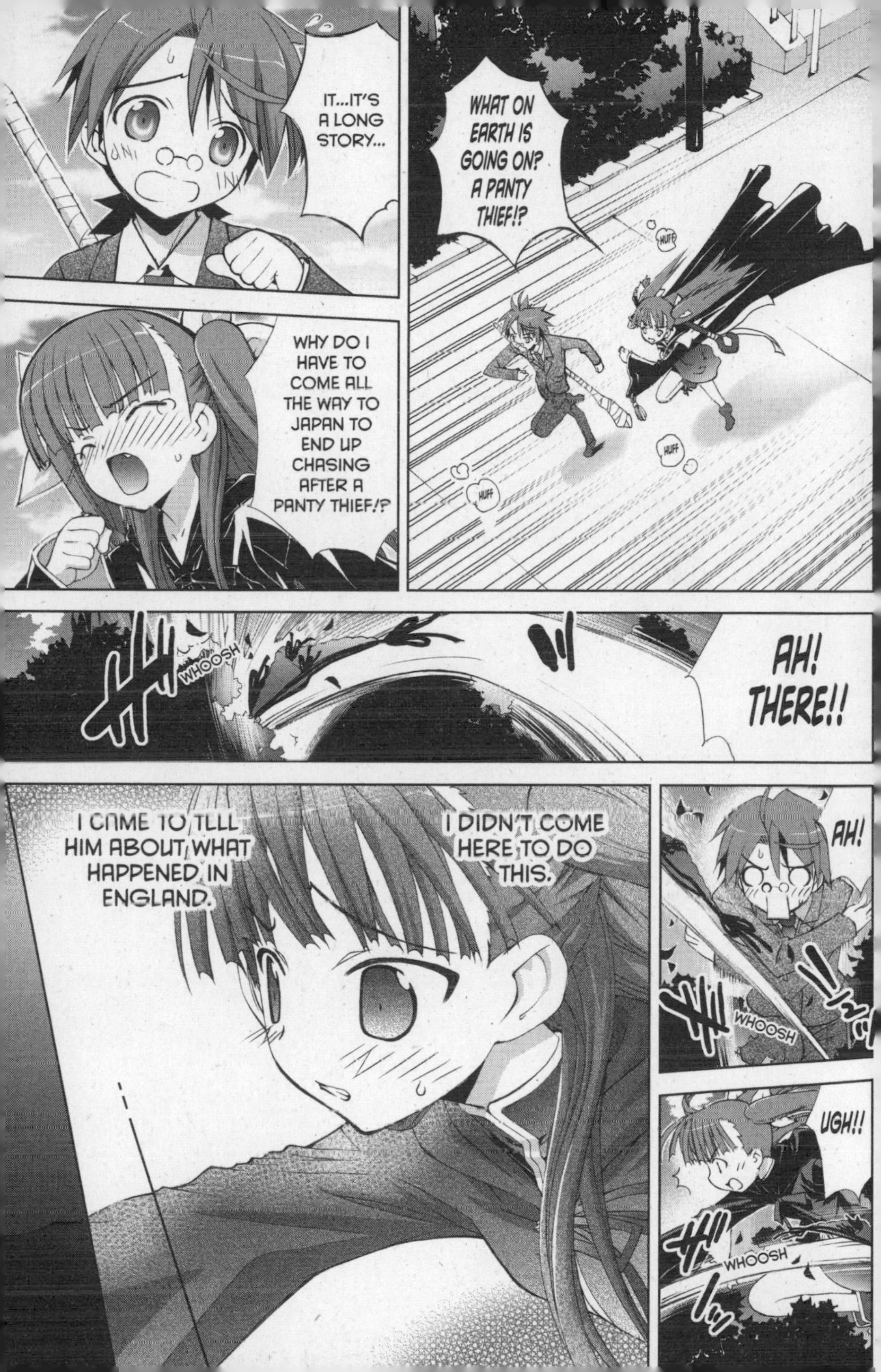
WHAT ON EARTH IS GOING ON? A PANTY THIEF!?
HUFF
HUFF
HUFF
IT...IT'S A LONG STORY...
WHY DO I HAVE TO COME ALL THE WAY TO JAPAN TO END UP CHASING AFTER A PANTY THIEF!?
AH! THERE!!
WHOOSH
AH!
WHOOSH
UGH!!
WHOOSH
I DIDN'T COME HERE TO DO THIS.
I CAME TO TELL HIM ABOUT WHAT HAPPENED IN ENGLAND.

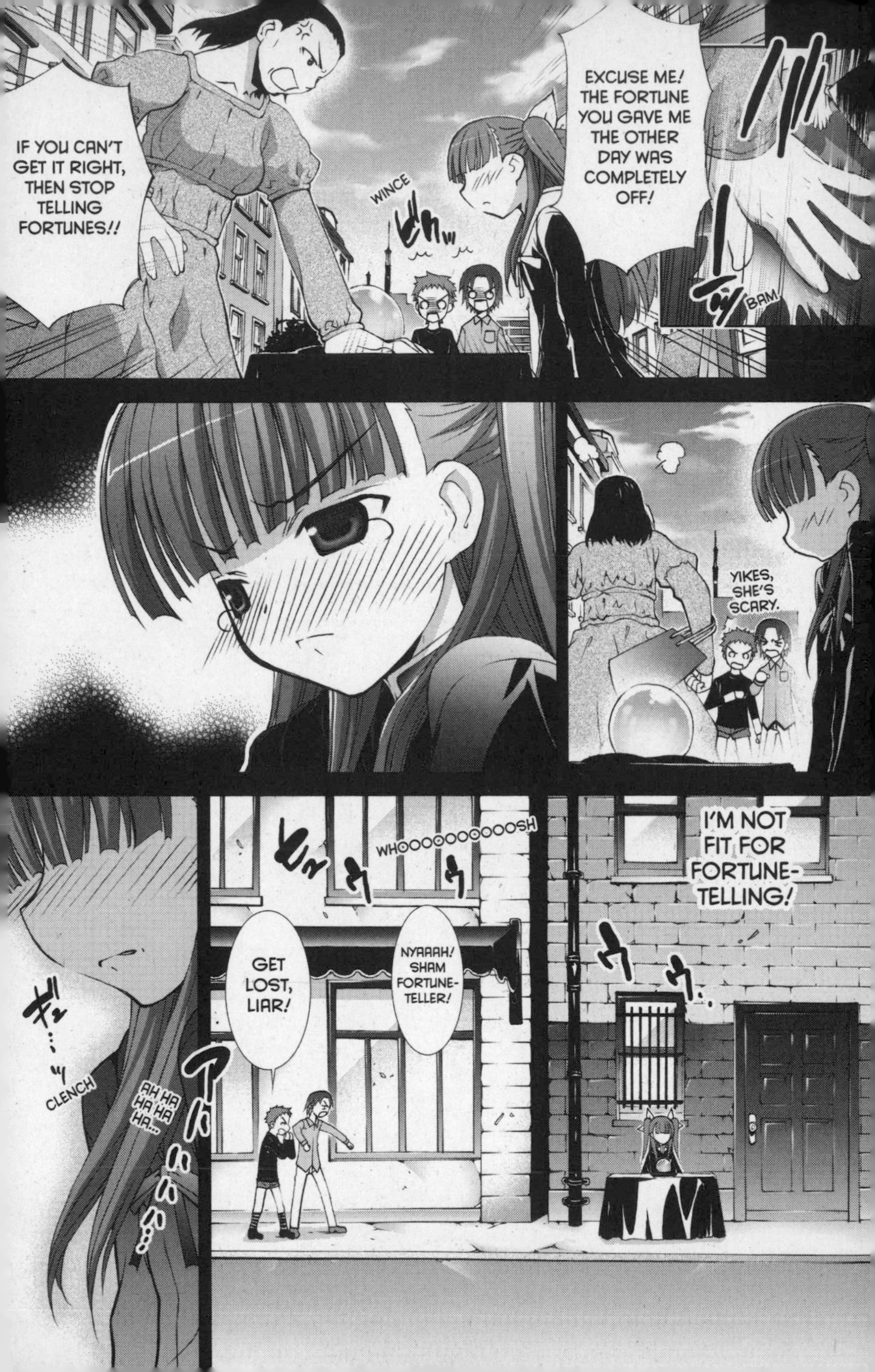
BAM
EXCUSE ME! THE FORTUNE YOU GAVE ME THE OTHER DAY WAS COMPLETELY OFF!
IF YOU CAN'T GET IT RIGHT, THEN STOP TELLING FORTUNES!!
WINCE
YIKES, SHE'S SCARY.
I'M NOT FIT FOR FORTUNE-TELLING!
WHOOOOOOOOOOOSH
NYAAAH! SHAM FORTUNE-TELLER!
GET LOST, LIAR!
CLENCH
AH HA HA HA HA...

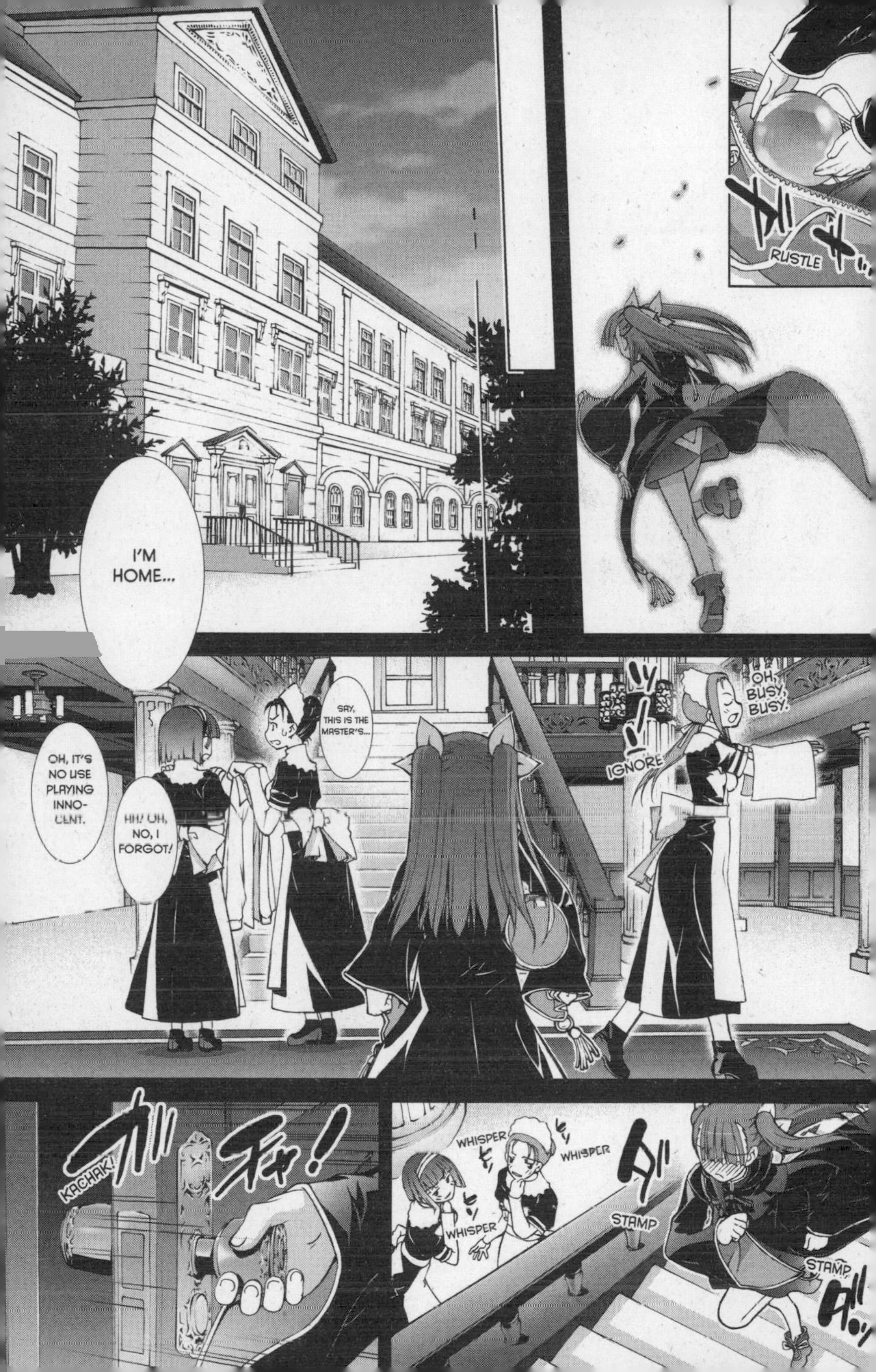
RUSTLE
I'M HOME...
OH, BUSY, BUSY.
IGNORE
SAY, THIS IS THE MASTER'S...
HH! OH, NO, I FORGOT!
OH, IT'S NO USE PLAYING INNOCENT.
STAMP
WHISPER
WHISPER
WHISPER
STAMP
KACHAK!

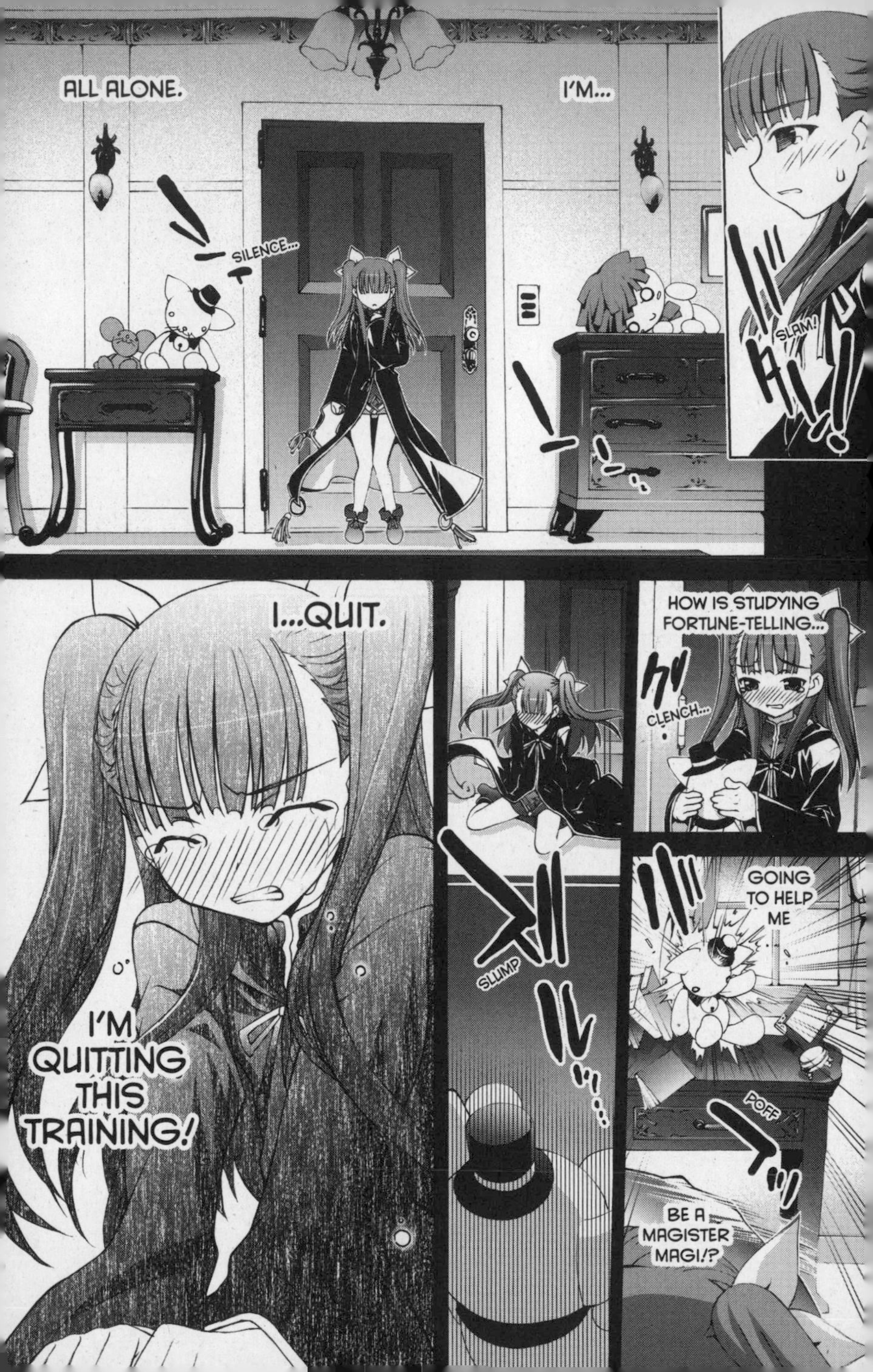
SLAM!
I'M...
ALL ALONE.
SILENCE...
HOW IS STUDYING FORTUNE-TELLING...
CLENCH...
GOING TO HELP ME
POFF
BE A MAGISTER MAGI!?
SLUMP
I...QUIT.
I'M QUITTING THIS TRAINING!

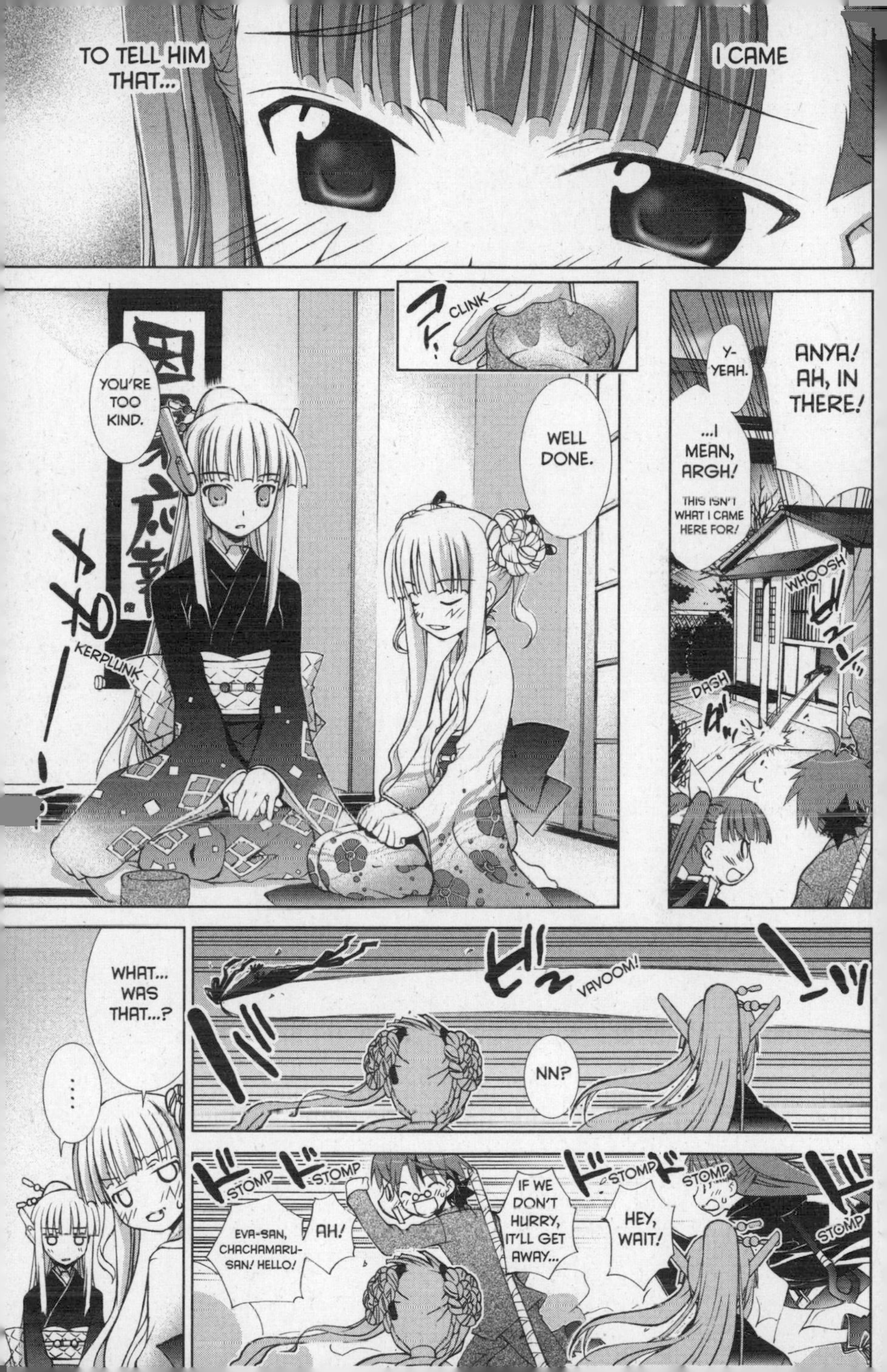
I CAME
TO TELL HIM THAT...
ANYA! AH, IN THERE!
Y-YEAH.
...I MEAN, ARGH!
THIS ISN'T WHAT I CAME HERE FOR!
WHOOSH
DASH
CLINK
WELL DONE.
YOU'RE TOO KIND.
KERPLUNK
VAVOOM!
NN?
STOMP
STOMP
STOMP
HEY, WAIT!
IF WE DON'T HURRY, IT'LL GET AWAY...
AH!
EVA-SAN, CHACHAMARU-SAN! HELLO!
STOMP
STOMP
WHAT... WAS THAT...?
....

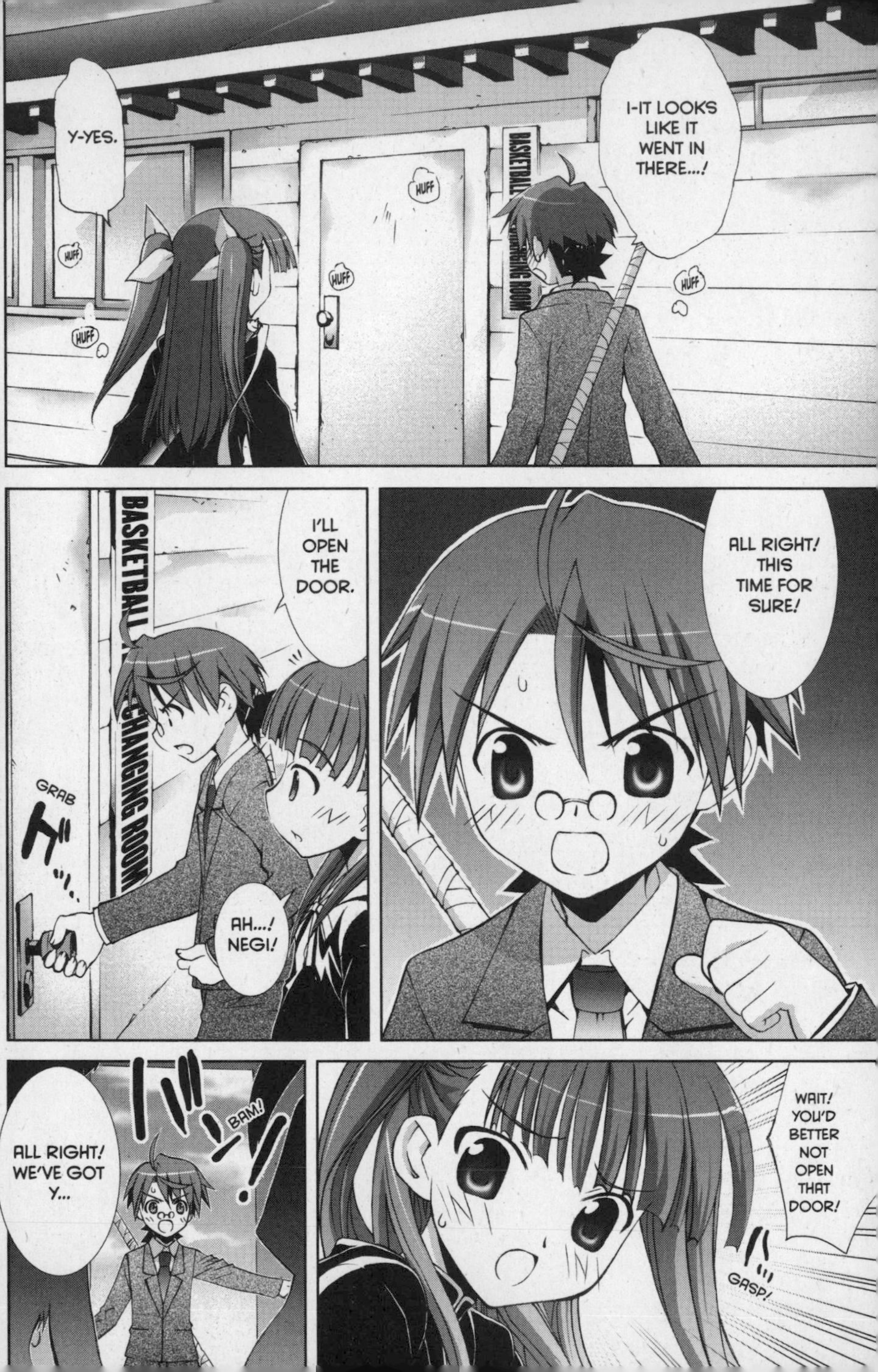
I-IT LOOKS LIKE IT WENT IN THERE...!
BASKETBALL CHANGING ROOM
HUFF
HUFF
HUFF
Y-YES.
HUFF
HUFF
ALL RIGHT! THIS TIME FOR SURE!
I'LL OPEN THE DOOR.
BASKETBALL CHANGING ROOM
GRAB
AH...! NEGI!
WAIT! YOU'D BETTER NOT OPEN THAT DOOR!
GASP!
BAM!
ALL RIGHT! WE'VE GOT Y...

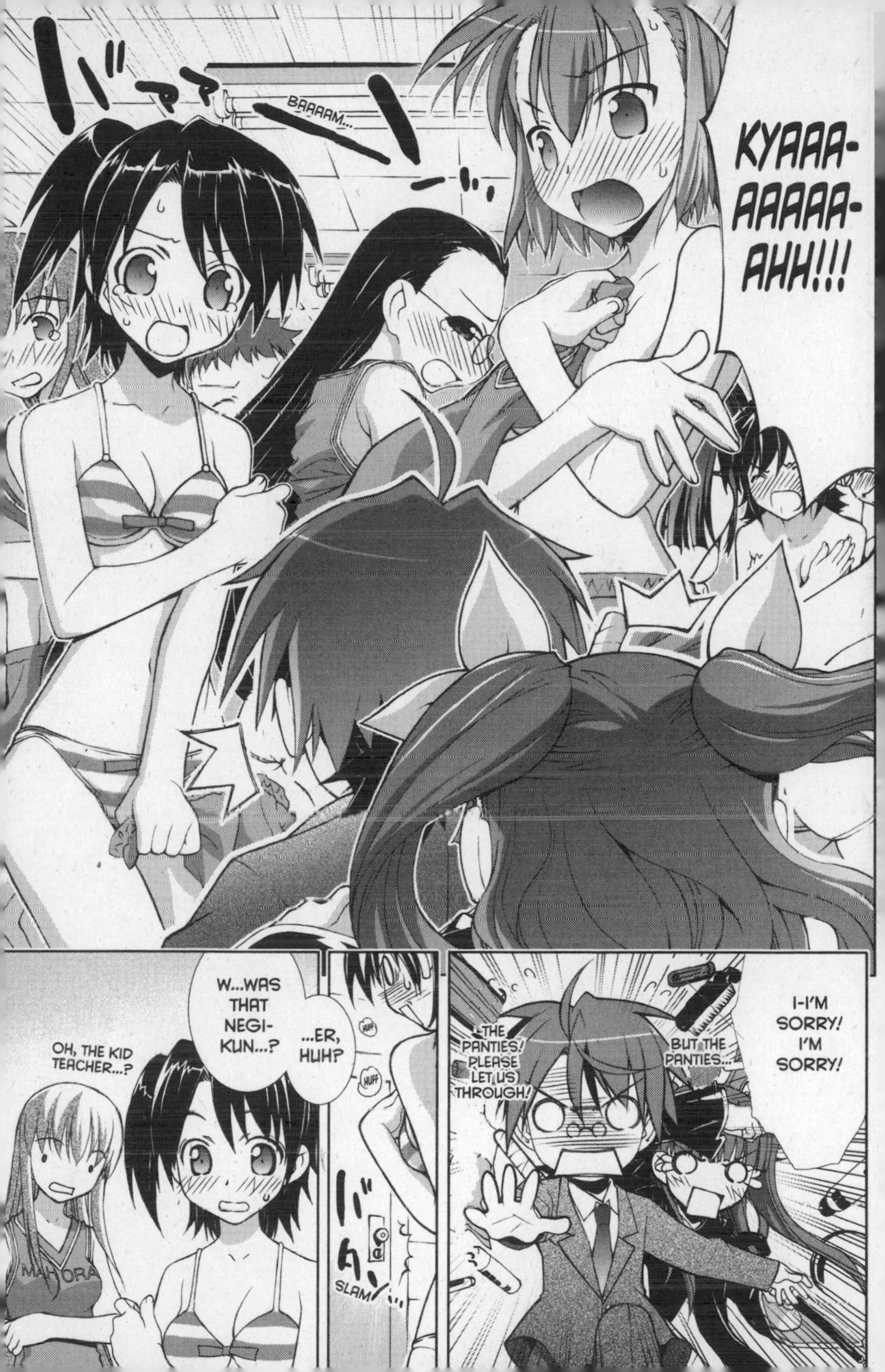
BRAAAAM...
KYAAA-AAAAA-AHH!!!
I-I'M SORRY! I'M SORRY!
BUT THE PANTIES...
THE PANTIES! PLEASE LET US THROUGH!
HUFF
HUFF
SLAM...
W...WAS THAT NEGI-KUN...?
...ER, HUH?
OH, THE KID TEACHER...?
MAHORA

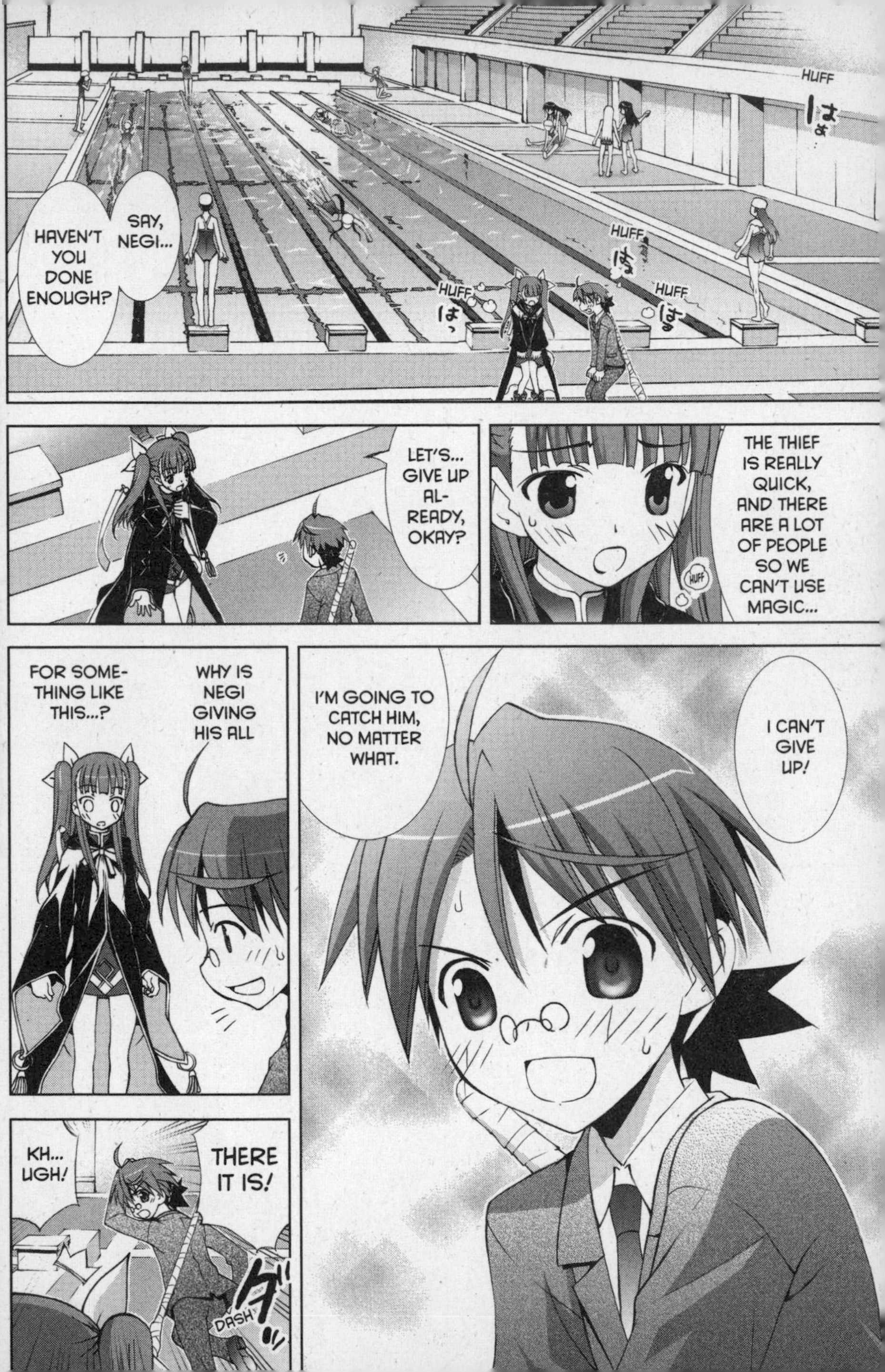
HUFF
SAY, NEGI...
HAVEN'T YOU DONE ENOUGH?
HUFF
HUFF
HUFF
THE THIEF IS REALLY QUICK, AND THERE ARE A LOT OF PEOPLE SO WE CAN'T USE MAGIC...
HUFF
LET'S... GIVE UP AL- READY, OKAY?
I CAN'T GIVE UP!
I'M GOING TO CATCH HIM, NO MATTER WHAT.
WHY IS NEGI GIVING HIS ALL
FOR SOME- THING LIKE THIS...?
THERE IT IS!
KH... UGH!
DASH

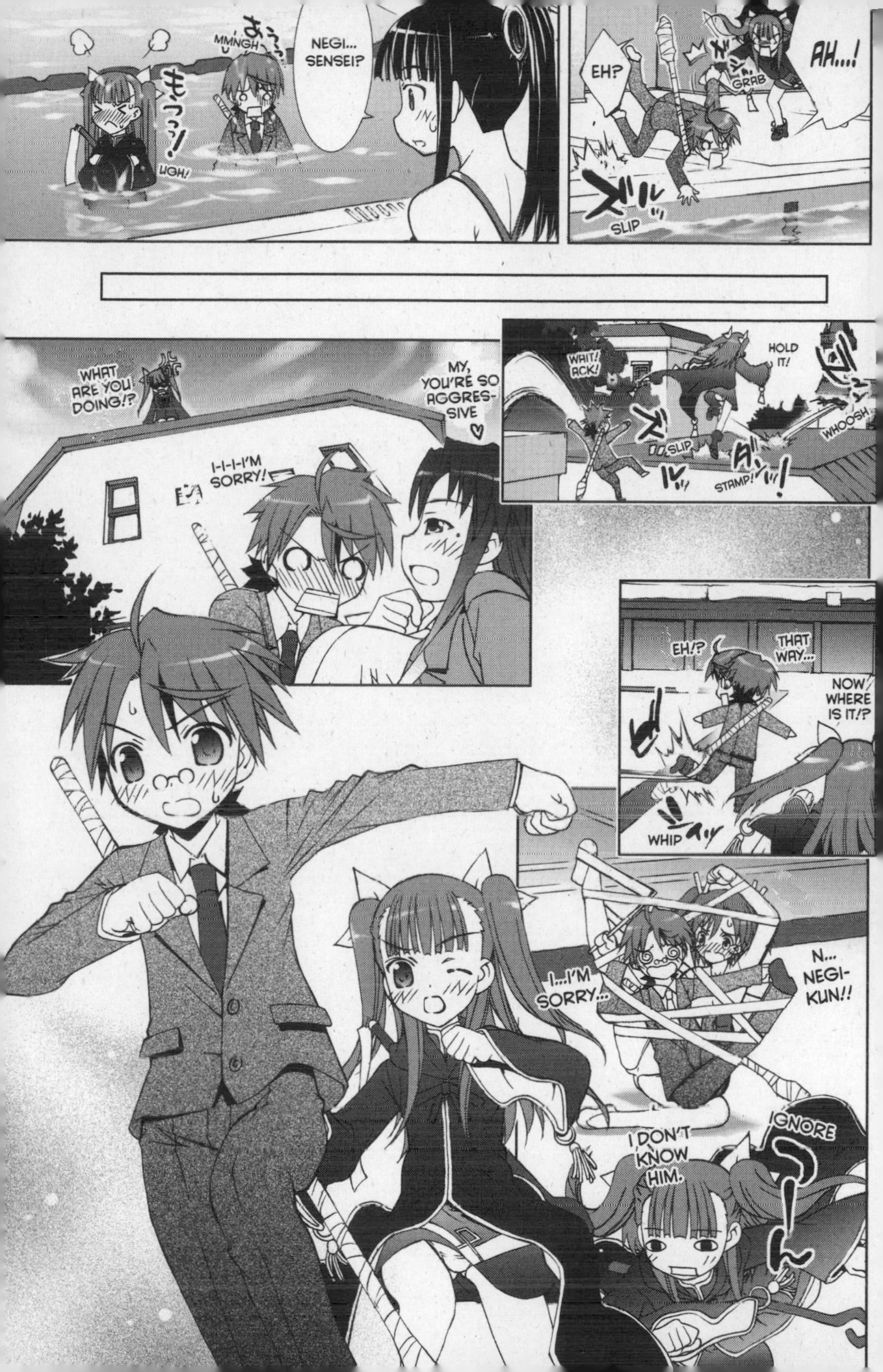
AH...!
EH?
GRAB
SLIP
NEGI... SENSEI!?
MMNGH
UGH!
HOLD IT!
WAIT! ACK!
WHOOSH
SLIP
STAMP!
MY, YOU'RE SO AGGRES-SIVE ♥
I-I-I-I'M SORRY!
WHAT ARE YOU DOING!?
THAT WAY...
EH!?
NOW WHERE IS IT!?
WHIP
N... NEGI-KUN!!
I...I'M SORRY...
IGNORE
I DON'T KNOW HIM.

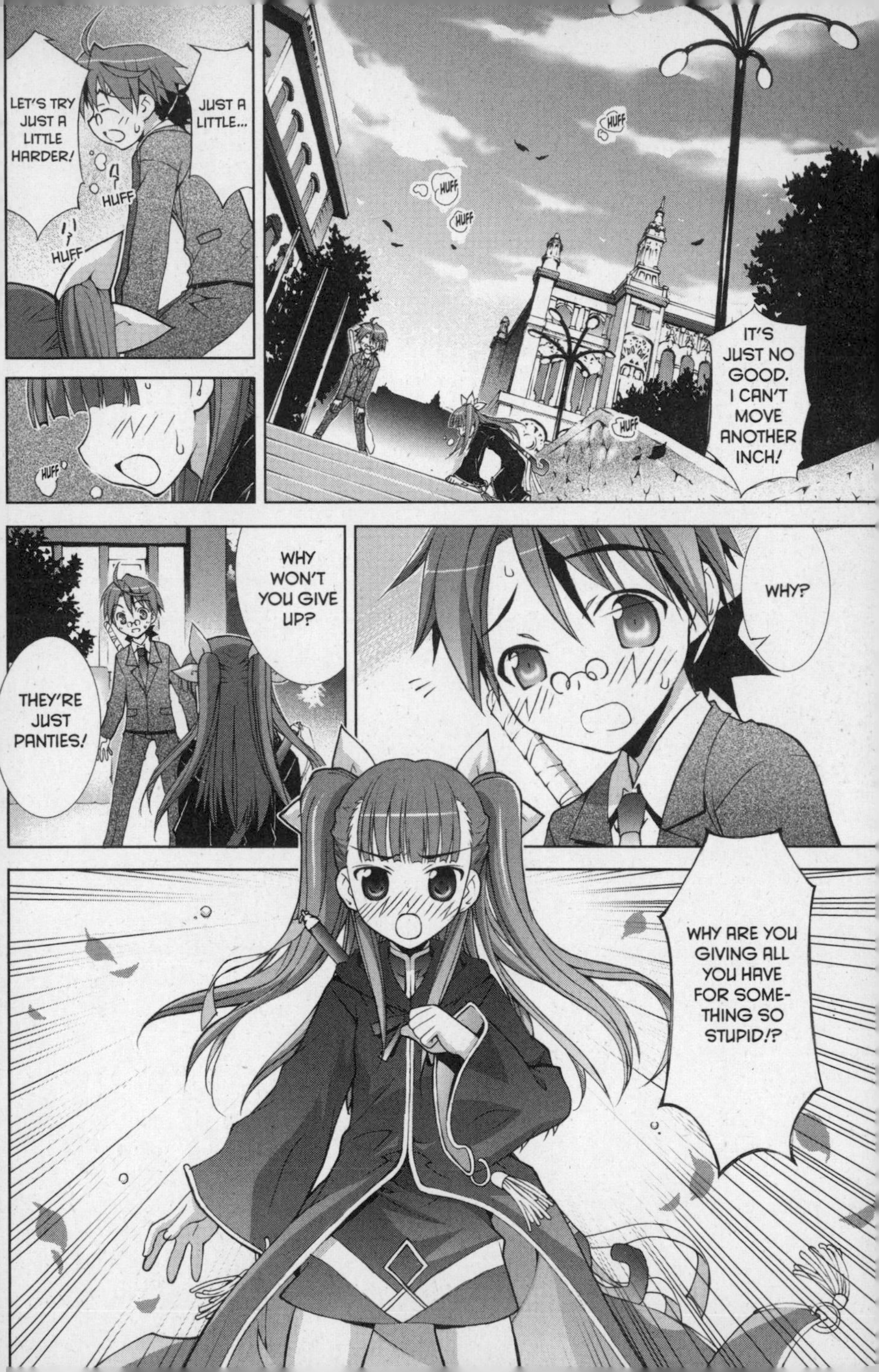
HUFF
HUFF
HUFF
IT'S JUST NO GOOD. I CAN'T MOVE ANOTHER INCH!
HUFF
JUST A LITTLE...
LET'S TRY JUST A LITTLE HARDER!
HUFF
HUFF
HUFF
WHY?
WHY WON'T YOU GIVE UP?
THEY'RE JUST PANTIES!
WHY ARE YOU GIVING ALL YOU HAVE FOR SOME-THING SO STUPID!?

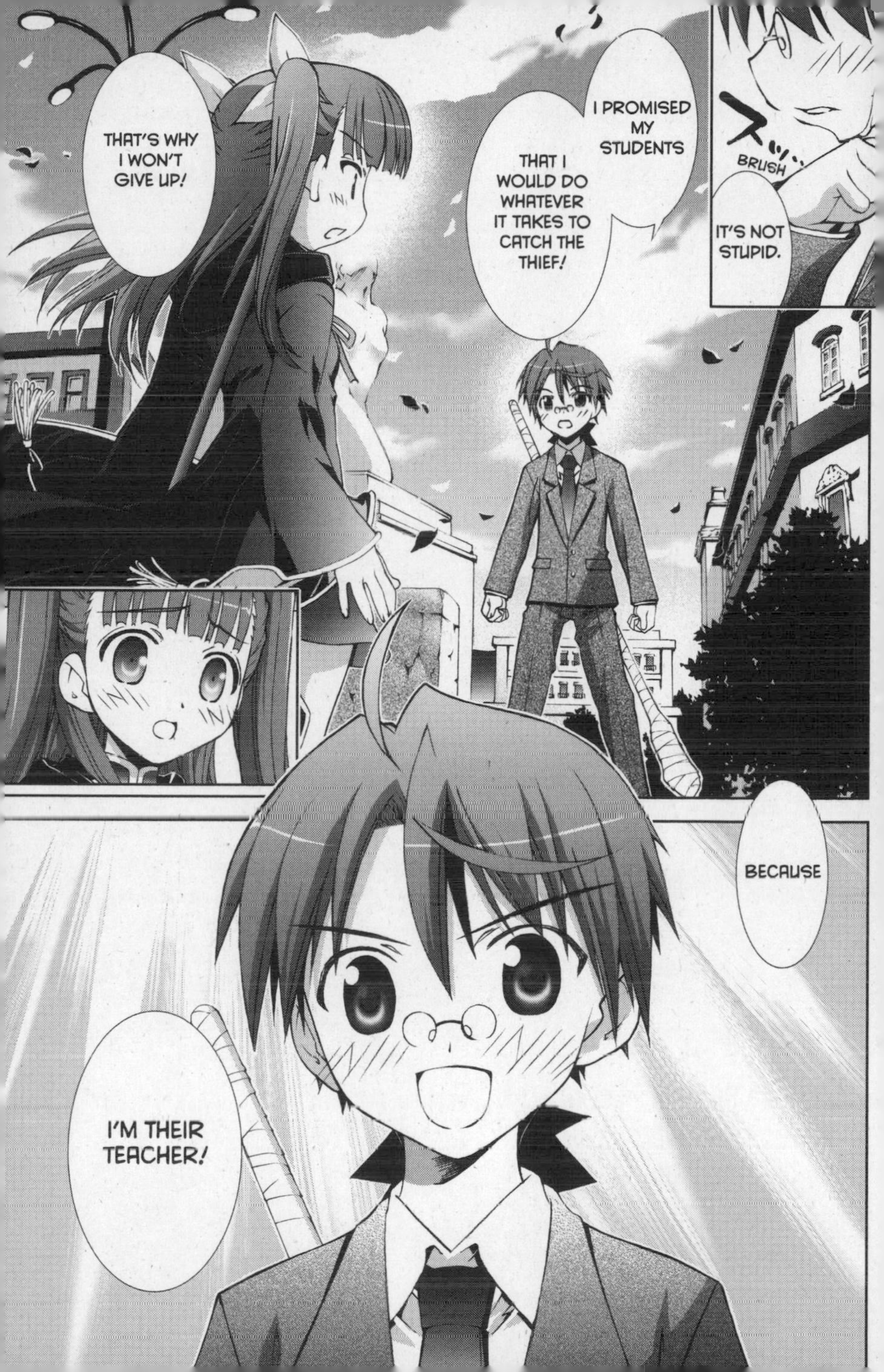
BRUSH
IT'S NOT STUPID.
I PROMISED MY STUDENTS
THAT I WOULD DO WHATEVER IT TAKES TO CATCH THE THIEF!
THAT'S WHY I WON'T GIVE UP!
BECAUSE
I'M THEIR TEACHER!

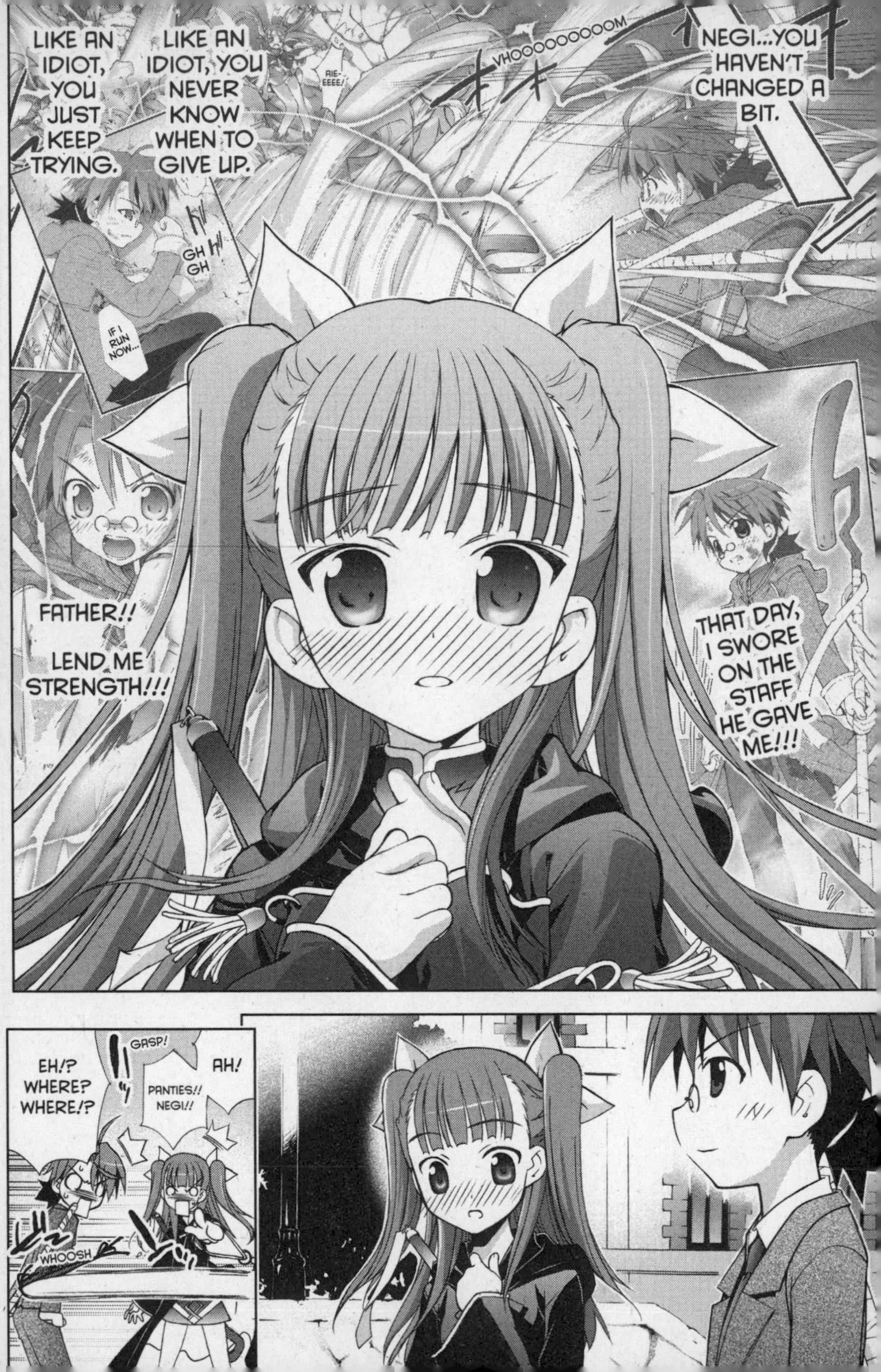
NEGI...YOU HAVEN'T CHANGED A BIT.
VHOOOOOOOOOOM
LIKE AN IDIOT, YOU NEVER KNOW WHEN TO GIVE UP.
AIE-EEEE!
LIKE AN IDIOT, YOU JUST KEEP TRYING.
GH GH
IF I RUN NOW...
THAT DAY, I SWORE ON THE STAFF HE GAVE ME!!!
FATHER!!
LEND ME STRENGTH!!!
AH!
PANTIES!! NEGI!!
GASP!
EH!? WHERE? WHERE!?
WHOOSH

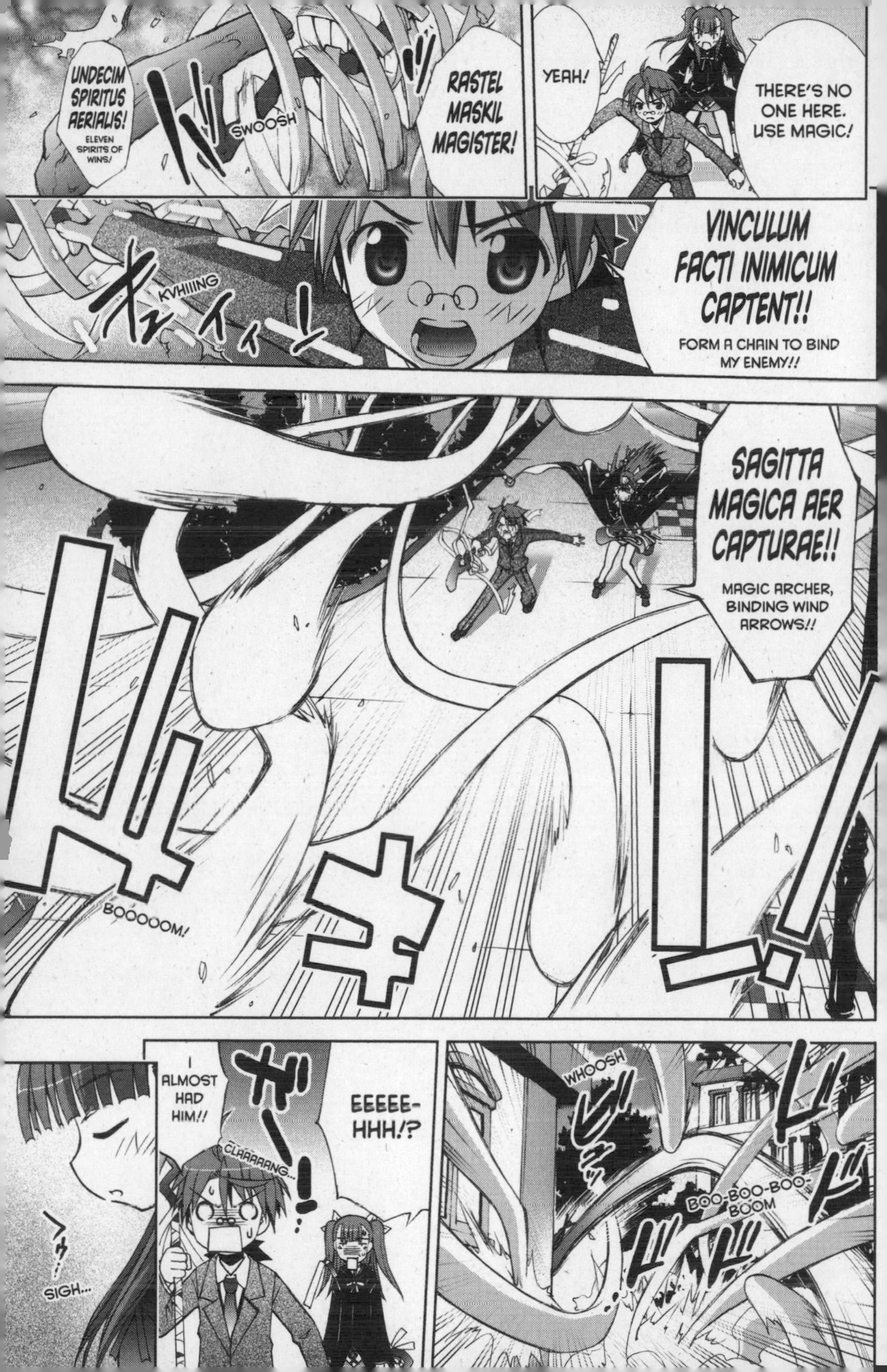
THERE'S NO ONE HERE. USE MAGIC!
YEAH!
RASTEL MASKIL MAGISTER!
SWOOSH
UNDECIM SPIRITUS AERIALIS!
ELEVEN SPIRITS OF WINS!
VINCULUM FACTI INIMICUM CAPTENT!!
FORM A CHAIN TO BIND MY ENEMY!!
KVHIIING
SAGITTA MAGICA AER CAPTURAE!!
MAGIC ARCHER, BINDING WIND ARROWS!!
BOOOOOM!
WHOOSH
BOO-BOO-BOO-BOOM
EEEEE-HHH!?
I ALMOST HAD HIM!!
CLAAAAANG...
SIGH...

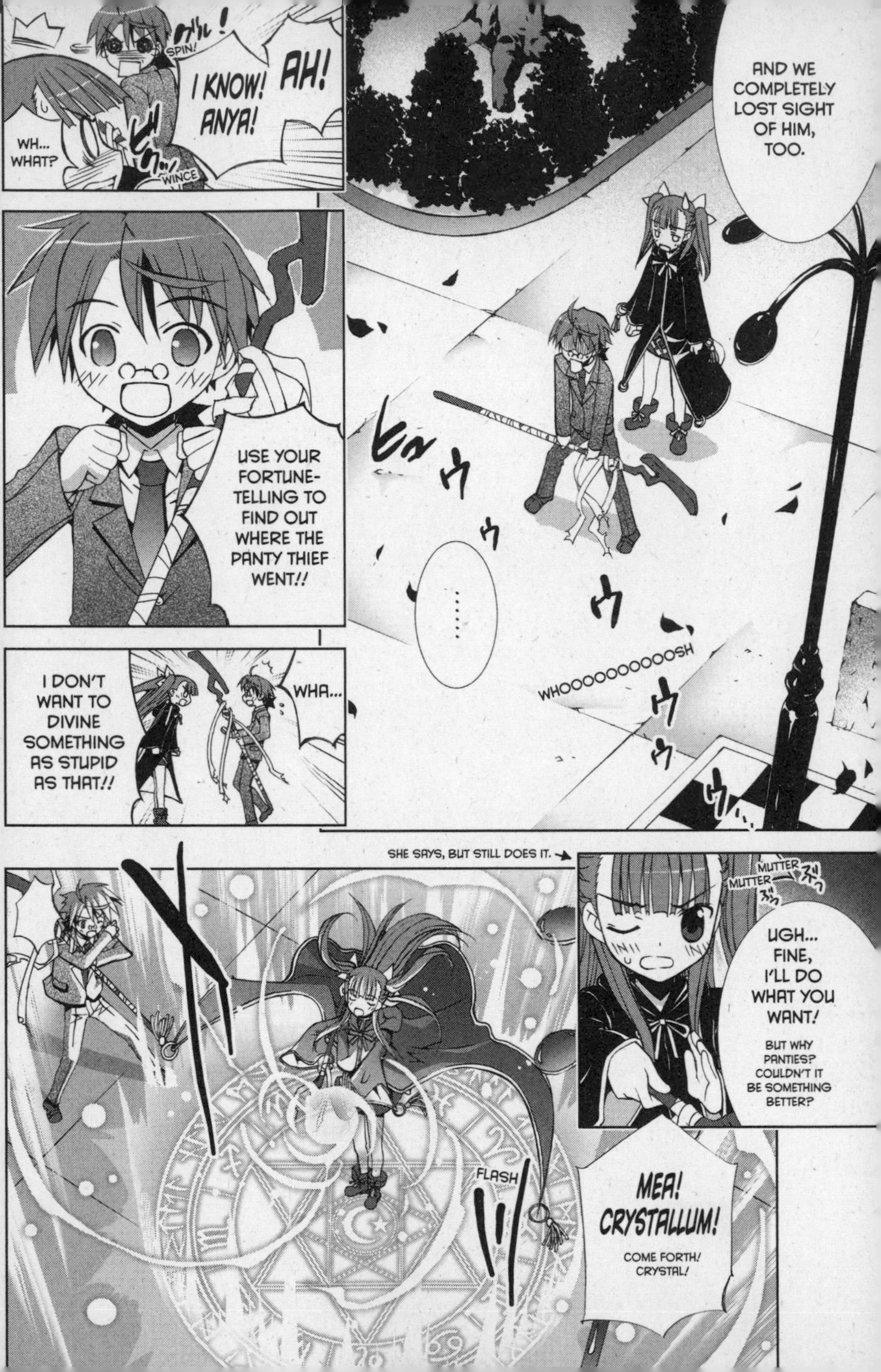
AND WE COMPLETELY LOST SIGHT OF HIM, TOO.
......
WHOOOOOOOOOOSH
AH!
I KNOW! ANYA!
SPIN!
WINCE
WH... WHAT?
USE YOUR FORTUNE-TELLING TO FIND OUT WHERE THE PANTY THIEF WENT!!
WHA...
I DON'T WANT TO DIVINE SOMETHING AS STUPID AS THAT!!
SHE SAYS, BUT STILL DOES IT.
MUTTER
MUTTER
UGH... FINE, I'LL DO WHAT YOU WANT!
BUT WHY PANTIES? COULDN'T IT BE SOMETHING BETTER?
MEA! CRYSTALLUM!
COME FORTH! CRYSTAL!
FLASH

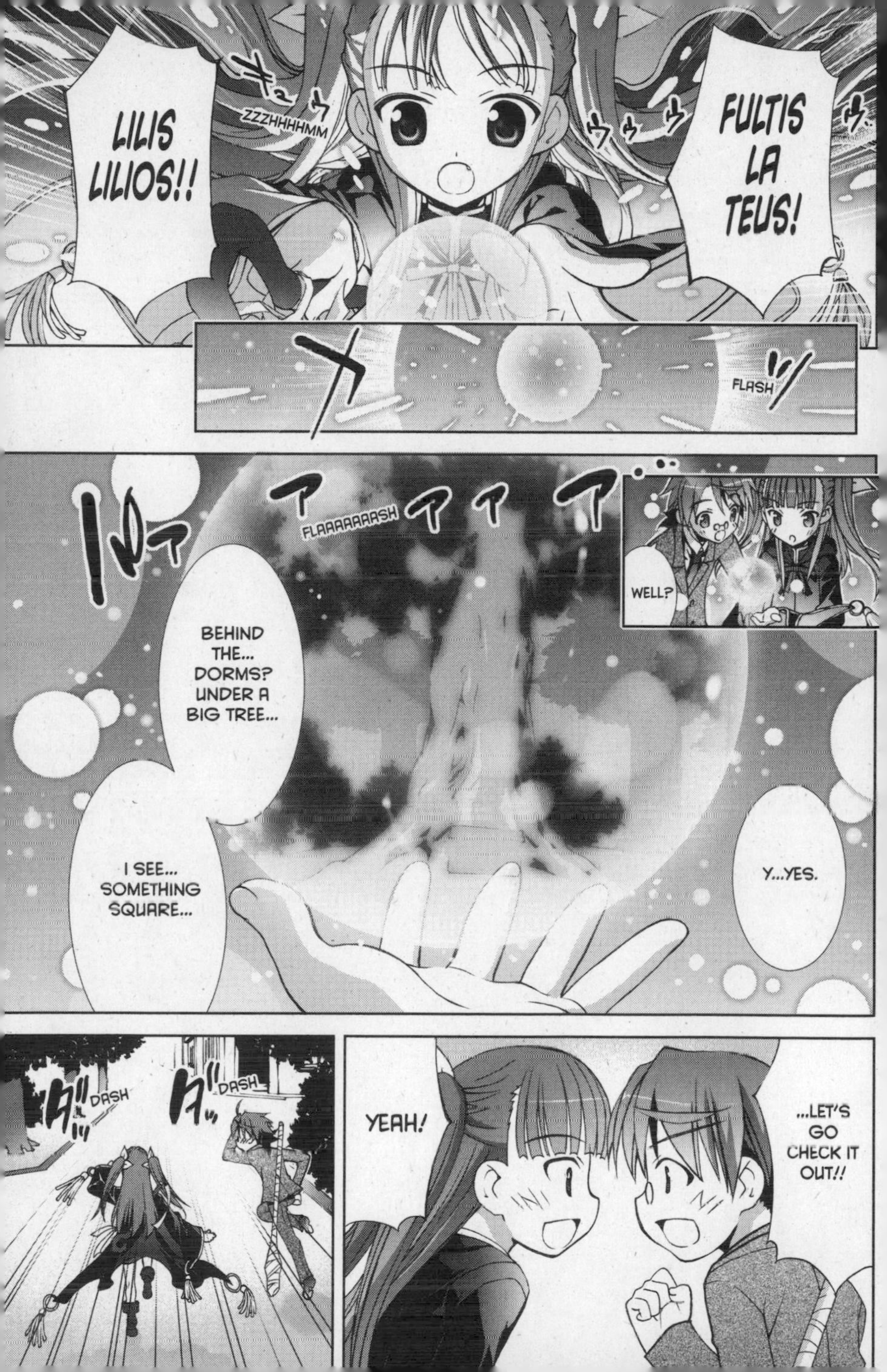
FULTIS LA TEUS!
LILIS LILIOS!!
ZZZHHHHMM
FLASH
WELL?
FLAAAAAAASH
Y...YES.
BEHIND THE... DORMS? UNDER A BIG TREE...
I SEE... SOMETHING SQUARE...
...LET'S GO CHECK IT OUT!!
YEAH!
DASH
DASH

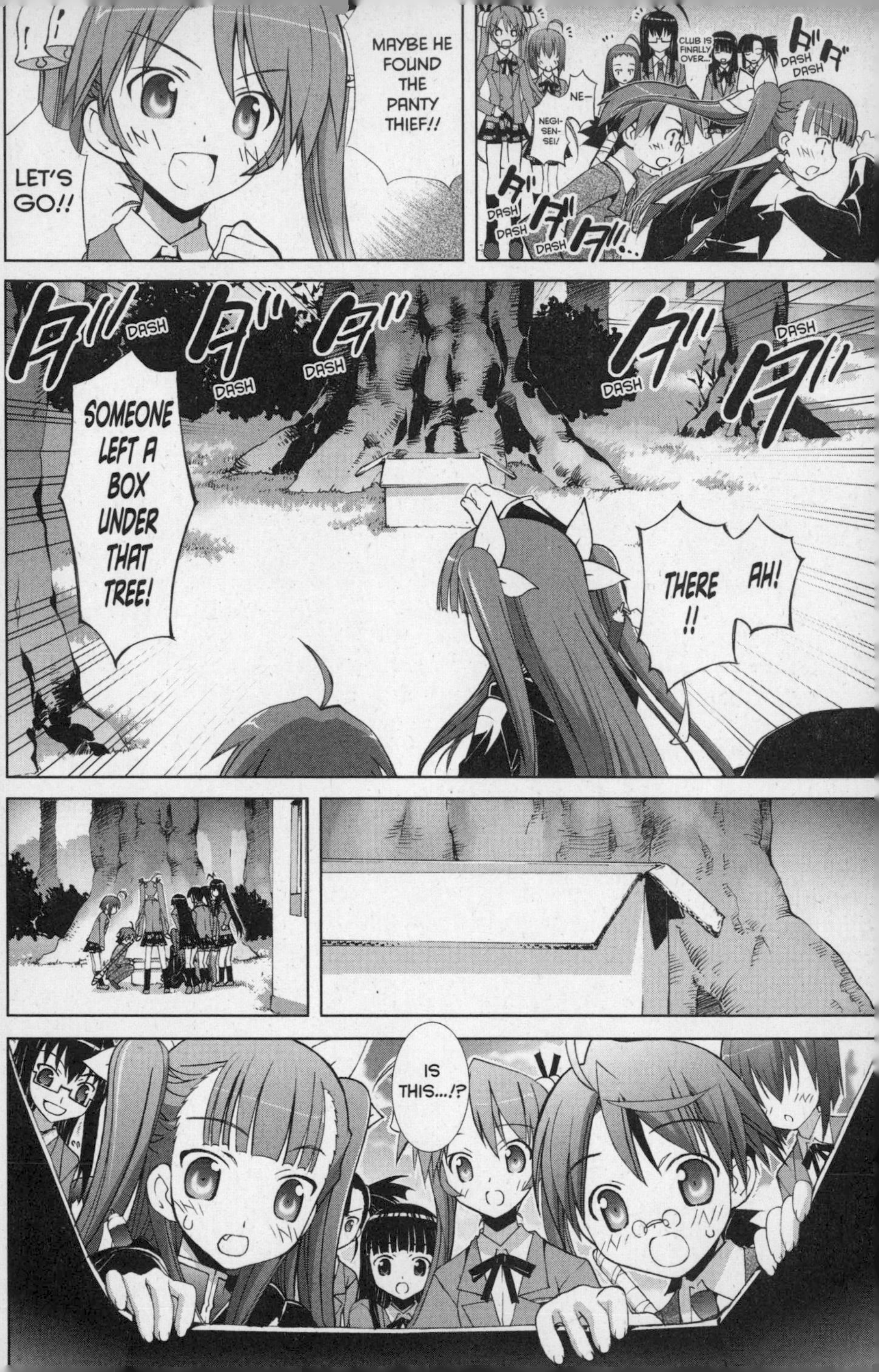
CLUB IS FINALLY OVER...
DASH DASH
NE—
NEGI-SENSEI!
DASH DASH DASH
MAYBE HE FOUND THE PANTY THIEF!!
LET'S GO!!
DASH DASH DASH DASH DASH
AH!
THERE!!
SOMEONE LEFT A BOX UNDER THAT TREE!
IS THIS...!?

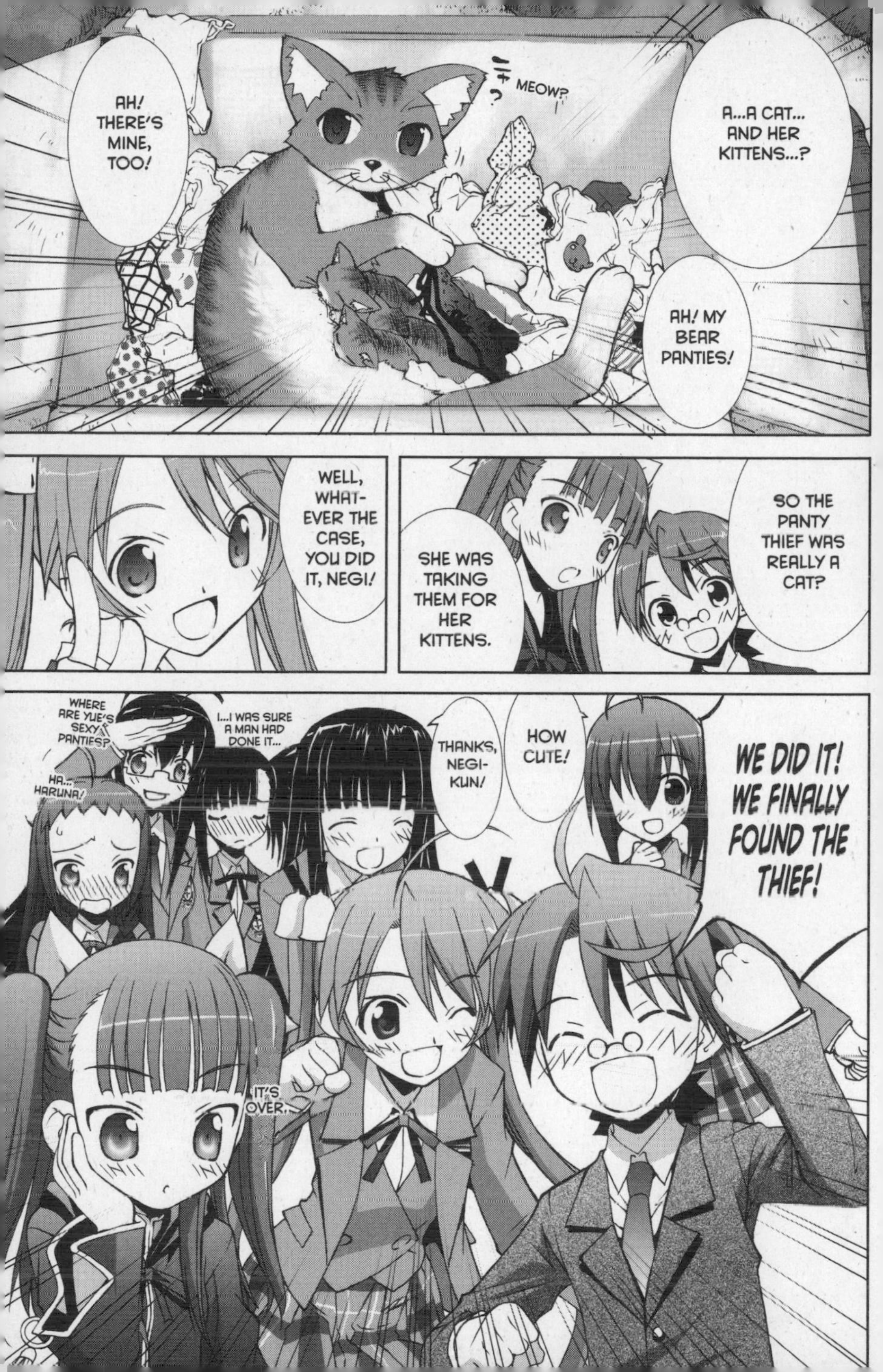
A...A CAT... AND HER KITTENS...?
AH! MY BEAR PANTIES!
MEOW?
AH! THERE'S MINE, TOO!
SO THE PANTY THIEF WAS REALLY A CAT?
SHE WAS TAKING THEM FOR HER KITTENS.
WELL, WHAT-EVER THE CASE, YOU DID IT, NEGI!
WE DID IT! WE FINALLY FOUND THE THIEF!
HOW CUTE!
THANKS, NEGI-KUN!
I...I WAS SURE A MAN HAD DONE IT...
WHERE ARE YUE'S SEXY PANTIES?
HA... HARUNA!
IT'S OVER.

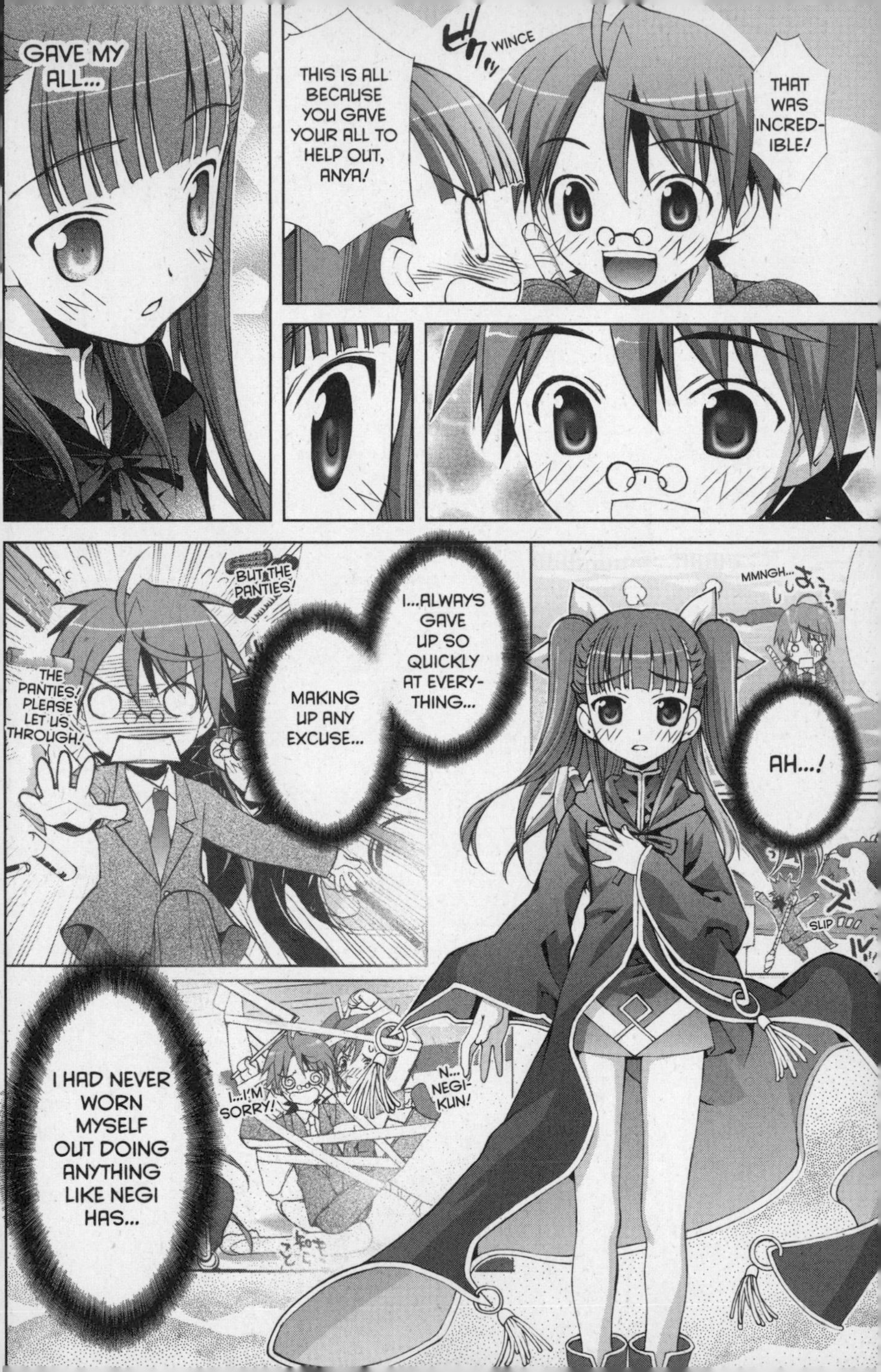
THAT WAS INCREDIBLE!
WINCE
THIS IS ALL BECAUSE YOU GAVE YOUR ALL TO HELP OUT, ANYA!
GAVE MY ALL...
MMNGH...
AH...!
SLIP
I...ALWAYS GAVE UP SO QUICKLY AT EVERY-THING...
MAKING UP ANY EXCUSE...
BUT THE PANTIES!
THE PANTIES! PLEASE LET US THROUGH!
N... NEGI-KUN!
I...I'M SORRY!
I HAD NEVER WORN MYSELF OUT DOING ANYTHING LIKE NEGI HAS...

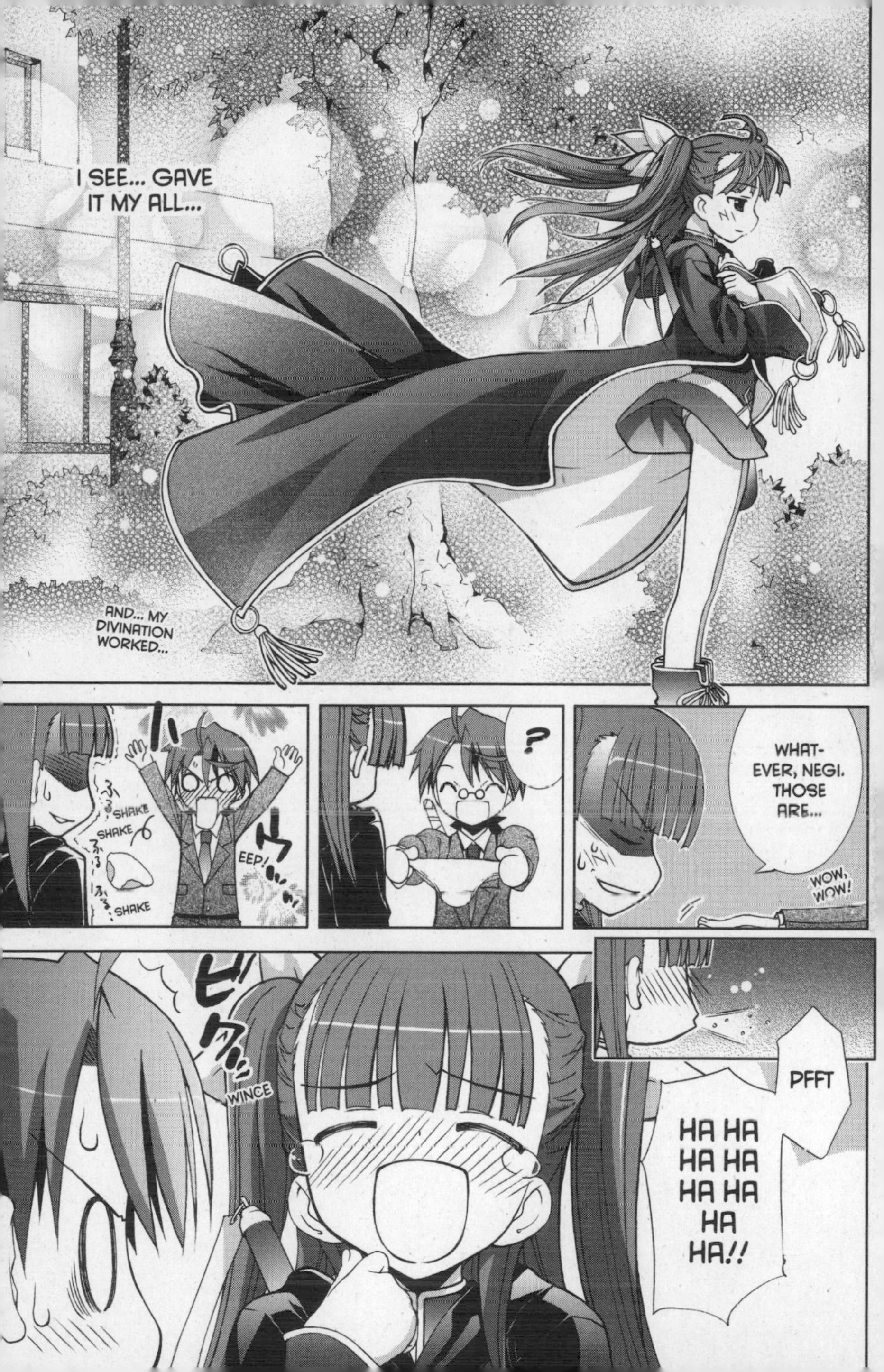
I SEE... GAVE IT MY ALL...
AND... MY DIVINATION WORKED...
WHAT-EVER, NEGI. THOSE ARE...
WOW, WOW!
?
SHAKE
SHAKE
SHAKE
EEP!
PFFT
HA HA HA HA HA HA HA HA!!
WINCE

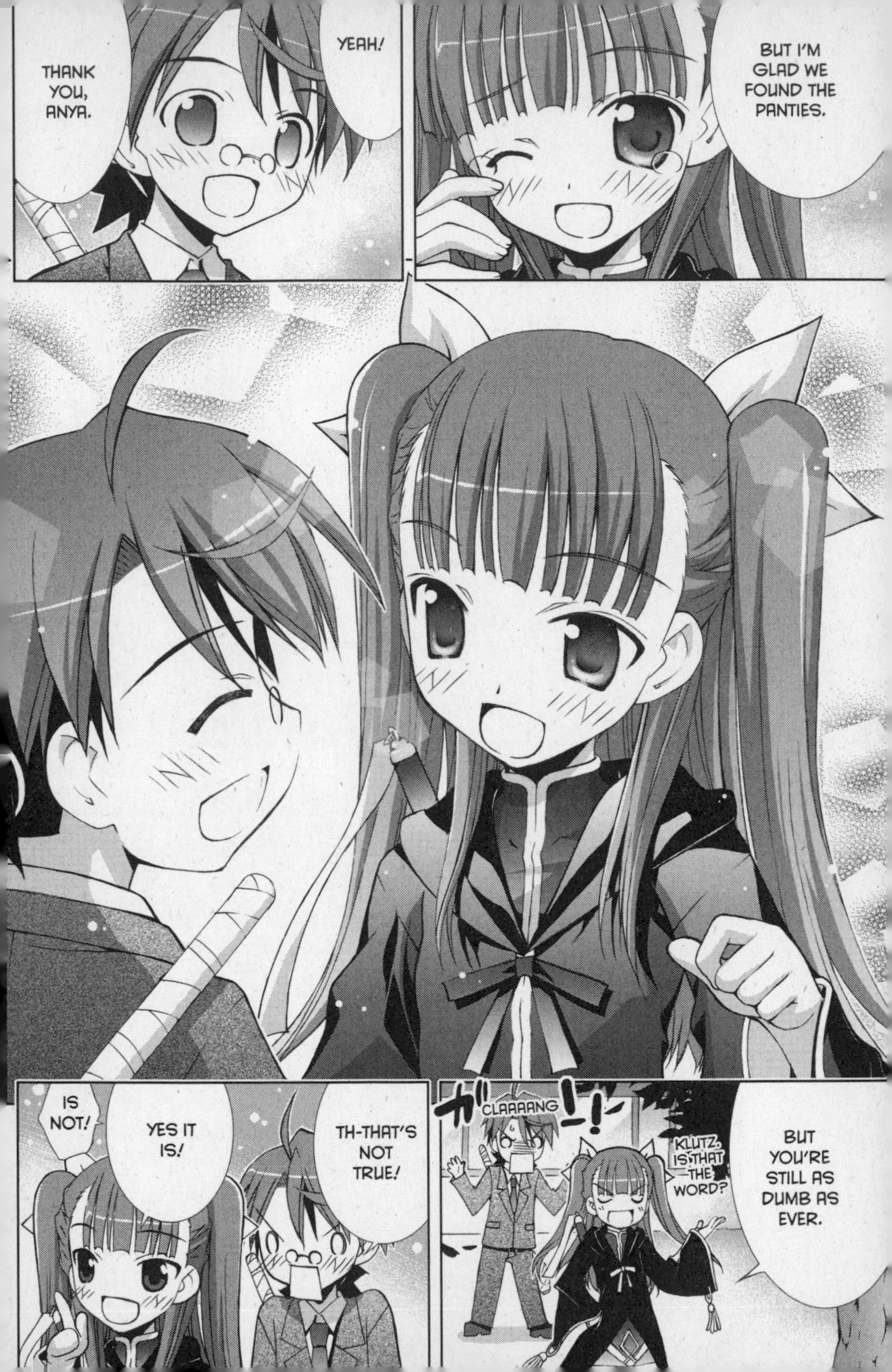
BUT I'M GLAD WE FOUND THE PANTIES.
YEAH!
THANK YOU, ANYA.
BUT YOU'RE STILL AS DUMB AS EVER.
KLUTZ, IS THAT THE WORD?
CLAAAANG
TH-THAT'S NOT TRUE!
YES IT IS!
IS NOT!

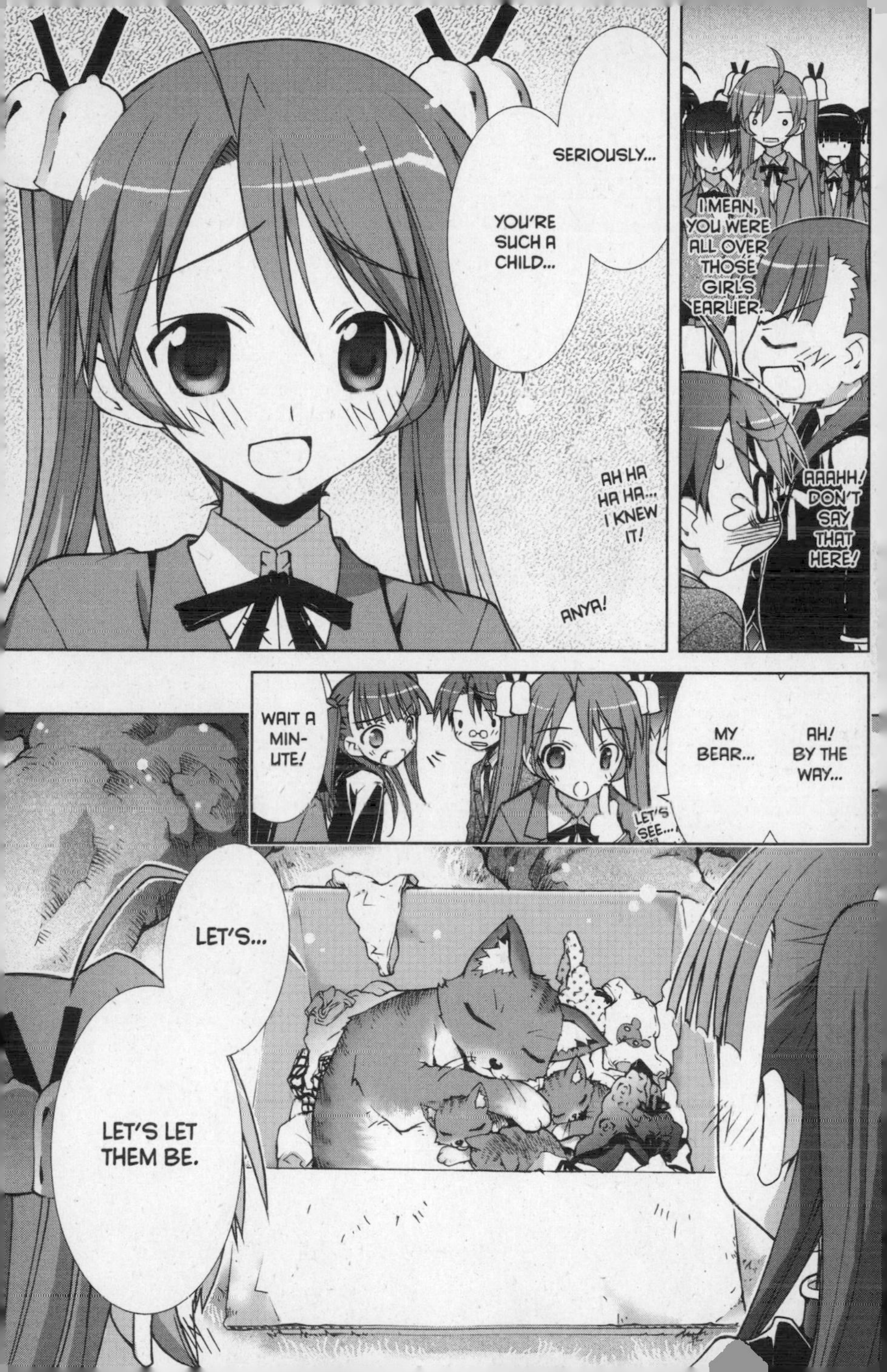
I MEAN, YOU WERE ALL OVER THOSE GIRLS EARLIER.
AAAHH! DON'T SAY THAT HERE!
SERIOUSLY...
YOU'RE SUCH A CHILD...
AH HA HA HA... I KNEW IT!
ANYA!
AH! BY THE WAY...
MY BEAR...
LET'S SEE...
WAIT A MIN-UTE!
LET'S...
LET'S LET THEM BE.

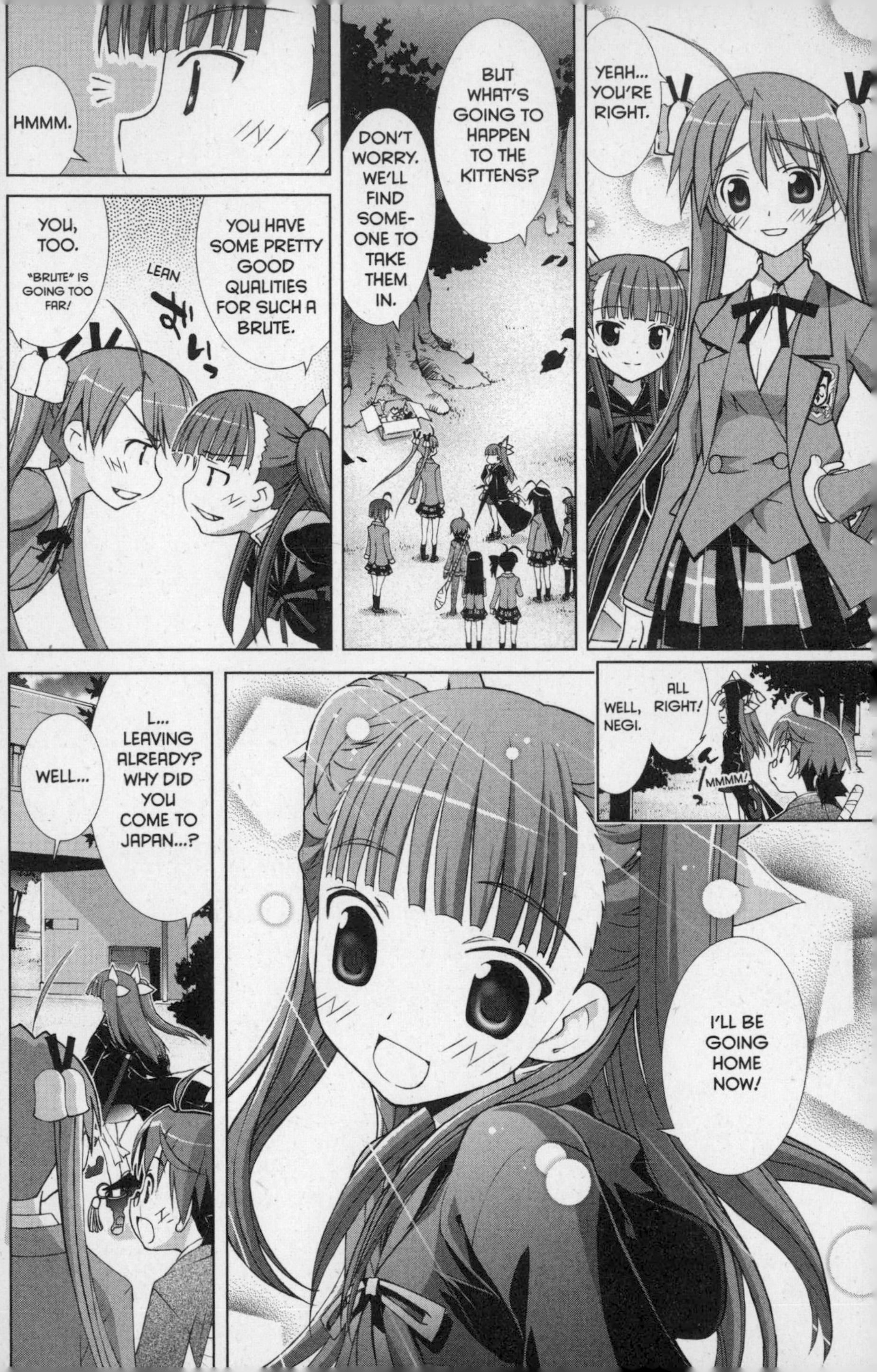
YEAH... YOU'RE RIGHT.
BUT WHAT'S GOING TO HAPPEN TO THE KITTENS?
DON'T WORRY. WE'LL FIND SOME-ONE TO TAKE THEM IN.
HMMM.
YOU HAVE SOME PRETTY GOOD QUALITIES FOR SUCH A BRUTE.
LEAN
YOU, TOO.
"BRUTE" IS GOING TOO FAR!
ALL RIGHT!
WELL, NEGI.
MMMM!
I'LL BE GOING HOME NOW!
L... LEAVING ALREADY? WHY DID YOU COME TO JAPAN...?
WELL...

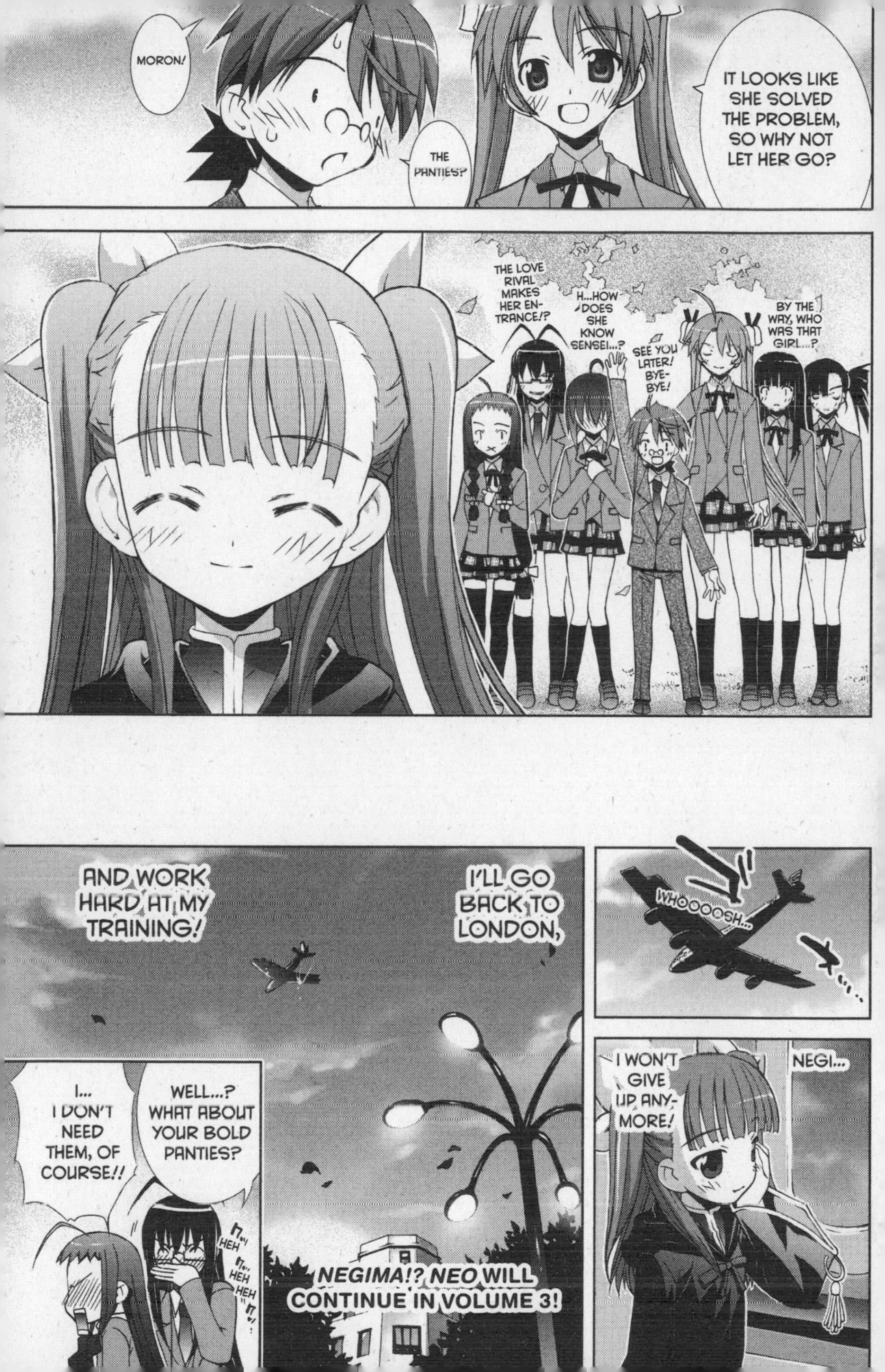
IT LOOKS LIKE SHE SOLVED THE PROBLEM, SO WHY NOT LET HER GO?
THE PANTIES?
MORON!
BY THE WAY, WHO WAS THAT GIRL...?
SEE YOU LATER! BYE-BYE!
H...HOW DOES SHE KNOW SENSEI...?
THE LOVE RIVAL MAKES HER EN-TRANCE!?
WHOOOOSH...
NEGI...
I WON'T GIVE UP ANY-MORE!
I'LL GO BACK TO LONDON,
AND WORK HARD AT MY TRAINING!
WELL...? WHAT ABOUT YOUR BOLD PANTIES?
I... I DON'T NEED THEM, OF COURSE!!
HEH HEH HEH
NEGIMA!? NEO WILL CONTINUE IN VOLUME 3!

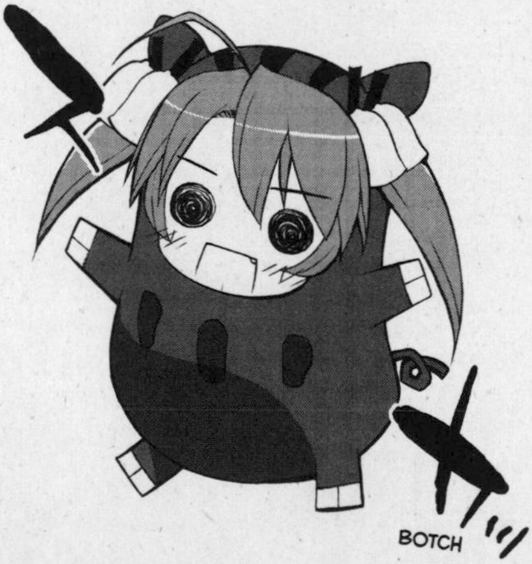
BOTCH

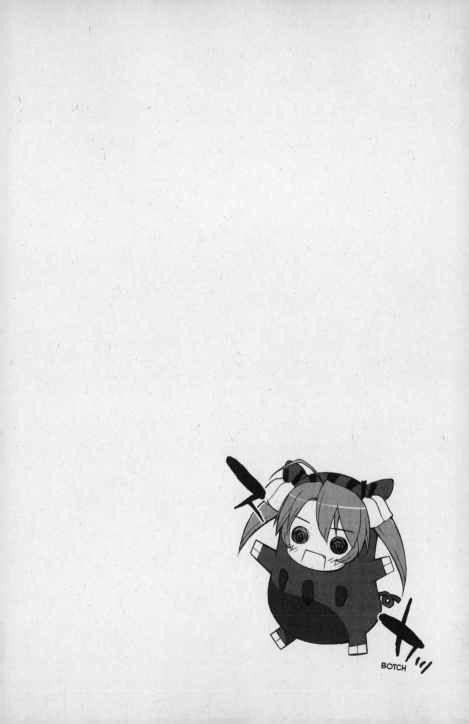

SPECIAL PERIOD / BONUS FOUR-PANEL MANGA

AH-AH-AH-AH-AH-AH...
SSSSSSIP
HOOOOOTTTT...

MAHORA SENTAI BAKA RANGERS

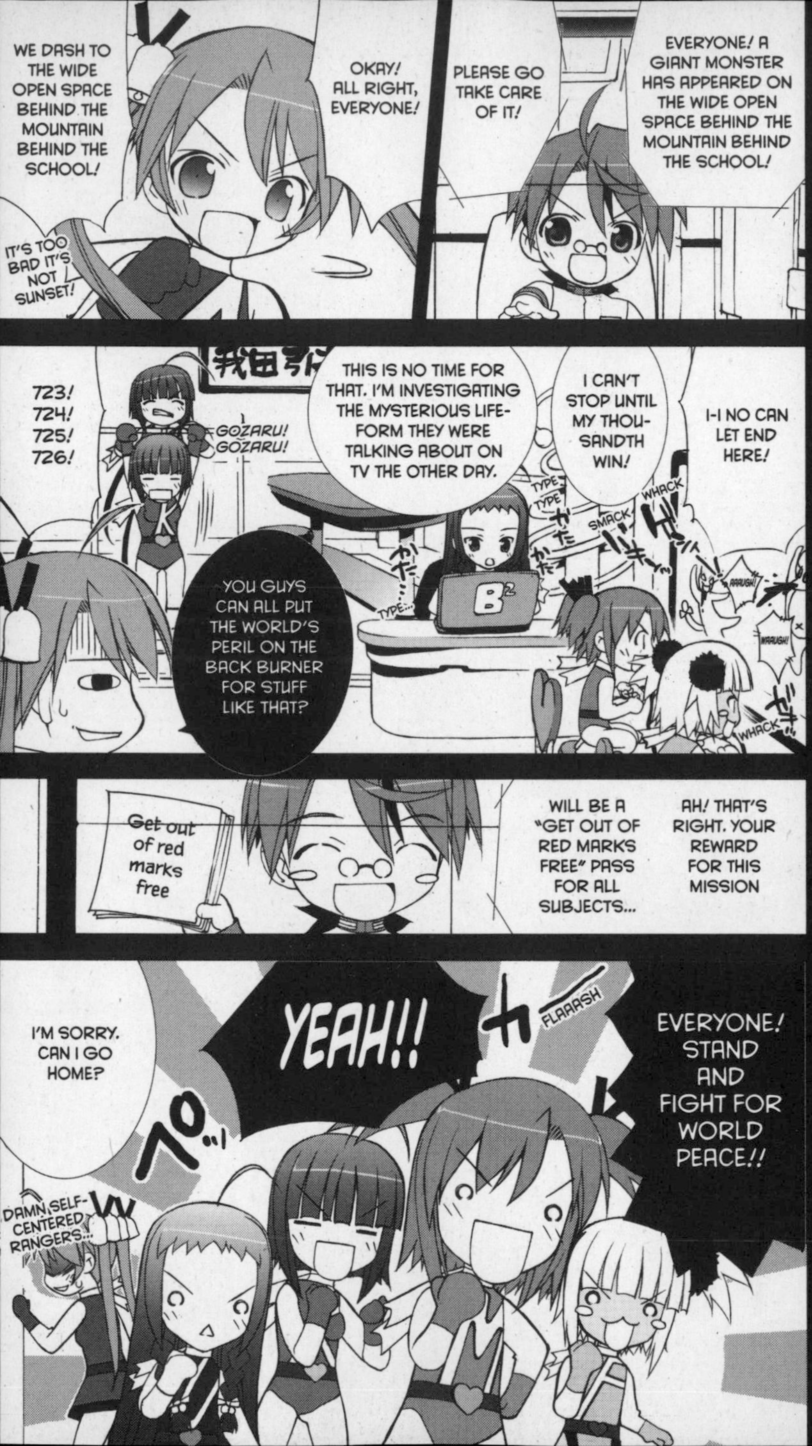
EVERYONE! A GIANT MONSTER HAS APPEARED ON THE WIDE OPEN SPACE BEHIND THE MOUNTAIN BEHIND THE SCHOOL!
PLEASE GO TAKE CARE OF IT!
OKAY! ALL RIGHT, EVERYONE!
WE DASH TO THE WIDE OPEN SPACE BEHIND THE MOUNTAIN BEHIND THE SCHOOL!
IT'S TOO BAD IT'S NOT SUNSET!
I-I NO CAN LET END HERE!
WHACK
SMACK
AAAUGH!
WAAUGH!
WHACK
I CAN'T STOP UNTIL MY THOUSANDTH WIN!
TYPE TYPE
THIS IS NO TIME FOR THAT. I'M INVESTIGATING THE MYSTERIOUS LIFE-FORM THEY WERE TALKING ABOUT ON TV THE OTHER DAY.
TYPE...
GOZARU! GOZARU!
723! 724! 725! 726!
YOU GUYS CAN ALL PUT THE WORLD'S PERIL ON THE BACK BURNER FOR STUFF LIKE THAT?
AH! THAT'S RIGHT. YOUR REWARD FOR THIS MISSION
WILL BE A "GET OUT OF RED MARKS FREE" PASS FOR ALL SUBJECTS...
Get out of red marks free
EVERYONE! STAND AND FIGHT FOR WORLD PEACE!!
FLAAASH
YEAH!!
I'M SORRY. CAN I GO HOME?
DAMN, SELF-CENTERED RANGERS...

BAKA RANGERS, HEAD OUT! 2

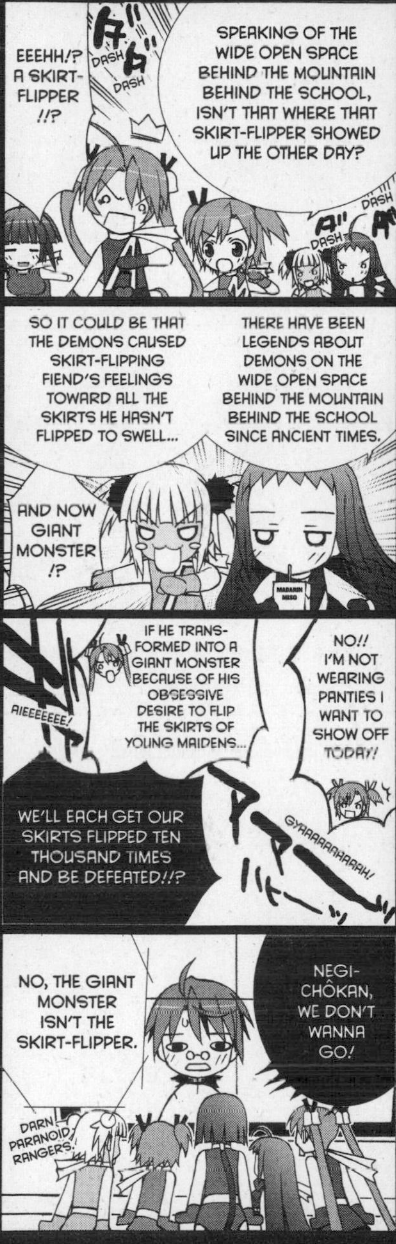

SPEAKING OF THE WIDE OPEN SPACE BEHIND THE MOUNTAIN BEHIND THE SCHOOL, ISN'T THAT WHERE THAT SKIRT-FLIPPER SHOWED UP THE OTHER DAY?
EEEHH!? A SKIRT-FLIPPER!!?
DASH DASH
DASH DASH
THERE HAVE BEEN LEGENDS ABOUT DEMONS ON THE WIDE OPEN SPACE BEHIND THE MOUNTAIN BEHIND THE SCHOOL SINCE ANCIENT TIMES.
SO IT COULD BE THAT THE DEMONS CAUSED SKIRT-FLIPPING FIEND'S FEELINGS TOWARD ALL THE SKIRTS HE HASN'T FLIPPED TO SWELL...
AND NOW GIANT MONSTER!?
NO!! I'M NOT WEARING PANTIES I WANT TO SHOW OFF TODAY!!
IF HE TRANSFORMED INTO A GIANT MONSTER BECAUSE OF HIS OBSESSIVE DESIRE TO FLIP THE SKIRTS OF YOUNG MAIDENS...
AIEEEEEEE!
GYAAAAAAAAAAH!
WE'LL EACH GET OUR SKIRTS FLIPPED TEN THOUSAND TIMES AND BE DEFEATED!!?
NEGI-CHÔKAN, WE DON'T WANNA GO!
NO, THE GIANT MONSTER ISN'T THE SKIRT-FLIPPER.
DARN PARANOID RANGERS.

WHOA!!

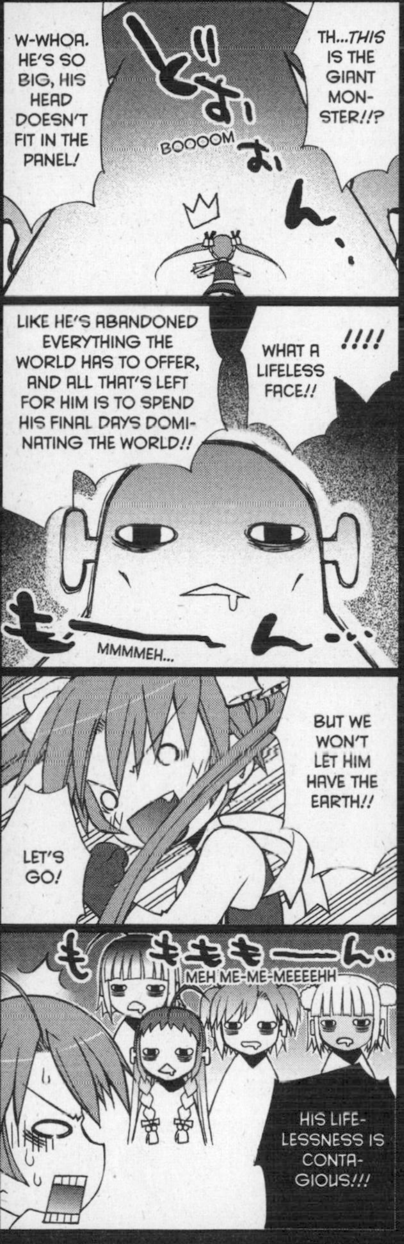

TH...*THIS* IS THE GIANT MONSTER!!?
W-WHOA. HE'S SO BIG, HIS HEAD DOESN'T FIT IN THE PANEL!
BOOOOM
!!!!
WHAT A LIFELESS FACE!!
LIKE HE'S ABANDONED EVERYTHING THE WORLD HAS TO OFFER, AND ALL THAT'S LEFT FOR HIM IS TO SPEND HIS FINAL DAYS DOMINATING THE WORLD!!
MMMMEH...
BUT WE WON'T LET HIM HAVE THE EARTH!!
LET'S GO!
MEH ME-ME-MEEEEHH
HIS LIFELESSNESS IS CONTAGIOUS!!!

“WHOA” RANGERS!

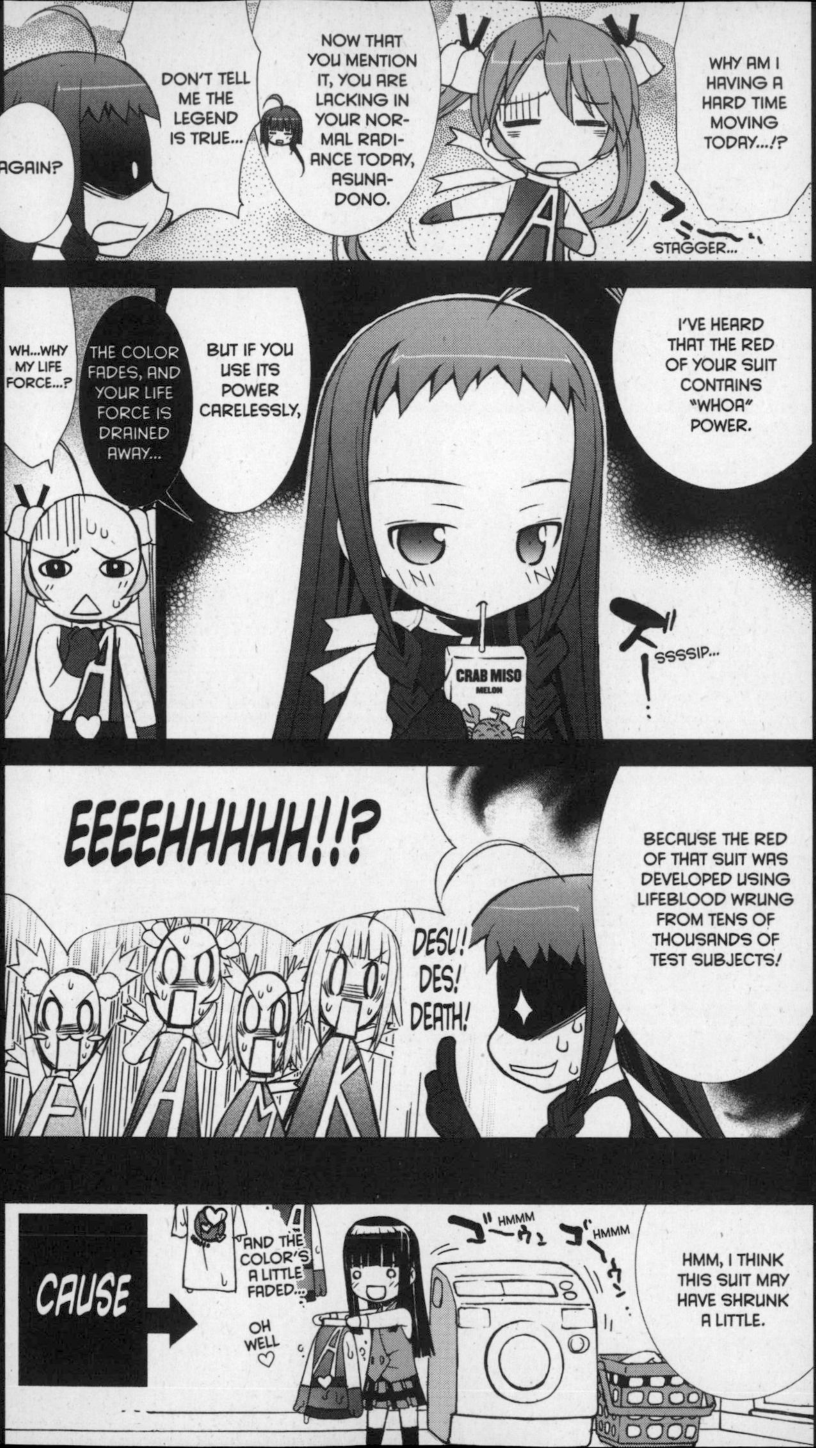

WHY AM I HAVING A HARD TIME MOVING TODAY...!?
STAGGER...
NOW THAT YOU MENTION IT, YOU ARE LACKING IN YOUR NORMAL RADIANCE TODAY, ASUNA-DONO.
DON'T TELL ME THE LEGEND IS TRUE...
AGAIN?
I'VE HEARD THAT THE RED OF YOUR SUIT CONTAINS "WHOA" POWER.
SSSSIP...
CRAB MISO
MELON
BUT IF YOU USE ITS POWER CARELESSLY,
THE COLOR FADES, AND YOUR LIFE FORCE IS DRAINED AWAY...
WH...WHY MY LIFE FORCE...?
BECAUSE THE RED OF THAT SUIT WAS DEVELOPED USING LIFEBLOOD WRUNG FROM TENS OF THOUSANDS OF TEST SUBJECTS!
DESU! DES! DEATH!
EEEEHHHHHH!!?
HMM, I THINK THIS SUIT MAY HAVE SHRUNK A LITTLE.
HMMM
HMMM
AND THE COLOR'S A LITTLE FADED...
OH WELL ♡
CAUSE

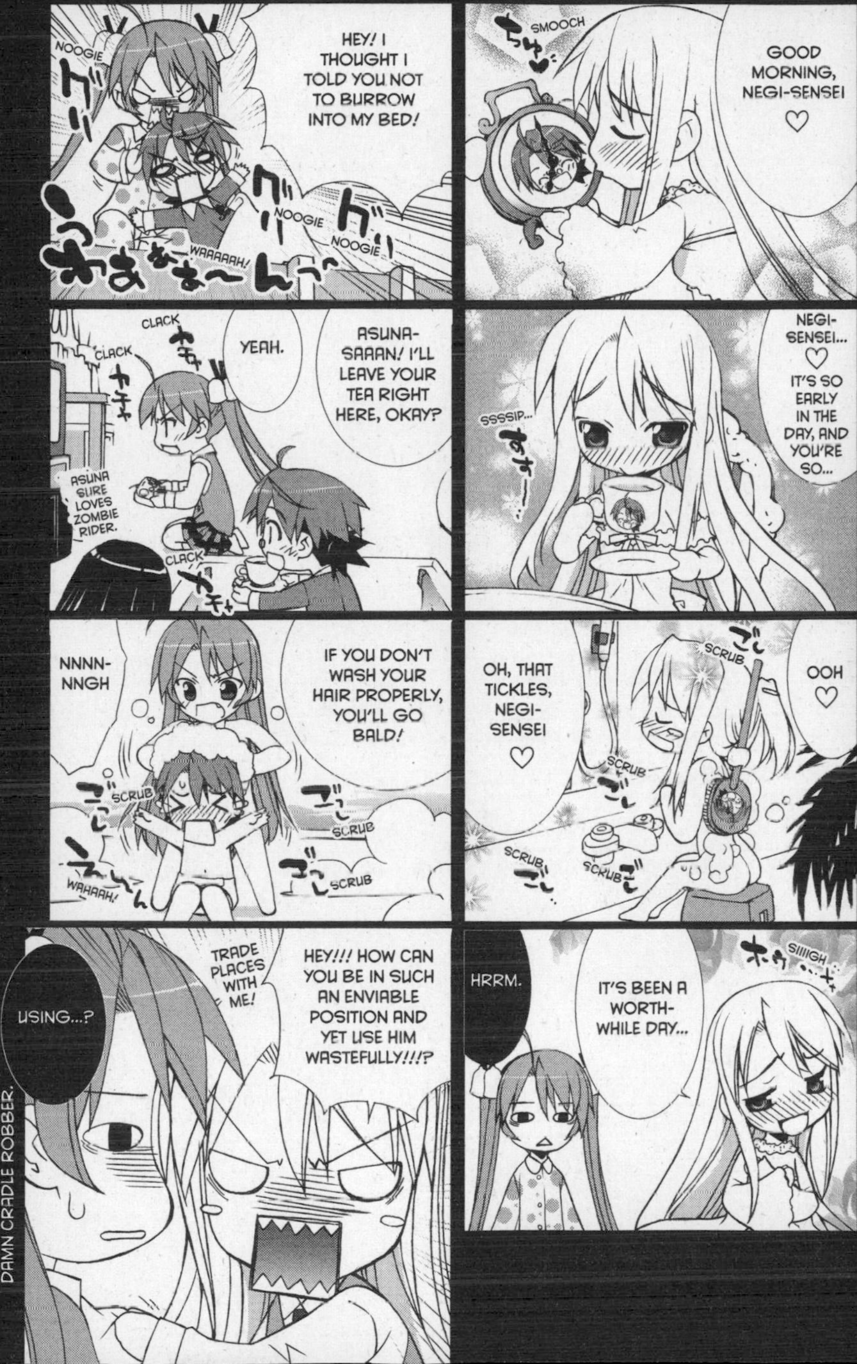
SMOOCH
GOOD MORNING, NEGI-SENSEI ♡
NOOGIE
HEY! I THOUGHT I TOLD YOU NOT TO BURROW INTO MY BED!
NOOGIE
NOOGIE
WAAAAAAH!
NEGI-SENSEI... ♡ IT'S SO EARLY IN THE DAY, AND YOU'RE SO...
SSSSIP...
ASUNA-SAAAN! I'LL LEAVE YOUR TEA RIGHT HERE, OKAY?
YEAH.
CLACK
CLACK
ASUNA SURE LOVES ZOMBIE RIDER.
CLACK
OOH ♡
SCRUB
OH, THAT TICKLES, NEGI-SENSEI ♡
SCRUB
SCRUB
SCRUB
IF YOU DON'T WASH YOUR HAIR PROPERLY, YOU'LL GO BALD!
NNNN-NNGH
SCRUB
SCRUB
SCRUB
WAHAAH!
SIIIIGH
IT'S BEEN A WORTH-WHILE DAY...
HRRM.
HEY!!! HOW CAN YOU BE IN SUCH AN ENVIABLE POSITION AND YET USE HIM WASTEFULLY!!!?
TRADE PLACES WITH ME!
USING...?
DAMN CRADLE ROBBER.

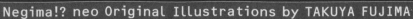

ASUNA KAGURAZAKA

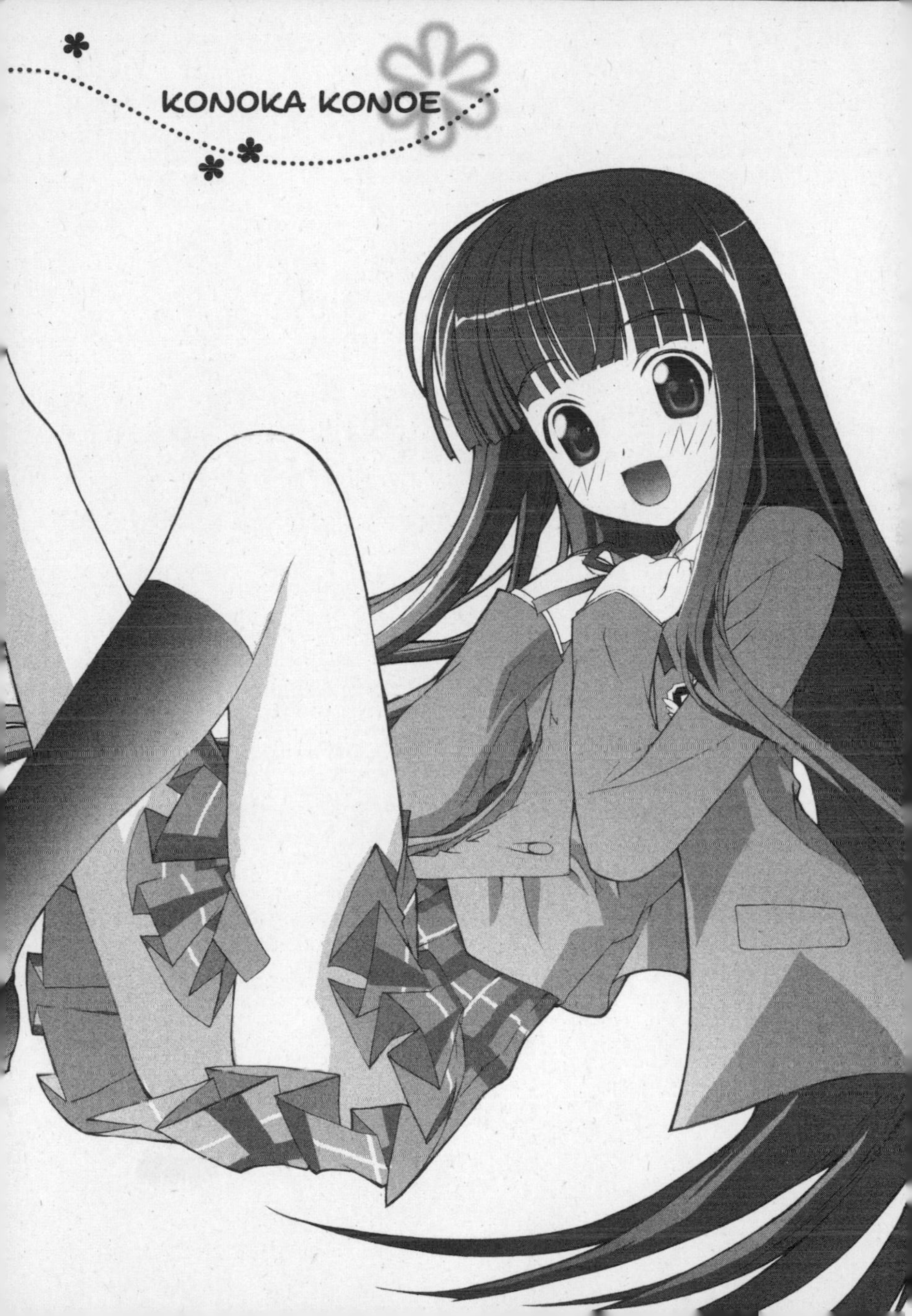
KONOKA KONOE

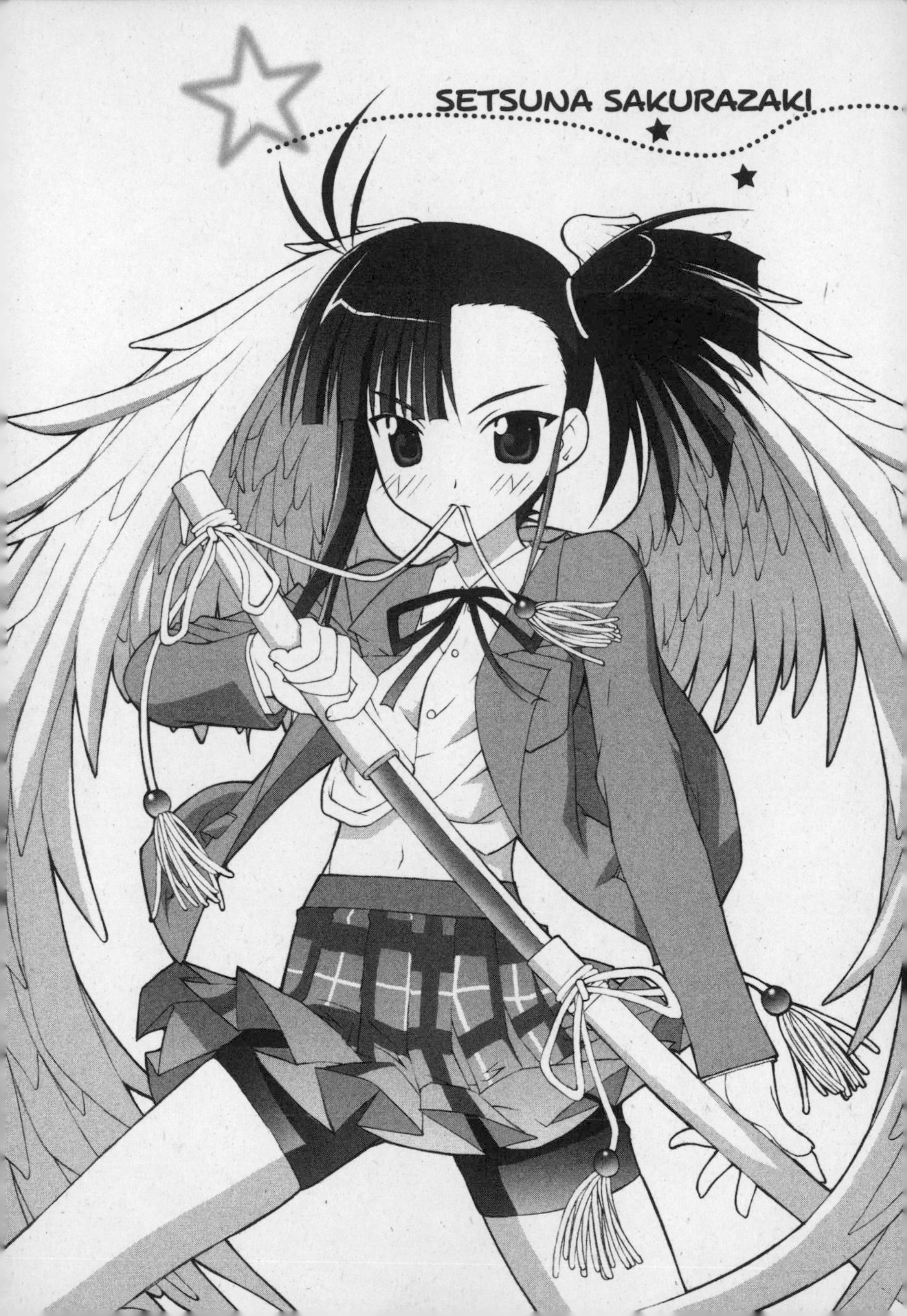
SETSUNA SAKURAZAKI

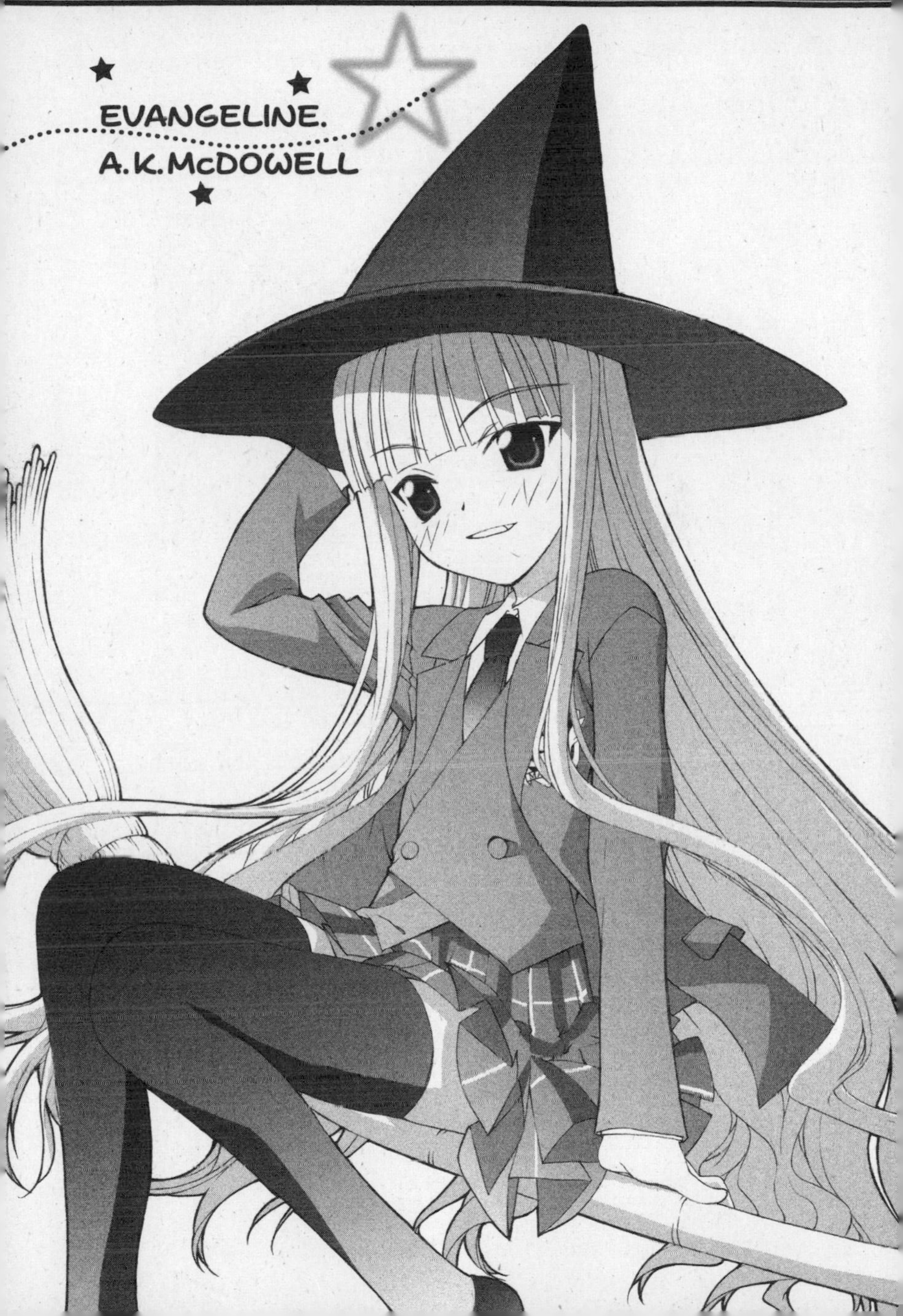
EVANGELINE.
A.K.McDOWELL

TAKUYA FUJIMA VERSION PACTIO CARDS

ASUNA KAGURAZAKA ARMOR CARD

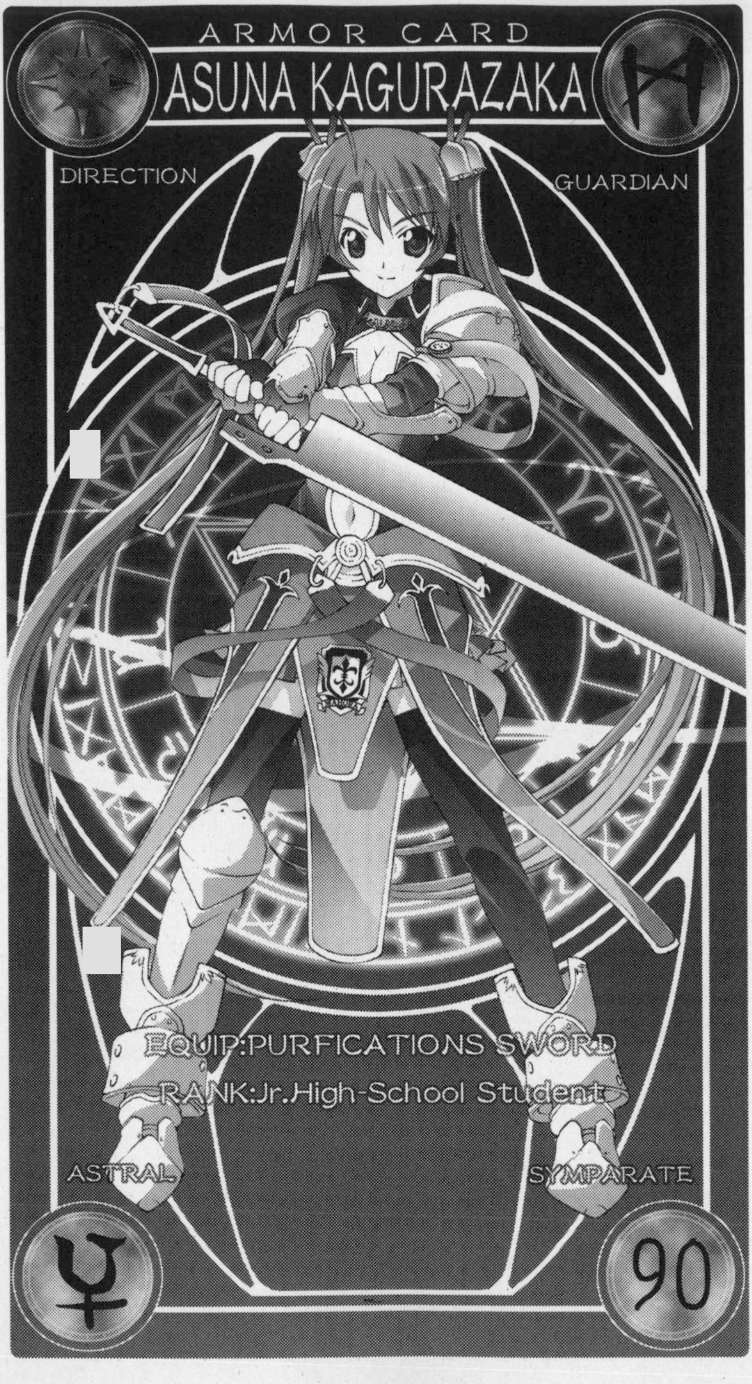
ARMOR CARD
ASUNA KAGURAZAKA
DIRECTION
GUARDIAN
EQUIP:PURFICATIONS SWORD
RANK:Jr.High-School Student
ASTRAL
SYMPARATE
90

TAKUYA FUJIMA VERSION PACTIO CARDS

KONOKA KONOE ARMOR CARD

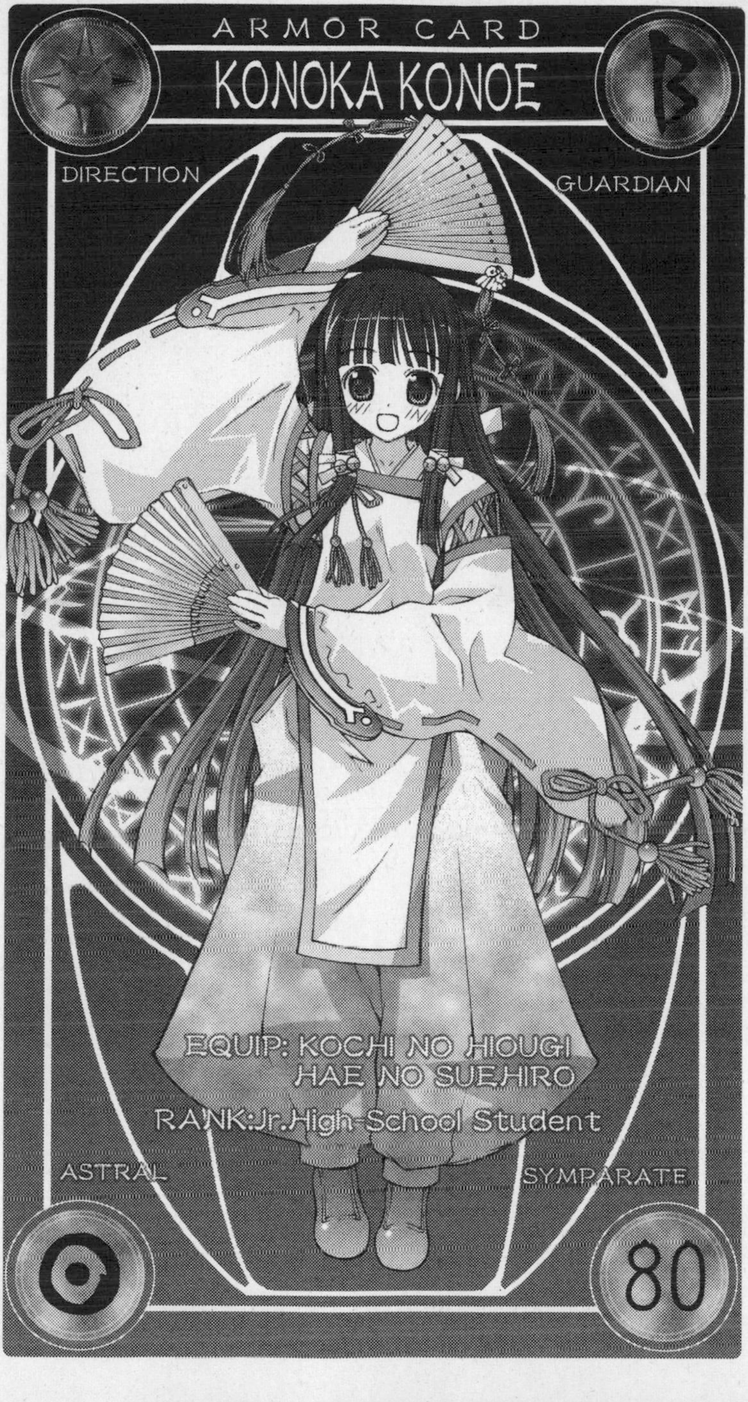

ARMOR CARD
KONOKA KONOE
DIRECTION
GUARDIAN
EQUIP: KOCHI NO HIOUGI
HAE NO SUEHIRO
RANK:Jr.High School Student
ASTRAL
SYMPARATE
80

HELLO, THIS IS TAKUYA FUJIMA. FOR VOLUME 2, A LIMITED EDITION WENT ON SALE! (PLEASED.) I'M HAPPY ABOUT IT, BUT IT WAS HARDER THAN I THOUGHT TO DRAW THE SAME COVER WITH A SCHOOL UNIFORM VERSION AND A SWIMSUIT VERSION [FACE] COUGH! THE NEGIMA!? NEO COVERS ARE VERY LOOOOOOONG ILLUSTRATIONS THAT INCLUDE THE COVER FLAPS, SO IT'S A LOT OF WORK DOING THE LAYOUT AND TRIMMING THINGS DOWN.

NEXT PAGE

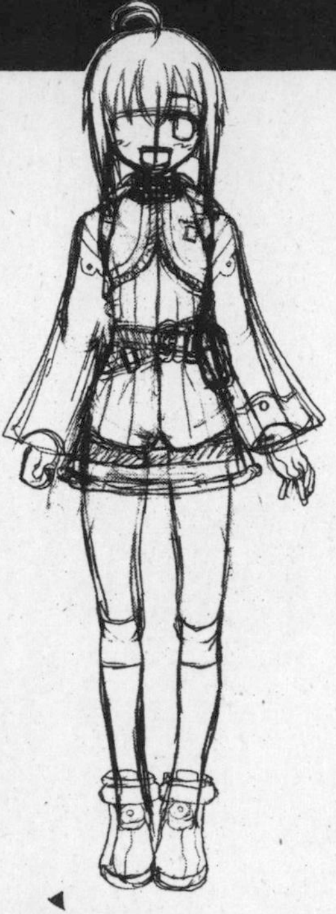

CHAPTER 8, PAGE 5. NODOKA ROUGH.

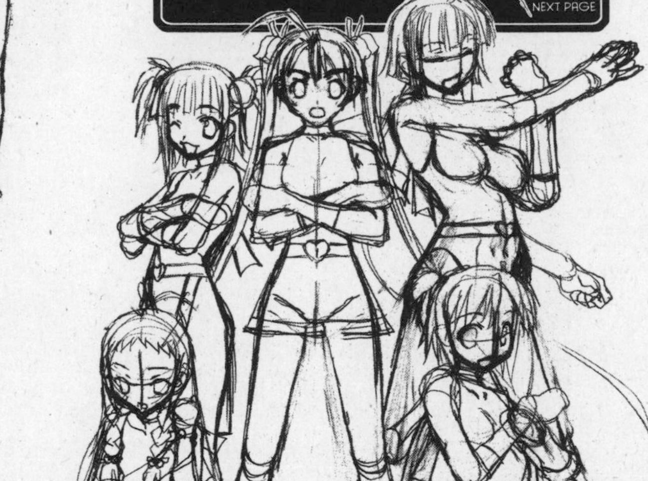

CHAPTER 8, PAGE 3. BAKA RANGERS ROUGH.

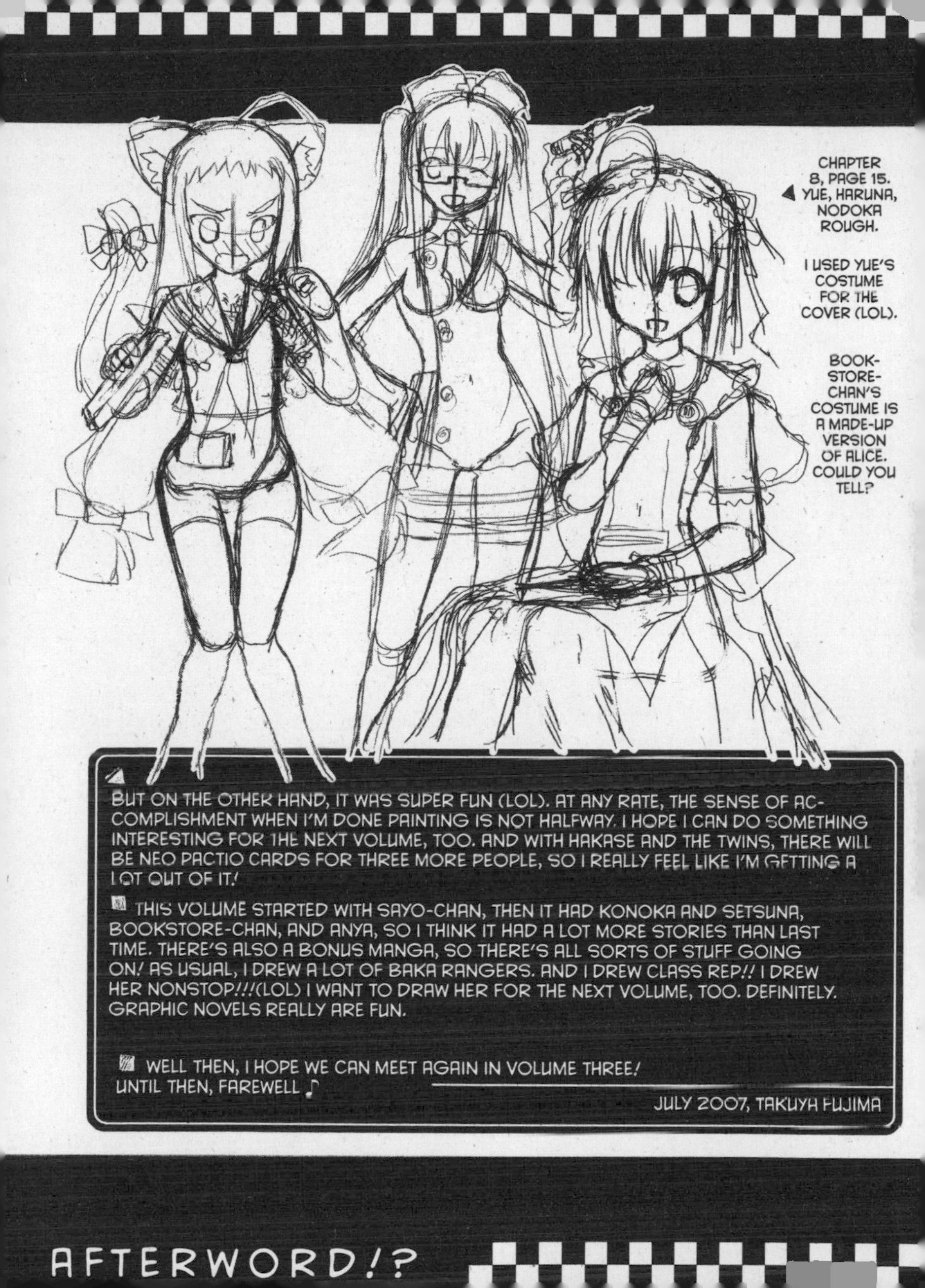

CHAPTER 8, PAGE 15. ◀ YUE, HARUNA, NODOKA ROUGH.

I USED YUE'S COSTUME FOR THE COVER (LOL).

BOOKSTORE-CHAN'S COSTUME IS A MADE-UP VERSION OF ALICE. COULD YOU TELL?

BUT ON THE OTHER HAND, IT WAS SUPER FUN (LOL). AT ANY RATE, THE SENSE OF ACCOMPLISHMENT WHEN I'M DONE PAINTING IS NOT HALFWAY. I HOPE I CAN DO SOMETHING INTERESTING FOR THE NEXT VOLUME, TOO. AND WITH HAKASE AND THE TWINS, THERE WILL BE NEO PACTIO CARDS FOR THREE MORE PEOPLE, SO I REALLY FEEL LIKE I'M GETTING A LOT OUT OF IT!

THIS VOLUME STARTED WITH SAYO-CHAN, THEN IT HAD KONOKA AND SETSUNA, BOOKSTORE-CHAN, AND ANYA, SO I THINK IT HAD A LOT MORE STORIES THAN LAST TIME. THERE'S ALSO A BONUS MANGA, SO THERE'S ALL SORTS OF STUFF GOING ON! AS USUAL, I DREW A LOT OF BAKA RANGERS. AND I DREW CLASS REP!! I DREW HER NONSTOP!!!(LOL) I WANT TO DRAW HER FOR THE NEXT VOLUME, TOO. DEFINITELY. GRAPHIC NOVELS REALLY ARE FUN.

WELL THEN, I HOPE WE CAN MEET AGAIN IN VOLUME THREE!
UNTIL THEN, FAREWELL ♪

JULY 2007, TAKUYA FUJIMA

AFTERWORD!?

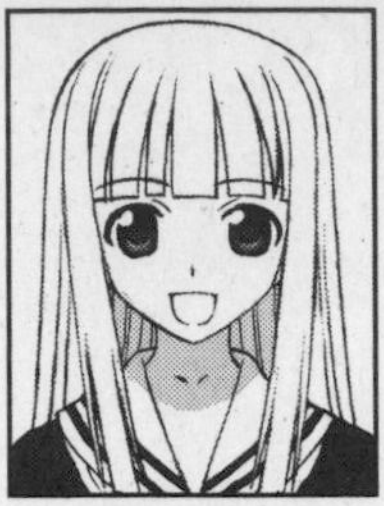

1. SAYO AISAKA

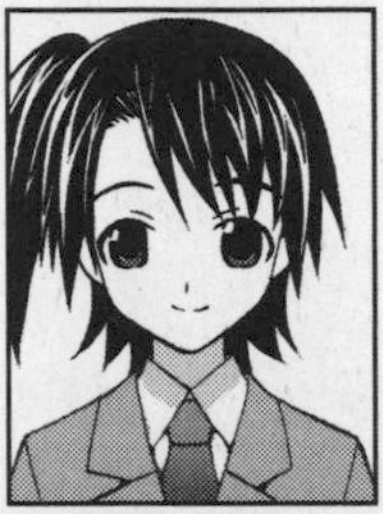

2. YUNA AKASHI
BASKETBALL TEAM

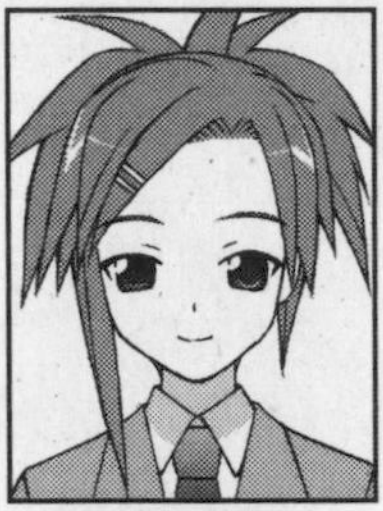

3. KAZUMI ASAKURA
SCHOOL NEWSPAPER

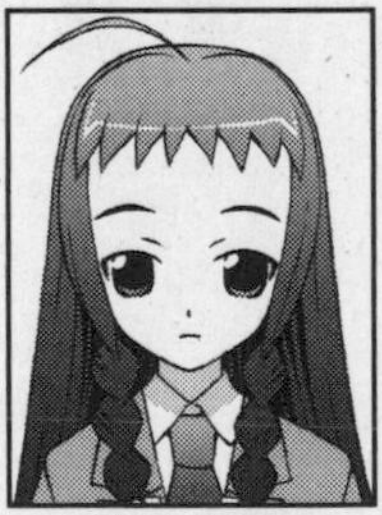

4. YUE AYASE
KIDS' LIT CLUB, PHILOSOPHY CLUB, LIBRARY EXPLORATION CLUB

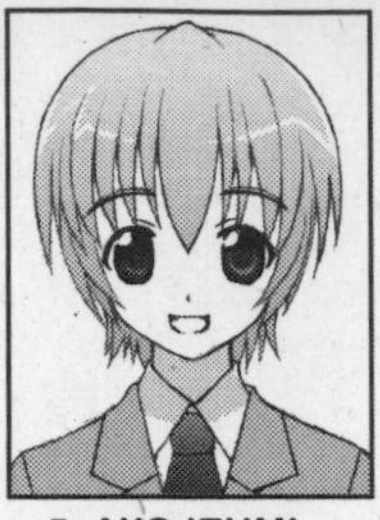

5. AKO IZUMI
NURSE'S OFFICE AIDE, SOCCER TEAM (NON-SCHOOL ACTIVITY)

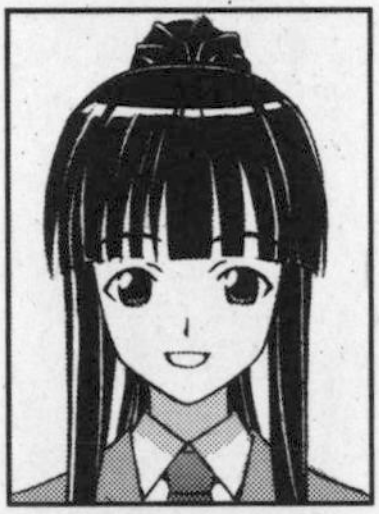

6. AKIRA OKOCHI
SWIM TEAM

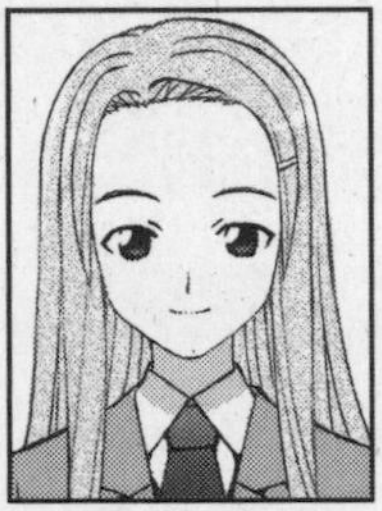

7. MISA KAKIZAKI
CHEERLEADER, CHORUS

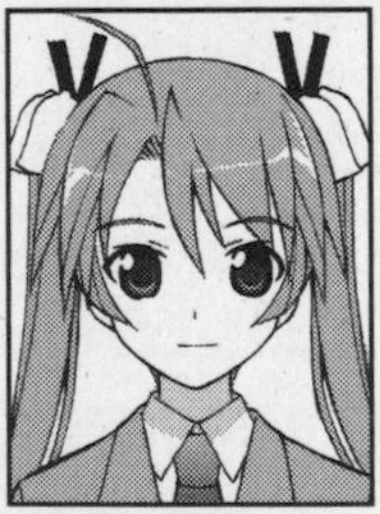

8. ASUNA KAGURAZAKA
ART CLUB

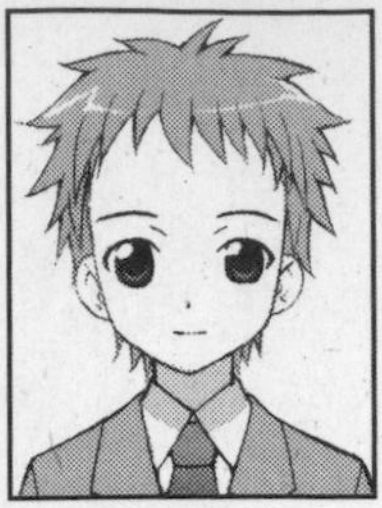

9. MISORA KASUGA
TRACK AND FIELD

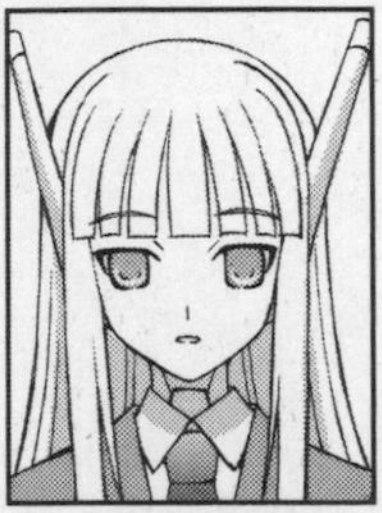

10. CHACHAMARU KARAKUI
TEA CEREMONY CLUB, GO CLUB

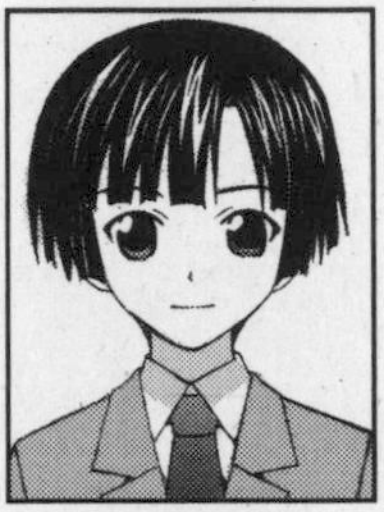

11. MADOKA KUGIMIYA
CHEERLEADER

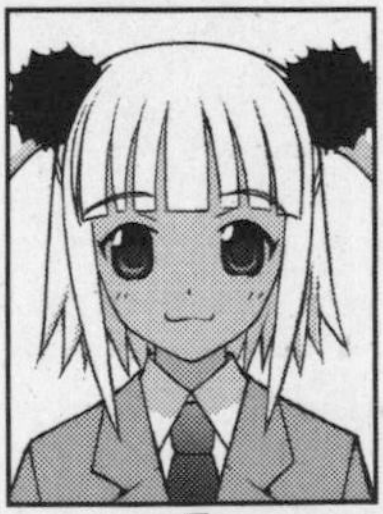

12. KŪ FEI
CHINESE MARTIAL ARTS CLUB

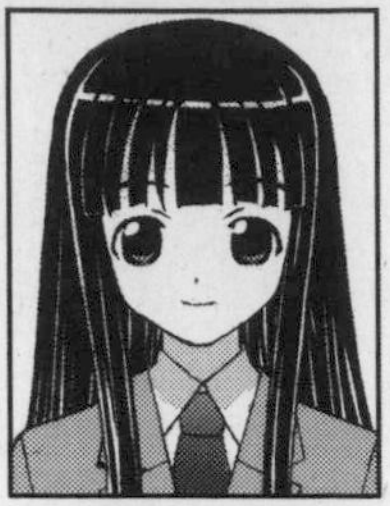

13. KONOKA KONOE
SECRETARY, FORTUNE-TELLING CLUB, LIBRARY EXPLORATION CLUB

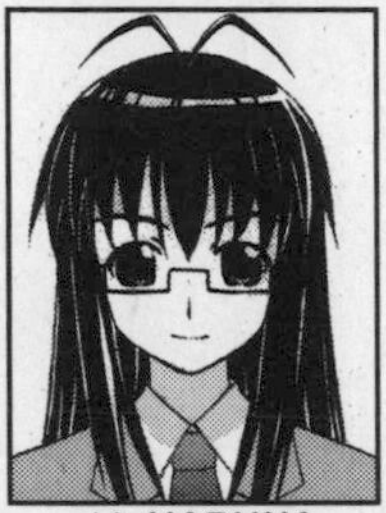

14. HARUNA SAOTOME
MANGA CLUB, LIBRARY EXPLORATION CLUB

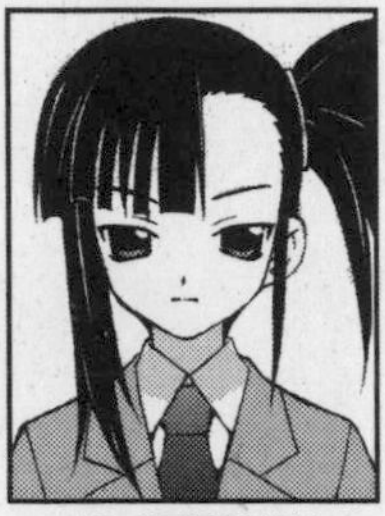

15. SETSUNA SAKURAZAKI
KENDO CLUB

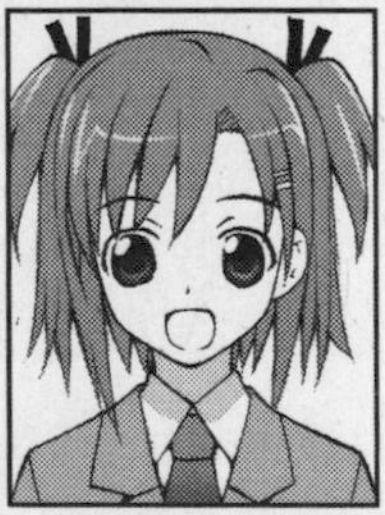

16. MAKIE SASAKI
GYMNASTICS

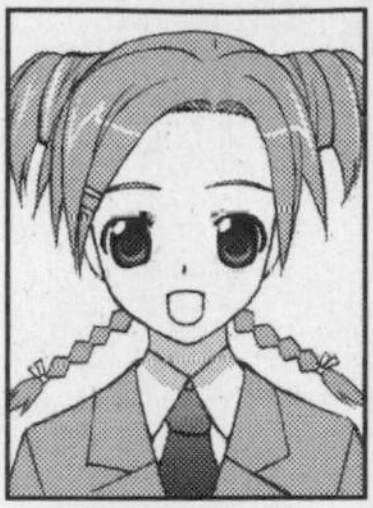

17. SAKURAKO SHIINA
LACROSSE TEAM, CHEERLEADER

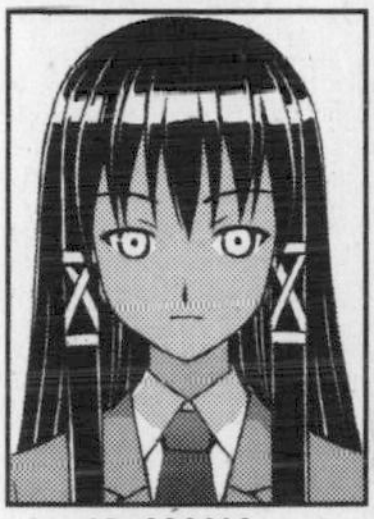

18. MANA TATSUMIYA
BIATHLON (NON-SCHOOL ACTIVITY)

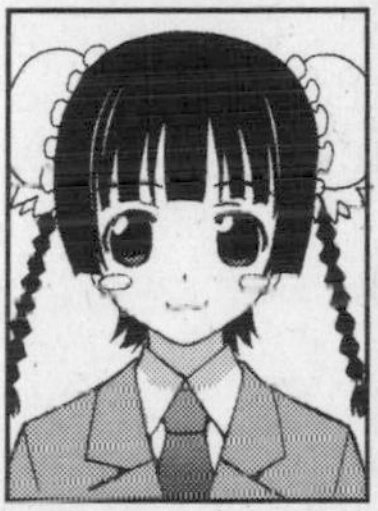

19. CHAO LINGSHEN
COOKING CLUB, CHINESE MARTIAL ARTS CLUB, ROBOTICS CLUB, CHINESE MEDICINE CLUB, BIO-ENGINEERING CLUB, QUANTUM PHYSICS CLUB (UNIVERSITY)

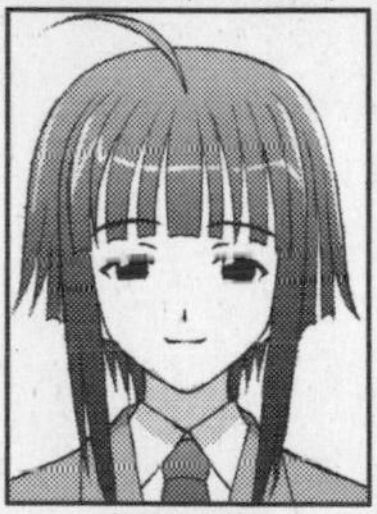

20. KAEDE NAGASE
WALKING CLUB

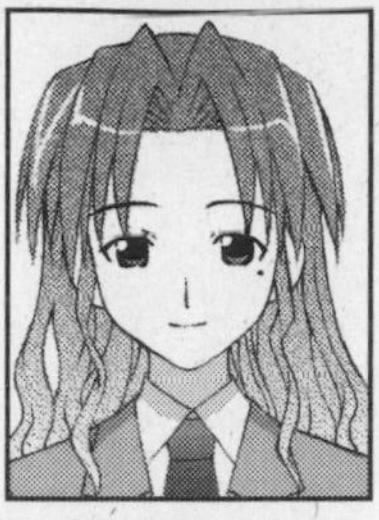

21. CHIZURU NABA
ASTRONOMY CLUB

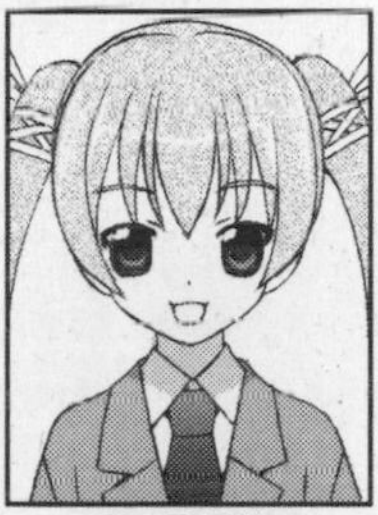

22. FUKA NARUTAKI
WALKING CLUB

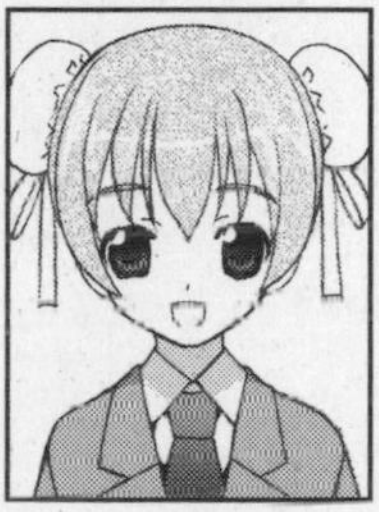

23. FUMIKA NARUTAKI
SCHOOL BEAUTIFICATION COMMITTEE, WALKING CLUB

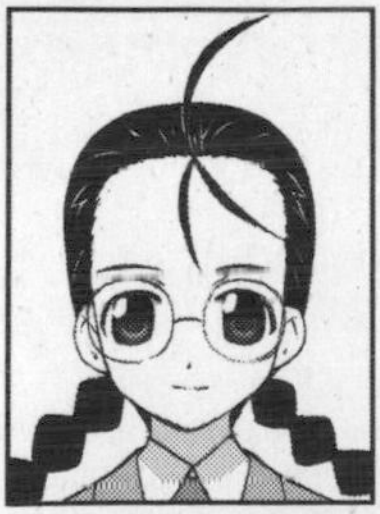

24. SATOMI HAKASE
ROBOTICS CLUB (UNIVERSITY), JET PROPULSION CLUB (UNIVERSITY)

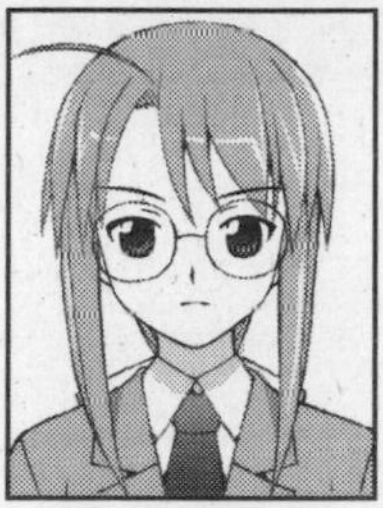

25. CHISAME HASEGAWA

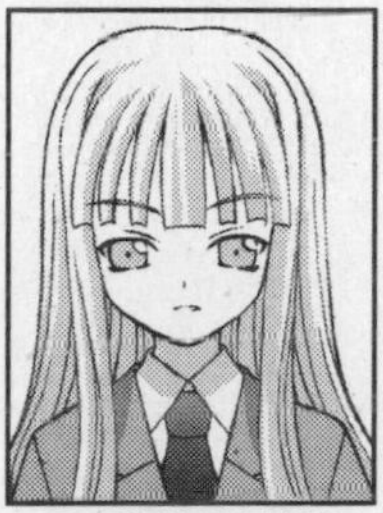

26. EVANGELINE A.K. MCDOWELL
GO CLUB, TEA CEREMONY CLUB

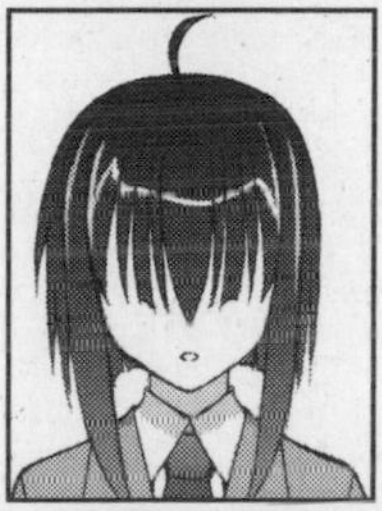

27. NODOKA MIYAZAKI
GENERAL LIBRARY COMMITTEE MEMBER, LIBRARIAN, LIBRARY EXPLORATION CLUB

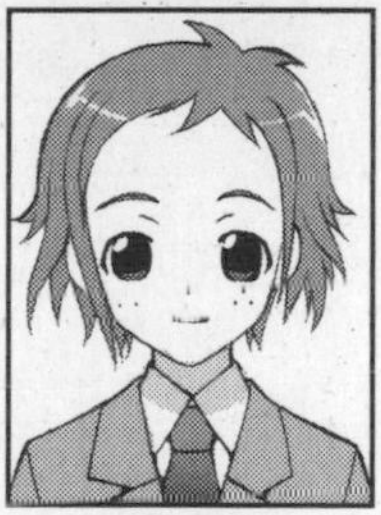

28. NATSUMI MURAKAMI
DRAMA CLUB

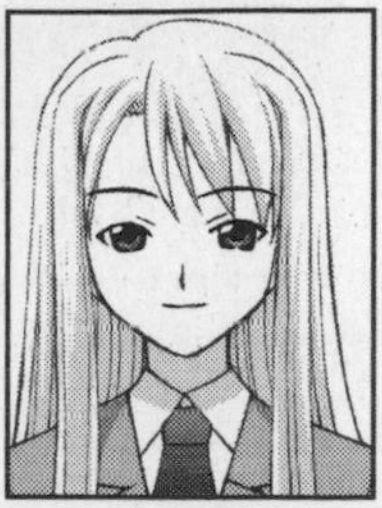

29. AYAKA YUKIHIRO
CLASS REPRESENTATIVE, EQUESTRIAN CLUB, FLOWER ARRANGEMENT CLUB

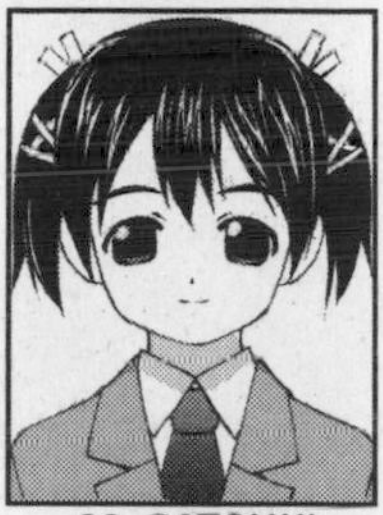

30. SATSUKI YOTSUBA
LUNCH REPRESENTATIVE, COOKING CLUB

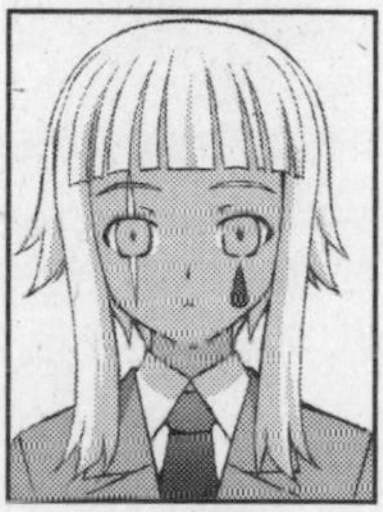

31. ZAZIE RAINYDAY
MAGIC AND ACROBATICS CLUB (NON-SCHOOL ACTIVITY)

Translation Notes

Japanese is a tricky language for most Westerners, and translation is often more art than science. For your edification and reading pleasure, here are notes on some of the places where we could have gone in a different direction in our translation of the work, or where a Japanese cultural reference is used.

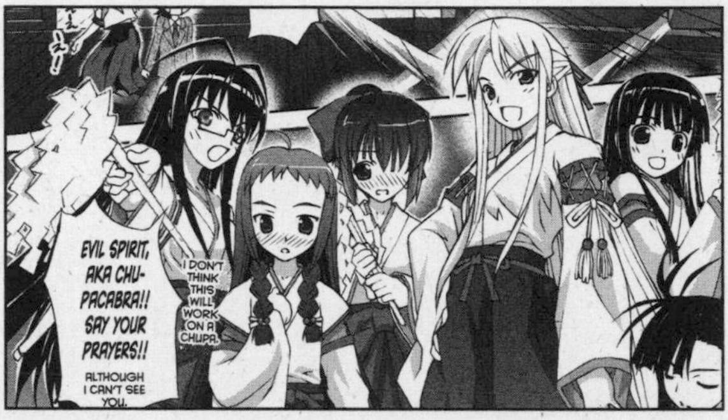
I DON'T THINK THIS WILL WORK ON A CHUPA.
EVIL SPIRIT, AKA CHU-PACABRA!! SAY YOUR PRAYERS!!
ALTHOUGH I CAN'T SEE YOU.

What you need for evil spirits, page 23

To rid the classroom of evil spirits, Ayaka and the others are dressed as Shinto priestesses. The wands with paper streamers they carry are waved as part of purification rituals.

Chizuru-nee, page 33

Nee is short for *Onee-san*, or "older sister." Natsumi must think of Chizuru as an older sister and so addresses her that way.

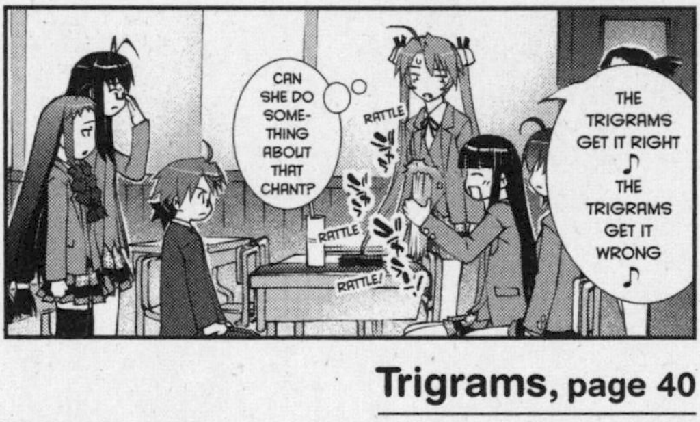
THE TRIGRAMS GET IT RIGHT ♪ THE TRIGRAMS GET IT WRONG ♪
RATTLE
RATTLE
RATTLE!
CAN SHE DO SOME-THING ABOUT THAT CHANT?

Trigrams, page 40

The trigrams are a part of *I Ching* and thus *I Ching* divination. A trigram is an arrangement of three parallel lines that represent different directions, elements, animals, etc. depending on which lines are broken and which are solid. Konoka uses the trigrams to tell fortunes. For an example of what they look like, there are four of them on the flag of South Korea.

Yūnagi, page 64

This is the name of Setsuna's sword. It means "evening calm."

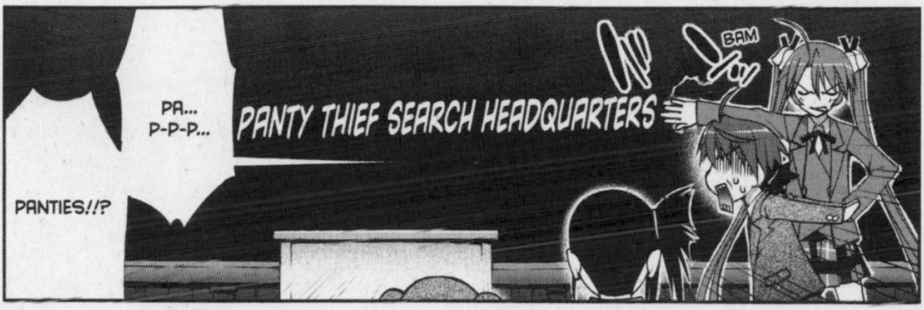
BAM
PANTY THIEF SEARCH HEADQUARTERS
PA...
P-P-P...
PANTIES!!?

Panty thief, page 142

Because most people hang their clothes to dry instead of using clothes dryers in Japan, sometimes it's not so hard (although extremely unethical) to see a certain item of clothing and just take it, so panty thieves show up a lot in anime and manga.

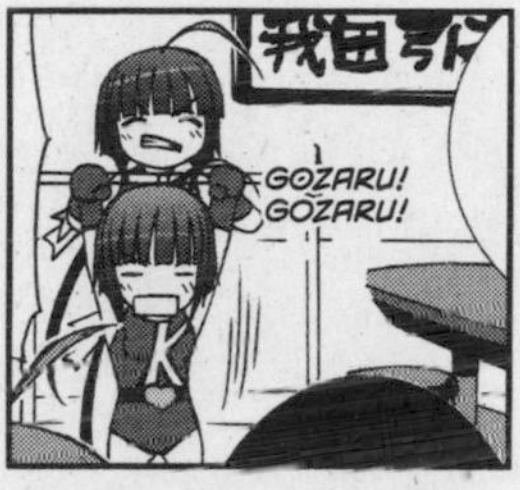
GOZARU!
GOZARU!

Gozaru, page 174

Gozaru is a very very humble way of saying "to be." (For example, "I [humbly] am.") It's not used in regular conversation very often these days, except by fictional ninja and samurai type characters like Kaede, who uses it frequently—so frequently that she doesn't even need a sentence to put it in. It is also used in ritual expressions like "*Ohayō gozaimasu*," which literally means (very politely) "it is early."

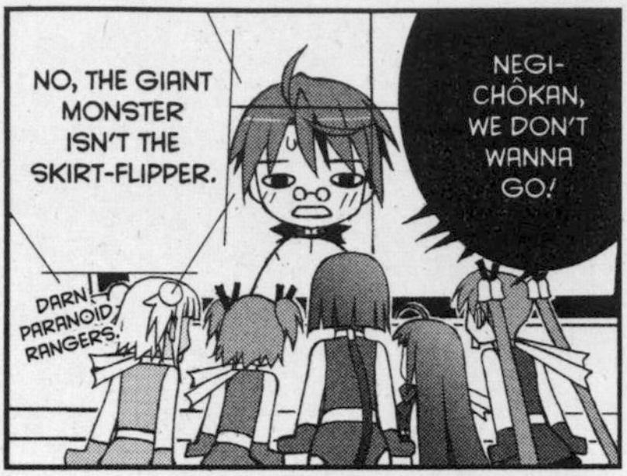
NEGI-CHÔKAN, WE DON'T WANNA GO!
NO, THE GIANT MONSTER ISN'T THE SKIRT-FLIPPER.
DARN PARANOID RANGERS!

Negi-chôkan, page 175

Chôkan means "chief" or "director." As the Baka Rangers' commander, it is a fitting title for little Negi.

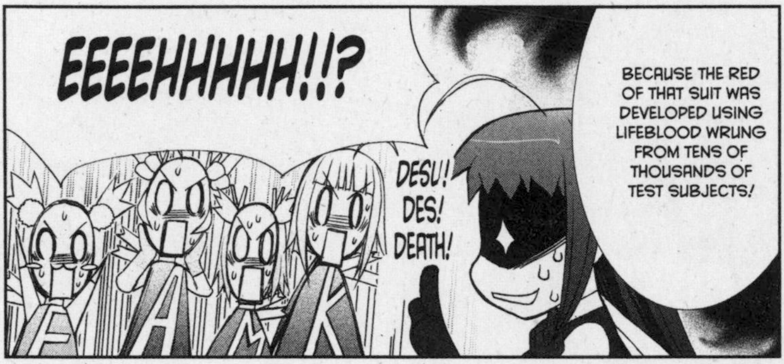
BECAUSE THE RED OF THAT SUIT WAS DEVELOPED USING LIFEBLOOD WRUNG FROM TENS OF THOUSANDS OF TEST SUBJECTS!
DESU! DES! DEATH!
EEEEHHHHH!!?

Desu, page 176

Desu is a polite way to end sentences in Japan, roughly meaning "it is." Yue uses polite language and so often ends her sentences in *desu*. Here, she repeats it, partly for emphasis, but partly for its similar pronunciation to the English word "death."

Preview of
Negima!? neo
Volume 3

We're pleased to present you a preview from *Negima!? neo*
volume 3. Please check our website (www.delreymanga.com)
to see when this volume will be available in English.
For now you'll have to make do with Japanese!

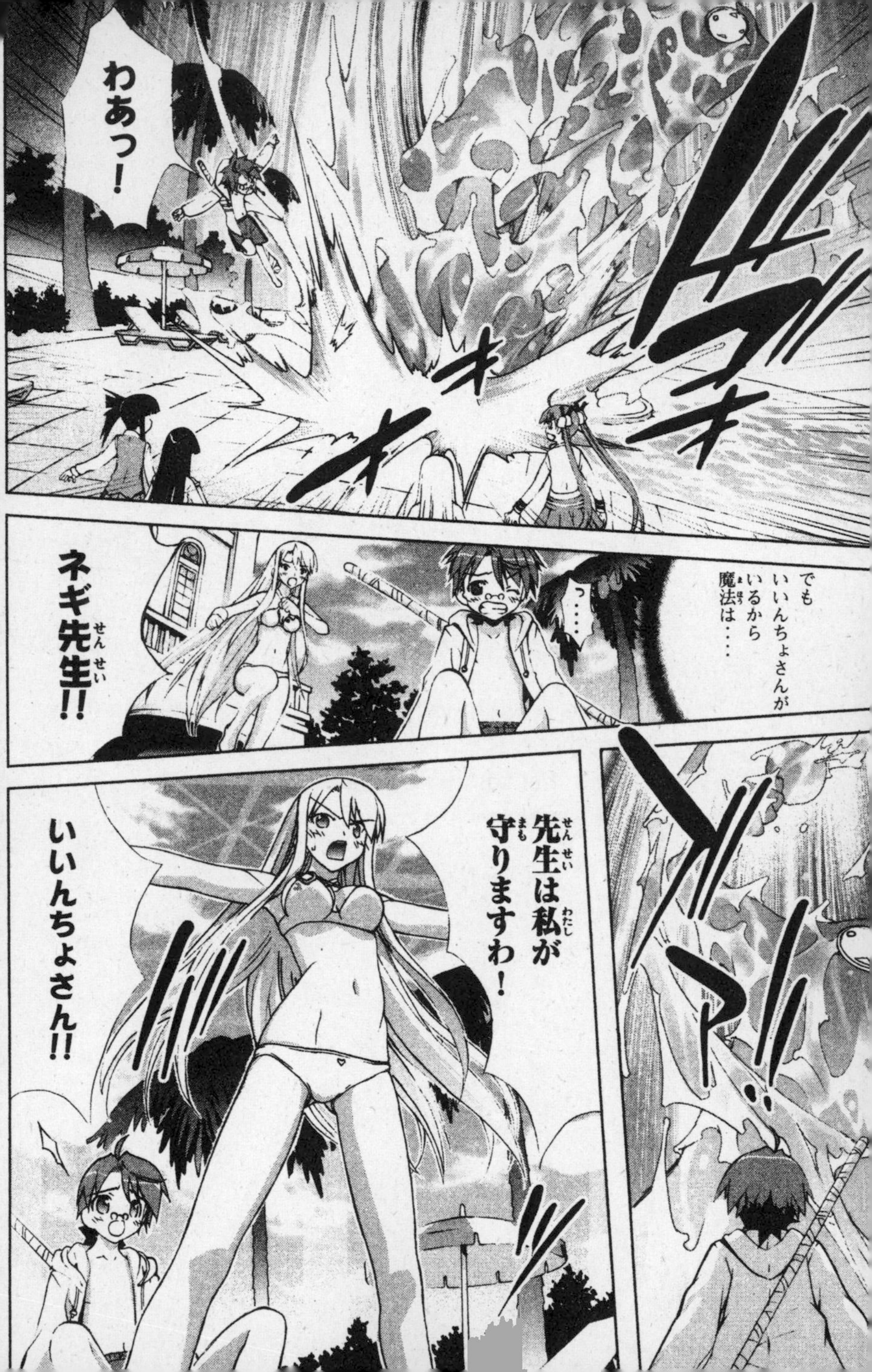
わあっ！
でも
いいんちょさんが
いるから
魔法は・・・・
っ・・・
ネギ先生!!
先生は私が
守りますわ！
いいんちょさん!!

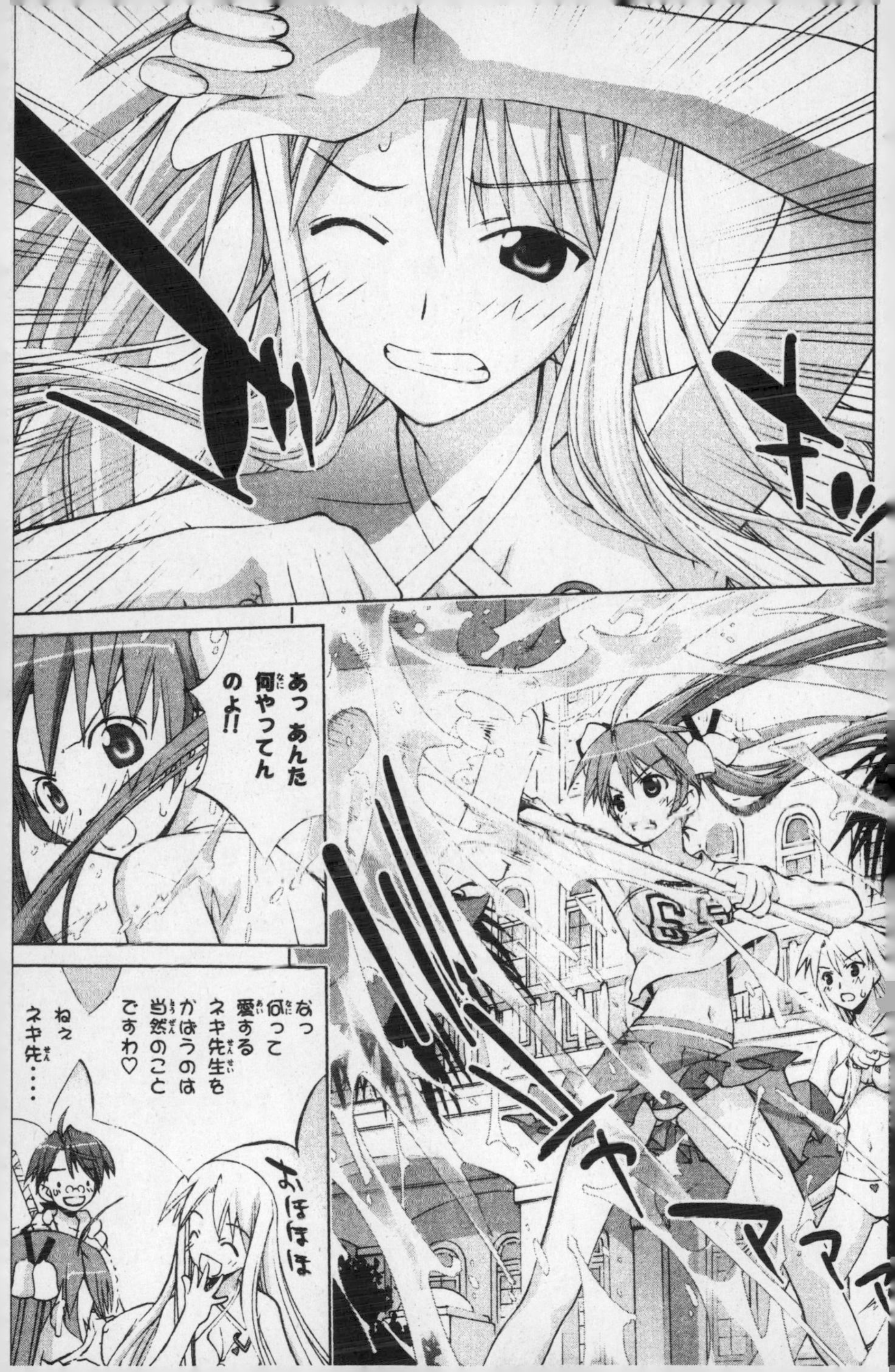
あっ あんた
何やってん
のよ!!
なっ
何って
愛する
ネギ先生を
かばうのは
当然のこと
ですわ♡
ねえ
ネギ先・・・・
おほほほほ

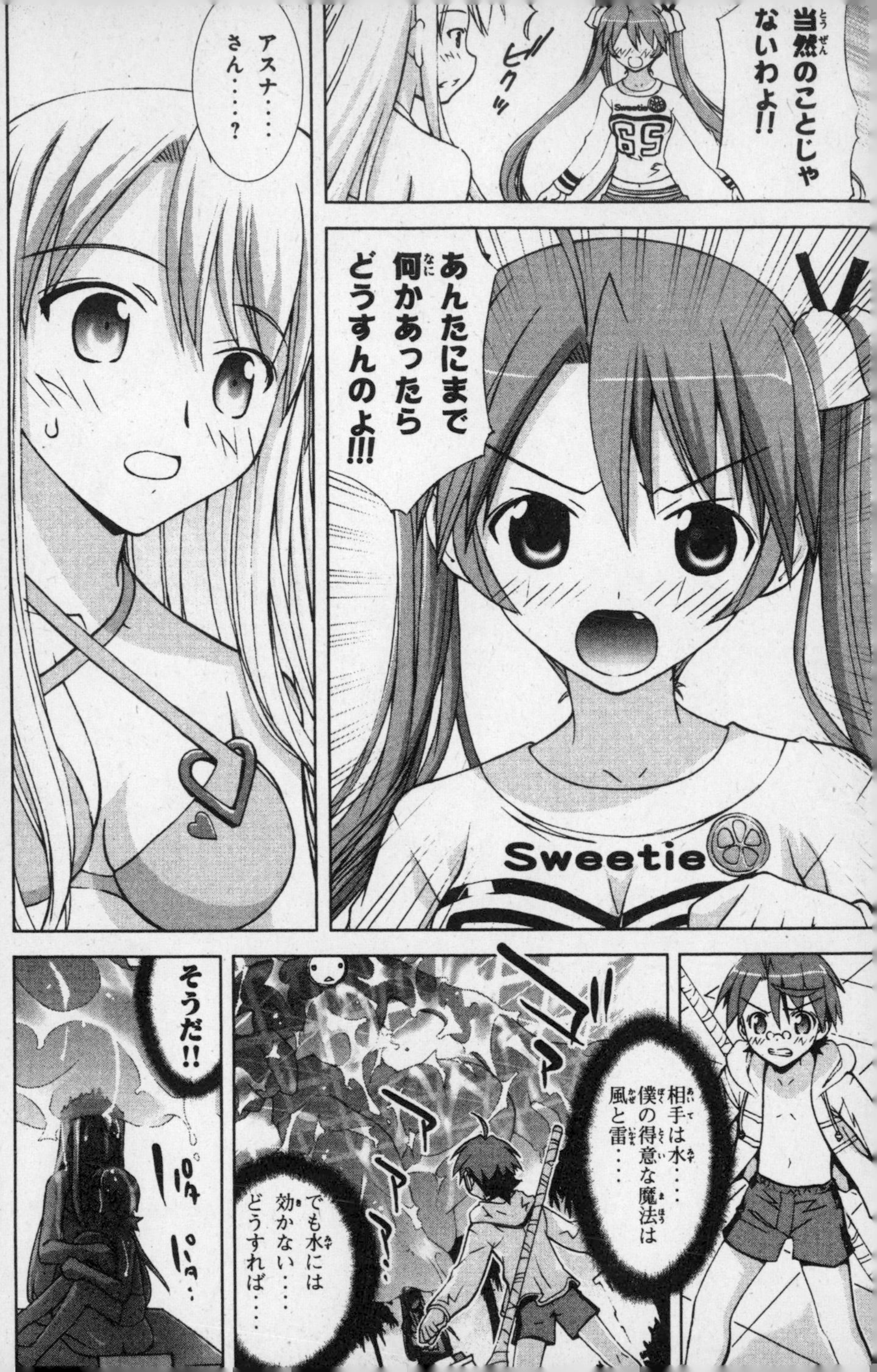
当然のことじゃないわよ!!
ビクッ
あんたにまで何かあったらどうすんのよ!!!
アスナ……さん……？
Sweetie
相手は水……僕の得意な魔法は風と雷……
ゴァァァァ…
でも水には効かない……どうすれば……
そうだ!!
パタ パタ…

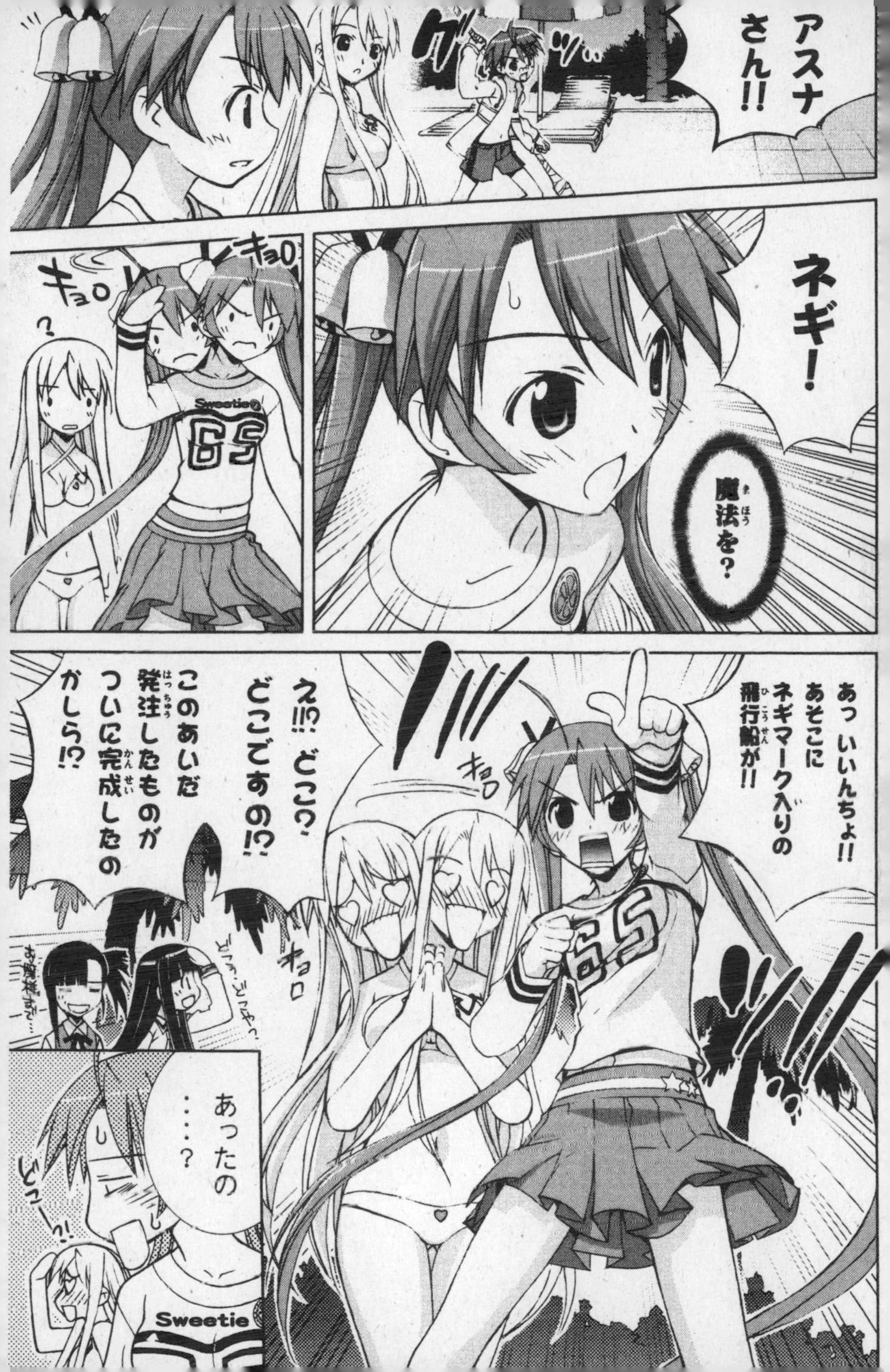
アスナさん!!
ネギ!
魔法を?
キョロ
キョロ
?
あっ いいんちょ!! あそこにネギマーク入りの飛行船が!!
え!!? どこ? どこですの!?
このあいだ発注したものがついに完成したのかしら!?
キョロ
あったの・・・?

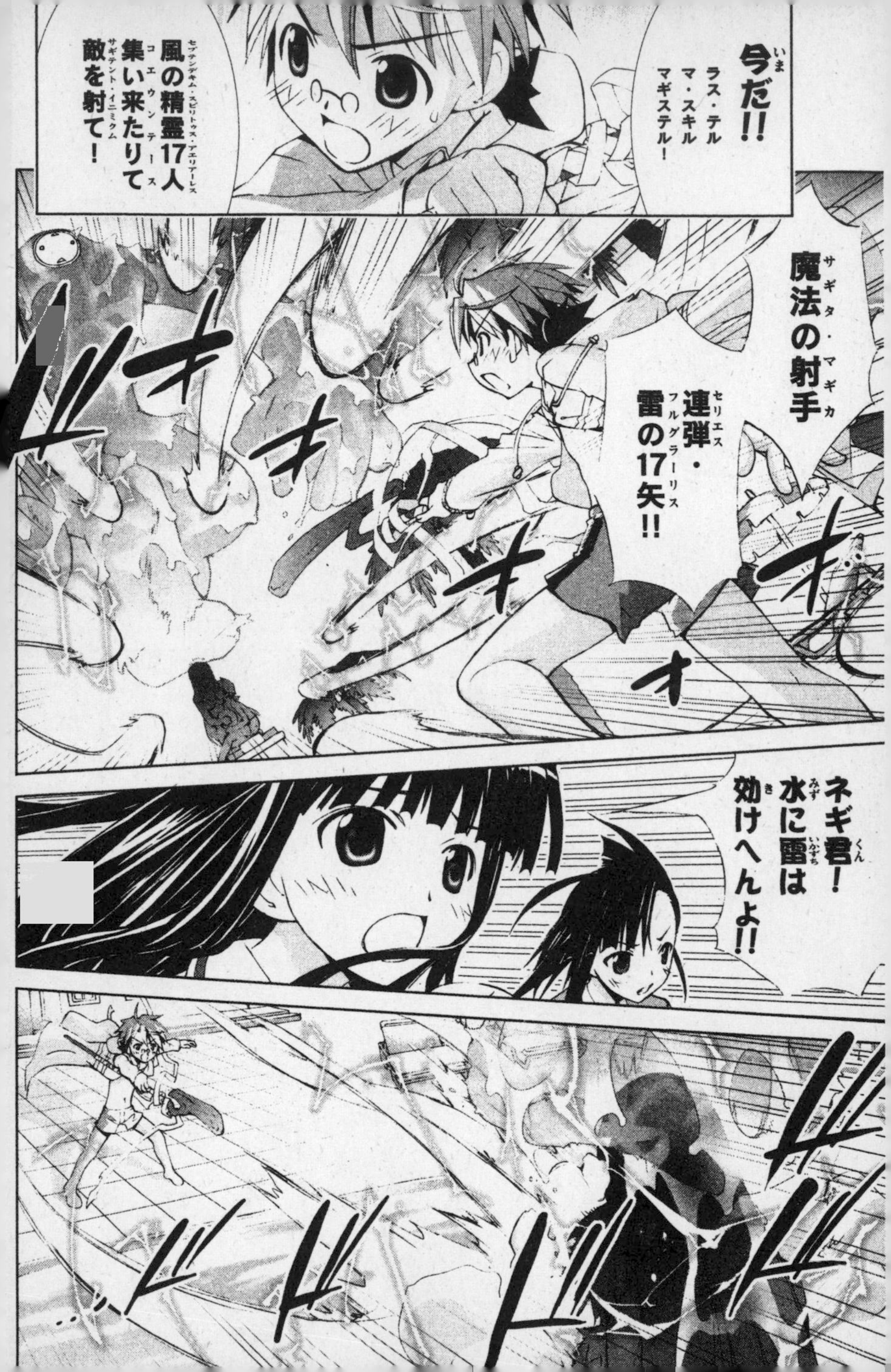
今だ!! ラス・テル マ・スキル マギステル!
風の精霊17人 集い来たりて 敵を射て!
魔法の射手 連弾・雷の17矢!!
ネギ君! 水に雷は効けへんよ!!

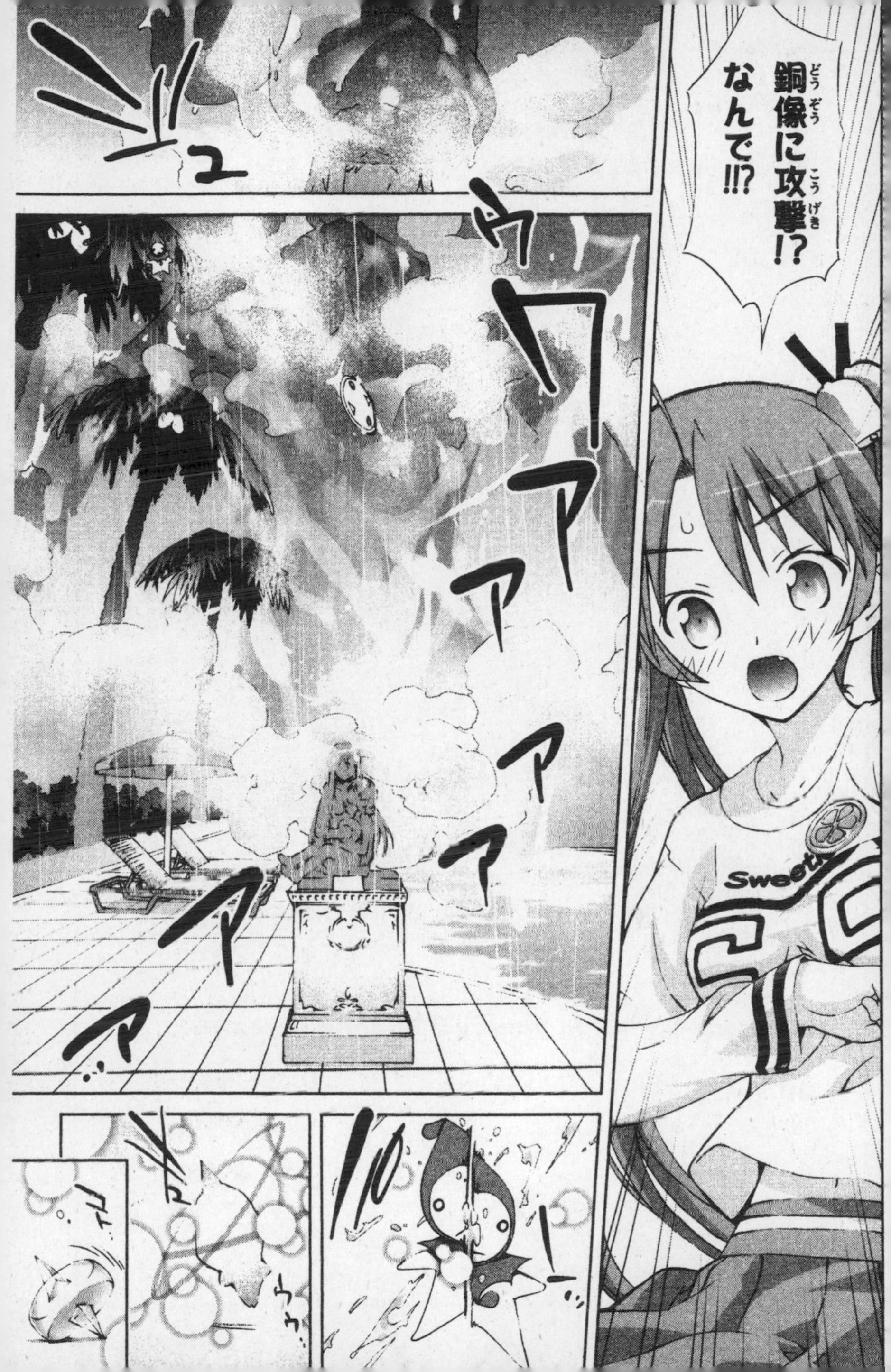
銅像(どうぞう)に攻撃(こうげき)!? なんで!!?
ウワアアアアアア…

FROM HIRO MASHIMA,
CREATOR OF *RAVE MASTER*

Lucy has always dreamed of joining the Fairy Tail, a club for the most powerful sorcerers in the land. But once she becomes a member, the fun really starts!

Special extras in each volume! Read them all!

VISIT WWW.DELREYMANGA.COM TO:
- Read sample pages
- View release date calendars for upcoming volumes
- Sign up for Del Rey's free manga e-newsletter
- Find out the latest about new Del Rey Manga series

RATING   T AGES 13+

The Otaku's Choice™

KITCHEN PRINCESS

STORY BY MIYUKI KOBAYASHI
MANGA BY NATSUMI ANDO
CREATOR OF ZODIAC P.I.

HUNGRY HEART

Najika is a great cook and likes to make meals for the people she loves. But something is missing from her life. When she was a child, she met a boy who touched her heart—and now Najika is determined to find him. The only clue she has is a silver spoon that leads her to the prestigious Seika Academy.

Kitchen Princess
1
custard pudding
taramasalata
rainbow colored jelly
christmas cookie
onion gratin soup
Story by
MIYUKI KOBAYASHI
Manga by
NATSUMI ANDO
Creator of Zodiac P.I.

Attending Seika will be a challenge. Every kid at the school has a special talent, and the girls in Najika's class think she doesn't deserve to be there. But Sora and Daichi, two popular brothers who barely speak to each other, recognize Najika's cooking for what it is—magical. Could one of the boys be Najika's mysterious prince?

Special extras in each volume! Read them all!

VISIT WWW.DELREYMANGA.COM TO:

- Read sample pages
- View release date calendars for upcoming volumes
- Sign up for Del Rey's free manga e-newsletter
- Find out the latest about new Del Rey Manga series

RATING T AGES 13+

DEL REY MANGA デルレイ

The Otaku's Choice

STORY BY TO-RU ZEKUU
ART BY YUNA TAKANAGI

DEFENDING THE NATURAL ORDER OF THE UNIVERSE!

The *shiki tsukai* are "Keepers of the Seasons"—magical warriors pledged to defend the planet's natural order against those who would threaten it.

When 14-year-old Akira Kizuki joins the *shiki tsukai*, he knows that it'll be a difficult life. But with his new friends and mentors, he's up to the challenge!

Special extras in each volume! Read them all!

TOMARE!

You're going the wrong way!

MANGA IS A COMPLETELY DIFFERENT TYPE OF READING EXPERIENCE.

TO START AT THE BEGINNING, GO TO THE END!

That's right!

Authentic manga is read the traditional Japanese way—from right to left—exactly the opposite of how American books are read. It's easy to follow: Just go to the other end of the book, and read each page—and each panel—from right side to left side, starting at the top right. Now you're experiencing manga as it was meant to be!